Husserl

'This is a first-rate volume...: The text is rich with historical background and comment. But it is the clarity and depth of understanding with which David Woodruff Smith explains the material that is so overwhelmingly present. An excellent work'.

Gayle Ormiston, Kent State University, USA

Routledge Philosophers

Edited by Brian Leiter
University of Texas, Austin

Routledge Philosophers is a major series of introductions to the great Western philosophers. Each book places a major philosopher or thinker in historical context, explains and assesses their key arguments, and considers their legacy. Additional features include a chronology of major dates and events, chapter summaries, annotated suggestions for further reading and a glossary of technical terms.

An ideal starting point for those new to philosophy, they are also essential reading for those interested in the subject at any level.

Hobbes	A.P. Martinich
Leibniz	Nicholas Jolley
Locke	E.J. Lowe
Hegel	Frederick Beiser
Rousseau	Nicholas Dent
Schopenhauer	Julian Young
Freud	Jonathan Lear
Kant	Paul Guyer
Husserl	David Woodruff Smith
Darwin	Tim Lewens

Forthcoming:

Aristotle	Christopher Shields
Spinoza	Michael Della Rocca
Hume	Don Garrett
Fichte and Schelling	Sebastian Gardner
Rawls	Samuel Freeman
Merleau-Ponty	Taylor Carman
Heidegger	John Richardson

David Woodruff Smith

Husserl

Routledge
Taylor & Francis Group

LONDON AND NEW YORK

First published 2007
by Routledge
2 Park Square, Milton Park, Abingdon, Oxon OX14 4RN

Simultaneously published in the USA and Canada
by Routledge
270 Madison Ave, New York, NY 10016

Routledge is an imprint of the Taylor & Francis Group, an informa business

© 2007 David Woodruff Smith

Typeset in Joanna MT by
Taylor and Francis Ltd
Printed and bound in Great Britain by
MPG Books Ltd, Bodmin

British Library Cataloguing in Publication Data
A catalogue record for this book is available from the British Library

Library of Congress Cataloging in Publication Data
Smith, David Woodruff, 1944-
    Husserl / David Woodruff Smith.
      p. cm. -- (Routledge philosophers)
    1. Husserl, Edmund, 1859-1938. I. Title. II. Series.
    B3279.H94S54 2006
    193--dc2   22006014634

ISBN10: 0-415-28974-2   ISBN13: 978-0-415-28974-0 (hbk)
ISBN10: 0-415-28945-0   ISBN13: 978-0-415-28975-7 (pbk)
ISBN10: 0-203-96843-3   ISBN13: 978-0-203-96843-7 (ebk)

For Doug and Glad
. . . and our Viennese heritage.

Illustrations

Below is a list of the figures appearing in the several chapters, usually with cartoon illustrations.

Preface

In this study, as befits the Routledge Philosophers series, I have sought to present Husserl's thought from a wide perspective in the 21st century. This reading presents Husserl not only as a 20th-century revolutionary who launched a radically new type of philosophy called transcendental phenomenology, but more fundamentally as an original thinker who takes his place along with Aristotle, Kant, et al., in the pantheon of great systematic philosophers in the history of thought.

Along the way, I lay out conceptual and historical details of Husserl's development of the new science of phenomenology (a reflective study of consciousness as experienced from the first-person point of view), assessing Husserl's role in the two traditions of continental and analytic philosophy in the 20th century. However, my main goal, in the course of the book, is to build an account of Husserl's overall *system* of philosophy. Accordingly, I have framed Husserl's philosophy as an integrated system of logic, ontology, phenomenology, epistemology, ethics, and more. In this account, the several parts of Husserl's system, including his phenomenology, are tightly interwoven, and this interweaving is itself conceptualized in the system. As we come to appreciate Husserl's unified philosophy, his originality becomes increasingly evident.

When referring to Husserl's works, I have cited the works in their extant English translations, where available, indicating the original German editions as well. I cite locations in Husserl texts by section numbers, which appear in all the respective editions.

Most of the quotations from Husserl that appear in my text are in my own translation, but I cite the relevant location in the extant English translations where available. The extant translations have been an invaluable guide even where I construct my own translations. If I vary the translation, it is because I want to ferret out a technical term and keep track of it in various texts. Husserl, the lapsed mathematician, kept to his choice of technical terms over decades of writing – expanding his overall theory rather in the style of a growing body of mathematical results.

For their work in conceiving and organizing the present series, I am grateful to Tony Bruce, editor-in-chief for Routledge's philosophy books, and Brian Leiter, editor of the Routledge Philosophers series. I wish to thank three anonymous reviewers of the penultimate manuscript, for their many helpful comments and observations. For detailed suggestions on the penultimate manuscript, I thank Jeffrey Ogle. For specific remarks on a key part of Chapter 6, I thank Martin Schwab and Amie Thomasson. For discussions of constructivist ethical theories pertinent to Chapter 8, I thank Aaron James. Also regarding Chapter 8, I thank Christopher Lay and Gary Hartenburg for discussion of passages on normativity in the Prolegomena of Husserl's *Logical Investigations*.

In more general terms, I would like to express my appreciation to the many colleagues and students who have engaged with me on ideas that have somehow found their way into the following interpretation of Husserl's thought. Especially, I would mention my colleagues in some three decades of discussion and writing related (more or less directly) to "California" phenomenology: Dagfinn Føllesdal, Jaakko Hintikka, Ronald McIntyre, (the late) Izchak Miller, Hubert Dreyfus, John Searle, Richard Tieszen, Martin Schwab, Dallas Willard, Allan Casebier, Amie Thomasson, Kay Mathiesen, Wayne Martin, Jeffrey Yoshimi, Paul Livingston, Jason Ford, Charles Siewert. I would also mention Anglo-Austrian colleagues whose studies of Brentano and Husserl have deepened my historical and ontological perspectives on Husserl: Kevin Mulligan, Peter Simons, and Barry Smith; also Edgar Morscher and Johannes Brandl. In the Parisian scene, I would mention Jean Petitot, Jean-Michel Roy, the late Francisco Varela, and Bernard Pachoud, who have looked to cognitive science, and Clair Ortiz Hill, who has looked to Husserl's ties into early philosophical logic. I've long benefited from J. N. Mohanty's perspectives on Husserl. My sense of Husserl's systematicity has benefited, indirectly, from many discussions with the late Charles W. Dement, exploring what we have called ontological systematics. Finally, the book has benefited further from studies of Husserl by a variety of scholars, including David Bell, Christian Beyer, David Carr, Richard Cobb-Stevens, Steven Crowell, John Drummond, Lester Embree, Denis Fisette, Klaus Held, Edouard Marbach, Dermot Moran, A.D. Smith, Robert Sokolowski, Robert Tragesser, Donn Welton, Dan Zahavi. Needless to say, Husserl's rich texts have occasioned significantly different lines of interpretation, and so, as my narrative progresses, I try to indicate alternative views of Husserl where appropriate, without losing the reader's focus.

Thanks for their excellent work to Lisa Williams for copy-editing, Jeffrey Ogle for preparing the index, Christina Chuang for crafting the Chinese script in Chapter 6, and Jason Mitchell for supervising production.

Finally, I wish to thank my wife Mary for her wonderful support in so many ways.

David Woodruff Smith
2006

A chronology of Husserl's life and works

1859	Edmund Husserl is born, 8 April, in Prossnitz (Prostejow), Moravia, second of four children.
1876–82	Studies at the Universities of Leipzig, Berlin, and Vienna. Studies mathematics with Kronecker and Weierstrass.
1882	Doctoral dissertation, "Contributions Towards a Theory of Variation Calculus", accepted 8 October.
1884–6	Studies with Franz Brentano in Vienna and Carl Stumpf in Halle.
1887	Marries Malvine Steinschneider, 6 August.
1887	*Habilitationschrift*, "On the Concept of Number, Psychological Analyses", accepted and printed.
1887–1901	Lectures as Privatdozent in the University of Halle.
1891	*Philosophy of Arithmetic, Psychological and Logical Investigations.*
1892	Frege published critical review of *Philosophy of Arithmetic.*
1892–5	The Husserls' children are born: Elli, 1892; Gerhart, 1893; Wolfgang, 1895.
1900	*Logical Investigations, First Part: Prolegomena to Pure Logic*, first edition.
1901	*Logical Investigations, Second Part: Investigations into Phenomenology and Theory of Knowledge Logic*, first edition.
1901	Appointed Professor Extraordinarius at the University of Göttingen.
1903	The Munich "school" of phenomenology is formed, with Johannes Daubert and Adolf Reinach.
1906	Advanced to Professor Ordinarius at Göttingen.
1907	The Göttingen Philosophical Society is formed, with Edith Stein and Roman Ingarden.

1903–15	Lectures on Time-Consciousness, 1905–10. Lectures on Thing and Space, 1907. Lectures on the Theory of Meaning, 1908. Lectures on Ethics and Value Theory, 1911, 1914. Lectures and exercises on various philosophers, including Leibniz, Locke, Berkeley, Hume, Kant, Fichte, and Lotze. Several courses of lectures on Kant's first and second Critiques, theoretical and practical reason.
1911	"Philosophy as Rigorous Science", in *Logos*, vol. 1 (1919/11).
1912	Drafts manuscripts of *Ideas* I, II, and III.
1913	*Ideas* I, that is, *Ideas toward a Pure Phenomenology and Phenomenological Philosophy, First Book: General Introduction to Phenomenology*.
1916	Appointed Professor Ordinarius at the University of Freiburg, 5 January to begin 1 April.
1916	Husserl's son Wolfgang is killed near Verdun, 8 March.
1917	Husserl's son Gerhart is wounded, April. His mother dies, July.
1916–19	Edith Stein serves as assistant to Husserl at Freiburg.
1919–23	Martin Heidegger serves as assistant to Husserl at Freiburg.
1922	Lectures at University College in London. Meets G. E. Moore.
1924	Rudolf Carnap attends Husserl's advanced seminar.
1925	Lectures on Phenomenological Psychology.
1928	Retires, becoming Professor Emeritus.
1928	*Phenomenology of Internal Time-Consciousness* (edited by Martin Heidegger after prior editing by Edith Stein).
1929	Lectures in Paris, introduced by Emannuel Levinas and others. Later published as *The Paris Lectures*.
1929	*Formal and Transcendental Logic*.
1929	Gilbert Ryle visits Husserl, summer.
1931	*Cartesian Meditations* (in French translation).
1933	Suspended from the University by Nazi decree (April). Decree later annulled (July). German citizenship later revoked.

1935	The Vienna lecture, "Philosophy in the Crisis of European Humanity".
1935	Offered a chair at the University of Southern California in Los Angeles, which Husserl declines.
1935–8	Manuscripts are drafted that would be published posthumously as *The Crisis of European Science and Transcendental Phenomenology*.
1938	Husserl dies, 27 April, 79 years old.

Introduction

Edmund Husserl, founder of phenomenology

Born in Moravia, educated in Vienna and Berlin, first in mathematics and later in philosophy, Edmund Husserl (1859–1938) taught and wrote philosophy at a succession of German universities. He is best known as the founder of phenomenology, defined as the study of the essence of consciousness as experienced from the first-person point of view. Husserl's phenomenology launched a philosophical program that changed the course of European thought. Not only the preeminent phenomenologist, Husserl was also one of the great systematic philosophers, akin to Aristotle and Kant. It is time for Husserl to take his rightful place in this pantheon. Accordingly, this study of Husserl will focus on his overall system of philosophy, in which phenomenology plays its special role.

There are two Husserls: the passionate, revolutionary philosopher who fits naturally in the dynamic "continental" tradition, and the exacting, mathematical, formalist philosopher who fits naturally in the "analytic" tradition. Both are equally real; both have exerted influence on different trends in 20th-century philosophy. Yet there is also a third Husserl, the one who integrates the revolutionary Husserl and the scientific Husserl. This is the systematic philosopher who sees all things as interdependent, the Husserl who even produced a theory of dependence itself, a theory that binds together his many other theories about consciousness, nature, society, number, ideal "logical" forms in all these things, and so on.

Husserl entered the intellectual scene near the turn of the 20th century, a time when psychology, logic, mathematics, and physics were taking giant leaps. He initiated a new philosophical discipline to join these diverse sciences, setting phenomenology amidst the other core disciplines of philosophy. Integrating theories in logic, ontology, phenomenology, epistemology, and social cum ethical theory – in a way that is not yet widely understood – Husserl developed a complex and wide-ranging system of philosophy, including a high-level philosophy of philosophy cum science, mathematics, and humanistic concerns. It is my hope that the portrait of Husserl presented in this volume will simultaneously portray the revolutionary phenomenologist, the scientific philosopher, and the traditional systematist.

Husserl played a significant role in the flow of ideas in two 20th-century traditions: "continental" (European) philosophy and "analytic" philosophy, the former inspired by humanistic concerns and the latter by logical-mathematical-scientific concerns. Husserl's impact on continental philosophy is well known, along with his impact on phenomenological philosophy in the Americas and Asia. His impact on analytic philosophy, however, is only gradually coming to light. (See Dreyfus 1982; Mohanty 1982; Coffa 1991; Dummett 1993; Richardson 1998; Friedman 1999; Hill and Rosado Haddock 2000; Fisette 2003; Livingston 2004; Ryckman 2005, 2006.) The present volume explores the place of Husserl's system in the long sweep of history from Plato and Aristotle through Descartes, Hume, and Kant into 20th-century philosophy, highlighting his significance for these three historical lineages.

I have sought to present Husserl's complex ideas – his methods, concepts, theories, and system – in as simple a form as possible. Still, Husserl's thought is complex, and I try to show its complexity as the different themes interact across the chapters to follow. Weaving in and out of these doctrinal discussions are observations about Husserl's relations to other historical figures, indicating the context of his ideas. Also informing the discussion are passing remarks about the development of his ideas in particular texts, indicating the history of views within his own corpus. These aspects of the presentation offer guides for reading Husserl, as our presentation of Husserl is to serve readers as a first stop at Husserl's door, in the spirit of the Routledge Philosophers series.

Thus, I am writing for several audiences at once. As I turn to each area of philosophical theory that Husserl entered, I sketch basic concepts, key alternative views, and main historical thrusts in the background of Husserl's own discussion. If you are an experienced reader of philosophy but relatively new to Husserl, you may read a given chapter without, at first, following the narrative that moves through the chapters one by one. If you are already well versed in Husserl, you will easily find your own way to the themes and issues that most interest you, not least in the two chapters devoted to phenomenology. Whatever your background may be, you will find in Chapter 2 a unified presentation of Husserl's overall system, featuring an analysis of how and why the various parts of the system are mutually interdependent. And if you want to study Husserl's system in detail, finding issues of phenomenology in that larger context, then kindly follow the narrative as it develops over the course of the book. If you are particularly interested in the history of Husserl's work, and its development through his voluminous writings over half a century, then you may follow the leads I have laid down about particular texts, outlined in Chapter 1 but recited along the way. Finally, if you are interested in specific texts in Husserl's corpus, and how they play in his phenomenology, ontology, and so on, or in his overall system, then follow the references to particular texts, which I include as I reconstruct particular ideas along the way.

REVOLUTIONARY PHILOSOPHER, SCIENTIFIC PHILOSOPHER

There is a tradition in European philosophy, from Rousseau and Kant to Nietzsche and Heidegger and recent cultural critics like Foucault and Derrida, a tradition that emphasizes radical change. History is a dynamic process, always changing from one contingent social reality to another, embracing abstract philosophical theories about mind and body and society, and concrete political movements promoting particular ideologies of self and polis. In this tradition of "historicity," Husserl plays his role of abstract revolutionary, pressing the cause of phenomenology in philosophy and beyond. Husserl's famous critique of the "life-world" holds that the European sciences have lost touch with everyday life, in their zeal for "mathematizing" nature. The result is a disastrous loss of respect for rationality in ordering human life, from science to politics, an irrationality Husserl saw as driving the hideous movement of National Socialism in his last years (1935–8) in his adopted land of Germany. Apart from politically revolutionary critique, Husserl's philosophy falls largely in line with the revolutionary "critique of reason" launched by Kant in so many words. Husserl saw transcendental phenomenology as a radical rethinking of our relation to the world, not simply a cognitive relation (conceptual representation infused with sensory input, per Kant), but an "intentional" relation guided by ideal meaning. Husserl's passion for this vision launched a large and continuing movement in European thought. Martin Heidegger, Maurice Merleau-Ponty, and Jean-Paul Sartre, inter alios, developed their own visions of phenomenology, dependent on Husserl's yet seeking fundamental changes, as their existential phenomenologies emphasized concrete practical and political engagements. In their wakes followed the social perspectives and cultural theories of language in Michel Foucault, Jacques Derrida, and Jürgen Habermas, still visibly moving in a philosophical space of meaning framed by Husserl.

But there is another tradition in European philosophy, the tradition that emphasizes not political, social, or cultural dynamics, but science, mathematics, and logic, with a very different dynamic. For decades, this tradition was seen as the legacy of logical theory developed by Gottlob Frege, Bertrand Russell, and then the logical positivists of the Vienna Circle in the 1920s and 1930s, especially Rudolf Carnap, who promoted the ideal of exact philosophy guided by the new logic. The positivists took mathematics and modern physics as exemplars of clear and objective philosophical thought, as opposed to the impressionistic, subjective, and emotional writing of what are today called the continental philosophers. What's wrong with this familiar picture? Decades before the Vienna Circle, Husserl promoted a model of rigorous, exact, and scientific philosophy, in line with the ideals of his teacher Franz Brentano and his hero Bernard Bolzano. At the turn of the 20th century, Vienna was the high point of European thought, in art, architecture, music, science, and mathematics. Husserl came of age in that Vienna, while studying also in Germany. His early work was entirely in mathematics and then philosophy of mathematics. His revolutionary zeal was similar to that of the European mathematicians of his day, including his friends Georg Cantor (pioneer in set theory) and David Hilbert (pioneer in formal axiomatic methods leading to the very idea of metamathematics). Even Albert Einstein evolved in this milieu, in direct contact with Hilbert and with the mathematician Hermann Weyl, who was directly influenced by Husserl. Carnap himself attended Husserl's lectures, which left an indelible imprint on Carnap's positivist treatise *The Logical Structure of the World* (1928). Husserl's place in the logical-mathematical-scientific turn of European philosophy is less well known but emerging in force, as the details of Husserl's role in this lineage are gradually coming to light. Stay tuned for references in the text to follow, especially Chapter 1 and Chapter 3.

SYSTEMATIC THINKER, HOLOGRAPHIC WRITER

The portrait I shall develop of Husserl's philosophy is that of an intricate philosophical system that ranges widely yet develops with an overall unity, at all points opening to still further exploration. Of the great thinkers in the West, the greatest systematic philosophers were arguably first Aristotle and then Kant. Husserl joins these two, I submit, on the short list of greatest systematic philosophers, those who produced a truly wide-ranging system of philosophy and worked out exceedingly careful details through the system. There are other systematic thinkers of great stature – Aquinas, Hegel, Whitehead. But my thesis here is that the greatest systematic philosophers are Aristotle, Kant, and Husserl – not least because each system in this sequence can be seen as a successor system that radically changes and improves on its predecessors.

What makes Husserl a systematic thinker is the way everything is related and interdependent as he writes about consciousness,

meaning, evidence, the natural world, time, space, cultural institutions, number, mathematical structure, science, objectivity and
subjectivity, objects and their properties, essences and categories,
and more. What is remarkable in Husserl's oeuvre is the natural
way in which one text ties into another, even if the texts were
written decades apart and are nominally aimed at different
themes. Trained as a mathematician, Husserl seems to have carried
the sense of cumulative results into his philosophical work.
Indeed, he rarely changed his views as he constantly expanded on
his previous results, much as a mathematician builds on previous
theorems. Few philosophers tie their results so tightly together,
and few develop their ideas in this theorem-by-theorem way.
Accordingly, Husserl's views about consciousness presuppose his
views about body and vice versa, his conception of logic presupposes his conception of "intuition" and vice versa, his theory of
essence joins with his theory of dependence, and so on.
Moreover, as is explained in Chapter 2, Husserl's system includes
its own *metatheory*, a theory about how the partial theories in the
system are bound together: they are parts of a well-defined whole,
and Husserl's theory of parts and wholes thus allows a theory of
how his overall theory of consciousness-and-world is tied
together.

Husserl's system of ideas is thus an instance of what he called a
"precise [*prägnant*] whole," where each part of the whole depends
on every other part. Husserl's choice of phrase is evocative.
Although the German "*pregnant*" is sometimes translated as "pregnant" (as in "a pregnant phrase," which is full of meaning), the
term derives from the verb "*prägen*," meaning to stamp or mint a
coin, producing a precise form, and so "*prägnant*" means precise,
concise, or terse. Thus, Husserl is saying that a *prägnant* whole is
one that is precisely formed, namely so that its parts are precisely
bound together. So it is with the parts of Husserl's philosophical
system: the partial theories – of experience, meaning, time,
culture, essence, number, and so on – are bound together tightly
into the whole theory that is his system.

Husserl's writing can be difficult. He wrote a series of books,
each of which was to be a new introduction to the new science of

phenomenology. Yet, somehow, he lacked the knack for laying out his theories so that one idea follows simply on another. He was not building his edifice one brick at a time. Husserl's pedagogy is thus challenging, with one text on one theme echoing another text on a different theme. In the end Husserl's writing, and thinking, is holographic. It is as if he is working, year to year, from an eidetic pictorial image etched in his mind, a broad canvas on which his system is painted. As he refines one part of the image, he preserves the rest, integrating the new work with the old.

Accordingly, Husserl's texts are like holographic plates, or rather chunks of the whole plate that contains Husserl's systematic philosophical image of consciousness and the world. Husserl's whole philosophical system is visible in each of his texts, although each text focuses on specific themes of phenomenology, ontology, logic, and so on. So the system is a hologram. Reading Husserl on one theme reignites the image of his whole system, inviting the reader to look more closely into other parts of the system. Hence, as I work through Husserl's system chapter by chapter, I frequently allude to other parts of the system, in other chapters, earlier or later, reconstructing the system to the best of my ability so as to show the whole in the parts. The same point or idea will thus appear in different guises in several chapters. This style of repetition is meant to show the interconnections among the various parts of Husserl's system, each reflected in the others. If I am right about the holographic character of Husserl's thought, there is no other way to lay out the systematic structure of his philosophy.

THE PLAN

The narrative of the book follows this vision of Husserl's overall system of philosophy. Chapter 1 introduces Husserl, the human being, his life, his work, his significance.

Chapter 2 then constructs an overview of Husserl's philosophical system, sketching the key parts and how they work together. This scheme follows the development of ideas in Husserl's first major work, the *Logical Investigations*, which appeared in three

volumes covering some 1,000 pages. It is not easy to see the forest
for the trees, and so I try to portray the structure of the forest
before describing in detail individual trees (concepts) or groves
(theories).

In the *Investigations* Husserl develops a constantly expanding
overall theory, as he progresses through specific theories in logic,
language theory, ontology, phenomenology, and, finally, epistemology. The same progression is discernible in his next book, *Ideas*
I, but phenomenology is there given the salient role. Husserl's
later books, and the many courses of lectures published posthumously, all expand on ideas or theories that fit into the
organization laid out in the *Investigations*. I have chosen to follow
that plan through the remaining chapters, each expanding on
Husserl's results in one of the core areas of philosophy, guided by
the overall structure of theory mapped in the *Investigations*. It is
sometimes said that Husserl moved through radical changes of
doctrine, from a realist ontology to a purely phenomenological
philosophy and on to a radical idealism. However, I concur with
those who say there is a deep continuity throughout Husserl's
corpus, for each subsequent body of work takes its place in the
plan of the *Investigations*. The resulting picture of Husserl's philosophy is then systematic, with phenomenology taking its place in the
system, interdependent with doctrines of logic, ontology, epistemology.

Chapter 3, accordingly, studies Husserl's conception of "pure
logic," especially bringing out his prescient vision of what would
later be called semantics (how meanings represent various types
of objects) and metamathematics (the mathematical theory of
mathematical theories). Husserl's philosophy of everyday language
enters here, as language expresses meanings, which play their
roles in relating expressions to the world.

Chapter 4 then pursues Husserl's views in ontology. These
include a theory of "essences" (species, properties, relations) as
ideal or abstract entities, and a theory of parts and wholes, in
which a theory of dependence arises (how one object may depend
on another for its existence). These theories play their roles in
other of Husserl's theories, including his theory of the relation of

consciousness to the external world, involving his so-called transcendental idealism.

Chapter 5 turns to phenomenology. Here I present Husserl's
new, first-person science of consciousness, couched in fairly
neutral terms, and I summarize his various results, including analyses of the structure of intentionality (consciousness "of"
something), the structure of our experience of space and time and
physical objects, and awareness of other persons.

Chapter 6 delves into the more technical details of Husserl's
formulation of phenomenology. These include his method of
"bracketing" or "epoché" (bracket the question of the existence of
objects in the natural world around us and thereby attend to the
way we experience them). Here we pursue details of Husserl's
theory of intentionality, as each act of consciousness is directed
toward an appropriate object via a certain ideal meaning or conceptual structure called a "noema" (from the Greek for what is
thought or known). His theory of intentionality harks back to his
conception of logic.

Chapter 7 follows with Husserl's theory of knowledge, featuring
his generalized doctrine of "intuition," or evidential experience.
We perceive or "intuit" physical objects around us, but we also
"see" or have insight about the natures or essences of things,
including mathematical forms. Husserl develops an analysis of these
various forms of "intuitive" experience, which ground knowledge
of various types of object. We also consider his account of systematic knowledge in the sciences, and the ways in which scientific
knowledge depends on everyday knowledge in the "life-world."

Chapter 8 purses Husserl's views on the foundation of ethics,
which are not so well known as his phenomenology and attendant
doctrines. Husserl views ethical norms as grounded in our experience in reason and love, yet objective, somewhat in the way that
meaning in logic is objective yet grounded in the intentionality of
consciousness.

Chapter 9 concludes with an appraisal of Husserl's legacy. The
impacts of Husserl's various views are indicated along the way in
various chapters and are here regrouped. Here will also be found a
sketch of Husserl's views in ethics and value theory.

SUMMARY

Edmund Husserl (1859–1938) was a Czecho-Austro-German philosopher best known as the founder of phenomenology, which he defined as the science of the essence of consciousness. In fact, Husserl was one of the great systematic philosophers of the Western tradition, joining Aristotle and Kant in the top rank of system-builders. This book presents Husserl's overall system of philosophy, in which his conception of phenomenology plays a central role. Historically, Husserl's phenomenology was the seminal force in 20th-century continental European philosophy, while his conception of logic and epistemology interacted also with the tradition of 20th-century analytic philosophy. Husserl's place in the longer history of philosophy is becoming apparent as we gain some distance from the preceding century.

FURTHER READING

A broad picture of the context in which Husserl wrote can be gained from the following works. Looking to the tradition of classical phenomenology, Dermot Moran expounds the results of Husserl, Heidegger, Merleau-Ponty, and other early 20th-century phenomenologists, while Simon Critchley offers a succinct perspective on the revolutionary style of continental philosophy that features phenomenology. Looking to the tradition of analytic philosophy, Alberto Coffa interprets the development of logical theory, especially semantic theory, in which Husserl plays a sometimes neglected role, while Michael Dummett appraises the growth of analytic philosophy, looking to the relations between Husserl and Frege. Barry Smith interprets the wider tradition of Austrian philosophy, featuring Brentano, inter alios, a tradition that gave rise to both phenomenology and analytic philosophy.

Coffa, J. Alberto. 1991. *The Semantic Tradition from Kant to Carnap: To the Vienna Station.* Cambridge and New York: Cambridge University Press.

Critchley, Simon. 2001. *Continental Philosophy: A Very Short Introduction.* Oxford: Oxford University Press.

Dummett, Michael. 1993. *Origins of Analytical Philosophy.* Cambridge, Massachussetts: Harvard University Press.

Moran, Dermot. 2000. *Introduction to Phenomenology,* London and New York: Routledge.

Smith, Barry. 1994. *Austrian Philosophy: The Legacy of Franz Brentano.* Chicago and LaSalle, Illinois: Open Court.

One

Husserl's life and works

In this chapter we outline the development of Husserl's philosophy over the course of his life. Writing for half a century, addressing richly varied themes, Husserl published just five books during his lifetime. Yet he left volumes of lecture texts and some 40,000 pages of shorthand notes, showing the philosopher at work on detailed analyses of consciousness, space, time, intersubjectivity, number, and so on, elaborating in finer detail the ideas unfolded in the texts he released for publication during his long career. From this *"Nachlass"* many further volumes of Husserl's writing have been produced, with many more to come. The historical development of Husserl's thought, in relation to the wider history of philosophy in his day and to the long philosophical tradition from Plato onward, will indicate the range of Husserl's thought and the wider context of his work.

A PORTRAIT OF HUSSERL

Edmund Husserl (1859–1938), Czecho-Austro-German mathematician turned philosopher, founded the discipline of phenomenology, a new approach to the study of consciousness and its role in constituting or giving meaning to the world. In the Europe of his day, mathematicians were laying new foundations for mathematics (in set theory and non-Euclidean geometries) and physicists were developing new foundations for physics (in relativity theory and quantum mechanics), while psychologists were setting psychology on a scientific foundation (from Franz Brentano to Wilhelm Wundt and, in a different direction, Sigmund Freud). Husserl shared this passion for new foundations, and he sought to put philosophy itself on a radical new path, with a new vision and new methods.

Husserl proposed that all philosophy, and indeed all science and all knowledge, be grounded in what he came to call transcendental phenomenology, seeking the ideal meaning of various types of experience, from perception and imagination to judgment and knowledge formation. The rationalists – Descartes, Leibniz, Spinoza, et al. – had held that knowledge is founded ultimately on reason; the empiricists – Locke, Berkeley, Hume, et al. – countered that knowledge is founded ultimately on sense perception; and then Kant's critique of pure reason (and of pure sensation) laid out a synthesis of rationalist and empiricist doctrines, mapping the mind's contribution to the structure of space, time, and things as we know them. Into this grand sweep of European philosophy entered Husserl. Deeper than the structure of either reason or sensation, or Kantian categories of the understanding, Husserl held, is the structure of consciousness itself: what he called intentionality, that is, the way that consciousness is "directed" toward or represents objects of various kinds in the world. Phenomenology studies just this structure, and thereby provides the proper foundation for knowledge.

In practice, however, Husserl's idea of philosophical foundation was different from that of prior thinkers such as Descartes and Kant. Husserl developed a systematic philosophy in which phenomenology, ontology, epistemology, and logic are interdependent parts, each founded upon elements in the other parts. For Descartes, all philosophy is founded on epistemology (the theory of knowledge) and all knowledge is founded in the "pure light" of reason. For Kant, all philosophy, from theory of knowledge to moral theory, is founded in reason, pure and practical, which operates in conjunction with sensibility. For Husserl, by contrast, all philosophy is founded on the phenomenological theory of intentionality, but phenomenology, logic, ontology, and epistemology are in certain ways mutually founding. Thus, Husserl's philosophy developed with a kind of structured holism, even as phenomenology became the avowed centerpiece and the proclaimed foundation for the whole system.

As Husserl's philosophy developed, and as his conception of phenomenology was extended and modified by later thinkers (especially Martin Heidegger, Jean-Paul Sartre, and Maurice Merleau-Ponty), the concerns of phenomenology spread from the foundations of logic, science, and knowledge to the meaning of human experience and its significance for social reality. Existentialism and later movements (structuralism and poststructuralism) carried phenomenology from mathematics and science to social analysis. (See Moran 2000 for a detailed appraisal of the varieties of phenomenology that evolved through the 20th century.)

Husserl was a philosophers' philosopher, engaging the large issues raised by Plato, Aristotle, Descartes, Hume, and Kant, along with the issues of logico-mathematical theory emerging in his day in Cantor, Frege, Hilbert, Carnap, Whitehead and Russell. Accordingly, Husserl's philosophy addressed in a systematic way the classical issues of universal and particular, mind and body, individual and society, fact and value, and especially the emerging issues of how mind and language represent the world. Today's techniques of computer science would have been at home in Husserl's model of mental representation, yet Husserl insisted that the techniques of formal modeling be grounded in bona fide activities of consciousness, as our minds present and engage things in our environment. And from this formal mathematical matrix of ideas emerged Husserl's conception of phenomenology, focused on concrete human experience and the importance of the world of everyday life.

A mathematician turned philosopher, Husserl's writing was complex and abstract, yet strangely engaging. The more you read, the more you see of his large vision. His complex prose is holographic: the more you read, the more you see in each part the larger scheme. In his early works you can see the same concerns that emerge in his later works, such as his humanistic concern for the life-world, which plays smoothly into the concerns of existential philosophy in later decades. And in his later works you can see the same concerns that launched his earliest work, such as his concern for logical theory as a scheme for representing the world.

There is a brief film clip of Husserl in a home movie (reproduced in a videocassette in Embree 1991). The film shows a rather small man, with full beard, round wire-rimmed glasses, and the three-piece suit of his day. He seems almost to be looking toward the Platonic heavens with an idealistic bearing as he walks in the garden behind his apartment in Freiburg, Germany. Husserl often received visitors, both students and famous philosophers, in his family apartment, sometimes talking with them in his garden, to which he refers in his writing. It is reported that his wife Malvine would sometimes escort a visitor to meet Professor Husserl in his study, where a long discussion would ensue, and then Frau Husserl would escort the visitor to the door, where she would quietly ask, "Is he as great as Plato?"

Husserl's writing shows his penchant for abstraction, for drawing the very large picture meant to be filled in by concrete details of experience. His lectures were said to be complex and demanding, and students found that Husserl was not gifted at understanding others, either in discussion or in reading other philosophers. These qualities do not sound like those of the leader of a great philosophical movement. Yet his passion for philosophy, for truth and objectivity, and for the new science of phenomenology, were clearly contagious. His writing and teaching drew many students, and the phenomenological movement was launched. This movement was the dominant force in 20th-century European philosophy, even as later phenomenologists diverged from Husserl's own strict path. Moreover, scholars today are discovering Husserl's role in the development of analytic philosophy, the other great movement launched in the 20th century. Furthermore, while Husserl was not a philological scholar of the classical philosophers, from Plato through Kant, his philosophy absorbed and reconfigured the concerns of these classical thinkers. The world has not often seen such a broad philosophical mind executing abstract theories with attention to exacting description of concrete detail. These are the traits of a mathematician put to work in the philosophy of a visionary, and they inform Husserl's conception of phenomenology, seeking ideal meanings in concrete everyday experiences. History will place him among the small number of greatest philosophers, though his full legacy will not be understood for another hundred years.

THE COURSE OF HUSSERL'S CAREER

The early years

Edmund Husserl was born on 8 April 1859 in Prossnitz, Moravia, which was then part of the Habsburg or Austro-Hungarian Empire and is now Prostejov, near Brno in the Czech Republic. He died on 27 April 1938 in Freiburg, Germany, near the French border, in the town where he taught and practiced philosophy at the zenith of his career.

Husserl was born into an assimilated Jewish family in the German-speaking community in the Czech region Moravia (part of what Germans called the Sudetenland, an area that would be the focus of German aggression in the 1930s). The family was not religious, and Edmund himself became a Lutheran as a young adult. The second of four children, Edmund was an uninterested schoolboy who nonetheless showed some ability in mathematics. At the age of nine he was sent to school in Vienna, then finished his Gymnasium (high school) studies at Olmütz, now Olomouc, in 1876. He entered the University of Leipzig, studying astronomy, mathematics, and physics. There he befriended Thomas Masaryk, a philosophy student (and later President of Czechoslovokia), who interested Husserl in the philosophy of Franz Brentano and in the empiricists. In 1878 he moved to Berlin, where he studied mathematics and philosophy. There he attended the lectures of two great mathematicians, Karl Weierstrass and Leopold Kronecker. In 1881 Husserl transferred to the University of Vienna and in 1882 earned his doctorate in pure mathematics with a dissertation on the calculus of variations. His dissertation was directed by a disciple of Weierstrass, and in 1883 Husserl returned to Berlin as Weierstrass' assistant. But Husserl's interests were turning toward philosophy. After a period of military service, he returned to Vienna, where his friend Masaryk was then teaching philosophy as a *Privatdozent* (unsalaried lecturer).

From 1884 to 1886 Husserl attended the lectures given in Vienna by Franz Brentano, a charismatic teacher of great renown. In these years Husserl turned firmly to philosophy, and Brentano's conception of descriptive psychology would be the formative influence on Husserl's later development of phenomenology. Through Brentano Husserl became interested in the empiricist philosophy of David Hume, whom Husserl always admired as a genuine forerunner of phenomenology, as Hume mapped the different kinds of mental activities. Brentano also introduced Husserl to the work of Bernard Bolzano, whose conception of logic proved a crucial inspiration in Husserl's development of phenomenology. Moreover, it was from Brentano that Husserl learned of the Medieval theory of *intentio*, the mind's aiming at objects in thought or perception. After a decade of incubation, Husserl's conception of intentionality would be the heart of his theory of knowledge and ultimately phenomenology.

The years in Halle: 1886–1900

Husserl was ready to begin work on his *Habilitation* (a kind of second doctorate in the German university system, the prerequisite for university positions). However, Brentano's conflicts with the Church forced him to resign his professorship in Vienna. So Brentano then sent Husserl to study with Brentano's former student Carl Stumpf at the University of Halle. In 1886 Husserl moved to Halle, and in 1887, under Stumpf's supervision, Husserl completed his *Habilitation* thesis, *On the Concept of Number, Psychological Analyses*. Sitting on Husserl's examination committee was the mathematician Georg Cantor, known today for his pioneering work in set theory and the foundations of mathematics. Husserl and Cantor became friends during Husserl's years at Halle, where Husserl continued in the post of *Privatdozent*. In the *Habilitation* thesis Husserl proposed to clarify the concept of number by tracing its formation in psychic acts of distinguishing multiplicities, or "manifolds" (a notion to which Husserl often returned, and a term that remains in contemporary geometry). In this early work Husserl had begun his intellectual migration from pure mathematics into philosophy and ultimately into pure phenomenology. That journey would take Husserl another 14 years.

Husserl remained at Halle until 1901, all the while teaching at the rank of *Privatdozent*. He was never happy in this position in Halle, living with little prestige and limited income (students paid for lectures). But his family life was begun in the Halle years and seemed quite happy. In 1887 he married Malvine Steinschneider. They had three children: Elli, born in 1892; Gerhart, born in 1893; and Wolfgang, born in 1895. Malvine, also from a Jewish family, had become a Christian shortly before they married. Though Husserl considered his philosophy "a-theological," he seems to have had some strong religious feelings. Perhaps that intensity of feeling was related to his pursuit of the purity of consciousness and the ego in his later phenomenology.

Husserl published his first book in 1891 while at Halle, *The Philosophy of Arithmetic: Psychological and Logical Investigations, Book I*, which he dedicated to Brentano. This book was an extension of his *Habilitation* thesis, and it marked Husserl's transition from mathematics into philosophy of mathematics, turning his eye to logical theory and an inchoate form of analysis of psychic activity – the kernel of his later vision of phenomenology. In the same era mathematicians, including his friend Cantor, were working toward new foundations for mathematics in the emerging theory of sets (then variously called *Inbegriffe*, *Mannigfaltigkeiten*, or *Mengen*: as it were, conceptual graspings or groupings, manifolds or multiplicities, and groups). Over the following decades, mathematicians and logicians would seek to ground all of mathematics in a combination of logic and set theory. Husserl's position in *The Philosophy of Arithmetic* has been widely taken as a form of "psychologism," reducing mathematics to patterns of psychic activity like mentally grouping things and counting or measuring the size or cardinality of the group. The subtitle of the book is illuminating, for we see Husserl beginning to wrestle with the relation between the psychological and the logical. (Recall that from Brentano Husserl had acquired an admiration not only for descriptive psychology, but also for logical theory, in Brentano's own exact philosophy and in Bolzano's prior logic.)

Husserl had corresponded in writing with Gottlob Frege, Professor of mathematics at Jena, whom we now know as one of the greatest logicians in history. When Husserl's book appeared, Frege wrote a critical review charging Husserl's philosophy of arithmetic with psychologism, or reducing logic and mathematics to psychology. Frege joined Hermann Lotze in attacking 19th-century psychologism and defending instead a Platonistic philosophy of mathematics, which would hold that numbers and other mathematical entities exist in their own right and are not created by psychological activities. Husserl readily accepted Frege's anti-psychologism, seeming to turn sharply in his tracks and to move in a different direction. In fact, Husserl's account of the origin of the concept of number was not a reduction of numbers to psychic acts; nonetheless, he did not yet have the tools to sort out the relevant issues concerning how thoughts or concepts of numbers are related to numbers themselves. Book II of The Philosophy of Arithmetic never appeared. Instead, over the next decade Husserl wrote his monumental Logical Investigations, published in 1900–1. That work opened with a book-length attack on psychologism and then moved through detailed studies in ontology, phenomenology, and epistemology.

The years in Göttingen: 1901–16

Husserl's Logical Investigations, the result of a decade of hard thinking about a rich complex of themes, earned Husserl at last a regular, salaried position in the German academy. In 1901 he was appointed Professor Extraordinarius (somewhat like Associate Professor in today's American academy) at the University of Göttingen. In 1906, despite faculty opposition, he was advanced to Professor Ordinarius (the rank of full Professor, which, in the German academy, is granted to only a couple of scholars in each field at each university). Husserl stayed at Göttingen until 1916, and during this period his philosophy evolved considerably.

During the Göttingen years, Husserl was actively involved with a group of scientists and mathematicians including the mathematician David Hilbert, who framed the problem of completeness for axiomatic systems in mathematics. Husserl's conception of logic as the theory of theories, mapped out early in the *Logical Investigations*, had already indicated the philosophical importance of logical completeness for a theory conceived as a system of propositions closed under logical deduction. (In the 1930s Kurt Gödel would prove theorems about completeness and incompleteness in certain axiomatic systems. Late in life Gödel would study Husserl's phenomenological theory of knowledge, finding himself in sympathy with Husserl's phenomenology.)

Throughout the 1890s, Husserl's conception of logic had developed in tandem with his emerging conception of phenomenology, as he wrote out some 1,000 pages of the *Logical Investigations*. On the heels of its publication, as he took up his new position in Göttingen, Husserl's phenomenology developed a strong following throughout continental Europe. In Munich in 1903 an informal "school" of phenomenology took shape following Husserl's work, organized in good measure by a farmer named Johannes Daubert (who died in the First World War) and including Adolf Reinach, who developed a phenomenological ontology for legal theory (he also died in the First World War). The Munich school promoted a realist ontology for phenomenology, in line with Husserl's ontology of parts/wholes and states of affairs. In 1907 the Göttingen Philosophical Society formed to advance phenomenology. This group included Roman Ingarden and Edith Stein. Ingarden, who contributed to the growth of philosophy in Poland, would later criticize Husserl's turn to transcendental idealism, and he would develop a phenomenologically informed ontology of art works, which remains influential today. Stein would go on to write a doctoral dissertation under Husserl, published as *On the Problem of Empathy*, a seminal work on the phenomenology of understanding others, after which she turned to religious writing. Though Jewish, Edith Stein converted to Catholicism, but died in the Nazi concentration camp at Auschwitz; in 1998 she was canonized by Pope John Paul II, becoming Saint Benedicta, in recognition of her ordeal and as testament to her faith.

In 1891 William James, Professor at Harvard University, published his monumental *Principles of Psychology*, which surveyed the mind in a proto-phenomenological way, distinguishing basic types of mental activity, while stressing the role of habit and bodily states, especially emotions, taken as extending into the body. Husserl read and admired James' work, but James did not have a proper theory of intentionality, of how consciousness is directed toward things in the world. James took a pragmatist approach to psychology, tying our consciousness to our bodily habits, and to our social practices, whereas Husserl, in his Logical Investigations, took a logical approach to the study of consciousness, featuring the role of ideal meanings in representing things we experience. Still, the godfather of American pragmatism, Charles Sanders Peirce, was a logician, and interacted with European logicians as contemporary logic was developing. (Peirce and Frege independently proposed theories of the quantifier words "all" and "some," thereby advancing logic beyond Aristotle's syllogism.) Unfortunately for the history of 20th-century philosophy, James recommended against an English translation of Husserl's Logical Investigations, mistakenly thinking it just another long text of logic.

During the 1890s, in a different research program than James' psychology, Sigmund Freud, in Vienna, was developing the foundations of psychoanalysis, launched in his Interpretation of Dreams, which appeared in 1900. Freud and Husserl had both attended Brentano's lectures on psychology, and both published groundbreaking studies of the mind in 1900. Freud's studies of dreams launched psychoanalysis, featuring the theory of unconscious psychic states and their causal influence on conscious emotions and actions. Husserl's studies of logic, by contrast, led into his phenomenology, featuring the theory of consciousness and intentionality. It does not appear that Freud read Husserl or vice versa. Yet, in a fortuitous division of labor, they championed, respectively, the unconscious and the conscious parts of the mind.

During the years 1905 to 1910 Husserl carried out some of his most important phenomenological analyses. He appraised the structure of our experience of time and of space, in works that were published much later, posthumously. In that context he studied the structure of sensation, of sensory experience as it unfolds in time, and the role of sensation in our experience of objects in space and time. In an important series of lectures on the theory of meaning

in 1908, he modified his earlier conception of meaning from the
Logical Investigations. These 1908 lectures launched his mature theory
of ideal meaning, for which he later introduced the famous terminology of "noema" (a Greek term for what is known). At the same
time Husserl studied Kant's philosophy and by 1913 presented his
own version of "transcendental idealism," adapting the Kantian idiom to
his conception of phenomenology, now called "transcendental"
phenomenology. In 1912 and 1913 Husserl tied together these
results, at a high level of abstraction, in his third book: *Ideas, Book One*.
The complete title was: *Ideas toward a Pure Phenomenology and a Phenomenological
Philosophy, Book One: General Introduction to Phenomenology*. This work is
known as *Ideas I*. In the same months in 1912 he drafted Books
One, Two, and Three of *Ideas*, though he published only Book
One. Book Two: *Phenomenological Studies of Constitution*, known as *Ideas
II*, was drafted at the same time, but Husserl never released it for
publication, a great misfortune since it contains some of Husserl's
most important concrete phenomenological analyses: analyses of
embodiment (the I or ego is not a disembodied spirit), kinesthetic
awareness (of one's bodily movement) in action, empathy (how I
experience another "I"), the world of everyday life (later called the
"life-world"), and the social structure of our experience (much
elaborated by later phenomenologists, including Martin Heidegger
and Alfred Schutz, and by the French poststructuralists, including
Michel Foucault). Book Three: *Phenomenology and the Foundations of the
Sciences, Ideas III*, elaborates on the relations between phenomenology,
ontology, psychology, and the social sciences.

In *Ideas I* (1913) Husserl's phenomenology took a "transcendental
turn." In the *Logical Investigations* Husserl's phenomenology was
developed in conjunction with a realist ontology, whereby
consciousness occurs in a world that exists independently of our
perceiving or thinking of it. In *Ideas I*, however, Husserl's
phenomenology was presented in conjunction with a neo-Kantian
doctrine of transcendental idealism, whereby the world is "constituted" in a multiplicity of actual and possible acts of consciousness.
What does it mean to say an object (a tree, another human being,
or whatever) is "constituted" in consciousness? As we shall see,
this is one of the thorniest issues in understanding Husserl. On

one reading of Husserl's transcendental idealism, every object in the world consists in a system of ideal meanings, or "noemata," which present it from an infinite variety of perspectives. Noemata take the place of Kant's "phenomena," or things-as-they-appear. Beyond that system of noemata, there is no "thing in itself," no object beyond the reach of all possible consciousness. The character of Husserl's idealism remains in dispute today. Some scholars find an idealism not unlike Berkeley's (the world reduces to ideas, though ideas are ideal noemata). Others find a transcendental idealism quite like Kant's (there is a world beyond our ideas, but we cannot know it as it is "in itself"). And some interpreters (including the present author) find a realist ontology joined with a methodological perspectivism (mundane objects exist independently of our consciousness of them, but we know them only through some particular conception or meaning). In any event, Husserl's position of "transcendental idealism" does not squeeze into any of the familiar pigeonholes. What is genuinely new in Husserl, and what makes his philosophy "transcendental," is his theory of intentionality, of how consciousness is directed via meaning toward objects that are (in most cases) independent of our consciousness of them. Husserl's conception of intentionality turns his phenomenology away from classical concerns of epistemology and ontology (what can we know and does it exist independently of our knowing it?), and toward 20th-century logical or semantic theory (how do meanings present or refer consciousness to objects in the world?). Thus, what makes Husserl's phenomenology transcendental, in his new conception of the transcendental, is the role of ideal meaning in the "constitution" of the world, as we interpret or understand things in the world only through the complex structures of meaning that characterize our myriad forms of consciousness of objects in the world.

The years in Freiburg

In 1916 Husserl was appointed Professor Ordinarius at the University of Freiburg. He would live out the rest of his life in

Freiburg, teaching, receiving famous philosophers from abroad, lecturing throughout Germany and in London, Paris, and Italy. Husserl was then the leading thinker in the German-speaking philosophy world, and phenomenology would remain the center of continental philosophy for the rest of the century, even as later philosophers modified or rejected aspects of Husserl's philosophy, especially its rationalism and its transcendentalism. (See Moran 2000 for a detailed study that ties many key European thinkers into phenomenology over the course of the past century.)

During the 1920s and 1930s the movement called "analytic philosophy" emerged, seeking to ground philosophy in logical and linguistic analysis, aligning philosophy with logic, mathematics, and natural science. The foundations of the new logic had been laid by Gottlob Frege in the late 19th century and were furthered by Alfred North Whitehead and Bertrand Russell in their monumental *Principia Mathematica* (1910–13). Husserl knew these works, but tied logical theory into phenomenology. Analytic philosophy took shape in the vigorous activity of the Vienna Circle during the 1920s, as the logical positivists sought to put philosophy on a firm empirical basis along with the physical sciences. Both Moritz Schlick and Rudolf Carnap, central figures in the Circle, addressed Husserl's work directly, and Ludwig Wittgenstein's famous *Tractatus Logico-Philosophicus* (1921) offers a somewise Husserlian analysis of how propositional meanings represent states of affairs in the world (it is not evident whether Wittgenstein knew of the similar picture of representation in the details of Husserl's *Logical Investigations*). Schlick resisted Husserl's Platonistic notion of ideal essences knowable by a special kind of intuition. However, Gödel, who studied in Vienna in the 1920s, would later argue for the role of abstract or ideal entities and for mathematical intuition, going against the 1920s positivism of Schlick *et al.* Carnap attended Husserl's lectures in 1924–5 while Carnap was writing *The Logical Construction of the World* (*Der Logische Aufbau der Welt*, 1928). This seminal work in analytic philosophy of science was clearly influenced by Husserl's doctrine of constitution (Carnap called his system "constitution theory," *Konstitutionstheorie*), but Carnap developed a formal logical language and its interpretation to model the way we conceptualize or "constitute" the world. Gilbert Ryle, one of the founding fathers of Oxford ordinary language philosophy with his The Concept of Mind (1949), visited Husserl at Freiburg in 1929. Ryle later reflected that The Concept of Mind could be viewed as a study in phenomenology, though the technique Ryle practiced was to analyze the ways we use mental verbs such as "think," "imagine," "see," "will," and so on. As the 20th century wore on, analytic philosophy took root in England and then America, reflecting in part the remarkable growth in science and technology. The traditions of continental phenomenology and Anglo-American analytic philosophy gradually diverged, leaving a famous cultural gap between philosophers in these traditions. Nonetheless, in the early 20th century the core concerns of the traditions overlapped, and key practitioners were engaged in fruitful interactions, which scholars are investigating today. And as philosophy of mind developed in the later decades of the 20th century, analytic philosophers returned to issues of intentionality and consciousness, which Husserl had explored earlier in his phenomenology.

During the 1920s a different sensibility was at work elsewhere in Europe, in the rise of existential philosophy, concerned with everyday human existence, including our social being and the role of choice and value in our world. Students in Freiburg joined Husserl in this emphasis. In Ideas II Husserl had analyzed the social or cultural (geistlich, "spiritual") aspect of the self or I, emphasizing the role of empathy in grounding social life and the personal and moral aspects of human life. In 1916 Edith Stein, as Husserl's assistant in Freiburg, edited the manuscript of Ideas II, but Husserl was not ready to release it for publication. From 1919 to 1923 Martin Heidegger, destined to become the leading German philosopher after Husserl, worked as Husserl's assistant, emphasizing our relation to the surrounding human world and its practices. In 1928–9 Emmanuel Levinas attended Husserl's (and Heidegger's) lectures in Freiburg, and took phenomenology back to Paris when he returned; Levinas would go on to develop a phenomenology of ethics, emphasizing the meaning of the "face" of the other. These themes would loom large in the existentialism cum phenomenology of Jean-Paul Sartre and Simone de Beauvoir, writing in 1940s Paris.

In 1928 Husserl retired. He was succeeded in the Chair of Philosophy by Martin Heidegger. Husserl continued to write and to lecture. In 1929 he published *Formal and Transcendental Logic*, returning to themes of the *Logical Investigations* but extending (or re-emphasizing) the foundation of logic in intentionality. In 1931, after his Paris lectures, he published a French translation of the *Cartesian Meditations*, casting his phenomenology in a revisionist Cartesian perspective and extending his epistemology with refined distinctions of types of evidence. Husserl was still pressing his conception of phenomenology, placing it in different contexts and introducing it differently in each of his principal books.

The final years: 1933–8

In 1933 the Nazis came to power in Germany and issued new regulations prohibiting Jews and other non-Aryans from holding positions in government or in the universities. Husserl was thereby effectively locked out of the University. The *Rektor* of the University of Freiburg in the spring of 1933, the official who enforced the Nazi decree, was none other than Martin Heidegger, Husserl's former assistant and now his successor. Although Heidegger remained as *Rektor* for only a few months, Husserl was shocked by the actions of both his former friend and his adopted country. Ethnically Jewish (though a Protestant), Husserl was loyal to Germany, noting that his son Wolfgang was killed and his son Gerhart wounded while fighting for Germany in the First World War. Heidegger's magnum opus *Being and Time* was dedicated to Edmund Husserl "in admiration and friendship" when published in 1927; subsequent editions dropped the dedication. Heidegger's actions and political ambitions in Nazi Germany remain a subject of scrutiny, but his acquired enmity for his forerunner was expressed in no uncertain terms in letters years later.

Husserl was prohibited from lecturing or publishing in Germany and his German citizenship was revoked, but in 1935 he delivered a lecture in Vienna that was incorporated into the posthumous book *The Crisis of the European Sciences and Transcendental Phenomenology* (known as *Crisis*, 1935–8). This book incorporates Husserl's thought during his final three years. The larger thesis is that natural science, since Galileo's "mathematization of nature," has lost touch with the level of understanding that we have in the *Lebenswelt* or life-world. This "crisis" in European culture, Husserl intimated, lay behind the rising irrationalism of the Nazi era. The Husserl children Elli and Gerhart had emigrated to the United States in 1933–4, but when Husserl died in 1938 he still had no plans to leave Germany. His widow was hidden in a convent in Belgium during the Second World War, and in 1946 she joined her children in the United States.

Husserl left a huge body of unpublished writing, or *Nachlass*, when he died. To protect this work from destruction by the Nazis, his supporters smuggled the whole *Nachlass* out of Germany through the Belgian consulate. These texts remain today in the Husserl Archives in Louvain (or Leuven), Belgium. Hermann Van Breda, a Belgian priest, arranged for the preservation of Husserl's manuscripts, and it was Van Breda who arranged for Frau Husserl to reach safety in Belgium.

THE TRAJECTORY OF HUSSERL'S WRITING

Husserl published relatively little for a major thinker with an academic career spanning half a century, from 1887 (when he completed his *Habilitation*, following rather quickly on his dissertation of 1883) until his death in 1938. Following the European tradition, most of his publication took the form of books, five books in 51 years. Yet Husserl wrote constantly, leaving a *Nachlass* of 40,000 pages of shorthand notes (in the Gabelsberg system commonly used in 19th-century German universities). Many of his lecture courses are preserved as texts. Moreover, he was constantly experimenting with philosophical ideas, "thinking through writing," often working out concrete analyses whose results are presented only abstractly in his published books. To some extent these are the habits of a pure mathematician, transferred to philosophy. Much of this massive output has yet to be transcribed from shorthand into German, much less translated into English. Decade by decade, though, a series of posthumous texts have appeared, forming further books in which Husserl is seen filling out the details of his overall philosophy.

Husserl's first book, published in 1891, was his *Philosophy of Arithmetic: Psychological and Logical Investigations*. The "logical" side of this work would remain in place throughout Husserl's career, but the "psychological" side would evolve into his subsequent conception of phenomenology. Husserl would soon consider this an immature work that bordered on psychologism by explicating the concept of number in relation to the psychology of grouping and counting. As noted earlier, Husserl was not wholly guilty as charged in Frege's critical review of the book, yet he took Frege's critique to heart.

Over the next decade Husserl composed what many regard as his magnum opus, the *Logical Investigations*, covering some 1,000 pages in the original German edition. (Note the title, and previous book's subtitle.) This work appeared in two parts:

- *Logical Investigations, First Part: Prolegomena to Pure Logic* (1900);
- *Logical Investigations, Second Part: Investigations in Phenomenology and Theory of Knowledge* (1901).

The Prolegomena is a book unto itself, a long critique of psychologism in logic and mathematics, including a critique of relativism in the theory of knowledge, and culminating in Husserl's positive account of logic as the "theory of theories." The Second Part comprises what today would appear as a series of six books or monographs, which he called "investigations." Investigation I is a philosophy of language, including a theory of sense and reference (compare Frege's famous doctrines on these topics) and a theory of speech acts (compare J. L. Austin's and John Searle's work in the 1950s tradition of Oxford philosophy). Investigation II is a theory of species or universals (in effect putting Platonic and Aristotelian views together). Investigation III is an ontology of parts and wholes, together with the important notion of ontological dependence (one thing cannot exist unless another does).

Investigation IV is a theory of "grammar," applying part–whole
theory to ideal meanings or propositions. *Investigation* V is a detailed
theory of intentionality, featuring carefully argued distinctions
among an act of consciousness, its ideal shareable content (ideal
meaning, in principle expressible in language), and the object
toward which the act is directed by way of its content. Here lies
the foundation of Husserl's phenomenology – buried in the
middle of the Second Part of the *Investigations*. Finally, *Investigation* VI
is a book-length study in the theory of knowledge, extending
Husserl's phenomenological theory of intentionality (how
consciousness represents) to a phenomenological theory of
knowledge (how consciousness forms genuine knowledge
through "intuition" or "evident" presentation of objects and states
of affairs).

Looking back, Husserl's *Logical Investigations* was a study in logic
widely construed, a philosophy of logic, mathematics, and scientific
theory that would be at home in the tradition of analytic philosophy – these were the concerns of Husserl's early career, moving
from pure mathematics through "pure" logic into ontology,
phenomenology, and epistemology. Looking forward, the *Logical
Investigations* launched Husserl's full conception of phenomenology,
for the theory of intentionality, the heart of phenomenology, was
laid out carefully and for the first time in Investigation V. Husserl
would later set phenomenology in a context of transcendental
philosophy (as distinct from naturalistic philosophy, based in
natural science). In 1913 Husserl published a revised edition of all
but the last Investigation, and in 1920 the revised edition of
Investigation VI appeared. The revised edition incorporated
remarks from Husserl's transcendental perspective. That edition is
what we have today (Routledge 2000 in English translation).

In 1913 Husserl published his third book, *Ideas* I, focused solely
on phenomenology. Its long title reads: *Ideas toward a Pure
Phenomenology and Phenomenological Philosophy, Book One: General Introduction
to Pure Phenomenology*.

This work was Husserl's mature manifesto of transcendental
phenomenology. Ironically, the abbreviated title that we use
informally, *Ideas*, would have been just right, since what the

empiricists called "ideas" are the proper subject matter of phenomenology, though Husserl drew crucial distinctions and developed a detailed theory not evident in his predecessors. (Recall that Husserl admired Hume, as did Brentano.)

In Ideas I Husserl presents his method of phenomenological "reduction": we are to study pure consciousness by "bracketing" the general thesis of the "natural standpoint," the thesis that there is a natural world of objects beyond our consciousness. By this method of bracketing, we turn our attention from the objects of consciousness (things in the surrounding world of nature) to our consciousness of these objects, regardless of whether they exist. At one point (§49), Husserl says that the world does not exist "absolutely" but only "relatively," in intentional relation to our consciousness. That at any rate is the doctrine of transcendental idealism often attributed to Husserl following his neo-Kantian transcendental turn. A more subtle interpretation holds instead that, for Husserl in Ideas I, any object in the world around us exists independently of our consciousness, but it exists "for us" – we know and experience it – only in acts of consciousness through specific meanings or "noemata," through which we understand it in a particular way. Then the point of bracketing is to turn our attention from the objects that normally concern us to our consciousness of these objects, and to the meanings through which we experience them.

Ideas I was written in a matter of months, and Books Two and Three, Ideas II and III, were drafted at the same time but never released for publication in Husserl's lifetime. These volumes, now published, not only provide detailed phenomenological analyses whose significance is touted in Ideas I. They also belie the tendency toward classical idealism that may be suggested by certain sections of Ideas I, (§§49ff.). Here Husserl details the structure of our experience of embodiment, of other persons, and of social practices and institutions. Here too lie the basics of the "existential" phenomenology developed later by Martin Heidegger and, in very different ways, Maurice Merleau-Ponty.

In 1929, shortly after his retirement, Husserl published his fourth book, Formal and Transcendental Logic, written in a few months.

Despite many years of work on phenomenology as opposed to logical theory, Husserl here returned to the nature of logic. Most of his phenomenological work is in evidence, as if presented here through the lens of logical theory, thus echoing the *Logical Investigations*. Husserl distinguishes formal logic, of the sort now familiar in symbolic or mathematical logic, from transcendental logic, by which Husserl means a philosophical account of formal logic. Basically, Husserl proposes that intentionality is the structure of thought or judgment in processes of reasoning. Where formal logic abstracts from these mental processes, to produce a logical calculus, transcendental logic analyzes the underlying intentional acts whose meanings are expressed by the symbolisms of formal logic. While mathematical logic was coming into full bloom, with Alfred Tarski's logical or semantic theory of truth and Gödel's incompleteness theorems still a few years off in the 1930s, Husserl was providing a philosophy of logic that tied logic into phenomenology.

In 1931 Husserl published his fifth book, *Cartesian Meditations*, in a French translation of the text of lectures he gave in Paris (the German edition would be published posthumously in 1952). Reflecting Descartes' epoch-making *Meditations on First Philosophy* (1641), Husserl here presents phenomenology with a focus on epistemology. Husserl says Descartes was close to discovering phenomenology but mistakenly held on to "a little tag-end" of the world, in the ego or I who thinks. Descartes sought to ground all knowledge in the certainty we each have of our own consciousness and our own self ("I think, therefore I am"). But Husserl develops a series of distinctions among types of evidence or certainty. The result is an approach to our own conscious experience, not unlike Descartes', but with a careful analysis of different kinds of evident knowledge: of my own experience, of myself as subject, of my body, of other objects in my surrounding world, and of other persons. In his *Meditations*, Husserl wrestled with the problem of solipsism as a challenge to phenomenology. Solipsism (meaning "one self") is the doctrine that there exists only what appears within my own mind – all else is illusion. Now, bracketing the world seems to leave one isolated within one's own consciousness, so that phenomenology may seem to lead to solipsism. Husserl tried to show how my experience of an "other I" undercuts the threat of solipsism, even within the bounds of phenomenology. Apparently unsatisfied with the force of this argument, however, Husserl continued to address the problem of intersubjectivity, or how things in the world are "there for everyone," reverting to a recurrent theme in Ideas I and Ideas II. Accordingly, Husserl produced a more compelling response to this problem in his last phase of work, gathered posthumously in the Crisis. In any event, Husserl's method of bracketing should have forestalled any threat of solipsism (as the method is explicated in Chapter 6).

In 1935 Husserl gave a lecture in Vienna titled "Philosophy in the Crisis of European Humanity." He extended the theme of that lecture in texts written between 1935 and his death in 1938. These texts were gathered in a posthumous volume published in 1954 under the title The Crisis of the European Sciences and Transcendental Phenomenology: An Introduction to Phenomenological Philosophy. This text is in effect Husserl's sixth and final book – still trying to introduce phenomenology to the world. On the face of it, Husserl broke new ground in the Crisis, configuring his conception of the life-world, modifying his prior "Cartesian" method of phenomenological reduction, and critiquing the "mathematization" of nature in physical science. In Husserl's analysis, (European) humanity was losing touch with its humanity as the scientific worldview was displacing our sense of the world in everyday life. In fact, the details of this analysis were already worked out in Ideas II, written in 1912. What was new in the Crisis was its direction: more humanistic, more existential, in some ways anti-scientist, with a nearly religious sensibility about the life-world. Some scholars see the Crisis as Husserl's response to Heidegger, who was actively seeking to replace Husserl as the great German thinker and the proper architect of phenomenology as fundamental ontology – and who had betrayed Husserl in enforcing the Nazi regulations that banned Husserl from the university. No one can miss Husserl's anguish over the crises of that time. In any event, beyond its 1930s political overtones, the

Crisis was a prescient work. For by the end of the 20th century the most active philosophical concern was arguably the new mind–body problem: how to understand mind and especially consciousness given the great advances in cognitive neuroscience, where psychic activity is to be explained in terms of computational processes executed in the neural network of the brain. How can we understand our own conscious experience and our everyday human activities in the life-world if everything reduces to physical and computational processes in fields of matter-energy mathematically defined by quantum mechanics and relativity physics?

Other manuscripts from Husserl's *Nachlass* have been edited to form further books of Husserl's work, filling out the picture we now have of Husserl's overall philosophy. These manuscripts show Husserl actively engaging basic issues throughout the rather long silences between his published books. Among these posthumous texts now available in English are the following, each of which has created a stir in the interpretation of Husserl's philosophy:

- *On the Phenomenology of Internal Time-Consciousness* (1893–1917);
- *Thing and Space: Lectures of 1907;*
- *Ideas II* and *Ideas III* (drafted in 1912 along with *Ideas I*);
- *Phenomenological Psychology: Lectures, Summer Semester,* 1925;
- *Analyses Concerning Passive and Active Synthesis: Lectures on Transcendental Logic* (lectures from 1920–6);
- *Experience and Judgment* (compiled from a variety of manuscripts over many years, said to complement *Formal and Transcendental Logic*).

Other volumes have been published in German but not yet translated into English, including:

- *Lectures on Ethics and Value Theory* (lectures from 1911, 1914).

The thing to note in this list is the combination of concrete phenomenological analyses with abstract logical and ontological theory. Throughout Husserl's career he combined these two types of philosophizing. On the one hand, we see analyses of time-consciousness, perception of things in space, the genesis of meaning (of such things) through active and passive synthesis (in intentional activity). On the other hand, we see Husserl framing these phenomenological analyses within a picture of logic that grounds reason in intentional acts of consciousness, in acts that carry ideal meanings through which we understand and experience things in the world around us – along with our selves and our experiences of these things.

THE EVOLUTION OF HUSSERL'S PHILOSOPHY

According to a prominent traditional interpretation, Husserl's philosophy evolved through some four periods separated by revolutionary turns of mind. (This traditional view is captured in some detail in Moran 2000; the view is perceptively summarized, then criticized, in Mohanty 1995. The secondary literature debates smaller twists and turns in Husserl's thought, but our concern is a broad evolution through four phases.)

The phases delineated by this view can be drawn from our account of Husserl's work. The first phase, in Husserl's early years at Halle, involved his foray into a seemingly psychologistic account of number, expressed in his *Philosophy of Arithmetic* (1891). Then Husserl reversed course, prompted in part by Frege's sharp criticism of that book. In his second phase, during his later years at Halle, Husserl carried out a detailed critique of psychologism in logic (and mathematics and axiomatic theories in general), developed in the Prolegomena to the *Logical Investigations* (1900–1). As we know, Husserl did not stop with logic: the *Investigations* continued with related studies in linguistic theory, ontology, phenomenology, and epistemology. In this quasi-Platonistic phase, emphasizing ideal species or essences, Husserl laid the foundations for his conception of phenomenology, articulated in the later parts of the *Investigations*. Therein, so the story goes, Husserl was beginning to change course again, returning to a descriptive psychology – the early phenomenology – as the foundation of knowledge. In the third phase, during his Göttingen years, Husserl is seen as taking a sharp transcendental turn, reconceiving and radicalizing phenomenology on a neo-Kantian transcendental foundation, seeking the conditions of the possibility of knowledge in pure consciousness alone. In *Ideas* I (1913) transcendental phenomenology led into a transcendental idealism that seemingly grounded all reality (not just knowledge, but being itself) in pure consciousness. Husserl's transcendental phase lasted into his Freiburg years and beyond his retirement, as the *Cartesian Meditations* (1931) grounded all the activities of consciousness in the pure or transcendental ego. By the end of the *Meditations*, however, Husserl was struggling with the problem of "transcendental solipsism," where the whole world seems to collapse into the solitary unit of being, "my" ego. In his fourth and final phase, then, Husserl changed course again, turning now to the social reality of the life-world. As we see in the *Crisis* (1935–8), the ego is born into the everyday life-world, where "I" live with others, and together we constitute the world as we know it. Scientific theories are them-selves formed by scientists working in the everyday world, their results "sedimented" into concepts inherited by others. And as "I," the practicing phenomenologist, turn to the transcendental acts of my own consciousness, I live still in the life-world, where my actions and commitments carry existential and social signifi-cance that undercuts any move toward classical idealism and solipsism. Here Husserl's philosophy comes to rest.

In this way, according to the traditional interpretation, Husserl rewrote the fundamentals of his philosophy at least three times, shifting from a psychologism of number to a Platonistic logical realism joined with a realist phenomenology, then to a transcen-dental phenomenology yielding a strong form of idealism, and finally to an existential (yet somehow transcendental) phenomenology grounded in the life-world.

There is excitement in the idea of the Master, the founder of phenomenology, radically and repeatedly changing course as his reflections move him onward. Moreover, a certain metaphilos-ophy is at work in the traditional interpretation of Husserl, a philosophy of radical change in the history of ideas, a perspective often invoked in continental philosophy (by Nietzsche, Heidegger, Foucault, Derrida). It is said that each great thinker must "kill off the father" (like Oedipus) in order to move on. Husserl is seen, accordingly, as killing off his former self at each of three great turning points in his philosophical evolution. Indeed, the traditional reading of Husserl begins in part with his successor, Heidegger. Nonetheless, if we look for the unity in Husserl's evolving philosophy, a very different picture emerges, and we come to see the continuity in the development of Husserl's thought. (See Mohanty 1995; Smith and Smith 1995.)

According to this alternative interpretation (followed in the present book), Husserl was constantly expanding his overall system of philosophy. The shifts observed in Husserl's writings were not radical (nearly schizoid) turns of mind, but rather recurrent efforts to get the large scheme right. In diverse explorations, Husserl moved back and forth across different levels and domains of theory in addressing different parts of the world of consciousness, nature, and culture. (See D. W. Smith 1995 on the relation between ontology and phenomenology in Husserl's system.)

A PREVIEW OF HUSSERL'S SYSTEM OF PHILOSOPHY

Husserl's system begins to come into view as we sketch how Husserl's corpus of work hangs together.

When Husserl moved from mathematics into philosophy of mathematics, in the *Philosophy of Arithmetic* (1891), his aim was not to reduce numbers themselves to patterns of mental activity like grouping and counting. Rather, he wanted to explain how our arithmetical concepts emerged, how they originated in and so rest upon such activities. Husserl would not be able to straighten out the relevant issues, however, until after he had developed his view of phenomenology and its relation to logic and ontology, in the complex story line of the *Logical Investigations* (1900–1). Much later, he would take up the genesis of mathematical concepts again, in a 1936 essay "The Origin of Geometry," included as an appendix in the *Crisis*. (That Husserl was not really or wholly guilty of psychologism as charged by Frege is evident in his early writings from the 1890s, well before he had completed his attack on psychologism in the Prolegomena of the *Investigations*. See Dallas Willard's introduction to his 2003 translation of Husserl's *Philosophy of Arithmetic: Psychological and Logical Investigations with Supplementary Texts from 1887–1901*; and see Husserl's texts gathered by Willard in the 1994 collection *Early Writings in the Philosophy of Logic and Mathematics*.)

Husserl's philosophy of logic, laid out in the Prolegomena of the *Logical Investigations*, was a deepening of his concern with the foundations of mathematics. In line with developments of his day (involving his friends in mathematics, Cantor and Hilbert), Husserl understood each mathematical theory as an ideally axiomatizable system of propositions that spell out a formal structure, a structure that can be applied to some domain of entities, such as the positive integers, or the points in Euclidean space, or the particles in physical space–time. The same form pertains to any type of theory, from physics to biology to empirical psychology. The task of "pure" logic, for Husserl, is to develop an account – a metatheory – about any such theory. Thus, for Husserl following Bolzano, logic is the theory of theories.

What Husserl calls logic, however, is a broader discipline than what we think of today. For Husserl, logic is a philosophical scheme that incorporates language systems, intentionality, and ontology – and, adding evidence, epistemology. This is the vision detailed in the *Logical Investigations* and amplified in later works. Husserl's philosophy develops, if you will, an onto-phenomeno-logic: a system that details and correlates structures of language, mind or experience, and world. The systematic correlation among these levels is basically the story of intentionality and its foundation in the world.

In *Ideas I* (1913) Husserl focuses more fully on the structure of intentionality, including the ideal meanings or noemata that embody the full structure of an act of consciousness and implicitly lead into intentionally related systems of noemata. In *Formal and Transcendental Logic* (1929) Husserl revisits his wide conception of logic, stressing the foundation of formal logic in intentionality and the structures of meaning that language expresses. In *Cartesian Meditations* (1931) he amplifies his account of evidence, of how intentional judgments bearing different types of intuitive evidence yield different kinds of knowledge – of consciousness, self, others, and the surrounding world.

In the *Crisis* (1935–8), Husserl focuses on the interplay between our everyday knowledge and our inherited scientific knowledge. The intentionality of the practicing scientist is founded on the intentionality of his/her everyday life (as Einstein works on relativity theory and its experimental support, he writes with a pencil and he breaks for lunch). Yet our everyday perceptions, judgments, and actions themselves carry meanings that are inherited as "sedimented" concepts that were developed by others long ago (we see trees and bees, we use hammers to strike nails, we think about the South Pole, we value human rights). Some of our inherited concepts are drawn from ancient cultural practices (like hammering); some are drawn from scientific theory (my computer runs on energy in a stream of electrons).

In Husserl's shifting emphases over the years and in different works, we should see an ever-expanding system of philosophy, seeking greater breadth and depth in ways indicated by the expansive range of ideas indicated above. In Husserl's varying claims about the world and its relation to consciousness, we should see not simply a vacillation between forms of realism and forms of idealism, but rather a struggle to specify relationships between act and object in the basic structure of intentionality. And in Husserl's concerns with social reality and the life-world, we should see not a latter-day rejection of the importance of consciousness and its intentionality, but rather a balancing (in line with his early work) of the subjective realm, the intersubjective or social realm, and the objective realm, especially the world of nature.

As the chapters proceed, we shall see in Husserl one of the great systematists in Western philosophy. His overall philosophy has a conceptual unity rarely matched over so wide a range of philosophical concerns. Our task shall be to explore the different parts of his philosophical system – logic, ontology, phenomenology, epistemology, and so on – while mapping out the ways in which all the parts hang together to form a coherent whole. Interestingly, this hanging-together (*zusammenhängen* – it sounds better in German) is itself an instance of the part–whole structure studied (almost buried) in the middle of the *Logical Investigations*. Husserl himself never explicitly recounted how his philosophy hangs together in light of his own theory of hanging-together, but that theorem of his philosophy remains a result to be drawn out by his readers. We, in this book, are those readers.

SUMMARY

Edmund Husserl (1859–1938) wrote voluminously over some 50 years. He studied mathematics initially, writing a doctoral dissertation on the calculus of variations, followed by a *Habilitation* (similar to a second dissertation in the German academic system) on philosophical aspects of number theory. The latter evolved into his first book, after which he moved with vigor into the development of a systematic philosophy that framed, and introduced, his new science of phenomenology.

Over the course of his career, Husserl published five books:

- *Philosophy of Arithmetic* (1891);
- *Logical Investigations* (in three volumes, 1900–1);
- *Ideas toward a Pure Phenomenology and a Phenomenological Philosophy* (Book One, 1913);
- *Formal and Transcendental Logic* (1929);
- *Cartesian Meditations* (1931).

Husserl regarded *Philosophy of Arithmetic* as an immature work, in which he had veered too close to "psychologizing" sets and numbers. A decade of intensive theorizing then produced the *Logical Investigations*, which many consider Husserl's magnum opus. In this 1,000-page work, Husserl presented his carefully wrought theory of intentionality (how an experience is directed via its content toward an appropriate object in the world). Here was the foundation of Husserl's conception of phenomenology, the science of the essence of consciousness. However, the *Investigations* also developed Husserl's conception of "pure" logic (where various forms of meaning represent appropriate forms of objects), his detailed categorial ontology (distinguishing "formal" and "material" essences), and his epistemology (featuring "intuition" as self-evident experience). Thus, the Investigations crafts Husserl's overall system of philosophy, in which phenomenology takes its place. Ideas then detailed Husserl's mature "transcendental" conception of phenomenology, employing his method of "bracketing" and his refined theory of intentionality. Husserl's fourth book reminds us of his continuing interest in logical and mathematical theory, even in his "transcendental" period. The Cartesian Meditations present Husserl's philosophy, centered on phenomenology, with a Cartesian twist. But Husserl worried, in the work itself, that this approach led into a "transcendental solipsism," whereby consciousness is enclosed unto itself rather than existing in significant relations to the world around one.

Although many years separated the appearance of his key books, Husserl wrote constantly. Posthumous volumes of his writing address the structure of time and space as we experience them, the relation between experience of oneself and empathic experience of others, and much more. Notably, his final phase of writing has been gathered as: The Crisis of the European Sciences and Transcendental Phenomenology (1935–8).

In his work Husserl addresses the sweep of thought from Galileo's inauguration of the modern sciences to the "crisis" of rationality Husserl saw in 1930s Germany. There Husserl developed the theme of the "life-world," in contrast with the "world of nature" as "mathematized" in modern physics.

In the course of his philosophical life, then, Husserl moved from an initial focus on the objectivity of knowledge (in mathematics, logic, and science) to a prominent focus on the subjectivity of our own consciousness (in pure or transcendental phenomenology), and on to a focus on the intersubjectivity of our collective experience of things (in the philosophy of the life-world). Husserl's oeuvre bears a remarkable unity even as he is constantly on the move.

Husserl's system of philosophy, framed in the Logical Investigations and refined in later works, shall be the focus of our presentation of Husserl in the present book.

FURTHER READING (AND VIEWING)

The following books include discussions of Husserl's life, works, and career. However, the more detailed discussions of philosophical issues in these books pertain to later chapters in this book. The videocassette shows Husserl in the flesh.

Bernet, Rudolf, Iso Kern, and Eduard Marbach. 1999. *An Introduction to Husserlian Phenomenology.* Evanston, Illinois: Northwestern University Press. A detailed overview of Husserl's phenomenology, its methods, its results, its development, and a detailed chronology of Husserl's life, work, and teaching.

Embree, Lester, ed. 1991. *A Representation of Edmund Husserl.* Videocassette. Boca Raton, Florida: Center for Advanced Research in Phenomenology, Florida Atlantic University, *circa* 1991. A videocassette representing Husserl, his life, and an account of his work, including a short film clip of Husserl from a home movie.

Mohanty, J. N. 1995. "The Development of Husserl's Thought." In Barry Smith and David Woodruff Smith, eds. *The Cambridge Companion to Husserl.* Cambridge and New York: Cambridge University Press. An appraisal of the development of Husserl's philosophy over the full course of his career, stressing the continuity of Husserl's development.

Moran, Dermot. 2000. *Introduction to Phenomenology.* London and New York: Routledge. An overview of classic work in phenomenology, including a chapter on background in Brentano, four chapters on Husserl's work and life, and several chapters on later phenomenologists (Heidegger, Sartre, Merleau-Ponty) and broadly phenomenological continental philosophers (Gadamer, Arendt, Levinas, Derrida), all presented in historical context and chronological development.

— 2005. *Edmund Husserl: Founder of Phenomenology.* Cambridge and Malden, Massachussetts: Polity Press. A presentation of Husserl's phenomenology and its development in Husserl's different stages, including the early phase, the later "transcendental" phase, and the final phase emphasizing other persons in the life-world.

Smith, Barry, and David Woodruff Smith, eds. 1995. *The Cambridge Companion to Husserl.* Cambridge and New York: Cambridge University Press. Essays on basic areas in Husserl's philosophy.

— 1995. "Introduction." In Barry Smith and David Woodruff Smith, eds. *The Cambridge Companion to Husserl.* Cambridge and New York: Cambridge University Press. An overview of Husserl's philosophy and its development.

Zahavi, Dan. 2003. *Husserl's Phenomenology.* Stanford, California: Stanford University Press. A short book giving an overview of Husserl's thought in the early logical period, the middle transcendental period, and the later life-world period, indicating Husserl's influence on subsequent figures in the continental tradition of Germany, France, and other locales.

Two

Husserl's philosophical system

Framing Husserl's overall system of philosophy, this chapter provides a preview and a conceptual roadmap of what is to come in Chapters 3–8. When read after those chapters, however, it serves as a summation and a retrospective on the unity of what went before. Accordingly, this chapter can profitably be read both before and after the ensuing chapters, with different perspectives in the two readings.

THE BIG PICTURE

Husserl's philosophy presents a unified account of our experience, the world we live in, our bodies, our selves, our knowledge (everyday and scientific), our values, our social institutions, and so on, explicating the forms or essences of these things and their interrelations. Within this philosophical system Husserl's phenomenology takes its place as a proper part of the whole, not (as often assumed) as the sole foundation and *raison d'être* of all the rest. To be sure, Husserl laid a passionate emphasis on his conception of phenomenology, the new science of consciousness and meaning. But his phenomenology is one specific part of his philosophical system, a part well integrated with other parts, including doctrines in ontology, epistemology, logic, and also ethics and value theory.

In brief, Husserl's philosophy develops a detailed account of: (1) our own conscious experience, especially its intentionality, or the way our experience represents things in the world around us; (2) the categories of things in the world in general, including

individuals, their properties or relations, their parts and dependencies, and how these entities form the states of affairs that
compose the world; (3) language, as a tool to express our
thoughts about the world, including our theories about the
natures of things, not least our mathematics and our sciences like
physics and psychology; (4) culture, including social or intersubjective practices, not least our shared norms and values, moral and
political. The details of Husserl's philosophy address the nature of
things as diverse as numbers, experiences, physical objects, and
values. These things take their places, however, within an abstract
structure of theory that we may approach almost as mathematicians might turn toward the concreteness of everyday life: for
Husserl was just that, a mathematician turning to the details of
our own experience and the most basic structures of the world in
which we live.

A philosophical account of a given domain of phenomena
(mental activities or electrons or numbers or what have you) is a
special kind of *theory*, a systematic statement about the nature of
things in that domain. Often a piece of philosophy reads more like
a short story or novel than a piece of physics or algebra. Yet
Husserl proposed that philosophy itself be treated as "science" (in
a 1911 essay titled "Philosophy as Strict Science"). In the *Logical
Investigations* (1900–1) Husserl defined logic as the theory of
theory, or alternatively the science of science. Accordingly, he
thought of philosophy as a science in a wide sense of the term,
thus a theory: not a formal or mathematical theory, and not an
experimental science like physics, but a certain kind of theory
drawing on different aspects of reason and experience,
constructing a disciplined explication of the things so studied.
Husserl's overall system of philosophy is, then, a wide-ranging
but unified theory. And our task in this chapter is to outline that
theory as a whole.

Husserl never presented his system in one clear and salient and
pedagogically ordered narrative, saying, "Here goes my theory of
everything, starting from the following axioms." Rather, his
system unfolded over a lifetime of writing. Nonetheless, there is a
roadmap of the philosophical terrain covered in his intellectual

journeys, and that map is his first major work, his magnum opus, the 1,000-page *Logical Investigations* – far more than "logical" investigations – published in 1900 and 1901. All of his later work, published and unpublished, takes its place in the framework detailed in the *Investigations* – as if he kept the big picture always in mind while he experimented with detailed analyses of this and that. Moreover, the unity of Husserl's system follows from principles detailed in the *Investigations*: the overall theory – of mind, world, form, value, and so on – entails a theory of its own unity. That well-defined structure of theory governs all of Husserl's subsequent work, including his full-throated presentation of "transcendental" phenomenology in *Ideas* I (1913).

Husserl's system comes into view as we survey his corpus (as in Chapter 1). But we can best appreciate the system, with its diverse motifs and motives, when we look at his work from a wide historical perspective.

In Husserl's eyes, and in his time, phenomenology seemed the obvious centerpiece of his philosophy, and arguably its proper and sole foundation. After all, phenomenology was a new discipline in philosophy, distinguishing itself from epistemology, ontology, ethics, and logic. Indeed, the perspective of 20th-century continental European philosophy remained focused on the role of phenomenology in Husserl's philosophy. On the one hand, Husserl's later "transcendental" conception of phenomenology ties into the tradition of German idealism reaching from Kant to Fichte and beyond, and neo-Kantian philosophy dominated German universities in the 1920s. On the other hand, Husserl's earlier foundational studies tie into the Viennese tradition of exact or scientific philosophy, and Husserl's logical conception of phenomenology, joined by his phenomenological conception of logic, interacted with the Vienna Circle's concerns in the 1920s and 1930s. In any event, from our perspective today, we may consider Husserl's philosophical ties into the 20th-century traditions of both continental and analytic philosophy, and into the longer sweep of European philosophy. From our contemporary, and more global, perspective, we see that Husserl's philosophy ranged much more widely than phenomenology. For the analytic philosopher, Husserl's philosophy of logic and mathematics (evident in his biography) stand out. For the continental philosopher, however, what stand out are Husserl's concerns with consciousness, existential meaning, and the life-world. As we take a broader view of Husserl's overall work, we begin to see the relations Husserl himself defined among logic, ontology, phenomenology, and epistemology. The trajectory through these four fields was mapped out in great detail, in that order, in the *Investigations* – with more to come, including views on social or cultural theory, ethics, and value theory.

When we look at Husserl's place in the history of Western philosophy, we then see the different parts of Husserl's philosophical system in contrast with the views of other great thinkers over the millennia. Husserl's philosophy of logic and mathematics (we saw) was a sharp reaction against 19th-century psychologism. Husserl's concern with the ontology of essences (eidos, species, or universals) takes its place in the debates that raged from Plato and Aristotle through the Middle Ages and continue today: debates over realism and nominalism in the theory of universals, starting with Plato's theory of forms. Husserl's concern with the foundations of knowledge picks up the debates that began in the 17th century, thus in the sweep of modern philosophy from Descartes and rationalism to Locke and empiricism, to Kant and his concern with Newton's new physics, and on into 20th-century philosophy of science (theory of knowledge in the special sciences). Husserl's phenomenological theory of intentionality has roots that reach from Brentano back through the Middle Ages (in Latin and Arabic–Islamic–Persian philosophy) and all the way back to Aristotle. And when Husserl addressed ethics (in lecture courses), he took up issues in moral theory or practical philosophy raised by Kant and Hume, amid the European Enlightenment, against the familiar background of Plato and Aristotle.

Husserl also briefly addressed Asian philosophy in a study of meditation in Buddhism. He contributed three articles to a Japanese journal, *Kaizo*, in 1923–4. Today phenomenology is studied in Japan and India, partly because it resonates with traditional philosophical themes of Zen and other forms of Buddhism, which stress the importance of reflection on one's experience and its place in the world. Even transcendental idealism seems at home in the traditional Buddhist concept of illusion, widely debated in Hindu and Buddhist philosophy over many centuries.

In the present chapter, then, we shall frame Husserl's overall philosophical system, stressing the unity in his philosophical theory of mind, language, world, form, knowledge, value, and the *interdependencies* among his theories in logic, ontology, phenomenology, epistemology, and ethics. In later chapters, we take up details of Husserl's doctrines in various areas of philosophy, including his methodology for phenomenology.

Importantly, this conception of Husserl's *doctrinal* system differs from the strictly *methodological* system that is supposed to characterize Husserl's transcendental phenomenology on some accounts. Husserl's passion for phenomenology and its method may encourage the view that Husserl was a revolutionary who would reduce all philosophy to the practice of transcendental reflection as we "phenomenologize" all that we encounter. Indeed, Husserl sometimes touted the method of "bracketing" or "phenomenological reduction" as his paramount achievement. In 1930, two years into retirement, Husserl instructed his assistant, Eugen Fink, to develop an outline of the "System of Phenomenological Philosophy" – note the word "system" (see Fink 1988/1995: xiii). No such work was ever written. Instead, with Husserl's approval, Fink drafted the *Sixth Cartesian Meditation: The Idea of a Transcendental Theory of Method* (published only posthumously in 1988, the first part translated in Fink 1988/1995). This work was designed to extend Husserl's five *Cartesian Meditations* (1929/1960), grounding Husserl's conception of phenomenology in a non-Cartesian, yet non-Kantian, transcendental methodology, in "a phenomenology of phenomenology, a reflection on phenomenologizing" (Fink 1988/1995: 1). The aim was to distinguish Husserl's approach to phenomenology from that of his successor, Martin Heidegger. Subsequently, in his last wave of work in the *Crisis* (1935–8/1970), Husserl revised his account of phenomenological method, emphasizing the role of the "life-world." Throughout his evolving conceptions of method, however,

Husserl's doctrinal system retained the structure that shall be our main concern. And within that system, no one part of the system is reduced to any other: the several theories that fall, respectively, in logic, ontology, phenomenology, epistemology, and ethics retain their own force, yet the several theories are *interdependent*, in ways we shall try to bring out.

HUSSERL'S SYSTEM

Philosophy has been traditionally divided into some four main areas, including logic, epistemology, metaphysics or ontology, and ethics. Social philosophy and political philosophy join ethics under the umbrella of value theory. Phenomenology – taking shape under Husserl's pen – forms a fifth main area of philosophy. Husserl's corpus addresses all these areas, as well as issues in philosophy of language and philosophy of mind, two specialized areas that developed over the course of the 20th century.

In the *Logical Investigations* Husserl worked from logic to philosophy of language, to ontology, to phenomenology, to epistemology. (Value theory would follow only later.) We trace the outlines of Husserl's overall system, then, as we outline the basic theories Husserl developed in these areas. We shall follow the course of development in the *Investigations*, reaching out from there into results in later works. However, we shall tread lightly over the texts and simply sketch Husserl's main ideas and views in these areas.

Logic

Logic is the study of valid reasoning, including deductive inference, as in mathematics (where inference logically preserves truth), and also inductive reasoning, as in experimental science or in a court of law (where inference confers only probability). The foundations of logic include semantics, the study of how language expresses meaning and represents objects in the world, specifically how various forms of sentence can be true, that is, the conditions under which sentences can be true. These logical-semantic concerns (as we call them today) were the focus of Husserl's philosophy of logic.

In Husserl's day Gottlob Frege's new logic of quantifiers (words like "all" and "some") advanced logic far beyond Aristotle's theory of syllogism. Meanwhile, the new logic was amplified with set theory in the new foundations of mathematics, laid in part by Georg Cantor (whom Husserl befriended during his years in Halle). Moreover, the axiomatic method of ancient geometry gained new form in the ideal of a deductive theory expressible in a formal or symbolic language; indeed, the ideal of a complete axiomatic theory, where all truths in its domain are entailed by its axioms, was charted by David Hilbert in particular (whom Husserl befriended during his years in Göttingen). All theories in mathematics, and in mathematical physics, were cast as logical systems of propositions. These new ideas of logic begat a logical view of scientific theory, especially in the work of Rudolf Carnap (who attended Husserl's lectures in Freiburg). Where others developed the details of mathematical logic and a coordinate methodology of science, Husserl turned his attention to the philosophy of such a logic and theory of science (broadly conceived).

Husserl considered the technical work of mathematical logic to be the work of clever technicians, whereas the philosopher ought to seek a further, philosophical explication of the foundations of logic and mathematics and science. In today's computer idiom, we might say Husserl considered the formidable technical constructions of logic to be the domain of "hackers" (not a pejorative term among computer scientists). By contrast, Husserl sought a "pure" (as opposed to applied) theory of the constructions of logic. ("What exactly is computation?" the philosopher today might ask of the computer scientist.) In this spirit, then, Husserl propounded his vision of "pure logic."

Bernard Bolzano was Husserl's inspiration. Bolzano's *Wissenschaftslehre* (1837), or *Theory of Science*, defined a science as a system of objective propositions "in themselves" (*Satz an sich*), composed of objective ideas-in-themselves (*Vorstellung an sich*). When we think that P, our mental activity takes the form of a subjective proposition, a subjective form of idea (*Vorstellung*) that we express in a sentence "P." Bolzano was critical of the prevailing Kantian account of representations or ideas (*Vorstellung*). For, Bolzano held, we must distinguish carefully between subjective and objective ideas. Subjective ideas transpire in our individual minds (in the temporal flow of our experience, Husserl would add), but objective ideas are not in space or time – they are rather like Platonic forms, only they are like ideal forms of thinking (rather than forms of animals or trees or what have you). When two people each think that dogs chase cats, there are two subjective ideas, existing in two different people, thinking at different places (in two people's heads, we say today) and perhaps at different times. Yet there is only one objective idea, the proposition that dogs chase cats, which both people think, or entertain in thinking. Following Bolzano, Husserl holds that logic is about objective ideas, not subjective ideas.

Propositions are ideas with a form expressible in language by a complete sentence, such as "Dogs chase cats." Each proposition is composed of ideas of appropriate form, such as the subject idea expressed by the noun "dogs" and the predicate idea expressed by the predicate "chase cats." Formal logic analyzes and systematizes the relevant forms of expression in a given language and, Husserl stresses, the relevant forms of ideas expressed thereby.

Husserl argued that we need to assume ideal objective meanings, like Bolzano's propositions-in-themselves (or, later, Frege's eternal "thoughts"), in order to account for the objectivity of logic. What makes a pattern of inference logically valid, Husserl held, is the relation of entailment or consequence among propositions-in-themselves. Without ideal meaning, logic can only be about the contingent ways that people happen to reason, incorrectly or not. And in that direction lies psychologism, the reduction of logic to psychology.

For Husserl, a theory is itself a system of propositions about a given domain or subject matter. Ideally, a group of these propositions are axiomatic, and together these propositions entail all propositions in the theory, thus, all truths about the domain. The ideal of a deductively complete axiomatic theory for any domain would find limits in the ingenious mathematical proofs produced by Kurt Gödel in the 1930s, but these incompleteness theorems of metalogic were not yet envisioned by Husserl. The domain of a theory may be the positive integers, in the theory of arithmetic. (Recall that Husserl's first book was Philosophy of Arithmetic.) Or the domain may be all dogs, for the theory of canines (a very specific part of biology). In the world of nature we do not expect to form a complete conception or theory of any type of object. Indeed, Husserl repeatedly stressed that the essence of a natural object such as a tree is transcendent of our knowledge of it, in that its nature outruns all possible perceptions of it (say, from different sides). In any event, the ideal of a theory about such a thing remains, even if the theory is in practice or sometimes in principle incomplete.

What bind together the propositions in a theory, on this model, are the relations of entailment whereby the axiomatic propositions entail other propositions in the theory. The theory of entailment Husserl called "consequence" logic (today logicians speak of "proof theory"). But Husserl's logical interests lay elsewhere.

In the 1930s Alfred Tarski developed a mathematical model of truth for certain types of language, a "semantic" conception of truth where the truth-conditions for more complex sentences are defined in terms of those for simpler sentences. This model furthered the development of semantics as a key part of logic. Since the 1940s logicians and philosophers of logic have divided logical theory into three areas: syntax, semantics, and pragmatics. (Carnap laid out the distinction in several works.) Syntax concerns the shapes of expressions; semantics concerns the meanings of expressions and what expressions represent or refer to; pragmatics concerns people's use of expressions in various contexts. In these post-Husserlian terms, Husserl's philosophy of logic was little concerned with syntax and the proofs defined by syntactic rules of inference. (A simple rule of propositional logic reads: "If P then Q. P. Therefore, Q." Syntax alone guarantees validity for any inference with this form.) Instead, Husserl's concern was with semantics. Frege's logic developed a detailed semantics of ideal sense, wherein sentences express eternal "thoughts," what Bolzano called propositions-in-themselves. Husserl's main focus was on ideal meanings, the propositions that make up a theory, and he was concerned with how meanings represent things in the world, assuming that certain forms of meaning represent certain forms of object. Where the proposition "That dog is angry" represents the state of affairs that a certain animal is in a certain state of agitation, the meaning "that dog" represents the particular animal itself, and the meaning "is angry" represents its property of agitation.

Practicing logicians, in the 20th century, worked with forms of expressions or sentences in a well-defined symbolic language. Their concern was generally with the computational properties of the predicate calculus or theories expressed in that symbolism. They did not need to turn their eyes toward a Platonic – or Bolzanoan or Fregean – heaven of ideal, objective propositions. Indeed, many logicians followed W. V. Quine's lead in rejecting Platonistic conceptions of propositions, settling instead for the linguistic entities we can see on the printed page. However, in Husserl's terms, these logicians or mathematicians were "technicians," not yet true "philosophers." For Husserl, "pure logic" is about the logical and semantic properties of ideal meanings, propositions and their constituents. And Husserl's challenge remains on the table for subsequent logicians of a more nominalistic persuasion: what makes an inference valid, if logic addresses only the forms of sentence that a given group of people happen to use in a certain way? This was the problem of psychologism against which Husserl and Frege argued so vehemently at the close of the 19th century.

For Husserl, the study of language is a different area of study than pure logic, and Husserl outlined what today we call a philosophy of language, coordinate with his philosophy of pure logic.

Language

Where logic goes, philosophy of language is not far behind. For Husserl, logic is about propositions (ideal meanings): their logical forms, their semantics (what they represent or mean, what makes them true or false), their entailments. For later logicians, we observed, the focus shifts to sentences in a well-defined language, their forms, semantics, entailments. That said, Husserl holds that propositions are expressed in language and thereby communicated, and shared, with other speakers.

Husserl distinguishes the sense (Sinn) of an expression (its ideal meaning) from its object, what it represents or stands for. Frege articulated the semantics of sense and reference (Sinn and Bedeutung) in a systematic way, for which he is now famous. To cite his familiar example, two expressions may have the same reference but express difference senses: "the morning star" and "the evening star" both refer to Venus, but they do so in different ways, expressing different senses with differing "cognitive" or conceptual values (as Frege put it). In the same era, Husserl sketched his own version of a semantics of sense and reference, with some criticisms of Frege's competing scheme. The point to observe here is the principle of distinguishing ideal sense from objective reference, thereby launching a semantics of two levels. (More on this in Chapter 3.)

How do the expressions in a language, carrying their sense and reference, relate to the people who use the language? Husserl elaborated a version of the traditional view that language expresses thought (as Aristotle originally theorized). When a speaker says, "The moon is on the horizon," the speaker expresses in English a sense that is the content of what he or she is thinking. When another person hears the utterance (and understands that language), the hearer understands the sentence uttered and grasps its sense, the proposition that the moon is on the horizon. Communication consists in this transfer of sense, this sharing of meaning, between a speaker and a hearer.

Husserl's model of communication here assumes more than linguistic activities of speaking and listening. The actors in communication themselves have experiences of perceiving, thinking, and wishing. In short, linguistic activity itself rests on a range of mental activities. And, as we shall see, the hallmark of mental activity, according to Husserl, is intentionality: the way in which an experience is "directed" toward various things. But we are ahead of Husserl's story.

Husserl joined with other 19th-century Platonistic logicians (Bolzano, Lotze, Frege) in assuming a range of ideal or (as we say today) abstract meanings, which include the "thoughts" or propositions expressed by a given language. Human languages are themselves social artifacts that serve the purpose of communication between people, along the lines just described. Here in a nutshell is Husserl's philosophy of language, which supplements his philosophy of logic.

Husserl posited ideal meanings in order to account for the objectivity of logic. And he proposed a theory of speech activities in order to account for human communication. In Husserl's theory of logic and language, then, activities of speech relate to ideal meanings.

But what exactly are these ideal meanings that language serves to express? In the first edition of the *Logical Investigations*, Husserl proposes a simple answer: the sense expressed by a linguistic expression (say, "the moon") is the ideal form of one's thinking about or "intending" an object in a certain way (say, conceiving or thinking about an earthly orbiter as "the moon"). Now, ideal forms or species are ideal entities along the lines envisioned by Plato (though Husserl's ontology will develop in ways different from the traditional interpretation of Plato's theory of forms).

Husserl assumes a theory of ideal types or species in part in order to identify the type of entity proposed as the sense or meaning of an expression, and so to account for the subject matter of logic and philosophy of language. Husserl here moves into the classical theory of universals. And so, as soon as Husserl has sketched his philosophy of language, on the heels of his philosophy of logic, he begins to move from meaning and language into ontology.

Ontology

Ontology is the theory of being, of what is and how things are. Ontology is also called metaphysics, though there are somewhat different usages of the terms. Some philosophers define metaphysics as speculative theory about reality beyond the reach of all evidence; the positivists and, before them, Kant rejected meta-physics in this pejorative sense. Other philosophers define ontology as the theory of what types of things exist and then define metaphysics as the further theory of time and space and causation, of whether there is a first cause of everything (perhaps God), of the special attributes of God, of whether there is life after death, and so forth; in this sense metaphysics is focused on certain specific issues of what exists and of the order of things. Here we shall make no distinction between metaphysics and ontology. We shall take ontology to be the theory of what there is. Further questions along the lines indicated as traditional metaphysics will simply take their place as special theories within ontology. However, in due course we shall address Husserl's special innovative conception of what he called formal ontology, considering what categories or structures of the world are particularly basic because they are "formal" structures that apply to wide ranges of things – all this in due time.

Early in the history of Western philosophy, Plato's theory of forms posited a realm of ideal forms or "eidos" to which earthly objects approximate, including, say, the form of humanity in which you and I participate. Aristotle called the forms "universals" and the things that exemplify them "particulars." But Aristotle wanted to bring the forms down to earth, down from the Platonic heaven of eternal forms. A particular human being, say Socrates, is a combination of form and matter, so the form of humanity is realized in Socrates when it informs or gives shape to the matter of which Socrates is composed. For Aristotle, the form of humanity exists in the world of nature, rather than in a heaven of ideal forms. There is much more to both the Platonic and the Aristotelian ontologies, but this brief parody sets the scene for Husserl.

Husserl combines elements of the Platonic and Aristotelian theories. In the case of an individual such as Socrates, Husserl proposes to distinguish three entities: the concrete individual Socrates, the form of humanity, and (here adapting an idea of Aristotle's) Socrates' own concrete instance of humanity. This latter entity Husserl calls a "moment" of Socrates. So how does Husserl account for the relation between the individual Socrates

and the form humanity? The ideal form of humanity is instantiated in a concrete instance of humanity that is a part or moment
of the concrete individual Socrates. Husserl calls this form an
"ideal species" (in *Logical Investigations*) or, alternatively, an
"essence" or "eidos" (in *Ideas* I). The concrete instance of the species
or essence is what he calls a "moment."

Why does Husserl think we need to assume a third entity here,
the moment of humanity in Socrates? Following Aristotle, we
need to distinguish Socrates' humanity from Plato's humanity.
Both individuals share the same form: humanity. But the
humanity in Socrates is numerically distinct from the humanity in
Plato. At any rate, that is how Husserl argues. It seems Husserl
never met a distinction he didn't like. And in the ontology of
species he thinks that we cannot do without any of these three
types of entity: species or essence, individual, and moment. The
challenge for alternative views is to explain "predication," how
individuals have essences or properties, without marking these
distinctions.

Husserl's doctrine of moments takes him from the theory of
universals into the theory of parts and wholes, since called "mere-
ology." For Husserl, the moment of humanity in Socrates is a *part*
of Socrates. Husserl distinguishes between dependent and independent parts. If Socrates were to lose his left little finger in an
accident while carpentering, the severed finger would still exist,
independently of the whole of which it was a part, namely,
Socrates or his body. But Socrates' humanity cannot be separated
from Socrates, on pain of nonexistence: his particular instance of
humanity cannot exist unless Socrates exists. Thus, Husserl holds,
a moment – here, Socrates' humanity – is a dependent part: a part
that cannot exist separately from the whole of which it is a part
(here, Socrates).

This distinction between dependent and independent parts is a
highly specialized piece of ontology, which most philosophers
prefer to avoid addressing. (There seem bigger fishes to fry, say,
in considering the essence of humanity, turning to ethics or
human rights.) Nonetheless, Husserl makes considerable use of this
notion of "moments," as we shall see.

One of the most innovative ideas in Husserl's ontology – arguably new in the history of metaphysics – is the distinction he draws between "formal" and "material" ontology. Husserl distinguishes between formal and material essences (think again of forms). Material essences, or "regions," are substantive (in that sense "material") domains of entities, including, on Husserl's appraisal, Nature, Culture (*Geist* or spirit), and Consciousness. Entities in these three regions are defined by very different properties: natural objects, by spatiotemporal location; cultural objects, by social relations, values, and institutions; acts of consciousness, by intentionality. Formal essences, or "categories," govern entities in any domain or region. Categorial forms include Number, Group, Part, Individual, Property or Relation, State of Affairs, and so on. Husserl's list is incomplete, but includes both mathematical forms and "logical" forms (understood as forms in the world, as opposed to forms of linguistic expression). Husserl's scheme of formal and material essences, or categories, shapes his whole philosophical system, and we shall return to the details of that scheme in Chapter 4.

One of the biggest problems in philosophy is the doctrine of realism: the thesis that the world around us – including trees, birds, buildings, other people, electrons, black holes, and so on – exists independently of whether we see or think about or know of these things. The opposite doctrine is called idealism: the thesis that the world depends for its existence on our seeing and thinking about it. George Berkeley, the famous idealist, held that this tree I see just is a bundle of ideas in my mind (or in God's mind). As noted in the Chapter 1, Husserl wrestled all his life with the problem of realism and idealism, settling on a novel position he called "transcendental idealism" – a term Husserl borrowed, with modification, from Immanuel Kant. This doctrine was closely allied with Husserl's mature conception of phenomenology.

The mind–body problem too lies just around the corner: how is mind related to body, especially the brain, given that mental activity depends on brain activity? This problem was to loom large in the years after Husserl's death. Yet it is very much a part of the problem space of phenomenology.

Phenomenology

Husserl defined phenomenology as the science of the essence of consciousness (*Ideas* I). Of all the things we encounter, consciousness is special because we experience it, we live through it. Indeed, the very essence of consciousness includes this first-person character: we each experience it in our own case; we know it as we experience it from our first-person point of view. This was the point of Descartes' famous proclamation, "I think, therefore I am." Consciousness is the medium of our existence as human beings who see and desire and cogitate. Three centuries of philosophy followed, and consciousness itself took center-stage with Brentano's psychology and soon Husserl's phenomenology and ultimately with neuroscience.

But what is the essence of consciousness? We begin an answer by example. Consciousness consists in our experiences of various types: seeing, touching, imagining, thinking, judging, desiring, feeling happy or angry, moving about in walking and doing things with our hands, willing and so acting. These and more are the types of conscious experience that populate our lives. These experiences are conscious. Are there basic features of these experiences that characterize them as conscious experiences?

The short answer from Husserl, extending Brentano, is: intentionality. On Husserl's analysis, consciousness is (almost always) a consciousness of something. In my present visual experience I see or am visually conscious of that tree out the window. My act of consciousness – my visual experience – is a consciousness of that tree. Husserl drew on Brentano's doctrine that every mental act is in this sense "directed" toward something. As Brentano put it, every act includes an object "intentionally" within it. But how are we to understand Brentano's idea that the object exists "in" the mental act? Husserl proposed instead that the act has a special property of being directed toward its object: the act itself is "intentional," or directed. What is the structure of this directedness, or intentionality?

The foundations of phenomenology lie in the distinction Husserl drew among an *act* of consciousness, its *content*, and its *object*. (This work was detailed in the *Logical Investigations*, Investigation V, and the full account of the science of consciousness followed in *Ideas* I.) Briefly: my act of seeing a tree is an event in my mind, in my stream of experiences. The tree I see is something very different, an object composed of roots, trunk, branches, leaves, photosynthesis, and flowing sap. Something very different still from both the act and the object is the content of the act, a certain idea or percept or concept of the tree. Husserl initially called this entity simply a "content" (in the *Investigations*); later he called it "noema" (in *Ideas* I), introducing a new technical term. The noema is utterly different in kind from both the act and the object, Husserl holds. For the tree it represents can burn down, but the noema or idea of the tree cannot burn. And while the act transpires over a minute or two of time, the noema is not a temporal entity. For the same idea or noema can be entertained in different acts or experiences at different times, say, when I see the tree today and you see it tomorrow, that is, provided we both see it in the same way (so far as possible). The content or noema of an act of consciousness, Husserl proposes, is an ideal meaning, which presents or represents or "means" an object in a certain way, as having these or those properties. There is also a fourth entity involved, namely, the individual having the experience. For the act is experienced by a subject or ego, "I," and is a part of the stream of consciousness that defines the (conscious) mind of that subject. (Husserl changed his view on the ego, but for the present discussion we note the role of the ego in consciousness.)

Brentano held not only that conscious experience is characteristically directed toward some object, but also that consciousness includes an "inner consciousness" of the experience itself, a kind of secondary directedness of the mind toward itself. Husserl followed suit, wrestling with the problem of what this inner consciousness consists in. It is not as though I am doing two things at once in a simple visual experience, seeing the tree and observing my seeing the tree. Philosophers today ask whether the mind or brain is monitoring its own activities, somewhat as a computer might keep a running log of what it is doing. We do not experience ourselves performing this sort of monitoring of our experience, and both Husserl and Brentano resisted this idea of inner observation or monitoring. Nonetheless, whatever its proper form, there is a kind of awareness (to use a neutral term) that essentially characterizes a conscious experience, an awareness that makes it conscious and thereby a consciousness of something (as in seeing a tree). There are in fact psychological experiments that show it is possible to see things without being aware of seeing them; this phenomenon is called blind sight, and its existence is frankly surprising to us because we are almost always aware of our seeing what we see. It is worth noting here, albeit in passing, that the theory of consciousness includes, then, not only the theory of intentionality (how consciousness is a consciousness of something), but also the theory of inner awareness (how we are aware of being conscious of something).

Phenomenology begins, like Brentano's descriptive psychology, with the classification of different types of experience, or acts of consciousness: perception, imagination, desire, thought of judgment, and so on. In Husserl's ontology, these types are ideal species, or essences. Now, a vital part of the essence of an act of a certain type, on Husserl's analysis, is the intentionality of the act. And what is the structure of intentionality? Given the distinction among subject, act, content, and object, Husserl proposes a basic analysis of intentionality. On Husserl's theory of intentionality, intentionality is a complex relation among subject, act, content, and object: *ego − act − content → object.*

This relationship is unique in kind, since the object of consciousness may in some cases not exist, as when I think about Santa Claus. In such a case, the ego, act, and content exist, and the content portrays a jolly bearer of presents, but no such object exists. Still, the pattern of intentionality, or directedness, exists. Alternative theories of intentionality propose possible or nonexistent objects at the terminus of the arrow, but Husserl's theory recognizes the work of content or ideal meaning even in the absence of the object "meant" or "intended."

"Pure" or "transcendental" phenomenology, for Husserl (in *Ideas* I), will study the "transcendental" structure of ego, act, and content or noema, while bracketing the question of the existence of the object intended. In Chapter 6, we shall discuss the debates about method that plagued Husserl. Here we may instead observe how Husserl tied phenomenology into ontology, language, and logic.

Contents of consciousness are, for Husserl, ideal meanings. In the case of judgment or discursive thought, as in a pattern of argument or inference, the meanings are propositions (expressible by grammatically complete sentences). Phenomenology studies the intentional force of these meanings, their role in the intentionality of consciousness. Logic studies their logical forms and their role in valid patterns of inference. Philosophy of language studies their role in speech activity and also semantics. Ontology addresses their ideal status. According to Husserl, phenomenology provides a crucial part of the foundations of logical and linguistic theory by tying logical theory into the theory of intentionality, of how the mind (and therewith language) represents things in the world.

In Husserl's hands, phenomenology also expands the foundations for all kinds of knowledge. Thus Husserl turns to epistemology, the familiar turf of three centuries of modern philosophy.

Epistemology

In epistemology, or the theory of knowledge, Husserl is known as a champion of "intuition" (*Anschauung*), or insight. Especially troubling for many readers is Husserl's notion of *Wesenserschauung*, or intuition of essence. The idea, in parody, is that we have a special ability to "see" ideal essences, as if we can pull up a periscope and peer into the Platonic heaven of forms, which do not exist in space–time but can yet be "seen" in the practice of intuition, a well-tutored insight into essence. Mathematicians can "see" abstract structures, in a way that the rest of us rarely do. Logicians can "see" logical form and the validity of forms of inference. Ordinary mortals can "see" the structure of more mundane essences, as we see that a bird has wings, a bachelor is unmarried, a ball cannot be red and green all over, and so on. Moreover, a trained phenomenologist can "see" that a visual experience is intentional, that consciousness has its own temporal structure, or that an action is motivated, as phenomenological reflection affords an intuitive insight into the structure and meaning or noema of each type of experience. Indeed, in the spirit of Cartesian rationalism, the phenomenologist might "see" that what gives us confidence in everyday perception is the phenomenological insight that vision normally puts us in touch with existing objects before us – so that seeing a tree rests on intuition about vision itself.

This parody of Husserl's theory of intuition is an intriguing if magical story. However, it overlooks the motives and details of Husserl's theory of knowledge. Moreover, it suffers from an anachronistic misunderstanding of how the term "intuition" (*Anschauung*) was used in the philosophical patois of Husserl's context (leading back through Kant into Medieval philosophy).

The *Logical Investigations* begins and ends with an account of the objectivity of knowledge in various domains, beginning with logical theory (in the Prolegomena) and ending with empirical knowledge (Investigation VI). Indeed, objectivity is precisely the aim of Husserl's theory of knowledge. Husserl was reacting to the subjectivity of psychologism in logic (the view that the validity of reason is just a matter of how we happen to go about thinking). More generally, he was reacting to the threat of subjectivity that he saw, following Bolzano, in the Kantian theory of knowledge as grounded in the a priori structure of our minds. Of course, Kant famously sought an account of objectivity *within* the structure of mind, but Bolzano and Husserl wanted a different and firmer ground of objectivity.

Husserl entered the dialectic about knowledge after three waves of epistemological theory. Beginning in the 17th century, the rationalists – Descartes, Leibniz, Spinoza – argued that knowledge must be ultimately based in reason, as sense perception provides no help to mathematics and logic, and reason itself must tell us where we can trust the testimony of our senses. In the 18th century, the empiricists – beginning with Locke, Berkeley, Hume – countered that all knowledge begins ultimately in sense perception. By the end of the 18th century, Kant proposed a synthesis of rationalist and empiricist principles. Roughly, for Kant, our experience and knowledge of the world are the result of joint mental activities of sensation and cognitive apprehension, or sensibility and reason, so that I see that green-leafed oak tree (I do not first see a patch of green and then reason that it is an oak before me). In the 20th century, many philosophers took natural science as the proper paradigm of knowledge, seeking a contemporary empiricism for our scientific age. Husserl, however, took a more complicated tack, developing what he called a phenomenological theory of knowledge.

As presented in the *Logical Investigations*, Husserl's theory of knowledge comes in two parts: the theory of theory and the theory of evidence. Our knowledge about any domain is systematic insofar as it is organized in the form of a theory, a system of propositions that hang together to tell a story about things in that domain. Objectivity comes with the way propositions support one another within a theory, deductively or inductively. But a theory, for Husserl, is a system of ideal propositions-in-themselves (Prolegomena), while knowledge consists in acts of judgment or settled beliefs (Investigation VI). Thus, logic alone leaves theories as propositions hanging together, without connection yet to our cognitive activity. The theory of intentionality ties propositions into acts of judgment or attitudes of belief, as the ideal contents of judgment or belief (Investigation V). What makes a system of judgments or beliefs *knowledge*, however, is the *evidence* that supports the propositions judged or believed, within the unity of a theory. And evidence is, on Husserl's analysis, a particular epistemic character in an experience of perception or, more generally, "intuition" (Investigation VI).

In Husserl's epistemology, "intuition" is the name for any type of experience that is an "evident" or "intuitive" experience of something "itself." In the *Logical Investigations* Husserl speaks prominently of intuitive (*anschaulich*) experiences of perception and judgment. Much later, in the *Cartesian Meditations*, he speaks prominently of different types of "evidence" (*Evidenz*), that is, in evident experiences. Over the course of his writings, Husserl recognizes some three types of intuition, or evident experience: sensory perception, eidetic or essential insight, and phenomenological reflection. In each of these types of experience, an object or state of affairs is experienced with "direct evidence." We can claim knowledge in or with that experience alone, that is, without further activities of inference. In perception, I see that tree over there, with direct evidence. In eidetic analysis, I grasp the form of number, as I "see" that succession (adding one to any number after zero) generates the positive integers. In logical analysis, I grasp the validity of a form of inference, among propositions in a pattern of argument. In phenomenological reflection, I grasp the structure of intentionality in my experience of hearing an aria from the opera *Tosca*. That is, I "see" that my act of hearing is a hearing of something (namely, a certain aria). As we attend to these various types of experience, and observe the evidential character in each, we may classify each as a type of intuition in Husserl's technical sense.

The air of magic in Husserl's theory of intuition gradually dispels as we adduce examples and analyze them. To be sure, the term tends to mislead, given its use in everyday parlance. ("The detective relied on sheer intuition.") But "intuition" entered our language through a technical idiom, introduced in the Middle Ages by William of Ockham and Duns Scotus, for whom *cognitio intuitiva* was direct knowledge, unmediated by inference. In short, knowledge begins in evidence, in evident judgments, which form knowledge insofar as evident propositions are organized into a logically structured piece of theory.

There is still a large task in characterizing and distinguishing types and strengths of evidence or intuitiveness in judgments about various kinds of phenomena. But there is no need to assume anything magical like a mental periscope that allows us to peer into a domain of seemingly inaccessible entities, from numbers to ideal species to ideal meanings. The task is, rather, one of carefully appraising many different types of experience that provide evidence. In practice, we do this as we develop expertise in different domains. In legal practice, as we follow the details presented in court in both civil and criminal cases, we develop an understanding of what counts as good and bad evidence in everyday affairs (Who pulled the trigger? What evidence has the jury of who did so?). In the practice of physics, refined over three or four centuries now, scientists assess the observational evidence for the hypothesis that light from a star is bent by gravity as it passes the sun toward our telescope; again, physicists assess the evidence proposed for the hypothesis that the universe began with a Big Bang 12 billion years ago, not 20 billion years as proposed earlier. In these practices of evaluating empirical evidence, for a hypothesis in physics or in a court of law, we find expertise rather than magic. And Husserl's phenomenological theory of intuition is best seen in exactly that light.

Husserl's theory of knowledge includes a general theory of knowledge, as outlined. But his specific analyses apply the general theory to three types of knowledge: (1) empirical knowledge about things in the natural and social world around us; (2) eidetic knowledge about ideal entities or "eidos," from numbers to essences; and (3) phenomenological knowledge about consciousness, intentionality, and noematic meaning. In each of these three types of knowledge Husserl finds a distinctive type of intuition: (1) empirical intuition or evidence, in sensory perception; (2) eidetic intuition or evidence, in insight about species, numbers, forms, and other ideal entities; and (3) phenomenological intuition or evidence, in reflection on consciousness, its intentionality, and its meaning or noema.

Ethics, value theory, social theory, political theory

Husserl is not widely known for his work in value theory, in ethical and political theory. Yet he lectured substantially on these topics in the years leading up to Ideas I (1913) and Ideas II (1912). Indeed, his phenomenology has ethical and political implications yet to be fully explored. Husserl explicitly addressed issues of ethics and aspects of value in lectures published as Lectures on Ethics and Value Theory: 1908–1914 (Vorlesungen über Ethik und Wertlehre: 1908–1914, 1988, no English translation to date). We cannot dig deeply into this material here, but I should like to sketch a line of interpretation of Husserl's promising contributions to ethics and value theory.

A major theme of Husserl's lectures on ethics (1908–14) is the *objectivity* of values, which Husserl approaches by drawing parallels between logic and ethics. Logic is a thoroughly objective discipline that studies the validity (logical goodness) of forms of inference. This value, validity, is something objective in the realm of propositions, which are ideal meanings. Similarly, ethics is a thoroughly objective discipline that studies the goodness or rightness of actions. This value, moral goodness or rightness, is something objective in the realm of intentional action, to be discerned in ethical judgment. Husserl considers what a "formal" axiology (theory of good) and a "formal" theory of practice ("*Praktik*") would look like. Here we may see Husserl's conception of formal ontology at work, appraising the form of a good action or a good practice (such as carpentry). The proper foundation of ethics, Husserl holds, involves the phenomenology of will, a study of the "constitution" of ethical values in acts of consciousness that include willing or wishing such-and-such as well as judging the moral worth of an action initiated by willing. In the background we may see the ethical theories of Aristotle, David Hume, and Immanuel Kant. Aristotle stressed the importance of virtue, or acting consistently according to a value; Hume stressed our feelings of sympathy with fellow actors as we evaluate actions; and Kant held that only the will is fundamentally good, in following the categorical imperative ("Act only on a maxim you could will to be a universal law"). Husserl's theory of "constitution" would analyze our consciousness of an action as good or right, where we will to perform what we take to be a good or right action and where we judge it good or right. In Husserl's idiom, we "constitute" objects in consciousness, meaning not that we bring them into existence through consciousness, but that they acquire meaning for us through consciousness. Thus, we will an action and judge that it is good or right. In that way, our experience presents an action with the objective value property of being good or right – applying Husserl's theory of intentionality to the experience of value, in willing and in evaluating actions.

When Husserl speaks of "practical" phenomena, meaning what we do (say, in building a table), he includes value properties and practical properties in the same breath. We commonly experience things in the world around us as having values even as we interact with them. Accordingly, I see and deal with things in "my surrounding world" (the life-world) as having evaluative and practical aspects. (*Ideas* I, §28.) I see a rose as beautiful; I will an action as good; I see a table as a surface to write on; I wield a hammer in driving a nail. In such familiar intentional activities, I experience objects as having value properties and practical properties. So ethical and practical properties belong to objects in our life-world: they are part of the region Husserl calls Culture (*Geist*, "spirit"). Now, cultural objects tie into our social or, as Husserl says, *intersubjective* engagement with objects. Thus, the table is "there for everyone," for me or you or anyone else, to write on. Moreover, we assume that it was crafted by someone; it is the product of intentional activities by others. Further, where a type of action is good, its value is "there for everyone" – its value is objective and intersubjective. Political values are a special breed. Where we hold individual liberty to be a good thing to be promoted by a political arrangement such as a national constitution or legal system, we hold that it is a good "for everyone" – at any rate, that is a key assumption of Enlightenment political philosophy. All these evaluative and practical features of things in the world around me, around us, are intersubjective, cultural phenomena. In particular, substantive moral *values* (it is wrong to kill, to steal, and so on) fall under the essence Culture, in Husserl's categorial ontology. (In *Ideas* II, Husserl defines the cultural realm as involving moral systems.) The point is not, for Husserl, that values are relative to a culture, simply created by a body politic, but rather that values are "constituted" in volitional activities in a social environment, and they are "constituted" as there for everyone. The character of intersubjectivity is tied into the character of objectivity, Husserl finds, for values around us as well as for natural objects around us.

Evaluative and practical phenomena presuppose my experience of "*others.*" In Husserl's analysis, *empathy* is the source of meaning whereby I experience a being as another "I," another subject, another "living" body acting by will, and so on. (Empathy is a running theme in *Ideas* II.) When we posit a value, holding that an action is morally good or right, or that a political institution is good, or that a painting is beautiful, we normally hold, within

appropriate limits, that this value is objective and so valid or
there "for everyone." My experience of something as having a
value normally depends, then, on my sense of "others," which in
turn is based in my ability to experience others through
empathy. The concept of empathy took shape in the late 19th
century, and Husserl's phenomenological analysis of empathy
depends on his theory of intentionality. Here are tools for a
Husserlian approach to value theory, to ethics, and to political
theory. Indeed, Husserl's successors in the phenomenological
movement pressed the importance of our experience of "the
other," in ways that lead into a rich theory of values. In Chapter 8
we shall return to the outlines of such a phenomenological theory
of values.

THE UNITY IN HUSSERL'S SYSTEM

Husserl ranged widely over the philosophical map. Yet he always
worked systematically, linking his ideas in different areas, and
constantly expanding his philosophical system. Given our survey
of the Husserlian system, we can spell out more explicitly the
unity in the system.

Over the course of the *Logical Investigations*, already summarized,
Husserl develops some seven ranges of theory. In their order of
appearances these are: a theory of logic (Prolegomena), a theory
of language (Investigation I), a theory of universals (Investigation
II), a theory of parts/wholes (Investigation III), a theory of
grammar or structures of propositions (Investigation IV), a theory
of intentionality and therewith phenomenology (Investigation V),
and a phenomenological theory of knowledge (Investigation VI).
Yet these pieces of philosophical theory do not stand alone. Each
presupposes and amplifies upon elements in each of the others.
Accordingly, they hang together in a system that addresses the
overall nature of the world, including – with special emphasis –
our place in the world: the place of our conscious experience in the
world of which we are conscious, thus the place of intentionality
in the world, its place as the crucial relation between ourselves
and other things in the world as we know them.

Thus, Husserl's theory of logic focuses on ideal meanings and how propositions join together to form theories. But ideal meanings are what we express in language. And the same meanings serve as ideal, shareable contents of thought or other types of intentional activity. Alternatively, the intentionality of an act of consciousness consists in a structure relating act, content, and object. But intentional contents are ideal meanings, the sort of thing studied in logic. And the contents of acts of consciousness are in principle expressible in language. And knowledge is formed as acts of judgment are supported by intuitive evidence for propositions asserted in coherence with other propositions that make up a theory or partial theory about a given domain of objects. In these ways Husserl links phenomenology – the theory of consciousness and its intentionality – with theory of language and theory of logic.

If meanings are ideal entities, what kind of entity are they? The early Husserl proposed that meanings are ideal species of acts of consciousness. That is, meanings are a particular type of species, what Aristotle called universals, what Husserl later called essences. Species or essences are the sort of thing shared by different individuals. For instance, two balls share the property of sphericality, and similarly two acts of thinking may share the same property of thinking-of-a-bird. Thus, two acts with the same content are individuals that share the same ideal species or essence. If you will, "what" I am thinking (the content of my thought) is how I am thinking, the ideal species of my thinking. In this way Husserl links the theory of intentionality, whence phenomenology, with the theory of species or universals, in the wider field of ontology.

The later Husserl (in *Ideas* I) distinguished meanings from essences or species. Both are ideal entities, but distinct types of ideal entities. Briefly, species group and qualify concrete individuals (you and I and Socrates are members of Humanity, or *Homo sapiens*), whereas meanings mean or represent things of different type (the sense or concept "human" represents the species Humanity, the sense or concept "the teacher of Plato" represents Socrates, the sense or proposition "Socrates is human" represents the state of affairs that Socrates is human). Both meanings and species are ideal, but they play different ontological roles. In this way the later Husserl expanded his theory of ideal entities. But essences, or species, continued to play their role in the structure of the world, in Husserl's ontology.

The theory of species leads Husserl further into ontology, into the theory of parts and wholes. For, on Husserl's analysis, a red ball instantiates the species or essence Red just in case a concrete instance of Red – this red in this ball – is a part of the ball: a dependent part, or moment, which could not exist apart from that particular ball. Husserl actually begins his work in phenomenology by focusing on moments of visual experience, distinguishing (say) the moment of seeing-red from the moment of seeing-round within an experience of seeing a red, round ball. In this way Husserl links phenomenology, or the theory of consciousness, with the theory of dependent parts, or moments.

Husserl also uses part–whole theory to amplify his theory of logic. For his theory of grammar is a theory of the parts of propositions and other complex types of meanings. Furthermore, this sort of analysis of parts of meanings is used in phenomenology, in the analysis of components of the content or noema of an act of consciousness. For example, when I think "Socrates taught Plato," the nominal meanings "Socrates" and "Plato" are joined by the predicative or relational meaning "taught" to form the composite meaning "Socrates taught Plato," of which the prior three meanings are parts. In these ways Husserl links part–whole theory with both logical and phenomenological theory.

When Husserl turns to epistemology, he links the theory of knowledge to both the theory of ideal meaning and the phenomenological theory of intuition, or intuitive-evidential characters of judgments that ground knowledge. If you will, the objective side of knowledge involves the way that propositions work in a logically well-formed theory, while the subjective side of knowledge involves the way that a proposition's truth is supported by evidence or intuitiveness, for example the sensory evident-ness in my seeing something before me. In this way Husserl links the theory of knowledge with both logical theory and phenomenological theory.

Logic itself is based on intuition. (How do we decide which forms of inference are valid? It is intuitively evident that the

following is a valid form of inference: If P then Q; P; therefore
Q.) Ontology too is based on intuition. (How do we decide for a
theory of universals? We look at examples, for instance observing
intuitively that there is a distinction between the species Red and the
particular moment of redness in this ball.) Indeed, in Husserlian
terms, the whole Husserlian system is a theory supported, as a
system of knowledge, by intuitive observation and intuitive
reasoning. And part of the system itself is a theory of knowledge
as based on intuition.

By now it should be clear, in outline, that Husserl's diverse theories in logic, ontology, phenomenology, and epistemology are
bound together as parts of a single, wide-ranging philosophical
theory of meaning, language, essence (species, form, number),
part–whole, consciousness (intentionality), and knowledge. It
would be a monumental task to ferret out all the important propositions put forth in these theories, to decide which propositions
are more fundamental, perhaps axioms, in each theory, to specify
the places where one theory presupposes concepts and principles
drawn from another theory, and so on. Nonetheless, the big
picture should now be clear. The partial theories are parts of the
grand theory, which is Husserl's philosophical system. Within the
system as a whole there are conceptual and logical links among
the partial theories of meaning, essence, part–whole, consciousness, knowledge, and so on, and these links bind the partial
theories together into a large theory of mind and world.

We have been talking about *parts* of Husserl's system. There is
method in this tactic. For, within Husserl's system, it happens that
Husserl's grand theory entails a theory of its own unity. To that
theory we now turn.

THE METATHEORY IN HUSSERL'S SYSTEM

Philosophers sometimes distinguish philosophy from metaphilosophy. Where philosophy studies the nature of being, mind, value,
and so on, metaphilosophy studies the nature of philosophy itself,
addressing the aims and methods of philosophy – and the difficult

question of just what sort of practice philosophy is (art, science, literature, or what?). Accordingly, within Husserl's philosophical system we may distinguish between his philosophy and his metaphilosophy. In the Husserlian scheme, moreover, this distinction takes a very specific form: separating Husserl's theory of theory from his other theories. The former constitutes Husserl's metatheory, which presumably applies to the other theories in his system, including the theory of theory itself, and to the whole system as a unified theory. Here we see a kind of recursion in Husserl's system, as the metatheory is a part of the system that applies to itself (somewhat as a computer program may apply a rule to a piece of data and then recursively apply the rule again to that result).

In the decades following Husserl's work, mathematical logicians developed a distinction between a theory (say, an axiomatic theory about a domain such as the natural numbers) and a higher-order metatheory for that theory. A theory's metatheory steps back (or up a step) from the theory itself and addresses the semantics of the theory, specifying what objects the theory talks about (say, numbers) and laying out the conditions under which a statement about such objects would be true. This metalogical notion of metatheory (part of what has been called model theory since the middle of the 20th century) is a mathematized version of Husserl's conception of "the theory of theories," itself inspired by Bolzano's conception of "logic."

For Husserl, philosophy itself is a science in the wide sense, that is, a disciplined form of theory. Accordingly, philosophy divides into theory of being (ontology), theory of knowledge (epistemology), theory of consciousness (phenomenology), theory of right action (ethics), and so on. Now, for Husserl, a theory is a logically well-formed system of propositions about a given domain: here lies his metatheory, his theory of theory, providing a pattern for any theory whatsoever. As we shall see, the unity of Husserl's philosophy is itself defined in terms of this metatheory. Husserl did not use the term "metatheory"; rather, he spoke of "pure logic" as the theory of theory, echoing Bolzano. (Only the name has been changed, to protect the innocent.)

In the decades that followed Husserl's writing, logicians and philosophers developed an articulate version of the distinction between theory and metatheory, assuming that a theory is expressed in a well-defined language. In the 1930s the logician Alfred Tarski distinguished between a language L and a metalanguage M of L. Suppose the language L talks about a given domain of objects, say, dogs and cats, as in the sentence "Dogs chase cats." Then the metalanguage M talks about L itself, as in the M sentence "The L sentence 'Dogs chase cats' is true." Tarski used the language/metalanguage separation in order to resolve the so-called liar paradox: the sentence "This sentence is false" (nicknamed The Liar sentence), cannot be true because it is true if and only if false; but this sentence cannot even be formulated in Tarski's system because it violates the boundary Tarski drew between language and metalanguage, as we can talk about the truth of a given sentence in a language L only within a distinct language M that serves as metalanguage for L. And so today, logicians generally distinguish between logic and metalogic, where logic designs systems of inference in a specified symbolic language, while metalogic operates in a higher level of language to prove theorems about what can be proved in a given system of logic in a specified language. More generally, philosophers today may distinguish between a theory and a metatheory about that theory.

Still, Husserl's metatheory is of a special character. There are many kinds of things that can be said about a given theory or range of theories. What exactly does Husserl's metatheory say?

First, a theory is a system of propositions, that is, ideal meanings expressible (in principle) by complete declarative sentences. Second, some propositions entail others in a theory, where the most basic propositions are axioms of the theory. (Ideally, all true propositions in the theory are entailed by the axioms, but in the 1930s the logician Kurt Gödel would prove that this type of completeness does not obtain for certain theories.) Third, the propositions are all about a common domain of entities. (The theory of dogs and cats is about entities in the given domain, the set of dogs and cats.) Since propositions are composed from concepts (such as "dog" or "cat"), the basic concepts in the theory semantically represent entities in the domain. In this way there is a semantic coherence to the theory. Here in a nutshell is Husserl's theory of theories, specifying the logical-semantical properties that define any theory whatsoever.

From this metatheory we can draw out a theory of the unity in Husserl's philosophical system. Husserl did not make the relevant points explicitly, but all the pieces of the analysis are in place. What then binds Husserl's several lines of theory together within his overall philosophy?

As we have seen, over the course of the *Logical Investigations* Husserl keeps expanding his system. His theory of theory focuses on ideal meanings, but ideal meanings also appear in his theory of language (meanings are communicated in speech), in his theory of intentionality (meanings are contents of conscious experience), and in his theory of knowledge (propositions are contents of judgment). Thus, the concept "meaning" appears in these four ranges of theory, so that each of these theories is tied into the others. That is, each presupposes concepts in the others, and so depends on the others, within Husserl's expanding system.

Again, Husserl's theory of intentionality addresses the quality of an act of consciousness, distinguishing the qualities of seeing, imagining, judging, and so on. And the specific quality of intuitiveness appears in his theory of knowledge. So the phenomenological concept of act-quality appears in Husserl's theory of intentionality and in his theory of knowledge, binding these theories together.

Husserl's theory of species draws on his theory of part–whole, as the concept of moment occurs in both theories: a moment is a dependent part of something, and a species is instantiated in a moment in a concrete individual (this instance of Humanity is a moment, or dependent part, of Socrates). Again, his theory of meanings draws on his theory of species, as (the early) Husserl proposes that a meaning is an act-species, or type of experience. Furthermore, his theory of grammar holds that meanings have parts, notably dependent parts. And his theory of intentionality holds that contents of acts of consciousness (meanings) have parts, including moments. So the concepts "species" and "part" and "moment" recur in Husserl's theory of universals (species, essences), in his theory of meaning, and in his theory of intentionality, thereby binding these theories together within his overall system.

According to Husserl's theory of theory, amplified by his theory of parts/wholes for meanings, a theory is a whole, where the propositions in the theory are parts of the theory. Husserl's philosophical system is itself, by this metatheory, a complex theory, of which Husserl's special theories are parts. Moreover, there is a variety of relations of dependence among the partial theories, some of which we have just noted. In this way we may view Husserl's system as a theory composed of appropriate parts, some of which are dependent on others. In this pattern of part–whole relations and dependence relations lies the unity of Husserl's system, according to Husserl's theory of theory, his metatheory.

We say that one proposition or theory logically *presupposes* another, in that the one cannot be true unless the other is true. In that sense, the one proposition or theory *depends* on the other: more precisely, the one's truth depends on the other's truth. This relation of logical presupposition is not usually considered a type of ontological dependence (where one thing's existence depends on another's existence). But such it is, given Husserl's model of intentionality. A thought or judgment is true just in case its content or sense, a proposition (say, that the rain has stopped), correctly represents an existing state of affairs (that the rain has stopped). Truth consists, then, in correspondence to an existing state of affairs in the world: that is, truth is a form of intentional relation, a successful or veridical intentional relation between a thought or proposition and its object, a state of affairs. This model of truth as a successful intentional relation is part of Husserl's theory of intentionality in general. (See D. W. Smith 2002 and 2005 for a detailed reconstruction of a Husserlian theory of truth as an intentional relation.)

So logical dependence is a form of ontological dependence: where one thought's veridical intentional relation (truth) cannot

obtain unless another thought's veridical intentional relation
(truth) obtains. Hence, according to Husserl's metatheory, the
several theories in Husserl's overall philosophical system are
bound together by relations of dependence, and dependence itself
is analyzed in Husserl theory of ontological dependence, or
founding (Fundierung).

Because Husserl's philosophy ranged so widely, with further
horizons of theory beckoning onward, it would be a virtually infinite task to chart the proper parts and dependencies within
Husserl's expansive system. Husserl once called phenomenology
itself "an infinite task." Moreover, we might anticipate theoretical
problems as philosophers pursue the details. How exactly are the
concepts and theories tied together, and are there limits on this
kind of systematic construction? At the close of the 20th century
many philosophers had given up on systematic thinking, leaving
the special theories in philosophy, science, and the arts as piece-
meal language-games. What remains remarkable, in any event, is
the vision of system that flows from Husserl's pen.

PHENOMENOLOGY IN HUSSERL'S EXPANDING SYSTEM

Phenomenology takes a paramount place in Husserl's philosophical system, with diverse connections to logic, ontology,
epistemology, and also ethical theory. What exactly is its place?

After the Logical Investigations (1900–1) Husserl focused increasingly on phenomenology. In Ideas I (1913) phenomenology may
seem to serve as the foundation of all philosophy, and indeed all
possible knowledge. But foundation is itself analyzed in his theory
of parts/wholes in the Investigations III, and he continues to use
his theory of foundation or dependence in all later works. For
Husserl, one thing is founded or dependent (ontologically) on
another just in case the first cannot exist without the second. But
dependence is not by definition a one-way street; two things may
depend mutually on each other, so that the one cannot exist
without the other and vice versa. Indeed, Husserl's leading
example (drawn from his teacher Stumpf) is of that sort: the color
and shape of an object are mutually dependent entities, two

moments (dependent parts) in the object, where (say) the instance of Red in this red round ball cannot exist unless the instance of Round in the ball exists, and vice versa. (Remember that "moments" are particularized instances of species – here, concrete instances of Red and Round.) Now, when we look at Husserl's philosophical system, we see mutual dependencies among the various theories falling in phenomenology, logic, ontology, and epistemology. One theory cannot do its work without the others: the logical or semantic force of the one simply cannot exist without the semantic force of the others – if you will, the intentionality of the one theory cannot exist without the intentionality of the other theories in the system. In that way, the several theories are mutually interdependent, mutually "founding." And so, within Husserl's system, phenomenology cannot be the sole foundation of the edifice. That is the picture which we have drawn.

It is often said that Husserl changed his worldview radically between the *Investigations* and *Ideas* I, migrating from an early position of realism to a strong form of idealism in his "mature" philosophy in *Ideas* I and later works. (Philipse [1995] and A. D. Smith [2003] argue that Husserl's later position was indeed a form of classical idealism; Føllesdal [1998] argues against an idealist reading of Husserl.) If Husserl became a confirmed idealist, for whom all the world exists only as idea or in a state of dependence on consciousness, then phenomenology ought surely to be the sole foundation of philosophy. For Husserl, all the world is "constituted" in consciousness, and if the world's very being depends on this "constitution," then everything we can say in philosophy ought to be grounded in phenomenology, the science of consciousness. However, when we turn to Husserl's doctrine of transcendental idealism (in Chapter 3) and to his theory of constitution (in Chapter 6), we shall find that his position is not what we normally think of as idealism. In brief, consciousness gives meaning, not existence, to the world around us. This doctrine of meaning-giving entails a crucial place for phenomenology in all philosophy, but not a place owed to classical idealism.

When Husserl sounds most like a classical idealist (in *Ideas* I, §49), he says that the natural world is "relative" to consciousness, that consciousness alone is "absolute," not "relative" to anything else. Unpacking his position, we find that every object in the world is "constituted" through its correlation with a system of meanings that present the object in various possible ways in actual or possible acts of consciousness. (See Chapter 6 on constitution.) This is not to say that the object is brought into being by consciousness, or dependent in its being on actual or possible consciousness of it. Questions of dependence are a further issue of ontology. Thus, Husserl may say that the world of nature and culture – our Umwelt or surrounding world – is in certain ways related to our consciousness, and indeed that the ways we understand things in the world depend on our consciousness of those things. But Husserl can also say that our consciousness depends in other ways on things in the world: on how our brains work and on how we have acquired concepts from our culture and our language. Dependence is not a one-way street, and there are very different kinds of ontological dependence running between consciousness and world. (These issues are dissected in Chapter 3.)

We should bear in mind the distinction between a piece of theory and its domain of objects. In particular, phenomenology is (in logical terms) the theory of the essence of consciousness as experienced (including, notably, the intentionality of acts of consciousness). By contrast, neuroscience is the theory of the essence of neural activities in the human brain. Now, we may ask whether phenomenology is dependent upon or independent of neuroscience: whether the one piece of theory depends on the other. Or we may ask whether consciousness itself is dependent upon or independent of neural processes in the subject's brain: say, whether acts of visual perception depend on neural information-processing in the visual cortex of the human brain. These are different sorts of question. The former is at stake in Husserl's metatheory. The latter is at issue in the question of Husserl's idealism. The two questions come together, however, where we observe that the practice of phenomenology is an activity of consciousness in which we reflect on our own activities of consciousness.

Husserl insists, in *Ideas* I and other works, that phenomenology is "presuppositionless." But given his systematic approach to philosophy, and given the opening set-up in *Ideas* I, this cannot mean that phenomenology is independent of all ontology, logic, and so on. It can only mean, instead, that we practice phenomenology as such without yet making use of concepts or principles drawn from other disciplines, specifically from the natural and cultural sciences. In his unified system, however, as he develops phenomenology in connection with logic, ontology, and so on, Husserl makes explicit use of presuppositions from formal ontology, notably the theory of ideal meaning or noema, the theory of species or essence, and the theory of part and dependence.

In Husserl's philosophical system, then, there is one particular way in which phenomenology founds other parts of philosophy: all of our meanings, through which we understand anything at all, are to be explicated in phenomenological analysis. Indeed, we may see a modernist motif developing from Descartes through Kant into Husserl: a vision of objectivity gained through subjectivity. For Descartes, our knowledge of everything begins in our knowledge of our own "thinking," which Descartes said we know with a special kind of certainty. For Kant, our knowledge of the spatiotemporal world around us is shaped by the a priori form of our own experience, by the forms of sensation or sensibility together with the forms of judgment or understanding, as our mind conceptualizes the deliverance of the senses. For Husserl, given his theory of intentionality, our experience of everything – including our knowledge of things in space and time – consists in acts of consciousness, which have a certain character of intentionality, the relational character of being directed via various types of meaning to appropriate objects. We experience things only in that way, and only through intentionality do we develop objective knowledge. But phenomenology is the philosophical discipline or theory that studies the intentionality of consciousness. In this way phenomenology is a special theory that founds all other theory in philosophy. Meanwhile, phenomenology itself presupposes and so depends on certain elements of logical, ontological, and epistemological theory.

So phenomenology occupies a special and central place in Husserl's overall system. The Husserlian system here involves a kind of recursion, as the phenomenology is both a part of the whole system and a kind of foundation for the whole system. For the theory of meaning or intentional content runs throughout his overall philosophical theory, as meaning is the heart of all theory. Nonetheless, given our analysis of Husserl's system and its metatheory, phenomenology is not the sole foundation of all philosophy, or of all strict "science."

We have already seen another recursion in Husserl's system, as the theory of theory is both a part of the system and a metatheory that applies to the whole philosophical theory and to the partial theories. Again, the theory of knowledge is a part of the system but also applies recursively to the evidential base of the several theories in the system and to the system itself. And, as we stressed, the ontological theories of meaning, species or essence, and part are a part of the system and also apply recursively to the theories in the system and to the whole system as a theory.

As Husserl continues to expand his philosophy throughout his career, phenomenology occupies a central place in the system, yet it stands in relations of mutual dependence to logic, ontology, and epistemology in the system. The overall structure of this system is mapped out in the _Logical Investigations_. That structure Husserl never abandoned.

HUSSERL'S SYSTEM AS TRANSCENDENTAL PHILOSOPHY

Around 1905 Husserl took a "transcendental turn." With this "turn" of mind, his conception of phenomenology took on certain motifs of "transcendental" philosophy, the tradition launched by Immanuel Kant in the _Critique of Pure Reason_ (1781/ 1787). Kant's influence on German philosophy extended from Fichte and Hegel, writing in Kant's immediate wake, into the milieu of German philosophy in which Husserl was writing as he moved from Vienna to Halle, Göttingen, and Freiburg. Ever the synthesizer, Husserl sought, characteristically, to adapt into his own system big ideas from the great thinkers: Plato, Aristotle,

Descartes, Leibniz, and now Kant – while retaining the seminal ideas he had drawn from Bolzano's logic and Brentano's descriptive psychology. Kantian "critique" of knowledge works its way back into the way the mind works through reason and sensation to produce our knowledge. Philosophy is thus "transcendental" where it seeks, in Kant's terms, "the necessary conditions of the possibility" of our knowledge, specifically our familiar knowledge of objects in space and time. Here Husserl finds a kind of proto-phenomenology, and indeed the term "phenomenology" had been coined in Kant's era. The task of phenomenology is thus to reflect on what Kant called "phenomena," that is, things *as* they appear in our experience, and so, for Husserl, to explore the *sense* or meaning things have in our experience. Transcendental phenomenology thus explores the space of meaning in our lived experience. (The felicitous term "space of meaning" is featured in Crowell [2001], exploring transcendental themes in Husserl and Heidegger.)

This transcendental form of phenomenology Husserl announced in the *Paris Lectures* (1907) and elaborated in *Ideas I* (1913). The adaptation of transcendental themes gave Husserl's mature phenomenology a distinctive thrust, vividly expressed in *Ideas I*. Indeed, Husserl's transcendental turn suggests a rather different approach to understanding Husserl's mature philosophy and its systematic character. In this approach, alternative to the present reconstruction of Husserl's system, Husserl's chief concern becomes methodological, rather than doctrinal. By practicing "transcendental" reflection through "transcendental-phenomeno-logical reduction," we suspend our concern with the natural and cultural world in which we live, and we address instead solely the ways things are given or "constituted" in our experience. Thereby, we appreciate the form or meaning of things just as we experience them. Husserl thus extended and radicalized Kant's conception of transcendental philosophy and, therewith, transcen-dental idealism, the latter term borrowed from Kant. (Moran [2005] traces the development of Husserl's philosophy, empha-sizing the ties to Kantian philosophy and its legacy in the tradition of German idealism. Other Husserl interpretations also stress the transcendental method of Husserl's mature philosophy, for instance Klaus Held in the lead essays in Welton 2003.)

But what exactly is transcendental philosophy for Husserl? What does Husserl make of transcendental method and transcendental idealism, and how does Husserl's transcendental phenomenology render his system, well, systematic? In Husserl's hands, in his philosophical system, the transcendental takes on quite a different significance than it has in Kant proper. Remember Husserl's origins in Bolzano (who actually wrote a book titled *Against Kant*). In Husserl's early work, preparing the way for the *Logical Investigations* (1900–1), Husserl joined in what Alberto Coffa has called "the semantic tradition" (Coffa 1991). Bolzano, Lotze, Frege, Husserl in their own ways each stressed the objectivity of sense, of ideas or thoughts or propositions, what Husserl called ideal intentional contents. In the eyes of this semantic tradition, objective meaning was precisely what was missing in the earlier varieties of logic and epistemology and their views of the mind. The rationalists had stressed the ideals of reason, the empiricists had privileged concrete sensory perception, and Kant had then worked to integrate reason and sensibility. All sought objective foundations for knowledge wrought from subjective experience, yet it remained for the "semantic" tradition to home in on ideal meaning per se.

For Husserl, accordingly, a transcendental critique of knowledge appraises our "constitution" of objects in the world by tracing our experience back to something more than the subjective mental processes in which we know or experience spatiotemporal objects – whether processes of reasoning (Descartes) or sensing (Hume) or a fusion thereof (Kant). By placing ourselves within our own first-person range of experience, in the practice of transcendental phenomenology, Husserl says, we "win a new region of being" (*Ideas* I, §33), namely, the region of "pure" consciousness. In our extended reflection on consciousness and its essential intentionality (*Ideas* I, §§84–131ff.), we unearth the range of sense (*Sinn*) or meaning in our experience, wherein we encounter objects just as we experience them. This range of sense embraces what Husserl calls "noemata," or "objects-as-intended" – replacing the Kantian notion of "phenomena," or "things-as-they-appear." For Husserl, then, transcendental philosophy focuses on the role of *ideal meaning* in our "pure" intentional experiences. Here lie the proper foundations, or conditions of the possibility, of all our intentional experiences, including those that lead into objective knowledge of things in the surrounding world.

Husserl's presentation, and practice, of "transcendental" method in *Ideas* I suggests an intriguing and radical picture of transcendental phenomenology and its place in Husserl's systematic philosophy. Husserl liked to talk of "breakthroughs": his breakthrough to objectivity in the *Logical Investigations* (1900–1), his breakthrough to transcendental subjectivity in *Ideas* I (1913), his breakthrough to intersubjectivity and the life-world in the *Crisis* (1935–8). The evolution of transcendental phenomenology, then, was a breakthrough to transcendental "constitution," to how the world as we know it is fashioned by the functioning of "pure" or "transcendental" consciousness. According to this radical picture of Husserl's philosophy, all objects in the world around us come into being and acquire their intended properties *through consciousness*. Stones, trees, dogs, my own body, other people, buildings – all things in our world come into being through consciousness, indeed through my consciousness, that is, so far as I can know from my own first-person, phenomenological perspective. Moreover, all of our scientific and philosophical theories are themselves products of consciousness, mine and others'. Whence all of phenomenology, logic, ontology, epistemology, and ethics, along with mathematics, physics, chemistry, biology, psychology, and sociology – all these ranges of *theory* are products of *consciousness*. And so are the *objects* studied in these disciplines. Accordingly, when we take the transcendental turn, on this radical picture, everything is ultimately seen as flowing from consciousness, whose provenance we come to appreciate only in the practice of transcendental phenomenology.

What is wrong with this exciting picture of Husserl's philosophy, however, is its disconnection from the core principles that unify Husserl's system. Even as Husserl is unfolding his conception of transcendental phenomenology, we shall see, he makes use of elements of logic, ontology, and epistemology that were detailed in the pre-"transcendental" *Logical Investigations*. What makes Husserl's philosophy systematic, then, is not the dedicated practice of the method of transcendental reduction, within which all parts of his system are grounded. Rather, what makes Husserl's philosophy systematic is the way in which the various parts of his system hang together, and it is only within that system that his method of transcendental reduction or reflection gains its significance.

SUMMARY

Husserl's philosophy takes the form of a unified system that integrates specific theories in logic, ontology, phenomenology, and epistemology – and also ethics. The framework of the system (*sans* ethics) is laid out in the long course of the *Logical Investigations* (1900–1). That framework remains in force as Husserl unfolds the themes and methods of transcendental phenomenology in *Ideas* I (1913) and later works. Husserl sees important changes in his thinking at certain points, notably in his later "transcendental turn" and again in his late emphasis on the life-world. Nonetheless, these important shifts take place within his expanding system of philosophy. Despite some heavy rhetoric among Husserl and his followers, Husserl remains firmly committed to the structure and details of his unfolding system, even as he adds new detail (rarely revoking earlier analyses), and even as he records dramatic overtures to Bolzanoesque logic, to Kantian transcendental philosophy, to Cartesian subjectivist philosophy, and to historical intersubjectivist philosophy.

Husserl's system is launched in the Prolegomena to the *Logical Investigations*. "Pure" logic, Husserl holds, maps the basic forms of thought or meaning, the basic forms of objects in the world, and the basic correlations between forms of meaning and the forms of objects represented by such meanings. Here is Husserl's sketch of what logicians have subsequently called formal or logical semantics. Husserl also addresses logical consequence or entailment, looking to the new system of logic developing in his day – but his own contribution lies in his conception of semantics.

Language expresses sense (*Sinn*) as meaning (*Bedeutung*). But the range of sense is itself that of intentional content: the ideal contents of various types or species of intentional experience such as seeing, thinking, imagining, and so on. In this way Husserl's conception of pure logic paves the way for his theory of intentionality, or the ways objects in the world are represented by contents of experience. And with the theory of intentionality Husserl launches his conception of phenomenology, the science of the essence of consciousness.

Husserl's ontology is part of the framework assumed by his conception of pure logic and by his conception of phenomenology. Key is Husserl's doctrine of essence, or ideal species, as he called essences in the *Investigations*. Husserl outlines a theory of essences or universals (species, properties, relations) that draws partly on Platonic and partly on Aristotelian theory. Thus, Socrates' being human Husserl analyses in terms of concrete individuals, ideal species, and concrete instances of species: the individual Socrates includes a "moment" or instance of the ideal species Humanity, and thereby the ideal species is tied into the concrete individual. Husserl's theory of parts and wholes is at work here, as a "moment" is defined as a dependent part, a part (Socrates' humanity) that cannot exist independently of the whole (Socrates).

Husserl's theory of intentionality, detailed first in the *Investigations*, features his distinction among an act of consciousness, its sense or ideal intentional content (which can be shared by other acts), and the object correlated with that sense. The act is thus intentionally directed toward its object by way of its content or sense.

Husserl's epistemology is a case of applied phenomenology. What forms knowledge, giving it objectivity or validity, for Husserl, is the "evidence" that supports our judgments. Evidence consists in the "intuitive" character of certain experiences. These experiences include reason and perception, each with its own type of evidence. Cognition, or "intuition" (*Anschauung*, the traditional term since Kant), consists in an "intuitive" or evident intentional experience. When I see that tree across the way, my conceptual sense "that tree" is supported or "fulfilled" intuitively by the sensory character of my seeing (as opposed to merely thinking) "that tree." When I "see" that $2 + 2 = 4$, my conceptualization "$2 + 2 = 4$" is supported or fulfilled intuitively. Such an "intuition" is not a mysterious peering into the Platonic heaven of numbers; it is rather a familiar form of experience as we enumerate things around us. When in reflection I "see" that thinking is an intentional experience, my phenomenological judgment about intentionality is supported intuitively, in my experience of reflection on the familiar essence of thinking.

As we have seen, Husserl's system of philosophy is bound together by relations of dependence among the several theories – logical, ontological, phenomenological, and epistemological theories. Behind this systematic unity lies Husserl's metatheory, his "theory of theories," the core of his logical semantics. Following Bolzano, Husserl says a theory is itself a system of propositions (propositional meanings or senses) bound together by relations of logical deduction and/or induction ("motivation"), and by relations of presupposition, or logical dependence. Husserl's metatheory, defining the unity of his system, is a philosophical vision that prefigured later logicians' mathematical theory of theories (notably in the work of Alfred Tarski, Rudolf Carnap, and later the style of possible-worlds semantics).

FURTHER READING

The systematic character of Husserl's philosophy is manifest in his full corpus, but the Logical Investigations lays out Husserl's system explicitly in one long treatise – though it is not easy to see the forest for the trees. Among the extant studies of Husserl's Investigations are two recent collections of essays (including my own accounts of the unity in Husserl's system).

Fisette, Denis. 2003. Husserl's Logical Investigations Reconsidered. Dordrecht and Boston, Massachussetts: Kluwer Academic Publishers (now New York: Springer). Essays on Husserl's Logical Investigations. Includes D. W. Smith, "The Unity of Husserl's Logical Investigations: Then and Now," offering an account of the unity of Husserl's system.

Zahavi, Dan, and Frederik Stjernfelt, eds. 2002. *One Hundred Years of Phenomenology: Husserl's* Logical Investigations *Revisited*. Dordrecht and Boston, Massachussetts: Kluwer Academic Publishers (now New York: Springer). Essays on Husserl's *Logical Investigations*. Includes D. W. Smith, "What Is 'Logical' in Husserl's *Logical Investigations?*," offering an interpretation of the interrelations between the parts of the *Investigations*, entailing the unity of Husserl's system.

Three

Logic: meaning in language, mind, and science

This chapter outlines Husserl's conception of logic and its relation to his overall philosophical system, including its role in the background of phenomenology. Readers unfamiliar with logic and formal semantics may find this chapter "heavier" reading than other chapters, though I have tried to lay out basic ideas along the way. These readers may want to browse more quickly through this chapter, returning to it as time permits.

HUSSERL AND LOGIC

By the second half of the 20th century logic and phenomenology were separated by a cultural chasm featuring "analytic" philosophy on one side, originally inspired by new logical theory *circa* 1900, and "continental" philosophy on the other side, originally inspired by new phenomenological theory *circa* 1900. Husserl is well known for his work in phenomenology, yet he was concerned with logic at all phases of his career, even before he "discovered" the new science of phenomenology. Indeed, as we observed in Chapters 1 and 2, Husserl's conception of "pure logic" led into his conception of "pure phenomenology." Moreover, he saw in phenomenology a foundation for logic in the theory of ideal meaning as intentional content. You might say that Husserl saw in logic far more than the logicians saw.

Logic – the theory of good or "valid" reasoning – was born in Aristotle's theory of syllogism (from the Greek word for inference, literally reckoning together). Aristotle posited exactly twelve forms of valid inference. Here is one form of inference or argument canonized in Aristotle's system:

All humans are mortal.	All *As* are B.
Socrates is a human.	*s* is an *A*.
Therefore, Socrates is mortal.	Therefore, *s* is a B.

On the left is a concrete inference; on the right is the form of that inference. To specify the form of the inference, the non-logical expressions in the example argument ("human," "mortal," "Socrates") are replaced by variable expressions, either predicate variables ("*A*" and "*B*" where "human" and "mortal" occur) or a name variable ("*s*" where "Socrates" occurs). The idea is that any appropriate replacement where these variables occur will produce a valid inference, that is, one in which the conclusion must be true if the premises are true. Aristotle's knack for classification led him to organize his results into twelve such model syllogisms or inference-forms.

The next leap forward in logic occurred in the late 19th century, along with coordinate developments in mathematics. Husserl came of age amid this upsurge of new ideas in logic and mathematics, and he either corresponded or worked directly with many of the seminal figures laying the foundations of the new mathematical logic, set theory, and non-Euclidean geometries. Mathematicians Boole, Schröder, and Peano joined philosopher-mathematicians Peirce and Frege in reconceiving the forms of language crucial for a wide range of the forms of inference used, not least in modern mathematics. Two key forms of symbol or expression emerged as basic to the new logic: the logical form of predicates and the logical form of quantifiers. In Aristotle's logic predicates invariably took the form of a predicate applied to a single term, the subject-expression in the sentence ("is mortal" applies to "Socrates" to form the sentence "Socrates is mortal"). However, mathematics regularly deals in relations and so does everyday language ("Socrates taught Plato," "Plato was shorter than Aristotle," "2 < 3," or "2 < x < 3"). Modern predicate logic thus allows for predicates that ascribe relations to more than one thing, whereas Aristotle's symbolism did not address relational predicates, arguably encouraging the view that relations are not real (where is the relation located, in one relatum or the other?). Function terms in mathematics already required application to as many terms as relevant ("$f(x,y,z) = 2x + (y - z)$"), and predicates ("$\_ < \_$") were naturally assimilated to function terms (sometimes predicates were called "propositional functions," as if a predicate carries terms into a sentence or proposition). More important still were the quantifier words "all" and "some." In Aristotle's logic, the subject-term "all humans" was treated as a single noun phrase. In the new logic, as developed (independently) by the American Charles Sanders Peirce and the German Gottlob Frege, quantifier words are treated as a kind of operator applied to sentences. Thus, "All humans are mortal" is reformulated as "For any individual x, if x is a human then x is mortal." And "Some mortal beings are humans" is formulated as "For some individual x, x is mortal and x is a human." Working with the logical forms of predicates and quantifiers as well as sentence connectives ("and," "or," "not," "if . . . then . . . "), the new symbolic logic was born, given full treatment by Alfred North Whitehead and Bertrand Russell in *Principia Mathematica* (1910). A wide variety of valid forms of inference were codified in the new system, far surpassing Aristotle's theory of syllogism.

Frege's work on the logic of predicates and quantifiers has drawn the interest of philosophers also because of his logic of "sense and reference" (*Sinn* and *Bedeutung*). For Frege the forms of names, predicates, and sentences are sharply defined, and appropriate forms of both sense and referent are correlated, respectively, with names, predicates, and sentences. Husserl himself outlined a system of correlations among expression, sense, and referent, as we shall see. Husserl's details are different at some points from Frege's, but the comparison between Husserl and Frege has proved useful in modeling Husserl's theory of intentionality, as we shall consider in due course. Indeed, with the semantical correlation of expressions with sense and with reference, logic addresses sense and reference in addition to validity of inference. This part of logic has come to be called *semantics*, formally so christened in the 1940s. As we shall see, Husserl's own contributions to theory of language address semantics, and specifically the role of intentionality in semantics. Here lies Husserl's innovation in logic.

As the new mathematical or symbolic logic was developing in Frege and Peirce (and Boole, Schröder, *et al.*), Georg Cantor was laying the beginnings of the theory of sets (*Menge*). Husserl was a colleague and friend of Cantor's at Halle for 14 years, and in his first philosophical works – his 1886 *Habilitation* manuscript and his 1891 book *Philosophy of Arithmetic* – Husserl analyzed several kinds of pluralities and how we conceive or represent them in the practice of arithmetic and geometry. Here are the seeds of Husserl's notion of "manifold," or *Mannigfaltigkeit*, resonant with Cantor's early theory of sets, sometimes called *Mannigfaltigkeitslehre* rather than *Mengenlehre*. When Husserl moved to Göttingen in 1900, he became a colleague and friend of the mathematician David Hilbert, who conceived all mathematics as purely formal axiomatic systems. Husserl had already worked with a similar model of mathematical theory in the Prolegomena to the *Logical Investigations* (1900–1). This conception of a "pure" theory, ideally a mathematical axiomatic system expressed in an appropriate language, Husserl envisioned as fulfilling Bolzano's idea of a theory as a system of ideal propositions. Husserl also had in mind the axiomatization of geometry: change the fifth of Euclid's axioms and you change the mathematical theory of geometry, whence alternative "geometries" emerge as formal axiomatic structures awaiting application to "material" domains.

All this mix of logical and mathematical terrain defined the soil in which Husserl laid down his *Logical Investigations*. Again and again in his career, Husserl returned to related logico-mathematical themes: in the structure of time (lectures from 1905–10 gathered in *On the Phenomenology of the Consciousness of Internal Time* (1893–1917)), the structure of space (lectures from 1907 gathered in *Thing and Space*, 1907), the relation of meaning to language and to thought (lectures on meaning in 1908; *Ideas* I, 1913), the relation between "formal" and "transcendental" logic (*Formal and Transcendental Logic*, 1929), and the "mathematizing" of nature (in his last writings of 1935–8 gathered in *Crisis*, 1935–8).

Husserl's contribution to logic, however, was not to craft a particular symbolic system with a formal language and formal rules of inference. That technical work Husserl left to others (Frege, Whitehead and Russell, et al.). Rather, Husserl's contribution was to address the *philosophical* character of the emerging conception of logic. Specifically, Husserl envisioned a system of what philosophers and logicians today call *semantics*: the systematic correlation among forms of expression, meaning, and objects in the world. Furthermore, Husserl appraised the relation of such a logical system, or semantics, to the intentionality of consciousness. For Husserl, a mathematical system of logic must be grounded in structures of intentionality, specifying the way meanings in our experience represent things in the world around us. Formal or symbolic logic is thus founded in our experience; it is not a system of free-floating symbols with no real meaning. Alternatively, we build formal systems of logic as *abstractions* from patterns of intentionality we find in acts of consciousness. With this grounding in intentionality, logic becomes not merely "formal" or mathematical, but also "transcendental."

Husserl proposed a division of labor between the "technicians" of logic and the "philosophers" of logic (Prolegomena, §71). The "technicians" develop mathematical symbolic systems of logic – formalized axiomatic theories – and prove results about their systems, whereas the "philosophers" develop the theory of what the mathematical systems of logic are about, especially how the symbol systems relate to our experience and to the world. Husserl clearly saw himself as a philosopher of logic, and following Bolzano he saw the conception of "pure logic" as the theory of theories. Husserl's theory of theories was not itself "mathematized," nor was it supposed to be. The mathematical theory of mathematical logical theories, later called metalogic, awaited the technical work of Alfred Tarski, Kurt Gödel, et al. By contrast, Husserl's theory of theories was itself a philosophical theory, specifically a theory of ideal meanings, of how propositions entail propositions, how concepts represent individuals, properties, and so on. These ideal meanings, on Husserl's theory, are intentional contents of appropriate experience, contents that are in principle expressible by appropriate linguistic signs.

Technical developments in mathematical logic, in the decades following Husserl's work, may be seen as working out the detail of the vision Husserl had laid out. This perception of Husserl's place in 20th-century logic may sound untethered to the actual history of logic. However, there are historical links from Husserl to seminal work in mathematical logic. Rudolf Carnap attended Husserl's lectures in 1924–5, during the period in which Carnap was writing *The Logical Construction of the World* (*Der logische Aufbau der Welt*, 1928, nicknamed "the *Aufbau*"). Carnap called his system in the *Aufbau* "constitution theory" (*Konstitutionstheorie*), and explicitly noted similarities to Husserl's system of transcendental phenomenology in *Ideas* I (1913). It was Carnap more than anyone who, by the 1940s, worked out the relations between syntax and semantics as basic parts of logical theory. Alfred Tarski, in the 1930s, developed a mathematical model of truth for a certain kind of formal language, and he called this model "the semantic conception of truth." Tarski persuaded Carnap of the importance and mathematical feasibility of a semantics of truth, beyond the syntax of an axiomatic system. Tarski cited Husserl's notion of categories in the *Logical Investigations*, and it should be noted that Tarski was educated in Warsaw by logicians in the Lvov–Warsaw school of philosophy. The Polish school (tradition) was founded by Kasimierz Twardowski, who with Husserl brought the theory of intentionality into its modern formulation based on a distinction among act, content, and object of consciousness. Furthermore, Kurt Gödel drew on Husserl's conception of our knowledge of ideal objects. The aforementioned are of course giants of 20th-century mathematical-philosophical logic. (See Coffa 1991; Richardson 1998; Friedman 1999; Roy 2004; Ryckman 2005, 2006, on Husserl and Carnap; and see Tieszen 2005 on Husserl and Gödel.)

A recurring theme in Husserl's writings, on very different topics, is his notion of a "manifold" (*Mannigfaltigkeit*). We shall observe Husserl's use of this notion as we proceed through the present book. This notion, Husserl said, was inspired by the mathematical theory of "manifolds" used in non-Euclidean geometries. The notion is also the precursor to the set-theoretic notion of a "model" (a structured set) that emerged from Tarski's work and led into connections with the Leibnizian notion of a "possible world." Suffice it to say that the architect of phenomenology, the science of the essence of consciousness, saw the world and our consciousness of it through eyes informed by the logic and mathematics of Husserl's youth.

THE STATUS OF LOGIC: HUSSERL'S CRITIQUE OF PSYCHOLOGISM

Husserl's *Logical Investigations* (1900–1) opens with a book-length study (volume I of the original German edition): *Prolegomena to Pure Logic*. Of the eleven chapters, the first ten are critical, unfurling lengthy arguments against a variety of philosophies of logic. The final chapter, which will be our main concern, outlines Husserl's positive conception of "pure logic," a conception that informs and integrates his subsequent accounts of ontology, phenomenology, and epistemology.

What kind of discipline is logic? That is the question Husserl addresses, posing a series of alternatives:

1 Is logic a theoretical or a practical discipline (a "technology")?
2 Is it independent of other sciences, and, in particular, of psychology and metaphysics?
3 Is it a formal discipline? Has it merely to do, as usually conceived, with the "form of knowledge," or should it also take account of its matter?
4 Has it the character of an a priori, a demonstrative discipline or of an empirical, inductive one?

(Prolegomena, Introduction, §3)

Similar questions linger today. Is logic a practical matter of efficient procedures of inference, or rather a theoretical matter of what makes an inference valid? Is logic independent of empirical psychology, which studies how we happen to argue, or even of metaphysics concerning the nature of the world we reason about? Is logic concerned only with the form of an inference, or must it address the content of the premises and conclusion? Is logic an a priori discipline like mathematics, where logic moves from axioms to theorems that characterize validity of inference, or is logic rather an empirical study of what probably (inductively) leads from premises to conclusion?

Husserl first considers whether logic is a "normative" and so a "practical" or "technical" discipline (Prolegomena: ch. 1). Logic cannot be only or primarily concerned with how we *ought* to reason, and thus with normative, practical, technical matters such as designing effective symbolic languages with rules of inference that are easy to follow. We ought to reason in accord with valid forms of inference, not for normative or practical or technical reasons, but because we would then be in accord with the objective standards of valid inference. So, Husserl finds, there is more to logic than normativity and practicality. Indeed, Husserl argues, every normative discipline must be founded on a theoretical discipline (Prolegomena: ch. 2), since the value or end of a discipline (what one ought to do therein) rests on an account of what the discipline is dealing with. For example, according to the discipline of automobile handling, I ought to drive my car with fuel in the tank. But this norm depends on the fact that my car runs on gasoline. Again, I ought to put in the clutch and shift into a higher gear when the tachometer reaches 5,000 to 6,000 rpm; but this norm depends on the fact that my car's piston-driven combustion engine has a limited range of rotation of the drive shaft. Thus, the discipline concerning how one *ought* to drive rests on the discipline concerning what an automobile is. Similarly, I *ought* to reason by following the appropriate rule of inference ("If you have 'P' and also 'if P then Q', you ought to conclude 'Q'"). But this norm of reasoning rests on the objective fact that the conclusion ('Q') *follows logically* from the premises ('P' and 'if P then Q'), that is, the conclusion must be true if the premises are true. Thus, the discipline of logic cannot be merely the normative or practical or technical discipline concerning how one ought to reason or how one can reason effectively by following well-crafted rules of inference in a well-designed language (Aristotle's logic or, better, Frege's). Rather, logic includes and is fundamentally grounded in a theoretical discipline – "pure" logic as opposed to technical-practical logic – that concerns what makes certain forms of inference objectively valid: namely, their logical form.

What sort of theoretical discipline would this be? Might it be an *empirical* discipline concerning how we think and reason? Perhaps the psychology of reasoning? Perhaps, in today's parlance, cognitive science or neuroscience, tracking how the human mind or brain tends to reason? We know Husserl's answer.

Husserl proceeds to a lengthy critique of psychologism (Prolegomena: chs. 3–9). *Psychologism* holds that logic is a theory about how the human mind works, moving from premises to conclusions of a given form. On such a philosophy of logic, shared by Mill and others whom Husserl addresses, laws of logic – laws of thought – are "laws of nature": empirical laws that govern the ways human beings happen to think, moving from such-and-such premises to such-and-such a conclusion. Logic then leads to a "subjective relativism," Husserl argues: laws of logic are merely subjective, relative to the ways we humans happen to find ourselves thinking – and so we have a mere "anthropologism" with regard to logic.

In *Philosophy of Arithmetic* (1891) Husserl had studied the mental activities of grouping and counting objects, seeking a theory of the "origins" of the concepts of plurality and number in such activities. Frege's review of the book charged Husserl thus with psychologism, and Husserl responded with a wide-ranging critique of psychologism that became the Prolegomena. The problem with *Philosophy of Arithmetic* was not actually psychologism. The problem was rather that Husserl was working with an inadequate model of intentionality, where (in the style of Brentano) an object is intentionally contained in our experience of the object. Husserl had not yet developed his theory of intentionality and so appeared to conflate object with content of consciousness, obscuring the distinctions he would later draw between (say) a plurality of objects (a group of birds on a wire) and our idea or concept of that plurality. Husserl looked back on *Arithmetic* as an immature, "childlike" analysis of number, and so the Prolegomena spent many chapters sorting out what he saw as errors in psychologism.

Nearing the end of the Prolegomena Husserl turns at last toward a positive conception of logic (ch. 10). Kant had sought an a priori objectivity for logic, and nearer Husserl's time Herbart and Lotze had urged an objectivity of logic that is linked with Platonism. What makes an inference *valid*, we should say, is the *objective form* of the inference. But Husserl's heroes in the objective conception of logic are Leibniz and Bolzano. We turn to Husserl's own conception of "pure logic."

"PURE LOGIC": THE THEORY OF SCIENCE AS THEORY OF THEORIES

In Husserl's estimate, Gottfried Wilhelm von Leibniz (1646–1716) was the first thinker to begin to see what logic as a science ought to be: what mathematicians would later call an algebraic formulation of systems of axioms and their deductive conclusions. Leibniz spoke of a *mathesis universalis*, a "universal mathematics," broadly conceived as a universal system of calculation of deductive inferences. (Leibniz was also the first to conceive of a computing or "reckoning" machine.) Husserl admired Leibniz's vision, speaking regularly of a "*mathesis universalis*." He applied the Leibnizian notion even to phenomenology as, in part, a "*mathesis* of experiences." (Compare *Ideas* I, §§72–5, where Husserl speaks of a "'geometry' of experiences" amid a discussion of "'definite' manifolds" [§72], prompting Carnap's reference to a Husserlian "*mathesis* of experiences.") However, the mathematical characterization of experience must be allied, for Husserl, with genuine "description" through intuition of experience (see Roy 2004 on Carnap's effort to mathematize experience).

Still, Leibniz had only begun to glimpse this possibility for logic as a *mathesis universalis*. In Husserl's eyes the first articulation of this conception was begun by Bernard Bolzano (1781–1848) in his *Theory of Science* (in German *Wissenschaftslehre*, 1837/1972), whose subtitle declares a "*Novel Exposition of Logic*." In the Prolegomena Husserl speaks of Bolzano in truly reverential tones, as he spoke of no other thinker in history. The proper vision of logic was not that in the commendable efforts of Kant, Herbart, and Lotze (§§58–60), but that begun by Bolzano in Leibniz's wake (§§59–61). "I am referring," Husserl trumpets, "to Bernhard Bolzano's *Wissenschaftslehre*, published in 1837, a work which, in its treatment of the logical 'theory of elements', far surpasses everything that world-literature has to offer in the way of a systematic sketch of logic" (§61, Appendix). Indeed, "[l]ogic as a science must . . . be built upon Bolzano's work, and must learn from him its need for mathematical acuteness in distinctions, for mathematical exactness in theories" (§61, Appendix). And yet the proper philosophy of logic remains to be fully grasped, and so Husserl sets out to try his hand at the task, precisely in the years when mathematicians around him were working on the technical mathematical details.

What is "theory of science," for Husserl? When we speak of "philosophy of science" today, we mean the philosophical study of sciences like physics, analyzing methods of modern physics (experimentation, mathematics, prediction and confirmation), and exploring the content of theories such as general relativity or quantum mechanics, what they say about space–time or quantum states of a system. In Husserl's day, however, "theory of science" had a rather different connotation. The term "theory of science," or "*Wissenschaftslehre*," was used not only by Bolzano, but before that by Johann Gottlieb Fichte (1762–1814). Fichte's *Wissenschaftslehre* was a post-Kantian epistemology in which objectivity of knowledge was to be sought within an ontology of radical subjective idealism (see Martin 1997). By contrast, Bolzano's *Wissenschaftslehre* theory of logic and knowledge developed within a doctrine of objective ideal meaning (a broadly Platonistic idealism of meaning). Husserl read Fichte during the years leading up to *Ideas* I (1913), in which Husserl incorporated ideas from Kant and Fichte. But in the first edition of *Logical Investigations* (1900–1), Husserl patterned his conception of *Wissenschaftslehre* after Bolzano. The term "science," or "*Wissenschaft*," was then used to mean any systematic discipline, whereas today the term "science" is used for empirical disciplines such as physics, biology, psychology, and so on. And so Husserl's "theory of science" was a theory of *theory* (Prolegomena, §§62–3): a theory of the structure of any unified theory (Theorie) about a domain of objects, such as spatiotemporal things (physics), or mental processes (psychology), or numbers (arithmetic), or geometric forms (geometry). Ultimately, philosophy itself is, for Husserl, such a "strict science," as he declared in "Philosophy as Strict Science" (1911). But our concern here is Husserl's conception of pure logic as "theory of theory" in the Investigations.

Briefly, Husserl's theory of science held that any science is a theory, understood as an ideal system of propositions about a domain of study. Thus "pure logic" is, strictly speaking, the theory of theories. "Pure" logic is implicitly contrasted with applied logic. Where applied logic develops systems of axioms, or theories, applied to a domain such as space (geometry) or mind (psychology) or material bodies (physics), pure logic studies only the way in which such theories represent, regardless of their intended application. Husserl's vision of a theory is thus the vision of a purely formal theoretical structure, the structure captured ideally by an axiomatic theory such as Euclid's five axioms of geometry. This formal or structuralist vision of a mathematical theory was taking shape around Husserl, and Husserl wanted to generalize this ideal, so that a theory is not intrinsically mathematical but follows the form of a systematic theory.

Briefly, Husserl's theory of theories holds:

1   A *theory* is any unified system of propositions about some given domain. Ideally, the theory is a system of axioms ("basic laws") and their deductive consequences.

2   A *proposition* is an ideal meaning, specifically, a meaning expressible by a grammatically complete sentence. A proposition is composed from simpler meanings, expressible by noun phrases (names, demonstrative pronouns, descriptions) or by predicates.

3   Meanings *represent* objects of appropriate types. Specifically, meanings are *contents* of intentional experiences, which are intentionally related to the objects represented by their contents.

4   Logic characterizes the *logical relations* among the propositions, and constituent concepts, in the theory.

5 In today's idiom, *proof theory* in deductive logic characterizes relations of entailment among propositions, and *semantic theory* characterizes the ways expressions *represent* individuals, properties, or states of affairs.

(cf. Prolegomena, §§62–6)

In Husserl's account, the proper focus of logic is on ideal meanings, including systems of ideal propositions, rather than the linguistic signs that we construct to express these meanings. Mathematical logic will of course work with these signs, in symbolic languages. However, as Bolzano had stressed, what gives logic its objectivity, what grounds the validity of inferences, is the essence of the ideal meanings expressed. Turning from the Prolegomena to the six investigations that follow, Husserl wryly observes:

> I assume . . . that no one will think it enough to develop our logic merely in the manner of our mathematical disciplines, as a growing system of propositions . . . , without, that is, gaining insight into the essence of the modes of cognition which come into play in their utterance and in the ideal possibility of applying such propositions. . . . Linguistic discussions are certainly among the philosophically indispensable preparations for the building of pure logic: only by their aid can the true *objects* of logical research [namely, ideal meanings in a theory] . . . be refined. . . . We are not here concerned with grammatical discussions, empirically conceived and related to some historically given language: we are concerned with . . . the *pure phenomenology of the experiences of thinking and knowing.*
>
> (*Logical Investigations*, vol. II: Introduction, §1)

In this way pure logic is grounded in phenomenology, and the six investigations develop the theory of that grounding.

HUSSERL'S LOGIC: A PHILOSOPHICAL-LOGICAL SEMANTICS

"The Idea of a Pure Logic": so reads the title of the final chapter (ch. 11) of Husserl's *Prolegomena to Pure Logic*. In this chapter Husserl outlines what a logic would look like were it a properly philosophical theory of theories. Husserl's outline of "pure" logic frames what later philosophers of logic came to call a *formal semantics*: a system that defines semantic correlations between language, thought, meaning, and the world. A Husserlian logic, or logical semantics, would specify correlations among:

1   the basic *forms of expression* in a language in which inference and representation are executed;
2   the basic *forms of meaning* expressible in the language, where meanings are ideal intentional contents of thought or judgment;
3   the basic *forms of logical laws*, or rules of inference, governing relations of entailment among propositions expressible by sentences in the language;
4   the basic *forms of objects* represented by the relevant meanings or expressions, including such object-forms as those of individual things, properties and species and relations, states of affairs, and ontological connections among these entities.

What is distinctive in Husserl's conception of such a logical system, what is largely missing from subsequent forms of semantics, is the role of intentionality in the system, and so the grounding of logic in phenomenology.

What exactly would such a system of logic look like? Husserl lists three basic "tasks of pure logic":

1   "the fixing of the pure categories of meaning, the pure categories of objects and their law-governed combinations" (§67);
2   the setting out of "the laws and theories which have their grounds in these categories" (§68);
3   the setting out of "the theory of the possible forms of theories or the pure theory of manifolds" (§69).

The first two tasks of logical analysis are familiar today, but the third is not. We'd best explain by example, since Husserl, in the grand style of German philosophy, does not always give examples (such trivia are left to the reader!).

Under categories of meaning, Husserl lists: the "forms" (*Formen*) represented by "the concepts: Concept, Proposition, Truth, etc." (§67). Thus (to offer an example), the elementary proposition "Aristotle is synoptic" is formed from the concepts "Aristotle" and "synoptic." Logically complex propositions are then formed by the "concepts of the elementary connective forms, . . . e.g. the conjunctive, disjunctive, hypothetical linkages of propositions to form new propositions" (§67). These connective forms are expressed by the standard sentence connectives "and," "or," "if . . . then . . . ," as well as "it is not the case that" (omitted in Husserl's list but standard in logic since Boole). So the proposition "Aristotle is synoptic, and Plato is intuitive" is formed by conjunction ("and") from the two simpler propositions: "Aristotle is synoptic," "Plato is intuitive." The concept "Truth" looks odd as a category of meaning, unless Husserl has in mind logical truths such as "If P, and if P then Q, then Q." We note that Bolzano had replaced Kant's notion of analytic truths, or truths by virtue of meaning ("All bachelors are unmarried"), with truths by virtue of logical form. The point, in any case, is that there are basic forms or categories of meaning, as suggested.

Correlated with forms of meaning, according to Husserl, are "formal *objective categories*" specified by "correlative concepts such as Object, State of Affairs, Unity, Plurality, Number, Relation, Connection etc." (§67). That is, *meaning categories* are correlated (by appropriate rules) with *object categories*. Whereas meaning categories are basic forms of meaning, object categories are basic forms of object: Object, Relation, State of Affairs (*Sachverhalt*), Unity, and so on. Here Husserl assumes results of his "formal" ontology, which posits forms of things in the world, forms of object that can be represented by appropriate meanings. There are "law-governed" combinations of meanings, defined by meaning categories, and there are law-governed combinations of objects, defined by object categories. In the first edition of the *Logical Investigations* (1900–1) Husserl spoke of "object theory" (*Gegenstandstheorie*), a term coined by his contemporary Alexius Meinong, fellow student of Brentano noted for championing the complete general theory of objects with or without being, objects that could serve as objects of thoughts (even thoughts about the golden mountain, which does not exist). By 1913, in the second edition of the *Investigations* (save for Investigation VI), Husserl spoke specifically of "formal ontology," coordinate with his ontology that opens *Ideas* I (1913). He did not endorse nonexistent objects à la Meinong, and he introduced the crucial distinction between formal and material aspects of objects.

Again we need some simple examples. The proposition "Aristotle is synoptic" is formed from the individual concept "Aristotle" and the general or predicative concept "synoptic"; these forms of concept are combined by the predicative form "is." On a logic such as Husserl envisions, this proposition, if true, represents the state of affairs that [Aristotle is synoptic]. Within that state of affairs, Aristotle has the form Object or (better) Individual, whereas being synoptic has the form Property, and these two forms combine to form the form State of Affairs. This pattern of logical formation was made famous two decades later in Ludwig Wittgenstein's *Tractatus Logico-Philosophicus* (in German, *Logisch-philosophisch Abhandlungen*, 1921, translated into English with the Latinate title). The *Tractatus*, as it is nicknamed, greatly influenced the course of logical philosophy for decades. Wittgenstein may or may not have known Husserl's *Logical Investigations*, but at the least both works were born into a common Viennese tradition including a conception of grammar shaped by Bolzano's work. (On the parallels and differences between Husserl's philosophical-logical system and Wittgenstein's, see D. W. Smith 2002.)

The most important notion in Husserl's vision of pure logic, as we look at its "first task," is the notion of form. We are used to looking for the logical or grammatical form of sentences in a language. But Husserl insists that we also look for the more fundamental form of meanings, including propositions, following Bolzano in positing ideal meanings with appropriate form. (Frege's notion of sense, or *Sinn*, is similar, where the sense expressed by a grammatically complete sentence is called a "thought," or *Gedanke*.) Moreover, Husserl assumes, we must also look for the basic form of objects that can be represented by meanings. Here, as we consider in Chapter 4, is the central notion in Husserl's conception of "formal" as opposed to "material" ontology. The recurrent lure of nominalism in philosophy (holding that the world includes only particular things, answering ideally to names) has discouraged many philosophers from taking seriously anything like objects with the form of properties (such as being synoptic), much less objects with the form of states of affairs (such as Aristotle's being synoptic). However, in Husserl's milieu, in early 20th-century Vienna, the ontology of states of affairs was widely assumed, as we see later on in Wittgenstein's *Tractatus*.

The "second task" of logic, Husserl says (§68), is finding laws of two sorts. On the side of meaning are "theories of inference, e.g. syllogistics"; on the side of objective correlates of meaning is "the pure theory of pluralities [*Vielheiten*], which has its roots in . . . the pure theory of numbers." Husserl is seeking the most abstract pattern of correlation between a theory and a domain of objects: the correlation between the inferential structure in a theory (axioms plus theorems) and the structure or distribution of objects (pluralities) to which it applies. "We are here concerned with the scope of laws [of logic], [laws] under which, by virtue of their formal respects, all possible meanings and all possible objects stand in spanning generality, [laws] under which every particular theory or science stands, which it must obey if it is to be valid" (§68 cont., translation modified.) What does Husserl have in mind here? Recall that his *Philosophy of Arithmetic* (1891) propounded a theory of number that grew out of an account of pluralities that also leads into set theory of the sort developed by his friend Cantor. Husserl's formal ontology far outruns set theory, but we can begin to see his point in terms of set theory. For example, in more recent "extensional" logics, the sentence "Aristotle is synoptic" is given a simple semantic analysis as follows:

- the name "Aristotle" is correlated with the object Aristotle;
- the predicate "[is] synoptic" is correlated with the set of all objects that are synoptic; and
- the complete sentence is correlated with the value True or, alternatively, with the set of all possible states of affairs in which (it is true that) Aristotle is synoptic.

A more complex sentence – including a highly complex sentence expressing a proper theory about some domain – will be treated in a more elaborate manner, in this style of semantics, yet the *formal objective structure* correlated with any sentence will be defined wholly in terms of objects and sets.

The "third task" Husserl assigns logic is the most difficult to understand, yet ultimately the most important for his overall philosophy. The third and final task of logic is to lay out the "theory of the possible forms of theories" (the term of art here is "*Theorie*") (§69). Since a theory is a system of propositions, which are ideal meanings, this task is a more abstract version of the second task. If we define the basic forms of meanings, the basic forms of connections among meanings, the basic forms of inferential ties among propositions in a deductive system – that is, if we define the parameters for any such form of theory – then we will have defined the *possible forms* of all formally possible theories. This is exactly what logicians have done, in Husserl's day and in subsequent decades. However, this task – now called metalogic – has been executed at the level of symbolic languages, which abstract from everyday languages like English, German, Chinese. In these technical constructions Husserl sees mathematical representations of ideal meanings themselves. So, in Husserl's view, modern metalogic would be a symbolic window on the real thing: any possible system of ideal meanings that come together in inferential relations to form a proper theory.

THE THEORY OF MANIFOLDS: FROM LOGIC TO ONTOLOGY TO PHENOMENOLOGY

In order to complete the ideal of a pure logic, Husserl holds, we must turn to the "manifolds" of objects that logic would correlate – in a proper semantics – with theories taken as ideal systems of propositions. Here is how Husserl introduces his conception of manifolds:

> The *objective correlate* of the concept of a possible theory determined only in respect of form [*Form*] is *the concept of a possible field of*

knowledge [Erkenntnisgebiet] over which a theory of such form will govern. Such a field [Gebiet] is, however, known in mathematical circles as a manifold [Mannigfaltigkeit]. It is accordingly a field which is uniquely and solely determined by falling under a theory of such a form, whose objects are such as to permit of certain connections [Verknüpfungen] which fall under certain basic laws of this or that determinate form. . . . These laws then, as they determine the field [Gebiet] or moreover the form of the field [Gebietsform], likewise determine the theory to be constructed, or, more correctly, the form of the theory [Theoriensform]. In the theory of manifolds, e.g., '+' is not the sign for numerical addition, but for any connection for which laws of the form a + b = b + a, etc., hold.

(Prolegomena, §70: 156–7, translation modified)

In brief, Husserl's visonary idea is this: (1) A theory depicts the essence of objects in a given domain or field; (2) the theory characterizes its field of objects by virtue of the system of deductive relations among its propositions about said objects, relations that hold by virtue of the logical form of these propositions; (3) the form of the theory is correlated systematically with the form of the field of objects characterized; (4) a manifold is defined as the form of a field, a field characterizable by a deductive theory about the field. Thus, a pure logic will include (what we today call) a semantics that specifies correlations between the form of a given theory and the form of a field of objects to which the theory can be applied. (The title of §70 reads "The theory of the possible forms of theories or the pure theory of manifolds." The "or" might suggest that manifold theory is the same thing as the theory of forms of theories. However, the text makes it plain that manifolds are not theory-forms but field-forms, forms of objective correlates of theories.)

The mathematical theory of manifolds, Husserl notes (§70), arose from "generalizations of geometric theory," specifically "the theory of n-dimensional manifolds, whether Euclidean or non-Euclidean." Relevant mathematical theories define "spaces" (Räumen) of appropriate form, and varieties of arithmetic and number theory likewise define appropriate fields or spaces. Husserl cites (§70) a number of mathematicians whose work relates to manifold theory: Grassmann, Lie, Cantor, Riemann, and Helmholtz. As we know, Husserl initially worked with mathematicians, he worked with Cantor as a colleague, and he began his philosophical career with the philosophy of number, publishing *Philosophy of Arithmetic* (1891) prior to the *Logical Investigations* (1900–1). From this intellectual base Husserl projected his own philosophical conception of a "manifold."

The key notion is that of a field of knowledge, that is, a domain of objects to which a theory applies. The theory of manifolds, however, defines only the form of such a field. This form must be realized, of course, in substantive objects in the field. If the field is that of the positive integers, then the form of the field is represented by the axioms and theorems of number theory for the integers, but the objects to which the theory is applied are the integers. If the field is the Euclidean plane, then the form of the field is represented by the axioms and theorems of Euclidean geometry, which is applied to points, lines, and shapes in the Euclidean plane. Now, in principle, the same form, or structure relating objects, could be realized in different fields featuring different objects. That is the point of the mathematical abstraction that defines a manifold, the form that is abstracted from a domain.

Consider Husserl's example in the above quotation. In the language of arithmetic, we find the sentence "$a + b = b + a$." The variable letters "a" and "b" range over numbers, let us say the positive integers. The sign "$+$" stands for the operation of addition, and "$=$" stands for the relation of identity or equality of numbers. But what if we interpret the letters as standing for people in an organization and we interpret "$+$" as standing for an operation that joins two people into a department in the organization. Then if all the axioms of the theory apply, including that expressed by "$a + b = b + a$," then the same relevant form would be realized in the field of positive integers and in the field of corporate life. This example is not realistic, but mathematicians work with related models (for instance treating numbers as either sets of sets or sequences, so long as the same axioms are satisfied by either interpretation of number terms).

Notice that a mathematical manifold is not a set. Whereas a set is a mere collection of objects (a collected "plurality"), a manifold involves a collection of objects together with relevant relations between them, as well as qualities and species inhering in them. Or, rather, a manifold is the form of such a structured collection of objects bearing relations. By the 1960s model theory would define a model (or structure) as consisting of a set of objects (the domain) and a set of relations between those objects (where a relation is further defined as a set of ordered tuples of objects from the domain). So the mathematical notion of model is a successor to the original notion of manifold, and can be seen as a "mathematization" of the more intuitive notion of manifold that concerned Husserl.

Husserl's notion of manifold, in any event, is wider than that used in mathematics, as Husserl's philosophical aims are wider. In Husserl's conception, a manifold is an *objective structure* defined as the *form* of a *field*. A field is characterized ideally by a deductive theory, but the field itself is an objective formation of objects. This notion of manifold would be explicated in ontology, and only then would it be put to use in "pure logic." Think of space. The natural world around us is spatial (and temporal). If space in nature has a certain formal structure, that structure is realized in the flow of matter and energy that nature comprises. Here we see Husserl's conception of ontology at work: "formal" ontology characterizes the forms of things, in this case the form of space in nature, while "material" ontology characterizes the substantive or "material" domain that is structured by a certain form, in this case mother nature herself. Indeed, this problem of distinguishing the material and formal sides of space or space–time was a difficulty in the development of relativity theory in physics, a difficulty addressed by Albert Einstein, Hermann Weyl, and Rudolf Carnap – the latter two bearing direct influence from Husserl (see Ryckman 2005).

Subsequent thinkers worked with a related doctrine of *structuralism*. On that view, only the structure of the world can be known, a structure consisting in the relations holding among things in the world. This view can be seen in the "logical atomism" of

Russell and Wittgenstein. But Weyl applied this sort of view specifically to relativity theory in physics. Moreover, Weyl drew explicitly on Husserl's transcendental idealism as a motivation for his structuralist conception of relativity. (See Ryckman 2005: ch. 7 on structuralism and its relation to Husserlian transcendental phenomenology.) However, Weyl joined Husserl in appealing to "intuition" in our knowledge of things in nature and also of the structures found in nature. For Husserl, knowledge of a domain always rests on "intuitive" experience, that is, a direct and evidential experience of objects in that domain and their essences. Intuition thus puts us in contact with the objects that are "determined" by the objective structure called a manifold, the objects to which that structure applies – be they objects in nature, experiences in consciousness, or artifacts in culture. In this way our knowledge of things, even our systematic theoretical knowledge, involves both the objects in the world and their structure called a manifold. (We take up Husserl's doctrine of intuition in Chapter 7.)

Husserl used the notion of manifold in all of his writings, but perhaps the most intuitive gloss is that in his last work, the *Crisis* (1935–8):

> "Manifolds" are thus in themselves compossible totalities of objects in general, which are thought of as distinct only in empty, formal generality. . . . Among these totalities the so-called "definite" manifolds are distinctive. Their definition through a "complete axiomatic system" gives a special sort of totality in all deductive determinations to the formal substrate-objects contained in them. With this sort of totality, one can say, the formal-logical idea of a "world-in-general" is constructed.
>
> (*Crisis* 1935–8/1970, §9f: 45)

This passage follows references to Leibniz's "highest form of algebraic thinking, a *mathesis universalis*" and "the algebraic theory of numbers," "analysis," "theory of manifolds," "logistics," the latter term referring to the new logic of Peirce, Frege, Whitehead, and Russell. Accordingly, the passage rings several historical bells. The references to mathematical theories hark back to the origin of Husserl's conception of manifolds. The theory of a complete axiom system harks back to Hilbert's concerns of metamathematics, Hilbert having been Husserl's colleague in Göttingen. Gödel's incompleteness results would call for some modification of the above notion of manifold (partial manifolds represented by incomplete axiom systems?). By the 1950s, following on Tarski's work, mathematical model theory took shape. And by the 1960s models were viewed intuitively as "possible worlds." A *possible world* is a structure of objects with appropriate relations (and properties and species), the way the world would be if such things were actualized. This intuitive notion falls smoothly in line with Husserl's ontological notion of manifold. Thus, we today might define a manifold as the *form of a possible world*. The most relevant notion of possible worlds is that found in Jaakko Hintikka's logic of belief or perception, which details a possible-worlds semantics for attributions of intentional attitudes (see Hintikka 1969, 1975). Husserl's theory of intentionality can be explicated as holding that each act of consciousness intentionally projects an array of relevantly possible "worlds" in which the object of consciousness is "determined" with various properties and relations. (See Smith and McIntyre 1982 on the systematic connections between Hintikka's logic and Husserl's phenomenological theory of intentionality.)

When Husserl turns to phenomenology, he extends to consciousness the model of representation he sees in "pure logic." Instead of a theory that represents a field of objects, Husserl addresses an act of consciousness that represents or intends a particular object in a field, if you will, comprising the object's relations to other objects. The "intended" object has a variety of species, properties, and relations. For instance, when I see a bird flying by a tree, the content in my experience represents the object as being a bird, having black plumage, and being in front of that tree (from my perspective). My background knowledge of such birds opens further possibilities of features that I might see from a different perspective, including possible relations to further objects. All this structure of meaning in my experience correlates with a *field* of what I see, a visual field comprising what I actually see amplified with a "horizon" of further possibilities compatible with the content of my experience. In other words, the "logic" of consciousness would depict a correlation between the *meaning* or content in my experience and the *structure* comprising the object and its array of "determinations" prescribed by the meaning or implicitly allowed by the meaning. That structure, in the horizon of the object as experienced, Husserl calls a manifold (see Smith and McIntyre 1982 for details).

As we shall find in Chapters 6 and 7, Husserl's phenomenology holds that the "constitution" of an object in consciousness – the way the object is conceptualized or put together for experience – is defined in terms of such a manifold of possibilities about the object, possibilities represented by the meaning in an act of consciousness together with implicit background meanings. Much as a theory is correlated with a field of objects, so an experience or its content is correlated with a field of phenomena centered on the object intended where the intended object is surrounded by an horizon of possibilities for that object as it is experienced. (See Yoshimi 2004 on the "field" of consciousness as analyzed by Aron Gurwitsch, an extension of Husserl's analysis of intentionality. See D. W. Smith 2004 on the structure of such a field.)

LANGUAGE, MEANING, AND EXPERIENCE

Like Bolzano and Frege, Husserl held that the proper medium of logic is not language but meaning. For Frege, logic ultimately concerns the realm of thoughts (*Gedanken*); for Husserl, following Bolzano's lead, logic is ultimately concerned with ideal meaning, including propositions (*Sätze*), which are similar to Fregean "thoughts." Subsequent logicians, however, have focused logic on language: on sentences in a well-defined language (usually cast in symbolic form), on deductive relations among sentences (defined by formal rules of inference), and on the domain of objects to which sentences may be applied. A modern logical semantics then defines the conditions under which a sentence of any form would be true. A theory is thus defined as a system of sentences that include axioms and theorems deducible from the axioms. Where are meanings in this modern scheme? Many philosophers of logic, joining W. V. Quine, have thought that ideal meanings, including

Figure 3.1 A Husserlian logic for a simple language or theory

	INSTANCE	TYPE
LANGUAGE	"Aristotle is synoptic" *expression*	"name + predicate" *form of expression: sentence*
EXPERIENCE	I think <Aristotle is synoptic> *act of consciousness*	entertaining the content <individual-sense + predicate-sense> *form of act: thought*
MEANING	<Aristotle is synoptic> *sense*	<individual-sense + predicate sense> *form of sense: proposition*
WORLD	[Aristotle is synoptic] *object*	[individual + property] *form of objective correlate:* state of affairs, more abstractly manifold

propositions or thoughts, are either obscure entities or Platonic objects that have no place in nature and are therefore, well, unscientific. Other philosophers join the likes of Frege and Husserl in embracing abstract or ideal entities such as propositions or senses, but frequently explicate a proposition, expressible by a sentence, in terms of the possible situations or "worlds" in which the sentence would be true. For Husserl's part, however, language, meaning, and truth in a state of affairs are all interrelated, as "pure" logic concerns meanings that are in principle expressible in language, which in turn "borrows" meanings from acts of consciousness. In this way pure logic is tied into the world, into acts of consciousness and their objects. Our task now is to explore Husserl's theory of the relations among language, meaning, and experience.

Let us begin with a greatly simplified example of how Husserl's ideal of pure logic would be extended to include the language that expresses a proposition and thereby represents an objective structure in the world. Take the simple sentence "Aristotle is synoptic." This piece of language *expresses* the proposition <Aristotle is synoptic>, which is formed from the concepts or meanings <Aristotle> and <synoptic>. This proposition *represents* the state of affairs [Aristotle is synoptic]. Suppose this sentence is a theory (a radically simple theory unworthy of the name). Then a Husserlian

I , the subject and speaker

My saying "Aristotle is synoptic" expresses the proposition <Aristotle is synoptic>, which is the content (sense or meaning) of my thinking <Aristotle is synoptic>, and which prescribes the state of affairs [Aristotle is synoptic], which is the object of my so thinking and thereby of my so asserting.

Figure 3.2 Husserl's model of language expressing thought

logic or semantics for this theory would consist of the correlation among language, meaning, and world as schematized as in Figure 3.1, where a *sentence* in a language expresses a *proposition* (an ideal sense) that semantically represents a *state of affairs* in the world, that is, if the sentence or proposition is true. This correlation among sentences, propositions, and states of affairs is the characteristic task of a logical semantics. But there is more. On Husserl's theory, the proposition (meaning) expressed by the sentence is the *content* of an act of thinking <Aristotle is synoptic>. Most 20th-century logics abstract away from thought or consciousness. (Many philosophers of logic and language were influenced by the neo-behaviorism of the mid-century, where language is treated on its own and consciousness is looked on with suspicion, or so the later Ludwig Wittgenstein was sometimes read.) For Husserl, however, a proper logic correlates structures of language, experience, meaning, and world. Thus Figure 3.1. (Notice how we are using quotation marks, angle brackets, and square brackets: for expressions, meanings, and states of affairs.)

A properly Husserlian logic or semantics would schematize the correlation among language, intentional experience, meaning, and world – in a very simple case, as in Figure 3.1. Here we assume the outlines of Husserl's theory of intentionality: an act of consciousness is directed via its content, a sense (*Sinn*), toward an object. Language supervenes on intentionality, in that language expresses thought, that is, the meaning (*Bedeutung*) of my sentence in *saying*, "Aristotle is synoptic," is precisely the content or sense of my *thinking* <Aristotle is synoptic>, that is, the proposition <Aristotle is synoptic>. Husserl developed a detailed account of this relationship among language, experience, meaning or sense, and objects in the world, as we see below. In the case at hand, the basic structure of this relationship is schematized in Figure 3.1. The same pattern of correlation is depicted, in a familiar cartoon form, in Figure 3.2.

In the narrative of the *Logical Investigations* (1900–1), the "Prolegomena to Pure Logic" is followed immediately by Investigation I, "Expression and Meaning," detailing Husserl's philosophy of language. Husserl joins in the classical view that language expresses thought, a view salient from Aristotle to Locke to Bolzano and Frege. What Husserl brings to the table, however, is both his theory of pure logic and his theory of the intentionality of consciousness. The details of these theories were not yet available to his illustrious predecessors in language theory, or to his contemporary Frege. In Husserl's philosophy of language we also see the holistic or holographic form of his philosophical system. For while Investigation I follows immediately on the Prolegomena, the account of language there given depends on results in Investigation V, where the basics of the theory of intentionality are laid out. Our reconstruction of Husserl's theory of intentionality occupies Chapters 5 and 6 in this volume. Like Husserl, we shall here assume, briefly sketched in passing, the rudiments of Husserl's theory of intentionality as we outline Husserl's theory of language.

Let us expand on the simple example we have already offered, now bringing in the full structure of language as an act of speaking, thereby expressing meaning, and thereby speaking about objects in the world. Consider the speech act wherein I say, "Aristotle is synoptic." The sentence uttered is a familiar enough piece of modern English. The speech situation consists in my addressing one or more hearers, taking for granted that we all understand the language spoken. In this circumstance, communication is virtually instantaneous as I say to you, "Aristotle is synoptic." This statement, let us suppose, is part of our discussion of which philosophers you and I find most systematic, and I tell you my thought, which you immediately comprehend.

Using Husserl's technical vocabulary, we analyze this speech act in the following terms. There is a *speaker*, myself. There is a *hearer* or *auditor*, yourself. I perform the *speech act* of saying, in assertive mood or attitude, "Aristotle is synoptic," thereby asserting the fact or state of affairs that Aristotle is synoptic. In this act I produce a concrete utterance of the *expression* "Aristotle is synoptic." This *expression* is an ideal species of spoken sound, and my uttered words are an *instance* of that expression type. In Peirce's familiar terms, the ideal expression is a sentence *type*, and the actual sound produced is a sentence *token*. In Husserl's idiom, the expression is an ideal *species*, a type of "universal" (the theme of Investigation II). Hearing my utterance, you understand what I am saying, resulting in communication between us. What is the exact structure of this communication? Husserl's answer draws on his theory of intentionality: an act of consciousness is directed via an ideal meaning or sense toward the object prescribed by that sense.

Focusing on the speaker, we note that my speech act involves more than my producing the sound of the sentence I utter (an acoustic blast, as John Searle puts it). In the normal circumstance, I think or judge what I assert in speaking. That is, in the case at hand, I perform an act of *judging* that Aristotle is synoptic, and in speaking I *assert* what I so judge. Thus, my speech act of asserting that Aristotle is synoptic rests on my *underlying* act of judging that Aristotle is synoptic. My judgment is an *intentional experience* or *act of consciousness*, which as such carries a certain *content*. This content is an ideal *sense* (*Sinn*), namely, the *proposition* (*Satz*) <Aristotle is synoptic>. This proposition prescribes the *state of affairs* [Aristotle is synoptic], which is thus the *object* of my judgment. That is, my judgment is directed via this proposition to that state of affairs. Whence, if that putative state of affairs exists, it makes my judgment, or its propositional content, *true*. Putting my judgment into language, my assertion is directed via this proposition to that state of affairs, and that state of affairs makes my assertion *true* if such a state of affairs exists. (Here we use the angle brackets to "quote" the proposition, as opposed to the words uttered. And we use square brackets to cite the state of affairs represented by that proposition.)

Turning from the speaker to the hearer, we see that communication consists, on Husserl's neo-classical model, in the speaker's *conveying* a meaning to the hearer. The proposition <Aristotle is synoptic> is the *meaning* (*Bedeutung*) of the sentence I utter. My utterance *expresses* (*ausdrückt*) this meaning or sense and *intimates* (*kundgibt*) my underlying judgment with that sense. (Husserl himself usually uses the noun forms "*Ausdruck*" and "*Kundgabe*.") The hearer, accordingly, understands what I am thinking and verbally asserting: the proposition <Aristotle is synoptic> is the content of my thought or judgment, and so the state of affairs [Aristotle is synoptic] is the objective correlate I am asserting to exist.

As Husserl puts it, my underlying act of judgment *lends* (*verleiht*) its sense to my speech act, or the speech act *borrows* that sense. Whence the *meaning* of my utterance is the *sense* of my underlying judgment, that is, as the sense is put to language. However, intentional content does not move perfectly from speaker to hearer. Husserl holds that language "stamps" sense in a certain way, so that there is or may be some difference between the sense in my judgment and the meaning expressed in my utterance. That is, the sense of my judgment is modified, shaped by language, in the process of linguistic expression: intentional sense is transformed into linguistic meaning – if you will, as the private becomes public, the subjective becomes intersubjective.

To be a bit more exact, then, Husserl holds that language "stamps" sense, partly modifying a sense as it enters language. The meaning of the sentence "Aristotle is synoptic," then, is the linguistic proposition <<Aristotle is synoptic>>. This meaning is a modification of the judgmental sense, the intentional proposition, <Aristotle is synoptic>. The meaning is not quite the same as the sense on which it is based. (Here we use double angles to "quote" the meaning, as opposed to the sense on which it is based.)

All that said: my uttering an instance of the expression "Aristotle is synoptic" expresses the meaning <<Aristotle is synoptic>> and intimates my judging that Aristotle is synoptic. The meaning expressed is a linguistically shaped variant of the sense <Aristotle is synoptic>, which is the content of my underlying judgment. That content is what I aim to convey to my auditor, within the limits of expressibility in the language. As the auditor hears my utterance, he grasps my meaning. In this way I convey the content of my judgment to my auditor. My judgment intends the state of affairs [Aristotle is synoptic]. And my auditor understands that I am asserting the existence of that state of affairs. The structure of communication lies in this complex scenario relating speaker and auditor in relation to appropriate the meaning conveyed and what object that meaning represents.

This model of linguistic communication is depicted, using Husserl's terminology, in Figure 3.3 – for "p" read "Aristotle is synoptic".

Much has been made of the difference between what I experience and what language can capture from my experience. But Husserl's chief example concerns perception. Suppose I see a black bird fly off, and I say, "That black bird is flying off." My hearer may not see the bird fly off, and even if he does his perspective is

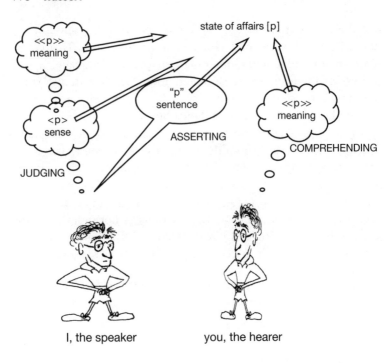

My uttering "p" intimates my judging <p> and expresses <<p>>, where the
meaning <<p>> is borrowed from the sense <p> in my judgment. The meaning
<<p>> is thereby conveyed to you, my hearer. The sense <p>, whence the
meaning <<p>>, prescribes the state of affairs [p]. The proposition <p> or
<<p>> is true if and only if the state of affairs [p] exists. Hence my judging <p>
is true and my asserting "p" is true if and only if the state of affairs [p] exists.

Figure 3.3 Husserl's philosophy of language

different. So, Husserl holds, there is something in the content of
my perception that cannot be brought to expression, we might
say something private or limited by my perspective and the
sensory experience I have in seeing the bird. Nonetheless, my
hearer understands what I say. By virtue of empathy, the hearer
can understand, within limits, what it is like for me to see a
black bird fly off. The context of speech indicates how the hearer
is to understand my sentence, namely, as oriented to my perceptual perspective on the bird and my sensory experience in seeing
the bird. All this is built into our everyday language, the ways we

understand one another in speaking of what we are seeing or have seen.

Many recent philosophers follow Ludwig Wittgenstein's remark to the effect that if you want to know the meaning of an expression, look at how it is used. Some philosophers of language take this remark a step further, declaring that the meaning of an expression just is its use, its use as captured in rules of usage. However, given the fleet of distinctions Husserl has drawn, in his account of linguistic communication, it should be clear that the rules of use of the sentence "That black bird is flying off" or "Aristotle is synoptic" are distinct from what is said, the meaning of the expression uttered, which is a linguistic modification of the content of the speaker's judgment.

FORMAL AND TRANSCENDENTAL LOGIC

In *Ideas* I (1913), in the middle of his career, Husserl folded into his conception of phenomenology certain themes of "transcendental" philosophy. Phenomenology was now called "transcendental phenomenology" and implicated in a form of "transcendental idealism" or "phenomenological idealism." The transcendental motif reflects Husserl's absorption of Kantian themes that were strong in German philosophy ever since Kant's *Critique of Pure Reason* (1781/1787) propounded a "Copernican revolution" in philosophy, as Kant emphasized the contribution of our mind to the ways we take the world to be. Husserl's views were different from Kant's on many key points, given Husserl's theory of intentionality. Nonetheless, scholars have commonly spoken of Husserl's "transcendental turn" that led into *Ideas* I. Since *Ideas* I is a treatise of "pure" phenomenology, appraising the structures of consciousness or "subjectivity," the impression may naturally arise that Husserl had left behind his concern with "pure logic" and its vision of a radical objectivity of knowledge grounded a *mathesis universalis*. It may be surprising, then, that Husserl returned to logic late in his career, publishing *Formal and Transcendental Logic* (1929/1969) as his fourth book. What was this work about?

Though Kant had introduced the terminology of "formal" versus "transcendental" logic, Husserl develops the distinction within his mature theory of intentionality, which is the basic framework of his transcendental phenomenology (see Chapter 6 in this volume). Briefly, for Husserl, *formal logic* is grounded in the purely formal structures of judgment-content (meaning) and correlated manifolds (Part I: chs. 1–3), whereas *transcendental logic* is grounded in intentionality (Part II: ch. 5), that is, in the role that meaning plays in directing consciousness, in particular judgment, toward its objects. Tracking the narrative of *Formal and Transcendental Logic*, we see that Husserl is reiterating the course of the *Logical Investigations*, while emphasizing the "transcendental" character of meaning as the "constituting" content of judgment based in "evidence."

Though we cannot here go into the details, Husserl's emphases in *Formal and Transcendental Logic* are worth noting. To begin, formal logic is an analytic "apophantics," that is, a theory analyzing ideal forms of judgment (*"apophansis,"* in Greek). This theory divides into "truth-logic" and "consequence-logic": truth-logic ties into the "theory of sense," while consequence-logic includes, for example, syllogistics (or "logistics," as the new logic was then called). Formal apophantics ties into formal mathematics and thus formal ontology, following – of course! – the Leibnizian ideal of a *mathesis universalis*. In this discussion Husserl cites both his *Philosophy of Arithmetic* and the Prolegomena of the *Logical Investigations*. In other words, Husserl reminds us that he has outlined the task of formal logic already in these earlier works: formal logic is "pure logic" grounded in the theory of manifolds. Where does logic turn "transcendental"? The rejection of psychologism marks the turn toward the transcendental – again following the course of the *Logical Investigations*. The theory of sense treats sense (*Sinn*) as ideal "judgment-content." But judgment also carries "evidence" (*Evidenz*). Here Husserl retraces the results of the Investigations V and VI of the *Logical Investigations*. Thus, formal logic is extended and grounded in the theory of ideal sense, especially propositions or judgment-contents, together with the theory of evidence (or "intuition"). But these two ranges of theory belong to transcendental phenomenology. So transcendental logic is formal logic grounded in transcendental phenomenology.

This abstract account of transcendental logic should be familiar, given our account of Husserl's conception of logic developed in the *Logical Investigations*. But we can indicate the force of Husserl's idea by returning to our simple example. Suppose I assert, "Aristotle is synoptic." Formal logic will appraise the form of the sentence I utter, the form of the judgment-content or sense <Aristotle is synoptic> expressed by the sentence, and the form of the objective correlate of the sentence and of the sense, the state of affairs [Aristotle is synoptic] – explicating all these formal structures ultimately in terms of manifolds. The "material" aspects of my judgment, whose content I so express, include the *intentionality* and the *intuitive* or *evidential* character of the judgment. That is, the content in my judgment prescribes the objective state of affairs [Aristotle is synoptic], and this judgment-content is supported by the evidence I have for the truth of this proposition. These aspects of my judgment ground the *objectivity* of the logic of such judgment-contents: the ideal character of the proposition itself, and the intuitive evidence it carries in my experience. These aspects of judgment, beyond the formal aspects, are appraised in transcendental phenomenology.

THE SEMANTIC TRADITION: BOLZANO, FREGE, HUSSERL, AND SUCCESSORS

The *semantic* tradition, it has been proposed, grew out of the 19th century as semanticists took a different path than Kantians, for whom the constitutive powers of the mind reign supreme, and positivists, for whom empirical science grounded in sense perception reigns over all knowledge. As Alberto Coffa puts it,

> The semanticists are easily detected: They devote an uncommon amount of attention to concepts, propositions, senses – to the content and structure of what we say, as opposed to the psychic acts in which we say it. The others cannot see the point of wasting so much time on semantic trivia.
>
> (Coffa 1991: 1)

Standout semanticists Coffa cites include Bolzano, Frege, and Husserl, followed by Carnap, Tarski, and their successors in logical theory.

Husserl is indeed a paragon of the semanticist, offering thousands of pages in praise of ideal meaning, drawing initial inspiration from Bolzano, with impetus also from Frege's critical review of Husserl's "psychologistic" *Philosophy of Arithmetic*. Nonetheless, Husserl's transcendental phenomenology is a full-blown theory of how consciousness "constitutes" objects in the world. For Husserl, however, unlike the "psychologistic" theories of both Kantian and positivist persuasion, the "constitution" of objects is achieved precisely through ideal meaning. As for the 19th-century positivists, Husserl quips, "If 'positivism' asserts as much as an absolutely presupposition-free grounding of all sciences on the 'positive', that is, on what is grasped originally [*originär*: with evidence], then *we* are the genuine positivists" (*Ideas* I, §20, translation modified). For Husserl, though, unlike the 19th-century positivists or the 1920s Vienna Circle positivists to follow, evidence comes not only in perceptual "intuition" (sensory perception), but also in "eidetic" intuition of ideal essences ("universals," also mathematical objects including numbers) and in "transcendental" intuition of ideal meanings. So Husserl would ground our cognition, starting with logical theory, in ideal meanings, which reside in acts of consciousness, some of which have the character of "evidence," and in ideal correlates of meanings including "manifolds." We turn to Husserl's theory of knowledge and experiential evidence in Chapter 7, the point here being that the very idea of *semantics* grew in logical theory, indeed in a historical context including Husserl's steadfast championing of meaning and form in "pure logic."

During the 1930s logical semantics evolved through the works of Kurt Gödel, Rudolf Carnap, and Alfred Tarski. David Hilbert, Husserl's colleague at Göttingen, had charted the ideal of a complete theory, where the axioms in the theory entail all that is true about the domain of the theory (perhaps the positive integers or the Euclidean plane). But Gödel's incompleteness results proved that, for certain languages, there are true sentences that cannot be proved by formal inference from axioms in the theory. This shows that truth is not a purely syntactic property of a sentence, determined by the form of the sentence. Carnap struggled to keep logic a matter of syntax, but Tarski's semantic theory of truth converted Carnap to semantics. Tarski's work showed how to construct a "definition" of truth for a specified language. In Tarski's theory of truth, we correlate a sentence with a condition that makes it true, for instance:

> The sentence "Grass is green" is true if and only if grass is green.

The sentence in quotation marks belongs to the *object language* for which truth is defined. The biconditional sentence belongs to the *metalanguage*, a higher-order language that talks about sentences in the object language, saying they are true under specified conditions. There is more to the Tarskian theory of truth than this schema, but the point to emphasize here is that the metalanguage specifies relations between an object-language *sentence* ("Grass is green") and a *condition* in the world (grass' being green). This relation is semantic. Within the development of mathematical logic after Frege and Hilbert, Tarski offered a mathematical model of the familiar notion of truth applied to a certain formal language. Tarski called his theory "the semantic conception of truth" (Tarski 1944, a philosophical account of his mathematical results in Tarski 1933). (Coffa 1991 traces the historical development of semantics through these logicians.)

In the 1940s the linguist Charles Morris proposed to divide the theory of language into three fields called *syntax, semantics,* and *pragmatics.* Syntax studies the forms of expression in a language (grammatical and logical form); semantics studies the meaning of expressions in the language; and pragmatics studies the use of expressions in the language. Logicians had been tilling soil in these fields for some time, but this distinction sharpened the division of labor. As noted earlier, Frege had developed a theory of logical form (featuring quantifier expressions, "all" and "some," along with relational predicates modeled on mathematical function symbols), launching the new symbolic logic: here was the syntax in Frege's logic. But Frege had also developed a theory of sense and reference, defining forms of sense and referent for basic forms of expression: here was the semantics in Frege's logic. Pragmatics would be developed only later. But Frege's logic already offered a detailed model for 20th-century logicians.

We have already indicated a structural similarity between Frege's logic and Husserl's logic grounded in intentionality. For Frege, a sentence expresses a sense that determines a reference. For Husserl, similarly, a sentence expresses a sense that prescribes an appropriate object if such exists. Furthermore, for Husserl, this linguistic relationship is itself grounded in an intentional relation wherein an act of consciousness has a certain content or sense that prescribes an appropriate object. The details are mapped out in our foregoing discussion, and indicated pictorially in Figures 3.1, 3.2 and 3.3. Putting aside differences of detail, Husserl envisions a semantics quite like Frege's, but Husserl joins this semantics of reference via sense with a model of intentionality via sense. And this "transcendental" grounding defines "transcendental" logic for Husserl: a richly *semantic* theory of both intentionality and language. (The connections between Husserl and Frege have been studied extensively. See Føllesdal 1969; Smith and McIntyre 1971; Dreyfus 1982; Mohanty 1982; Smith and McIntyre 1982; Cobb-Stevens 1990; Drummond 1990.)

In Tarski's wake, mathematicians developed *model theory*, defining truth "in a model." As noted earlier, a model or structure is defined as an ordered pair consisting of a domain of objects and a set of relations between those objects (where a relation is treated extensionally as an ordered tuple of objects in the domain). This notion of model is a set-theoretic version of what Husserl called a mathematical manifold, that is, a collection of objects structured by appropriate relations (such as points standing in geometric relations). Thus, a sentence is said to be true in a model if and only if certain conditions hold for objects in the model, that is, bearing appropriate relations. By the 1960s Jaakko Hintikka and others were treating models more intuitively as "possible worlds." Given these developments, it was possible to recast Husserl's theory of intentionality in terms of possible worlds: thus, my thinking that Aristotle is synoptic is directed via the sense <Aristotle is synoptic> toward Aristotle cum synopticity in all possible worlds in which Aristotle is indeed synoptic. In some worlds Aristotle lacks this property, so the worlds in which he has the property display, if you will, the intentional force of the content of my thought: these worlds display what my thought-content semantically prescribes. Indeed, this complex structure unfolds the "constitution" of Aristotle according to my conscious-ness, wherein I think <Aristotle is synoptic>. In Chapter 6 we will elaborate on this model of phenomenological "constitution." (The details of a Husserlian possible-worlds model of intentionality are developed in Smith and McIntyre 1982.)

We add one final stop in our story of Husserl's connections with subsequent logical theory. The philosophical logician David Kaplan (1989) has developed an influential logic of demonstrative pronouns. When I say, "That is a eucalyptus tree," my saying "that" refers to the object I am demonstrating on the occasion of utterance, typically the object I am pointing at. Frege had strug-gled with the problem of reference for terms like "I," "that," "today," and so on, as his theory of sense and reference did not seem to allow for the context in which a speaker utters such a pronoun. Addressing this problem, Kaplan proposed in effect two levels of meaning for such a sentence. We cannot explore the details of Kaplan's logic of demonstratives here, but we note that Husserl had already found the problem of demonstrative reference and proposed a similar solution. On Husserl's analysis, when I say "that" as in the sentence above, I refer to the object of my percep-tion on that occasion, to which I may be pointing. The expression "that" is accordingly an "essentially occasional expression," and it is keyed to my perception of the object to which I am referring. The general, "indicating" meaning of the word "this" then indi-cates the sense in my perceptual experience on the occasion of utterance. That sense is part of the content of my experience, a perceptual "intuition" of the object. Part of the force of my seeing "that [tree]" is that the object is intuitively before me. In any event, on Husserl's approach to the logic of "this" we see that my referring to a certain tree by saying "this" is grounded in my perception of the tree. So the formal logic of demonstratives depends on the "transcendental" structure of perception. (These problems of demonstrative reference and perception, in Husserl and Kaplan, are studied in the present author's article in Dreyfus 1982. The problem of perception as an "indexical" form of consciousness is studied, in its own right, in D. W. Smith 1989.)

In the semantic tradition Husserl occupies a special niche: it was Husserl who primarily, and most clearly, charted the role of intentionality in logical theory, specifying the role of ideal sense or intentional content in the relations among language, experience, and objects in the world.

THE PROBLEM OF "MATHEMATIZATION"

In his last writings, gathered posthumously as *The Crisis of European Sciences and Transcendental Phenomenology* (1935–8/1970), Husserl explored the problem of the "mathematization" of nature. Modern physics, from Newton to Einstein and beyond, has realized Galileo's ideal of a mathematical description of the essence of nature. Gravity was first characterized in Newton's mathematical laws of motion, as the law of gravity calibrated the force of attraction between any two massed bodies, such as the Earth and a falling apple. Einstein's general theory of relativity, launched in 1915, has since radically altered the mathematical characterization of gravity, now depicting gravity itself as a *geometrical* property of the space–time in which reside systems of matter-energy such as Mother Earth and Newton's apple. The problem Husserl poses, in the *Crisis*, is that nature herself is something distinct from the mathematical form our physics espies in nature, say, in the force of gravity found in nature. We experience nature in very different ways: when we *see* and *catch* the falling apple, say, and when we *conceive mathematically* the force acting on the apple, that is, when we do physics, working with mathematical equations. The mathematical theory of gravity can be cast, according to Husserlian "pure logic," as a system of propositions that represents a manifold of points in space–time inhabited by bits of matter-energy. But this manifold of space–time, depicted by our physical theory, is a mathematical *idealization* of the nature we encounter in everyday life. Here is the problem Husserl sees in modern "European" sciences, that is, mathematical theories about nature.

But what's the problem? I see "the morning star" at dawn, and I see "the evening star" at dusk (Frege's example). Again, I think of "the victor at Jena," and I think of "the vanquished at Waterloo" (Husserl's example). In such cases my experience is directed toward the same object via different senses, in the first example to the planet Venus, in the second example to Napoleon. So what is the problem with our thinking of something in nature, say, gravity, in two different ways, via very different senses? In everyday life I look up and see a falling apple, and I reach out and catch it. Thus, in the world of everyday life, the "life-world" or *Lebenswelt*, an apple falls, that is, there is an object we experience as "that apple falling toward the Earth." In the practice of physics, by contrast, we describe in mathematical terms the trajectory of an object drawn to the Earth by the force of gravity (say, a rocket ship falling toward Earth). In the world of physics, if you will, there is an object that we represent in the mathematics of gravitation theory as moving toward the Earth under a certain force. What, then, is the problem of "mathematization"? After all, we do want to use mathematics to build bridges and send airplanes around the globe.

Husserl sees a kind of alienation setting in with modern mathematical science: a disconnect between the way we experience things in everyday life and the way we represent things in mathematical theories. Our mathematical theories abstract away from the essence of the things they describe, forming an idealization of the real essence in nature. Well, that is the point of mathematics, to abstract out a more precise characterization of, say, the trajectory of an object falling to Earth; that is the only way we could send a rocket into space and bring it back to Earth (as with the Space Shuttle program). Indeed, Husserl's formalist conception of manifolds maps this idealization quite deliberately. The problem Husserl sees is our forgetting that our mathematical characterization of things is precisely an idealization, rather than a mirror of the essence of things themselves. The implication is that we might come to confuse the objects of our everyday concern with their proxy mathematical forms.

Indeed, if we turn from nature to consciousness, we find that Husserl's worry has been realized half a century after his death. What would it be to "mathematize" not physical objects like apples and planets and their motions, but our *own mental processes*? When Husserl distinguishes phenomenology from psychology, he classifies psychology along with physics as sciences of nature. For psychology studies the mind as part of nature, part of human beings that are animals in nature, biological organisms with brains that somehow produce or subserve our conscious experiences. As it happened, since the 1970s empirical psychology, or its kindred philosophical theory of mind, has sought to "naturalize" the mind. The dominant motif in "the cognitive sciences" has been the computer model of mental process, where the mental processes are characterized as information-processing realized ultimately in the brain. Now, a computer process is described by a *mathematical* characterization: a system of algorithms that describe the transition from one state of the computer system – presumably a mind or brain – to another. So if mind is to brain as software is to hardware, then the computational model of mind is a "mathematization" of mental process. What is the problem with this mathematization of mind?

A robust debate since the late 1980s has charged that the functionalist, and ultimately reductive, model of mind as computation is unable to account for the *subjective* aspects of our mental processes. Our mathematical model of mind fails to capture some of the most salient properties of our own consciousness. These properties include: (1) *what it is like* to see red or feel pain, known as the subjective "feel" or "qualia" of a sensation; (2) the *awareness* we have of our own consciousness, arguably the very structure of "self-consciousness" that makes our experiences conscious; (3) the *intentionality* of our acts of consciousness, how we experience things via intentional contents or meanings that outrun computational algorithms. There is a celebrated "explanatory gap," then, between the acts of consciousness we experience and the mathematical theory that is supposed to explain them, that is, to deliver an adequate characterization of these phenomena. Were Husserl alive today, he would find the "crisis" of modern sciences vividly exemplified in the theory of mind. What is missing in the neuro-computational theory of consciousness is precisely what Husserl's transcendental phenomenology was supposed to deliver! In Chapters 5 and 6 we shall dig into the results of Husserl's analyses of consciousness, its subjective characters, its intentionality, and more – the fruits of phenomenological investigation.

What then of mathematical logic? Has the "mathematization" of logic – in Frege, Whitehead and Russell, Gödel, Tarski, et al. – produced a crisis? In the Prolegomena, Husserl already distin-guished the "technical" and the "philosophical" aspects of logic. Mathematization itself is a good thing, vigorously endorsed in Husserl's conception of pure logic and the theory of manifolds. The problem, again, is not mathematization, but forgetting that mathematical idealization is precisely a technique of abstraction from that which is "mathematized." Hence, Husserl would insist, if we practice mathematical logic cut off from the phenomenolog-ical theory of intentionality, then we alienate logic from our own rational processes of thinking, even the very processes in which we practice mathematics and mathematical logic, producing mathematical model theory as, if you will, a development of Husserlian "pure logic." Indeed, just such a gap developed between logic and phenomenology in the second half of the 20th century. And, Husserl would cry from his grave, there is today an explanatory gap between the structures of symbolic language characterized by mathematical logic and the structures of experi-ence on which logic is based. We need to see, to keep in mind, the connection between formal logical structures and lived struc-tures of intentional experience. That is why Husserl wrote a book called *Formal and Transcendental Logic*.

A GRANDE HUSSERLIAN METATHEORY

As semantic theory in logic developed after Husserl's day, mathe-matical and philosophical logicians worked out technical details of a logical semantics. This genre of logic can be seen as unfolding something like Husserl's own vision of logic as just sketched. Within mathematics, metamathematics developed as a mathematical theory about mathematical systems, including results about consistency, completeness, incompleteness, and more. Within philosophy, metaphilosophy has long weaved in and out of the views of various philosophers, declaring the task of philosophy to be this or that, say, seeking foundations of ethics or knowledge, seeking social change, seeking wisdom rather than technical results, applying the methods of empirical science to philosophical questions, or whatever. How should Husserl's metaphilosophy be drawn? How, in light of his overall philosophical system, charted in Chapter 2? And how, in light of his conception of logic, as drawn in the present chapter?

In the prominent writings of phenomenology, in Husserl and in his immediate successors from Heidegger to Merleau-Ponty, philosophy was to reflect on our own human experience, beginning with our activities of consciousness in perception, thought, action, and so on, seeking the meaning of things as we experience and engage them. By contrast, in the Vienna Circle movement of the 1920s and 1930s, philosophy was to follow the empirical sciences and, furthermore, to express its results in the language of the new logic. Husserl's vision of philosophy, as charted in Chapter 2 in this volume following the *Logical Investigations*, is more wide-ranging than these views from either phenomenological or logical philosophies in Husserl's wake. Yet his vision of philosophy – and so his metaphilosophy – begins with his vision of pure logic. Where the technical logicians moved into work with particular symbol systems and their application, Husserl moved instead into ontology, phenomenology, and epistemology, working within the framework of his vision of pure logic. From this perspective, how should we understand Husserl's metaphilosophy?

As the *Logical Investigations* unfolded, a *grande metatheory* emerged: a philosophical theory about philosophical theories and their interrelation. Husserl did not gather the metatheory in one place; he did not even indicate it explicitly, yet it is there to be drawn out of his philosophical system (as sketched in Chapter 1). Look at

Husserl's theory of theories in the Prolegomena, already elaborated. Then look at the several theories he developed in the ensuing Investigations: (1) a theory of language expressing meaning as content of thought or experience; (2) a theory of essences or species, properties, and relations; (3) a theory of part and whole and ontological dependence; (4) a theory of parts of propositions and other forms of meaning; (5) a theory of intentionality and how sense directs consciousness toward objects; (6) a theory of evidence or "intuition" in knowledge. Look, along the way, at the *interdependencies* among these theories. The domains of these theories are parts of the world: *fields* of language, meaning, essence (including relation), wholes and dependencies, consciousness, and knowledge. Further down the road are cultural objects, values, and more. These domains are importantly linked, and we can see many of the links as Husserl proceeds. The partial theories take their place in a *grande* theory of consciousness, language, meaning, and objects of many types, all within the fabric of the world. This unified theory of consciousness-and-meaning-and-objects remains a *theory* in Husserl's full sense. And the *semantics* of that theory follows the contours of the structure of theory–meaning–field that Husserl recounts in his story of pure logic. So a part of Husserl's *grande* theory of everything is his pure logic, which is a theory of theories and how they mean various types of things in the world. This theory is a *grande* metatheory governing his overall philosophical theory. Moreover, that metatheory is itself a part of the *grande* theory, and its status as part-of-theory is analyzable within the theory of parts of meanings.

It is only within this *grande* philosophical theory, governed by this *grande* metatheory, that the more famous parts of Husserl's philosophy go to work: phenomenology, with Husserl's analyses of consciousness and intentional content; epistemology, with Husserl's account of "intuition"; ontology, with Husserl's account of formal and material categories; social theory, with Husserl's account of the life-world. The indicated structure in Husserl's philosophical system is precisely mapped, however, only in his theory of logic. That is why we have begun our detailed account of Husserl's philosophy with his work in or, better, on logic.

SUMMARY

Husserl's concerns with logic traversed his full career. His early work in mathematics was related to developments of number theory, set theory, and manifold theory, which played out in the subsequent results of mathematical logic and model theory. His anti-psychologistic view of logic led into his conception of phenomenology as distinguished from empirical psychology. His outline of a logical semantics prefigured the mathematical development of formal semantics in Tarski, Carnap, and possible-worlds semantics, while mirroring the formal structure of intentionality.

Inspired by Bolzano and later Frege, Husserl argued against 19th-century versions of psychologism, the view that logic is about psychological processes of reasoning, about how we happen to think and draw inferences. Rather, Husserl held, logic is about objective properties of ideal forms of sense or meaning, including propositions. Logic studies relations of consequence among various propositions, and semantic relations between such ideal meanings and what they represent in the world. "Pure" logic, for Husserl, is the "theory of science," the "theory of theories." Thus, pure logic maps basic forms or categories of sense (Concept, Proposition, Connective), basic forms or categories of objects (Individual, Property or Relation, State of Affairs), and semantic correlations between forms of sense and forms of object. For instance (in our terms), the *proposition* <Aristotle is synoptic> correlates with the *state of affairs* [Aristotle is synoptic] – and this proposition is *true* just in case the corresponding state of affairs exists. Here, the proposition is composed of concepts of appropriate form (the individual concept <Aristotle> , the property concept <synoptic>); the state of affairs is composed of objects of appropriate form (the individual Aristotle, the property synopticity); and there is a semantic correlation between the constituents of the proposition and the constituents of the state of affairs represented by the proposition. Here we see the beginnings of a semantic theory of truth, which Tarski developed in the 1930s. Central to Husserl's conception of logical semantics is his conception of *categories* of sense and *categories* of objects in the world.

Later 20th-century logicians focused on forms of language, shying away from "Platonistic" theories of sense shared by Husserl and Frege. However, Husserl offered an elaborate account of the relation between language and ideal sense. Language serves communication, for Husserl, because language serves to express forms of sense that are shareable intentional contents of thought. (More precisely, for Husserl, language modifies sense, in bringing intentional content to public expression as linguistic meaning.)

Adapting Kantian terminology, Husserl distinguished "transcendental" logic from "formal" logic. Formal logic addresses the proper forms of language, sense, and object, and correlations among these – including consequence relations among propositions and semantical relations between propositions and states of affairs. Here is the familiar domain of modern logic. But transcendental logic, according to Husserl, goes further, by grounding formal logic in laws of thought or its ideal intentional content – thus grounding logic in the theory of intentionality.

In Husserl's last phase of work, he worried about how our mathematical formulations of laws of nature abstract away from our everyday experiences of things in nature. His early conception of logic foreshadowed this problem of "mathematizing" what we experience in pre-mathematical forms. Pure logic, accordingly, includes more than formal logic, as it opens into the theory of intentionality and thus to a "transcendental" phenomenological conception of logic itself.

FURTHER READING

Below are studies of Husserl's relations to logic, semantics, mathematics, and the analytic tradition, together with studies in the historical background of logic and semantics that are especially relevant to reading Husserl in relation to logical semantics.

Beaney, Michael, ed. 1997. *The Frege Reader*. Oxford and Malden, Massachusetts: Blackwell. Contemporary readings on Frege's work.

Bolzano, Bernard. 1837/1972. *Theory of Science: Attempt at a Detailed and in the Main Novel Exposition of Logic with Constant Attention to Earlier Authors*. Edited and translated by Rolf George. Berkeley and Los Angeles: University of California Press, 1972. A partial translation of Bolzano's *Wissenschaftslehre*; original German 1837.

Cobb-Stevens, Richard. 1990. *Husserl and Analytic Philosophy*. Dordrecht and Boston, Massachusetts: Kluwer Academic Publishers (now New York: Springer). A phenomenologist's view of Husserl in relation to analytic philosophy.

Coffa, J. Alberto. 1991. *The Semantic Tradition from Kant to Carnap: To the Vienna Station*. Edited by Linda Wessels. Cambridge and New York: Cambridge University Press. A seminal history of the "semantic" tradition, including Bolzano, Frege, Husserl, Carnap.

Dreyfus, Hubert L., ed. 1982. *Husserl, Intentionality and Cognitive Science*. In collaboration with Harrison Hall. Cambridge, Massachusetts: MIT Press. A classic collection on Husserl's relation to Fregean semantics and cognitive science.

Dummett, Michael. 1993. *Origins of Analytical Philosophy*. Cambridge, Massachusetts: Harvard University Press. An astute history of early analytic philosophy, comparing Frege and Husserl in particular.

Fisette, Denis. 2003. *Husserl's* Logical Investigations *Reconsidered*. Dordrecht and Boston, Massachusetts: Kluwer Academic Publishers (now New York: Springer). Contemporary essays on the *Logical Investigations*, including a number of essays relevant to logical theory.

Frege, Gottlob. 1892/1997. "On *Sinn* and *Bedeutung*." In Michael Beaney, ed. *The Frege Reader*. Oxford and Malden, Massachusetts: Blackwell, 1997. German original, 1892. Key terms sometimes translated as: sense (*Sinn*) and reference (*Bedeutung*). Frege's seminal model of a semantics keyed to the new logic that Frege largely created.

Friedman, Michael. 1999. *Reconsidering Logical Positivism*. Cambridge and New York: Cambridge University Press. An astute appraisal of logical positivism, addressing relations to Kant and, at crucial points, to Husserl.

Grattan-Guinness, I., ed. 1994. *Companion Encyclopedia of the History and Philosophy of the Mathematical Sciences*, vols. 1 and 2. Baltimore, Maryland, and London: The Johns Hopkins University Press. See Parts 5, 6, and 7 on the history of logics, geometries, and number theories relevant to Husserl's era.

Hill, Clair Ortiz, and Guillermo E. Rosado Haddock. 2000. *Husserl or Frege? Meaning, Objectivity, and Mathematics*. Chicago and LaSalle, Illinois: Open Court. Essays setting the record straight on Husserl's relations to Frege and early logicians and mathematicians.

Hill, Claire Ortiz. 2002. "Tackling Three of Frege's Problems: Edmund Husserl on Sets and Manifolds". *Axiomathes* 13: 79–104, 2002.

Hintikka, Jaakko. 1969. *Models for Modalities*. Dordrecht and Boston, Massachusetts: D. Reidel Publishing Company (now New York: Springer). Classic essays by one of the founders of possible-worlds semantics, with relations to Fregean semantics.

——. 1975. *The Intentions of Intentionality*. Dordrecht and Boston, Massachusetts: D. Reidel Publishing Company (now New York: Springer). Hintikka's essays addressing Husserlian phenomenology and related semantic views.

Mohanty, J. N. 1982. *Husserl and Frege*. Bloomington: Indiana University Press. A careful history of the relations between Husserl and Frege, by a leading contemporary phenomenologist.

Mulligan, Kevin. 1990. "Husserl on States of Affairs in the Logical Investigations". Epistemologia, special number on Logica e Ontologia, XII, 207 234, (Proceedings of 1987 Genoa conference on Logic and Ontology).

Mulligan, K., Simons, P. M., and Smith, B. 1984. "Truth-Makers". In *Philosophy and Phenomenological Research* 44, 278–321.

Richardson, Alan W. 1998. *Carnap's Construction of the World: The Aufbau and the Emergence of Logical Empiricism*. Cambridge and New York: Cambridge University Press. A study of Carnap, including relations to Husserl.

Roy, Jean-Michel. 2004. "Carnap's Husserlian Reading of the *Aufbau*." In Steve Awodey and Carsten Klein, eds. *Carnap Brought Home: The View from Jena*. Chicago and LaSalle, Illinois: Open Court. A study of Carnap's system in light of Husserl, prompted by Carnap's own remarks.

Ryckman, Thomass. 2005. *The Reign of Relativity: Philosophy in Physics 1915–1925*. Oxford and New York: Oxford University Press. A remarkable study of the early philosophy of relativity theory, including relations to Husserlian transcendental phenomenology.

——. 2006. "Husserl and Carnap." In Richard Creath and Michael Friedman, eds. *The Cambridge Companion to Carnap*. Cambridge and New York: Cambridge University Press. A study of Carnap's relation to Husserl, addressing "bracketing" *vis-à-vis* "methodological solipsism" (Carnap) and the variant accounts of "constitution" in Husserl and Carnap.

Simons, Peter. 1987. *Parts: A Study in Ontology*. Oxford: Oxford University Press. A study in the ontology of part–whole relations, reflecting studies of Husserl's ontology.

——. 1992a. *Philosophy and Logic in Central Europe from Bolzano to Tarski*. Dordrecht and Boston: Kluwer Academic Publishers.

——. 1992b. "Logical Atomism and its Ontological Refinement: A Defense". In Mulligan, Kevin. editor. *Language, Truth and Ontology*. Dordrecht and Boston: Kluwer Academic Publishers, 1992, pp. 157–179.

Smith, Barry, ed. 1982. *Parts and Moments: Studies in Logic and Formal Ontology*. Munich and Vienna: Philosophia Verlag. Essays in ontology, informed by studies of Husserl's ontology of part–whole in the *Logical Investigations*.

Smith, Barry. 1994. *Austrian Philosophy: The Legacy of Franz Brentano*. Chicago and LaSalle, Illinois: Open Court. The only detailed study of the history of Austrian philosophy, including Brentano and Husserl and much more.

——. 1996. "Logic and the Sachverhalt". In Liliana Albertazzi, Massimo Libardi, and Roberto Poli, editors. *The School of Franz Brentano*. Dordrecht: Kluwer Academic Publishers.

Smith, David Woodruff. 2002. "Intentionality and Picturing: Early Husserl vis-à-vis Early Wittgenstein." In Terry Horgan, John Tienson, and Matjaz Potrc, eds. *Origins: The Common Sources of the Analytic and Phenomenological Traditions* (proceedings of the Spindel Conference 2001). *Southern Journal of Philosophy*, vol. XL, supplement 2002; published by the Department of Philosophy, the University of Memphis. A dialogue setting Husserl and Wittgenstein in conversation about propositions and states of affairs.

——. 2005. "Truth and Experience: Tarski vis-à-vis Husserl." In M. E. Reicher and J. C. Marek, eds. *Experience and Analysis. Erfahrung und Analyse. The Proceedings of the 27th International Wittgenstein Symposium*. Vienna: öbv a hpt. A study integrating Husserl's theory of intentionality with Tarski's groundbreaking "semantic" theory of truth.

Smith, David Woodruff, and Ronald McIntyre. 1982. *Husserl and Intentionality: A Study of Mind, Meaning, and Language*. Dordrecht and Boston, Massachusetts: D. Reidel Publishing Company (now New York: Springer). A book-length study of Husserl's theory of intentionality in relation to semantic theories.

Tarski, Alfred. 1944/2001. "The Semantic Conception of Truth and the Foundations of Semantics." In Michael P. Lynch, ed. *The Nature of Truth*. Cambridge, Massachusetts: MIT Press. 2001. Reprinted from *Philosophy and Phenomenological Research* 4 (1944). On Tarski's seminal work on truth, setting the style of contemporary logical semantics in terms of truth-conditions.

Tieszen, Richard. 2004. "Husserl's Logic." In Dov M. Gabbay and John Woods, eds. *Handbook of the History of Logic*, vol. 3. Amsterdam and Boston, Massachusetts: Elsevier BV. A monograph detailing Husserl's varied contributions to logic.

——. 2005. *Phenomenology, Logic, and the Philosophy of Mathematics*. Cambridge and New York: Cambridge University Press. A series of essays on relations between phenomenology and logic and philosophy of mathematics, including studies of Gödel's relations to Husserlian phenomenology.

Wittgenstein, Ludwig. 1921/1974. *Tractatus Logico-Philosophicus*. Translated by D. F. Pears and B. F. McGuinness. Atlantic Highlands, New Jersey: Humanities Press International, Inc., 1974. Original German edition, 1921, under the title *Logisch-Philosophische Abhandlung* (*Logical-Philosophical Treatise*). Wittgenstein's classic treatise, which may be read as a compact development of ideas in *Logical Investigations*, which Wittgenstein may never have seen, though both Husserl and Wittgenstein shared a background in Viennese thought.

Zahavi, Dan, and Frederik Stjernfelt, eds. 2002. *One Hundred Years of Phenomenology: Husserl's Logical Investigations Revisited*. Dordrecht and Boston, Massachusetts: Kluwer Academic Publishers (now New York: Springer). Contemporary essays on the *Logical Investigations*.

Four

Ontology: essences and categories, minds and bodies

In the prior chapter we explored Husserl's conception of logic. In his account of "pure logic," we found an articulate view of semantics, proposing a style of correlation between categories of meaning (or corresponding categories of linguistic expression) and categories of objects. This correlation flowered in Husserl's conception of intentionality, the structure wherein experience is directed toward objects in the world via meanings that represent such objects. Husserl increasingly addressed issues of ontology, as he moved from logic toward phenomenology, and into epistemology. In the present chapter we study the details of Husserl's ontology.

ONTOLOGY IN HUSSERL'S PHILOSOPHICAL SYSTEM

Ontology is the theory of what there is, assessing what are the basic kinds of things in the world, how they are interrelated, what are their essences, their modes of being, and so on. The term "metaphysics" is often used synonymously with "ontology," but there is also a more special sense in which metaphysics is defined as speculation about what lies beyond the range of empirical evidence (the nature of God, the gods, life after or before death, and so on). Husserl uses "metaphysics" in a variation on this special sense; he uses "ontology" in the generic sense we are following but with an expanded conception of ontology that distinguished formal and material ontology.

Husserl addressed issues of ontology throughout his career. In his early *Philosophy of Arithmetic* (1891) he considered what numbers are and how they are related to our mental activities of grouping and counting. In *Logical Investigations* (first edition 1900–1), he assumed ideal meanings and their logical correlations with basic forms of object; then he outlined a theory of ideal species (what Aristotle called universals), followed by a theory of part–whole structures; then he turned to the intentional relation of consciousness to its objects, looking to the role of ideal contents or meanings in intentional experiences. All these issues belong to ontology, while the structure of intentionality is also central to the analysis of conscious experience in phenomenology (as we see in Chapters 6 and 7). The structure of space and time occupied Husserl further (in lectures of roughly 1905–10), especially in relation to our experiences of time and space. Soon Husserl returned to the nature of ideal meanings (in lectures of 1908). *Ideas* I (1913) opens with a statement of his mature ontology. The nature of mind or consciousness, including its relation to the body and to the natural and social world, weaves through Husserl's ontology and phenomenology in *Ideas* I and *Ideas* II (both written in 1912). Similar concerns appear in his later writings. Finally, in the *Crisis* (1935–8) Husserl worried about the essence of nature, contrasting our "mathematized" conception of space–time and things in nature with the ways we understand space, time, and material objects in everyday life. Again, the issue – the essence of space, time, and material things – is ontological, though phenomenology enters the analysis.

In the present chapter we explore Husserl's systematic ontology in its own right. We shall outline his basic conception of ontology, featuring a novel system of categories both "formal" and "material." We shall pursue the implications of Husserl's ontology for the mind–body problem, which has been a robust area of research in recent philosophy. We shall look into his conception of "ideal" or abstract entities, from numbers to essences to meanings. Finally, we shall dig into Husserl's mid-career doctrine that the world stands in a certain relation to potential consciousness, central to his so-called "transcendental idealism."

FORMAL AND MATERIAL ONTOLOGY: FACTS, ESSENCES, REGIONS, CATEGORIES

The ontology of categories

Systematic ontology began with Aristotle's theory of categories. After Plato had explored a theory of particulars and "forms" (things and their ideal types or properties), his student Aristotle developed a more elaborate and systematic ontology. Aristotle proposed that everything there is falls under exactly one of ten maximally general *categories* – or is a combination of things in these categories. The concrete things of the world, called "primary substances" or "beings" (*ousia*), are characterized by several different types of things that are "said" or "predicable" of primary beings. (The Greek "*kate-goria*" originally meant what can be said of someone, what one can be accused of in a court of law.) To get an idea of how general these categories are, just look at Aristotle's list of categories, with some subcategories, compiled with examples in Figure 4.1.

Aristotle's scheme of categories reigned for many centuries. Then in the "modern" era of European philosophy, in the 17th to 19th centuries, ontological categories were replaced by epistemological categories, featuring in effect categories of concepts of objects rather than categories of objects themselves. The most influential system of conceptual categories was Kant's, put forth in his *Critique of Pure Reason* (1781/1787). Kant presented his scheme of categories, with four groups of three, in the form reproduced in Figure 4.2.

Other historical figures produced systems of something like categories or categorial concepts (Boethius, Suarez, Descartes, Hume, Locke, Hegel, Whitehead, to name a few). However, Husserl's background in the emerging mathematics and logic of his day, together with his emerging conception of phenomenology, prepared him for a radical rethinking of categorial ontology – to which we now turn.

Husserl's new system of ontological categories

A novel and distinctive system of categories emerged in Husserl's philosophy, both synthesizing and transcending the rival approaches

CATEGORIES			EXAMPLES
1	Substance		
	a	Primary Substance, i.e. Individual	this man, Socrates, this horse
	b	Secondary Substance, i.e. Species	man (mankind), horse (kind)
2	Quantity		four cubits, much (water)
3	Quality		
	a	State/Condition	grammatical (in the soul)
	b	Capacity	rational (in the soul)
	c	Affective Quality	white
	d	Shape	square
4	Relative (better, Relation)		double, half, larger [than]
5	Where, i.e. Place		in the Lyceum, in the marketplace
6	When, i.e. Time		yesterday, last year
7	Position, i.e. Arrangement		lying, sitting
8	Having		has shoes on, has armor on
9	Doing, i.e. Action		cutting, burning
10	Being Affected, i.e. Acted Upon, "Passion"		being cut, being burned

Figure 4.1 Aristotle's system of categories

Source: This table of categories and examples thereof is drawn from Aristotle's *Categories*, reprinted in Aristotle: Selections, translated by Terence Irwin and Gail Fine (Hacket Publishing Company, Inc., Indianapolis/Cambridge, 1995).

of Aristotelians and Kantians, developed with a keen eye to mathematical forms. For the Aristotelian, we categorize the most general or basic kinds of entities in the world. For the Kantian, we cannot get at ontological categories themselves, because, Kant held, we can know only things-as-they-appear, never things-as-they-are-in-themselves. So, for the Kantian, we categorize instead the most general or basic kinds of *concepts* we have, which we take to represent things in the world. Husserl, however, insists on categorizing both concepts, or meanings, and the objects they represent, holding that our experiences are intentionally related to objects via meanings that represent such objects.

Husserl forayed into categorial ontology early in the *Logical Investigations* (1900–1). In the Prolegomena (§§67ff.), as we saw in Chapter 3, Husserl specified that "pure logic" will include a semantic correlation between "pure categories of meaning" – hence categories of expression bearing such meanings – and "pure categories of objects." Categories of meaning include: "Concept, Proposition, Truth, etc." (§67) – also Connection ("and," "or," "if . . . then,").

CATEGORIES

1 Of Quantity
  Unity
  Plurality
  Totality

2 Of Quality
  Reality
  Negation
  Limitation

3 Of Relation
  Of Inherence and Subsistence (*substantia et accidens*)
  Of Causality and Dependence (cause and effect)
  Of Community (reciprocity between agent and patient)

4 Of Modality
  Possibility – Impossibility
  Existence – Non-existence
  Necessity – Contingency

Figure 4.2 Kant's system of (conceptual) categories

Husserl demands a *correlation* between categories of meanings (or concepts) and categories of objects, with attention to these two types of category in their own rights. Husserl thus requires a theory of *categories of objects* (going beyond Aristotle's), a theory of *categories of meanings* (going beyond Kant's), and then – in the semantic part of pure logic – a theory of how meanings in various categories *correlate* with objects in various categories (going beyond Frege's semantics, not in technical but in philosophical detail). The theory of object categories is thus presupposed by the semantic – and ultimately phenomenological – theory that correlates meaning categories with object categories.

In the first edition of the *Logical Investigations* (1900–1) Husserl spoke of the theory of objects (*Gegenstände*), noting the term "*Gegenstandstheorie*" championed by his contemporary, and fellow Brentano student, Alexius Meinong (Meinong 1904/1960). (The Meinongian approach to ontology is studied in Findlay 1963; D. W. Smith 1975; Parsons 1980.) In the second edition (and its English translation), Husserl uses the term "formal ontology" for the maximally general, or rather formal, theory of *objects of all types*. By "object" Husserl always means object of any type whatsoever, in whatever category: from birds and trees to numbers and sets, from physical objects to conscious experiences, from the blue in the sky to the glint in a person's eye, from works of art like Puccini's *Tosca* to political upheavals like the French Revolution, from the movements of the planets to the Einsteinian curvature of space–time, and – of course – from ideal species or properties (universals) to ideal meanings including concepts, propositions, and axiomatic theories. It is important to see how wide this notion of "object" is, for its range is precisely the domain of Husserl's emerging theory of categories of objects. (Husserl cites his shift in terminology from "theory of objects" to "formal ontology" in *Ideas* I, §10, final footnote.)

Husserl's systematic presentation of formal ontology appears only in the first chapter of *Ideas* I (1913). Since *Ideas* I is a book-length presentation of "pure" phenomenology, it is remarkable that Husserl chose to lay out his systematic ontology before proceeding with his account of the new "transcendental" discipline of phenomenology, in which we study consciousness and its representation of objects regardless of whether such objects exist. But Husserl's sketch of a systematic ontology is not merely (as some scholars have held) a paean to his early students who loved his realist ontology and disliked his "transcendental idealism" (see Ingarden 1975), for Husserl explicitly uses details of his ontology as he develops his account of "pure" or "transcendental" phenomenology (see Chapter 6).

In the opening two chapters – Part One – of *Ideas* I (1913), Husserl organizes his myriad ontological views into a systematic ontology. Although he imports much of the ontology already developed in *Logical Investigations*, there are some changes of detail (as meanings are given their own niche, distinguished from species of acts of consciousness). Most important, there is a wholly new *architecture* to the system. What is revolutionary is the distinction Husserl there develops between *formal* and *material* ontology, positing distinct types of *formal* and *material* categories. Some of the details we have seen in Chapter 3 of this volume, but we now pursue the organization of the system of categories.

Our task is to summarize, in its own right, Husserl's "big picture" of the categorial structure of the world, embracing objects of various type, notably including acts of consciousness, intentionality, meaning, and the objects of experience.

The doctrine of essence or eidos (Ideas I)

Part One (§§1–26) of *Ideas* I is titled "Essence and Cognition of Essence" (*Wesen und Wesenserkenntis*). "Essence" is Husserl's term for *what* an individual thing *is* (§3), including its kinds or species, its qualities or properties, and its relations to other things – what "determines" and so is predicable of something. (The German "*Wesen*" derives from "*was + sein*," or "what + is." Keep this in mind and we will not over-inflate the notion of essence, despite Husserl's high-sounding rhetoric.) Under Essence Husserl groups all "ideal" objects. These include species, qualities, relations – so-called "universals" – but also mathematical entities such as numbers, sets, and so on. Like Plato, Husserl insists that essences are *ideal* entities, or *eidos* (§3, adapting Plato's term), meaning they are not *real*, that is, concrete-spatiotemporal entities like rocks, tables, thunderstorms. Yet Husserl resisted "Platonic realism," the doctrine (in something of a parody) that Platonic "forms" or eidos exist in a Platonic heaven beyond space and time. Husserl famously held that we have ways of grasping or knowing essences in "eidetic intuition," or intuition of essences (§§3–4). This doctrine of eidetic intuition has been widely misunderstood, producing a serious distraction from the phenomenology and ontology in *Ideas* I. Intuition of essences is not a magical faculty for the gifted few, although Husserl insisted its practice is a skill that requires training. Rather, intuition of essences is a kind of abstraction wherein we focus on features shared by different instances of, say, the essence Tree. (Today cognitive scientists speak of "pattern recognition.") Thus we speak of "seeing" that a tree has limbs, or of "insight" that a triangle has three sides totaling $180°$. The epistemology of intuition will be laid out in Chapter 7, but for now our focus remains on the ontology of essences.

The opening chapter of *Ideas* I, "Fact and Essence" (*Tatsache und Wesen*) (§§1–17), is a dense presentation, unfolding a systematic structuring of Husserl's overall ontology, save for the theory of ideal meaning, which is developed much later in the book. The second chapter, "Naturalistic Misinterpretations" (§§18–26), then wards off criticisms. We shall focus here on Husserl's system of ontology and its novel types and organization of categories (§§1–16).

In Husserl's ontology, the first division of objects (of whatever type) is that between Fact and Essence (§2). Under *Fact* fall all "real individuals," that is, concrete individual objects ("individua," plural of "individuum") occurring "contingently" in space–time and/or time (see §2). Here are enduring objects such as stones, trees, birds, bears, humans, planets, stars. Here too are events or processes such as earthquakes, tsunamis, sports events, political revolutions, and elections – and particular experiences or acts of consciousness, the theme of phenomenology. Here also are concrete states of affairs such as my being 75 inches tall or Socrates' sitting under a certain olive tree. Under *Essence* fall all "ideal" objects or eidos that "determine" concrete objects. Here are the species, qualities, relations, and quantities that inhere in concrete objects: for example, humanity (humankind), cleverness or obstreperousness, unity (oneness), and being-a-teacher-of-Plato – these being ideal, shareable features that inhere in the concrete individual Socrates. Here too are mathematical eidos such as unity, plurality, and number (see §§10–12). Terminology: Husserl uses the German "*real*" for spatiotemporal objects, and "*reell*" for temporal objects including experiences (which are not properly spatial but are temporal); in English we have only the one word "real" to translate both.

Broadly, Husserl's categorial distinction between Fact and Essence is a variation on the Platonic–Aristotelian division between particulars and universals. However, Husserl goes on to develop a series of distinctions that form an innovative and original system of categories, separating *formal* from *material* categories, and featuring interesting choices for each. With these distinctions, there emerges Husserl's conception of "formal" ontology, assumed in his conception of pure logic and ultimately of pure phenomenology as well.

Material and formal essences: regions and categories

Husserl divided essences into two types: "material" essences, concerning substantive matters of "fact"; and "formal" essences, concerning the mere forms of objects of any type. Material essences at the highest level of generality he called *regions*; essences at the highest level of formality he called *categories*. Although he sometimes calls all high-level essences "categories," his strict usage is reserved for formal categories, which govern material regions or domains. That would leave Fact and Essence themselves as Ur-categories or super-categories, though Husserl offers no such name.

What, then, are regions and categories?

Consider an object in nature, say, this individual tree, a particular eucalyptus tree located at a certain time on a certain street in California. The tree is one thing, a concrete individual. Its essence is something else, an ideal formation comprising its species (Eucalyptus), its qualities (how it is colored), its spatial shape (how tall it is and how its limbs reach out in specific directions), its relationships (to me across the street), its structure with botanic parts (limbs, sap, bark, leaves), its unity, and so on. Such properties, each in principle shareable by other objects, make up its *"material" essence* as a spatiotemporal-physical thing in nature. The specific essence of this individual tree falls under the more generic essence Eucalyptus, which in turn falls under the more generic essence Tree, under Plant, and so on, up to the highest "material genus," Nature. To stay for a moment with this example, biological classification would specify these groupings precisely, and the theory of speciation has changed importantly since Husserl's day, but let us assume Husserl's overarching view that natural species and genera are "determined" by a type of essence, a type of "material" essence, to be detailed by careful empirical research. We will then need to distinguish the natural "species" *Eucalyptus globulus* from its corresponding "ideal species" or essence. The natural species is a botanical population distributed in space–time, with an evolutionary history on Earth, while its "ideal species" would be an "eidetic" formation including what biological systematists call its phenotype (characteristic observable qualities), its holotype (paradigm instances), and its phylogenetic clade (the tree of descendence relating the current natural species to prior species in its evolutionary descent). Husserlian ontology would ramify the extant debate among biologists over the definition of species, but we note here the ambiguity of the term "species" and how Husserlian eidos relate to naturally occurring species-populations. Note how empirical research interweaves with abstract ontology, on such an approach.

The "highest material genus" under which an individual object falls Husserl terms a *region* (*Region*) (§§9–10). In *Ideas* I Husserl works with Nature as a region (§9) and then homes in on the region Consciousness (*Bewusstsein*) (§33 and §§45ff., with the title "The Region of Pure Consciousness").

In *Ideas* II Husserl analyzes relations between the region Consciousness and the region Culture or Spirit (*Geist*). Consciousness is central to phenomenology in later sections of *Ideas* I, while Culture figures centrally in *Ideas* II but appears along the way also in *Ideas* I. So Husserl's ontology recognizes three, and presumably only three, proper *regions*: Nature, Consciousness, and Culture. These three kinds or domains – with their own distinctive and irreducible properties – were distinguished by other philosophers in the 19th century and indeed in earlier centuries. What is new in Husserl, however, is their place in his novel system of categories.

Each region embraces many lower, or more specific, essences or essence-domains. Under Nature are Plant, Animal, and so on. And under Plant are many different genera and their species, including *Eucalyptus globulus* (in botany's terminology). Each material region is studied in an appropriate *material ontology*. Thus, the ontology of Nature (§9) fans out into more specific ontologies of trees, of eucalyptus trees, of animals, of bears, of fishes, of swordfish, and so on. Of note to Husserl, given his mathematical background, is the way *applied geometry* figures in the material ontology of spatiotemporal objects in nature: the ancient *pure geometries* were followed in modern times by applied geometries in physics (§9). But pure geometry, as opposed to applied physical geometry, is part of pure mathematics or "formal *mathesis*" (§9). As we know from the *Logical Investigations*, Husserl saw in the ideal of a *mathesis universalis*, or universal mathematical theory, the ideal of a purely formal ontology. And in *Ideas* I Husserl lays out his notion of formal ontology as governing the variety of material ontologies of various regions and their more specific subdomains.

Husserl's key idea – defining his conception of *formal* ontology – is that all objects falling under material essences, from the most specific essences up to the most general regions, are further determined or governed by strictly *formal essences*. Whereas material essences define the substantive nature of an object, formal essences define the pure *forms* of objects, forms that are filled out in substantive ways by their material essences. For example, this particular tree is, "materially," a eucalyptus, but it is, "formally," an individual or "substrate" (§11), that is, something capable of bearing properties. It cannot bear the material essence Eucalyptus unless it bears the formal essence Individual. Further, the material species *Eucalyptus globulus* falls under the formal essence Species; the concrete species cannot be a species unless it falls under the formal essence Species. And the concrete state of affairs that consists in this tree's being a eucalyptus is itself a concrete object (a "fact") that falls under the formal essence State of Affairs. Formal essences such as Species Husserl calls "essence-forms" (§10); that is, they are forms – types – of material essences, "empty" forms that are filled by material essences such as *Eucalyptus globulus*.

Because these forms apply to objects in any relevant material domain, Husserl calls them "logical categories" (§10): logic applies everywhere. However, he explains that they are not "*meaning categories* [*Bedeutungskategorien*]" but "*formal objective categories* [*gegenständlichen Kategorien*] in the precise [*prägnanten*] sense" (§10, Husserl's italics and scare quotes). This distinction between objective categories and meaning categories is that drawn in the Prolegomena of the *Logical Investigations*, as Husserl states in the footnotes. Recall Husserl's conception of logic, which is wider than that of a symbolic language of inference.

Husserl offers slightly different lists of formal essences or categories. Here is one of his longer lists, from the Investigation III of the *Logical Investigations* (§11): the formal essences (corresponding to formal concepts) "Something, One, Object, Quality, Relation, Connection, Plurality, Number, Order, Ordinal Number, Whole, Part, Magnitude, etc." are contrasted with material essences (corresponding to material concepts) such as "House, Tree, Color, Tone,

Space, Sensation, Feeling, etc." Returning to Ideas I, we find Husserl listing these characteristic formal or "logical" categories: "Property, Relative Quality, State of Affairs [Sachverhalt], Relation, Identity, Similarity, Set [Menge] (Collection), Number, Whole and Part, Kind [Gattung] and Way [Art], and so forth" (§10). At the beginning of this list, the categories Property, Quality, Relation, and State of Affairs ramify the traditional theory of particulars and universals (where Aristotle's theory of categories began). However, the notion of a category of states of affairs was developed by Husserl and others around the turn of the 20th century. A Sachverhalt − literally "things-related" − is a structure consisting in two or more objects standing in a relation, or in a single object having a property or kind (as it were, a one-place relation). This structure would be the featured "logical form" in Ludwig Wittgenstein's famous Tractatus Logico-Philosophicus (Logisch-Philosophische Abhandlung, 1921), which may well be read as a study in formal ontology. In Wittgenstein's system of "logical atomism" (as Bertrand Russell called his own version of the doctrine), the world is the totality of "facts," or existing states of affairs, rather than objects, which merely appear as constituents in states of affairs. That is, the world is built up, formally, from states of affairs, "complexes" in which objects are bound together by relations.

Next on Husserl's recited list of formal categories are Identity and Similarity. Then come the mathematical categories including Set and Number − we may add Manifold (see Chapter 3). Husserl had devoted his first book to the theory of numbers, but after that "immature" effort in Philosophy of Arithmetic (1891) he spent an industrious decade working up to the system of the Logical Investigations (1900−1), radically extending his conception of ontology. Notice that he counts Number as a formal essence, while he counts geometric essences like Shape or Triangle as material essences, presumably because they apply only to objects in space or space–time.

Next on Husserl's list are the categories Whole and Part. In the midst of the Investigations Husserl devoted an extended study (Investigation III) to the ontology of part and whole. Notice, here, that he specifically includes the essences Whole and Part as formal essences, applicable to any material domain. Part and Whole apply to spatiotemporal objects (this table has parts including four legs and a table-top), but they also apply to conscious experiences (my seeing the table has parts as my visual field includes visual presentations of the table, the book on the table, and the chair behind the table). The forms Part and Whole also apply to expressions and their meanings, which have grammatical parts. A simple sentence is composed, say, of a name and a predicate; the proposition expressed thereby is composed of an individual concept and a predicative concept. (Investigation IV is Husserl's application of part–whole ontology to meanings.) Phenomenology itself turns on the analysis of the parts composing the ideal meaning that serves as the content of an intentional experience. (Investigation V pursues this "formal" analysis of the parts of intentional experiences and contents, and *Ideas* I carries such analyses further into the structure of noemata, as we see in Chapter 6.) We will return to wholes, parts, and dependence.

Whatever goes on the list of formal ontological categories, the assumption is that the forms listed apply to all domains of objects. Notably, Husserl's assumption is that the categories – Individual, Property, State of Affairs, Number, and so on – apply to any domain under any of the regions Nature, Consciousness, and Culture. (If this assumption proves too strong, the leading idea remains that formal categories apply to various material categories, however these be ordered. See the contrasting category schemes studied in D. W. Smith 2004.)

According to Husserl's epistemology, we grasp essences by *abstraction*, sifting through possible cases for shared essences and thereby coming to "see" what is shared. But formal and material essences are grasped by two different types of abstraction. In *generalization* we grasp a shared material essence, a species or genus (*Ideas* I, §12) at some level of generality, say, Tree or Plant or Material Thing, that is, Thing in Nature. In *formalization*, by contrast, we grasp a shared formal essence at some level of formality, say, Individual (Substrate), Property, State of Affairs, or Number. Generalization is practiced in everyday life as we look for generalities (Knife, Fork, Spoon, and Chopstick are species under Eating Utensil). In a more theoretical vein we practice generalization in empirical science as we look for higher theoretical generalities (in biology we find: Eukarya, Animalia, . . . , Mammalia, . . . , Homo, Homo Sapiens). By contrast, we practice formalization in mathematics and logic as we look for formal structures found in arithmetic, geometry, calculus, mathematical logic, and computer science, say, Number, Set, Manifold, Integral, Decidability, Algorithm, and so on. (See *Ideas* I, §13 on the contrast between formalization and generalization.)

"Syntactic" categories and "substrates"

Within the domain of objects overall, Husserl writes (§11), there is an important distinction between what he calls "syntactic forms" and "syntactic substrates," or "stuffs" that fill the forms. There is thus an important "formal-ontological" distinction between *syntactic categories* and *substrate categories*. In an Aristotelian idiom we might say that, in their "syntactic" form, substrates (primary substances) are the ultimate bearers of essences (universals), where essences are predicable of or borne by substrates but substrates are not predicable of anything. These formal categories "mirror" (*widerspiegeln*) the "pure-grammatical" distinction in the formal theory of meaning, the distinction between predicative concepts and individual concepts, which are expressible, respectively, by predicates and singular terms such as names and pronouns. In logic, *syntax* is defined as the theory of the forms of expressions in a language, or for Husserl the corresponding forms of meanings. Thus, the syntactic form of a sentence consists in the shapes and order of symbols occurring in the sentence, including their forming words. For instance, the sentence "Socrates is wise" has a left-to-right order of letters forming words separated by spaces, and a grammatical combination of the words, here that of a name and an adjective joined by the copula "is." Strikingly, Husserl transfers this notion of syntactic form not only to the forms of *meanings* expressed by the sentence, but to the forms of *objects* represented in the sentence.

In Chapter 3 we already worked with this sort of ontological distinction, looking to the correlation between forms or categories of meanings (or corresponding expressions) and forms or categories of objects represented by those meanings. We can chart, in the following scheme, the "syntactic" categories in a simple case for types or forms of expression, meaning, and object represented:

Expression type "[Name] + [Predicate]" = Sentence
Expression   "Socrates is wise" – this particular sentence
Meaning type   <[Individual Concept] + [Property Concept]>
□= Proposition
Meaning   <Socrates is wise> – this particular proposition
Object type   [Individual + Property] = State of Affairs
Object   [Socrates is wise] – this particular state of affairs

(Here I use the square brackets for a state of affairs formed from an individual and a property, I use the angle brackets for a meaning, a proposition formed from an individual-concept and a property-concept, and I use quotation marks for a sentence so formed from a name and a predicate.)

Husserl's vision of ontological *form* (*Form*) – objective formal structure in the world – may seem a simplistic projection of the logical forms of sentences or propositions on to the world, where ontological forms mirror linguistic forms. To be sure, he clearly promotes just such a projection, positing the ontological categories of State of Affairs or *Sachverhalt* (corresponding to a simple complete sentence), Species and Quality and Relation (corresponding to predicates in the new logic), and of course Individual (corresponding to the names or variables in the new logic). And Aristotle's early doctrine of categories already aligned categories with language. However, as we saw in Chapter 3, Husserl sees "pure logic" in relation to a more abstract range of theory, namely, the conception of mathematics and metamathematics emerging in his day. There we saw Husserl's pet concept of *manifolds* at work. At any rate, as we look for the implicit architecture in Husserl's ontology, we follow the trail of his fascination with *formal structure* in the world, a type of structure that can be characterized in a mathematical theory or *mathesis universalis*, a theory whose domain of study takes the form of a "manifold."

To see how syntactic categories reach beyond the mirror images of everyday grammatical categories and into mathematical structures, consider the list of examples Husserl offers:

> The categories corresponding to these [syntactic] forms [*Formen*] we call *syntactic categories*. Here there belong as examples the categories State of Affairs, Relation, Property, Unity, Plurality, Number, Order, Ordinal Number, and so forth.
>
> (*Ideas* I, §11)

The last four categories govern the mathematical theories of set, number, and so on, and lead into metamathematics, and accordingly Husserl soon returns to the category Manifold (*Mannigfaltigkeit*), mentioning "Euclidean Manifold" (§13). As we saw in Chapter 3, Husserl conceives a manifold as a structure that is the *form* of the *field* of an axiomatic theory. Even these forms are "syntactic," we infer, insofar as the form Manifold governs all mathematical domains characterized (here is the "grammar" model) by *theories*, which are systems of propositions (whose structure is defined in logical syntax or grammar).

The simplest syntactic form is that of *individual* objects, which Husserl calls "substrates." The "formal region" Object – comprising "objectivities" of any type whatever (*"Gegenstandlichkeit-überhaupt"*) – divides into two categories: Substrate and Syntactic Object (or Objectivity) (§11). *Substrates* are the ultimate bearers of essences at any level of formality. Essences at any level have syntactic forms, ontological forms that are correlates of "thought-functions" such as asserting ("x is wise"), denying ("x is not wise"), relating ("x is a teacher of y"), connecting ("A and B"), counting ("1, 2, 3, . . . "), and so forth. Essences may have considerable syntactic structure, as does the essence [Greek & Wise & Teacher of Plato], which corresponds to the predicative structure of judging or thinking "x is Greek & x is wise & x is a teacher of Plato." By contrast, substrates are, formally, objects that have no syntactic complexity but rather serve as the ultimate "termini" of syntactic structures leading up from substrates to all higher levels of essence (§11). Husserl calls these substrates "individuals" (§11), but prefers the Aristotelian idiom "*tode ti*," or "this there" (§14), because the term "individual" implies indivisibility and so a part–whole structure that is formally distinct from the structure of bearing essences. Thus we have the form of a syntactically complex essence predicated in the complex sentence "x is a Greek & x is wise & x is a teacher of Plato": the individual this-there (Socrates) is the substrate that has the syntactically structured essence predicated of it by this syntactically complex sentence.

By the way, when Husserl occasionally speaks of "categorial intuition," he has in mind "seeing" the syntactic, categorial structure of a syntactically complex object, especially a state of affairs such as Socrates' being Greek and wise and a teacher of Plato. Our concern at present, however, is with ontological structure, not intuition of such structure.

Parts, "moments," dependence, foundation, necessity

Among formal categories, we noted, Husserl includes Whole and Part.

In Investigation III of the Logical Investigations, Husserl develops the outlines of a theory of part and whole, a theory of these formal essences, that is, of how parts and wholes of various types are related. What is most important for our purposes is the distinction he draws between two types of part (Teil) called "piece" (Stück) and "moment" (Moment) (§17). A piece of an object is an independent part, a part that could exist apart from the whole: for instance the leg of a table. A moment of an object is a dependent part, a part that could not exist apart from the whole: for instance, this white – this particular instance of whiteness – in this vase (to borrow an example from Aristotle's Categories). (See B. Smith 1982; Simons 1987; Fine 1995 on Husserl's ontology of parts and wholes.)

Husserl's formulation of these notions is unfortunately complex. In effect, he packs Necessity into Dependence and Dependence into Moment. But we ought to factor out the distinct albeit connected formal essences: Part, Dependence, and Necessity. Accordingly, I think it is fair to simplify Husserl's story as follows.

First there is the essence of being a *dependent* (*unselbständig*) object, hence *dependence* or *foundation* (Fundierung) (§§2ff., 14). An object A is *dependent*, or *founded*, on an object B if and only if A could not exist unless B existed, that is, *necessarily* A exists only if B exists. Now, dependencies are governed by "laws of essence." So Husserl specifies that A is dependent or founded on B if and only if, according the laws of the essences of A and B, necessarily A exists only if B exists. (As Husserl puts it, an object of type A "requires foundation" in an object of type B, according to the relevant laws of essence (§17).) So let us isolate the formal category Dependence. This category applies to very different types of object. For example: a tree depends on sap flowing, according to the laws of botany governing the essence Tree; the numbers 1, 2, 3, . . . depend on the numerical relation of succession, according to the laws of arithmetic governing the essence Number; the truth of the proposition "The earthquake has ended" depends on the truth of the proposition "The earthquake began," that is, the former proposition presupposes that latter, according to semantic theory governing the essence Meaning. Notice that the term "foundation" may mislead, since dependence can be a two-way street where A and B are mutually dependent on each other. For example, some biological organisms are mutually parasitic, and the roles of Husband and Wife are mutually dependent, that is, A cannot be a husband to B unless B is a wife to A. So let us speak simply of dependence.

Assuming the distinct categories of Part and Dependence, then, a moment is defined as a dependent part: A is a *moment*, or *dependent part*, of B if and only if A is a part of B and the essences of A and B are such that necessarily A exists only if B exists. Husserl's leading example (§4) is drawn from psychology or, rather, phenomenology. Thus, the color and extension (shape) of an object of vision are mutually dependent. For instance, this rectangular white sheet of paper has two visible qualities, its whiteness and its rectangularity. This whiteness in the paper could not exist unless this rectangularity in the paper existed, and vice versa, according to the laws governing the essences Visible Color and Visible Extension. This sheet of paper is, then, a *whole* including as moments, or dependent parts, this-color and this-shape. Following Aristotle, this-whiteness and this-rectangularity in this sheet of paper are particulars existing in space and time where the sheet of paper exists.

Husserl evidently assumes that dependence occurs only where one object is a dependent part of a whole. But one whole object may be dependent or founded on another whole object. If I carve a statue from marble, the statue is a work of art that depends or is founded on my intentional activity (see Ingarden 1961/1989; Thomasson 1998). Perhaps Husserl assumes that the work and the activity that produces it are themselves parts of some whole, say, the artistic process. But if we do not go that route with Husserl, then we would simply distinguish two formal categories: Dependence and Part. We must return to the issue of dependence as we analyze the status of consciousness and the world – is one dependent on the other, and if so in what ways?

Husserl applies the theory of parts (and wholes) to very different types of object: things in nature (trees), acts of consciousness (my seeing that eucalyptus tree across the street), meanings (the structured proposition <that tree is a eucalyptus and it was planted 100 years ago>), even essences (Tall Bipedal Vertebrate Animal). We shall find implications of the theory of parts as we explore Husserl's analyses of parts of experience and meaning in Chapters 5 and 6, and in pursuing implications for philosophy of mind and for transcendental idealism later in this chapter. Keep in mind that Part is a formal category, and so is (or should be) Dependence.

The definition of dependence presupposes the notion of necessity, as A cannot exist unless B exists, that is to say, necessarily A exists only if B exists. Husserl seems to assume that Necessity is a category that governs relations among essences, that is, according to "laws of essence." Perhaps he thinks necessity resides only in aspects of essences. Here is a large topic we cannot pursue in detail. Briefly, Husserl offers a corrective to Kant's conception of "analytic" and "synthetic" propositions, the former true by virtue of meaning ("A bachelor is unmarried") and the latter true by virtue of contingent matters of fact ("Grass is green"). Husserl ramifies these traditional notions by appeal to the distinction between formal and material essences, which generate necessities on different grounds. "The cardinal distinction between 'formal' and 'material' spheres of Essence," he writes, "gives us the true distinction between the *analytically a priori* and the *synthetically a priori* disciplines (or laws and necessities)" (Investigation III, §11). Necessities, or necessary states of affairs, are the objective correlates of a priori propositions, but we are to distinguish two types of necessity. We may say that *formal necessities* are posited by *analytically a priori* propositions such as "3 > 2" or "Every whole has parts" or "A relation binds objects into a state of affairs." By contrast, *material necessities* are posited by *synthetically a priori* propositions such as "Every bird has wings" or "A house has at least one room" or "There cannot be a king without subjects" (compare §11).

Possibility is the counterpoint to Necessity. Husserl speaks often of possibilities. Notably in his account of the "horizon" of possibilities – in effect, possible states of affairs – left open by the content or sense of an experience. He occasionally speaks of "possible worlds" (*Ideas* I, §47), adapting the term from his hero Leibniz. We consider these things in Chapter 6. For now, let us allow that Possibility and Necessity take a place in Husserl's scheme of formal categories.

Meanings, senses, noemata

For Husserl, meanings are ideal objects that play a key role in both logic and phenomenology. But what type of ideal objects are meanings?

The ideal intentional content of an experience Husserl calls a *sense* (*Sinn*). A sense expressed in language he calls a *meaning* (*Bedeutung*). According to Husserl's logic, we know, a sense or meaning is correlated with an appropriate object, as the role of meaning is precisely to represent, logically, an appropriate object – for instance as the sense "the vanquished at Waterloo" represents Napoleon. And, according to Husserl's theory of intentionality, the sense in an act of consciousness is correlated with an appropriate object, as the sense represents the object of consciousness. These principles are developed at length in the *Logical Investigations* and reappear in *Ideas* I (with some variation on the expressibility of sense). In *Ideas* I, in his presentation of phenomenology as a discipline, Husserl introduces the Greek term *"noema"* for the ideal intentional content of an act of consciousness, and the core of the noema is called a *sense* or *noematic sense*. The details of Husserl's doctrine of noema emerge in Chapters 5 and 6 of this volume.

In the *Investigations* Husserl categorized sense with species. The sense, or ideal intentional content, of an act of consciousness, he held, is the *ideal species* of the act of consciousness. If I think that "the vanquished at Waterloo was Corsican," the content "the vanquished at Waterloo" embodies the way I am thinking of the object (who is in fact Napoleon): the *type* or *species* of presentation of the object in my experience. To categorize meanings with species explains in what way they are ideal (in the way that species are ideal), and no new categories are assumed.

However, by the time of *Ideas* I, Husserl had come to think of meanings or senses as their own kind of ideal object, deserving their own name, "noema." Husserl does not give an explicit argument for this change of status; he merely specifies that there is a correlation between an act and its noema, where the noematic sense in an act is cited as "the object as intended." The best argument for Husserl's new position, it seems to me, is that species and senses have different ontological roles. A species is *instantiated* by a moment in an object that is a member of the species. By contrast, a sense *represents* or *means* an object, that is, it semantically or intentionally prescribes an object, and often prescribes it as having certain "determinations" or properties. Instantiation is part of the structure of essences in general, while semantic representation is part of the structure of intentionality, quite a distinct feature of the world. In Chapter 6, we shall dig into the significance of Husserl's characterization of a sense as "the object as intended," a characterization that has led to some divergent interpretations of Husserl's theory of noemata and their role in intentionality. Whatever else we are to say of noemata, for Husserl an act's noema is an ideal meaning entity, distinct in kind from any ideal essence. (See Simons 1995 on Husserl's theory of meaning and his change of ontology in lectures of 1908.)

If meanings or senses have this distinctive role in intentionality, they deserve their own categorial niche in the structure of the world. Accordingly, in Husserl's ontology, there should be a distinct category Meaning, or Sense. And since the role of meanings is logical (semantic), this category should be a formal essence, or category proper. For every object of whatever type is subject to logical or semantic representation by appropriate meanings that range over objects in accord with the laws of essence for meanings. "Pure logic" defines the semantic correlations among various types of meanings and appropriate types of objects. Intentionality theory follows suit. The category Meaning is not specified as Husserl opens Ideas I with his scheme of formal and material ontology. But the thrust of his long presentation of phenomenology as the book proceeds surely demands that we distinguish this category amid the structure of the world.

Husserl's system of object types or categories

I propose to systematize Husserl's novel category scheme as in Figure 4.3 (compare D. W. Smith 1995). Husserl did not present his system of categories in an explicit diagram (as did Kant); nor did he offer an explicit architecture governing the categories. There is always the sense that Husserl's system is (unlike Kant's) a work forever in progress, reflecting a sense of the "transcendence" of the world and our incomplete knowledge of even the most basic structures of the world: there is always more to come. With this caveat in mind, I offer a reconstruction of the system of categories Husserl presented in Ideas I against the background of the Logical Investigations.

Husserl separated ideal meanings from ideal essences as he developed his theory of "noema," the type of ideal content that inheres in an act of consciousness. We study meanings, ideal intentional contents of experiences, in Chapters 5 and 6, here noting their place in Husserl's overall category scheme.

In Chapter 8 we consider Husserl's views on ethics and the theory of values. Husserl takes values to have a certain objectivity while, in the case of ethical values, they are related to our

TYPES OF OBJECT

Fact [Real Object: in time or space–time]
 real individuals
  independent individuals
  dependent individuals, i.e. moments
 states of affairs [*Sachverhalte*]
 events
  natural events
  mental events, experiences, acts of consciousness
  cultural events

Essence [Ideal Object: not in time or space–time; bearable by objects]
 Formal Essence
  Category (highest level of formality)
   Individual or Substrate (*Tode* Ti, This-There)
   Species, Quality or Property, Relation
   State of Affairs
   Connection [And, Or, Not, If-Then]
   Necessity, Possibility
   Dependence, Independence
   Whole, Part
   Unity, Plurality, …
   Number
   Set, Group, …
   Manifold
   Value
   …
 Material Essence
  Region (highest level of generality)
   Nature
    …, Plant, Animal, …, Human, …
   Consciousness
    Subject ("I"), Act of Consciousness, Stream of Consciousness
   Culture or Spirit (*Geist*)
    Person, Society, Value, Artifact, …

Meaning or Sense [Ideal Content of Intentional Experience]
 Individual Sense – "this tree"
 Predicative Sense – "is a eucalyptus," "is taller than that oak"
 Proposition(al Sense) – "this tree is a eucalyptus"
 Connective Sense – "and," "or," "not," "if …then"
 Quantifier Sense – "all," "some"

Figure 4.3 Husserl's system of categories

emotions and our social life. Where should values appear, then, in Husserl's category scheme? Morality and ethical values Husserl places under the material region Culture, as our values regarding actions and what counts as a good person are part of our everyday life-world. However, I have placed Value as a category under Formal Essence, since values should apply to objects in the different material regions. For instance, a good will should fall under the region Consciousness, while a good or well-developed oak tree should fall under the region Nature, as should a good pattern of psychological development for a human infant.

THE STATUS OF IDEAL OBJECTS

Ideal — as many today say, *abstract* — objects are a controversial lot. By hypothesis or definition, they do not exist in time or space. But how then are they related to *real* objects, which exist in time or space–time? How can ideal objects like properties or kinds be instantiated or realized or borne by real objects, since that realization relation must span the gap between real and ideal? How can ideal objects such as properties or numbers or sets play any role in causal relations in the real world? How can ideal meanings relate to real experiences, which carry meanings as contents? How can ideal meanings represent real objects, where the intentional relation of representation must reach from the realm of ideal meanings into the realm of real objects like trees or hilltops? And is it plausible that ideal objects exist in a Platonic heaven that is outside space, time, and nature? These are the problematic issues long posed for ideal objects, since their inception in Platonic philosophy.

The classical doctrines on universals (species, properties, and so on) run roughly as follows. *Platonic* (extreme) *realism* says that eidos are real or existent entities that do not exist in time or space–time, yet are instantiated in real, concrete objects (the eidos wisdom is instantiated in the concrete individual Socrates). *Aristotelian* (moderate) *realism* brings universals down to earth, saying that universals exist only insofar as they are instantiated in concrete particulars, whence they exist in time or space–time as "accidents" inherent in particulars (wisdom "inheres" in Socrates insofar as this particular instance of wisdom is "in" Socrates). *Nominalism* or, better, *particularism* holds that only concrete particulars exist, so a predicate such as "is wise" is a purely nominal affair (we truly say, "Socrates is wise," but there is only Socrates of whom the predicate holds though the predicate does not represent any additional entity). (Armstrong 1989 surveys the classical and contemporary positions, *sans* Husserl.)

Where does Husserl stand *vis-à-vis* the classical positions on universals?

In Investigation II of the *Logical Investigations*, Husserl assesses a variety of traditional issues about "ideal species," and in Investigation III he develops an ontology of parts and wholes that plays a role in his account of ideal objects and their instances in concrete objects. As far as I can see, Husserl's theory of ideal objects and their instances carries over intact into *Ideas* I, where the theory is used in Husserl's articulation of phenomenology. (See the account of noesis and noema addressed in Chapter 6 of this volume.) Here is a summary of Husserl's view, as I would reconstruct it.

Start with species (or properties or relations), that is, universals. Husserl's ontology of universals distinguishes three types of object (in the formal sense of object). Take a simple case: Socrates is a man. Husserl distinguishes: (1) the *ideal species* Man; (2) the *concrete individual* Socrates; and (3) the *concrete instance* of manhood in Socrates. The latter is what Husserl calls a "moment," or dependent part, of Socrates – in that sense it is "in" Socrates. Then: Socrates *instantiates* the species Man if and only if Socrates' manhood *is a moment of* ("in") Socrates, and that moment *is a concrete instance of* the species Man. In effect, Husserl borrows from Plato in positing ideal species and from Aristotle in positing concrete instances of species.

What is novel is the ontology of part that Husserl puts to use in a synthesis of Platonic and Aristotelian views. The particular instance of manhood, of Man, in Socrates is a concrete particular, an *individual*. But it is a *dependent* object, an individual dependent for its existence on the individual Socrates. Further, it is a dependent *part*, or *moment*, of Socrates. *This-manhood-in-Socrates* exists in time and space, as a part of Socrates, who exists in time and space. Presumably, Socrates' manhood exists when and where Socrates exists. By contrast, Socrates' left foot is an independent part, or "piece" of Socrates. If that foot were (gods forbid) cut off in an accident, the foot would exist apart from Socrates; and, whether attached or detached, the foot exists in a spatiotemporal expanse distinct from the spatiotemporal expanse occupied by the whole Socrates. In effect, Husserl's notion of moment is an extension of Aristotle's notion (in the *Categories*) of a particularized quality "in" an individual, but Husserl explicates the core notion within a detailed theory of part and whole.

The relation between the concrete individual Socrates and the ideal species Man is thus mediated by the particular instance of Man(hood) that exists spatiotemporally in Socrates, a moment of Socrates. We still find the ideal species Man instantiated by a concrete individual in space–time, albeit an individual that is a dependent part of Socrates. How does this more complex relation solve the ancient problem of crossing the ontological chasm between ideal and real objects? How does Husserl's theory avoid the problematic Platonism attacked ever since Aristotle? The answer, I propose, lies with Husserl's distinction between formal and material essence.

We must understand Husserl's ontology of ideal objects within the context of his formal ontology. *Objects* include any formal type of object whatever. Species, individuals, moments are all objects, but objects falling under different formal categories or subcategories: under Essence (Material Essence), Substrate, and Dependent Part, or Moment. The link between a concrete individual and an essence, I take it, is itself a *formal* link, just as the grammatical link of predication is a formal linguistic link ("Socrates *is* a man," reformulated in predicate logic as "Man (Socrates)" or "M(s)," on the model of the application of a function term to an argument term). Thus, this-manhood *is a moment of* Socrates, and this-manhood *is an instance of* Man(hood), and so Socrates *is a member of* the species Man. These three formal linkages bind objects of appropriate formal types – different types. Here are the grounds of a response to traditional worries about ideal objects, and Husserl gestures in this direction, with an air that he does not suffer gladly these fools who misunderstand his doctrine.

After laying out his ontology of formal and material essences in opening *Ideas* I, Husserl dismisses the critics who would charge him with a misbegotten "Platonic hypostasizing" of essences (§22).

If *object* and *real object* ("*Gegenstand*" and "*das Reales*") are distinguished, as in *Logical Investigations*, Husserl retorts, "if object is
defined as anything whatsoever, for example, as subject of a true
(categorical, affirmative) statement, then what offense can
remain?" In short, the objection to Husserl's doctrine of essence
as Platonic hypostasizing rests on a confusion of formal and material categories. To fill in the argument, we might say: if you object
to essences because they are ideal and so cannot be in space–time
and thereby tied into real objects, you have made a category
mistake. Real objects fall under the material essence or region
Nature. Essences (of whatever type) do not – that would be an
utterly confused claim, given Husserl's ontology. So, if you think
that an eidos must be in space–time if it is to be tied to a real
object, then you have missed the point of the categorial distinction between Fact and Essence. There is a link of instantiation
between the concrete individual Socrates, or his particular
manhood, and the ideal species Man, but that tie is not a
spatiotemporal relation, much less a causal relation. Indeed,
though we readily use the word "relation," we do not take this
Socrates–Manhood link to fall under the formal essence Relation.
In grammar we speak of the linking verb "is," the copula, and we
do not take it to stand for a *relation*, say, like being taller than or
being a teacher of. We say "Socrates is wise," where the copula is
said to be syncategorematic, that is, it does not stand for anything
(in any category), but merely links subject and predicate. (In the
syntax of predicate logic, the sentence is rendered as "W(s),"
where the predicate "W" is applied by parentheses to the name
"s" – with no suggestion that the parentheses represent anything
at all.) Similarly, we must see the ties between objects in different
categories, or between a "fact" and an essence, as a distinct formal
feature of life in a world structured by Husserlian categories.

MIND AND BODY AND CULTURE

Framing his conception of phenomenology, Husserl's ontology
has interesting implications for philosophy of mind. On many
issues, arguably, he was a good century ahead of his time.

The mind–body problem – how our conscious experience is related to our body and to the physical world in general – has been with us for millennia. Yet philosophy of mind, in the tradition of analytic philosophy, has been perhaps the most vigorous area of philosophical activity in recent decades. As 20th-century physics produced amazing empirical-mathematical results in relativity theory and quantum mechanics, revising Newtonian mechanics and electromagnetism theory, many philosophers stepped in to argue for a scientific *materialism* or *physicalism*, holding that the mind must somehow reduce to purely physical processes, like everything else in the known universe. In the 1920s and 1930s the logical positivists of the Vienna Circle promoted a vision of philosophy based in empirical science informed by the new logic, and in the 1950s materialism was pressed explicitly as analytic philosophy moved its focus from language to mind. By 1950, furthermore, the digital computer had arrived, and in the 1960s many scientists and philosophers came to see the computer as a mechanical mind, storing information in memory, drawing inferences, and even guiding the movements of a robot. *Functionalism* emerged as the dominant "naturalized" model of mind: as software is to hardware, so concepts and their logic are to neural architecture, or "wetware" – that is to say, mind simply consists in rule-governed processing of information, real-time computation running in a brain or even, some say, in a silicon-chip computer. By the 1980s, techniques of brain-imaging were demonstrating, graphically, the way mind is grounded in neural activity, showing which parts of the brain are at work during perception, memory, emotions, and so on. The new physicalism – armed with physics, computer science, and neuroscience – seemed to have a clear lock on our ultimate understanding of the mind. Yet by the late 1980s, many naturalistic philosophers were arguing that the functionalist-physicalist model does not adequately account for some of the most salient properties of mind: the "qualia," or subjective characters, of sensation; the intentionality of thought, involving meaning as well as the manipulation of purely syntactic symbols (the 1s and 0s of a digital computer); and the very character of consciousness, whereby we experience and are aware of our own mental states. How, then, can we give credence to the well-established results of contemporary science and yet accommodate the *phenomenological* characters of our own experience? This is the state of play in current philosophy of mind – to which Husserl's results can speak in an articulate way. (Summaries of the basic positions in philosophy of mind are expounded in Churchland 1988; Kim 2000; Searle 2004. Studies addressing phenomenology as well are Petitot *et al.* 1999; Smith and Thomasson 2005.)

There is another type of philosophical theory of "mind," growing out of the 19th century's concern with *Geist*, or "spirit," in the sense of *Zeitgeist* or the spirit of the times. This range of philosophical theory involves both subjective personal experience and objective historical, social activity. G.W.F.Hegel's *Phenomenology of Spirit* (*Phänomenologie des Geistes*, 1807/1977) brought these issues to the fore. By 1900 social theorists distinguished two kinds of "science": natural science, including physics, and cultural science, including social and political theory. (The German terms are "*Naturwissenschaft*" and "*Geisteswissenschaft*.") Like the philosophers of the Vienna Circle, Husserl saw Hegel's writing as the antithesis of "scientific" philosophy, though recent philosophers have been more sympathetic. In any event, in Husserl's day social theorists such as Wilhelm Dilthey held that social or cultural phenomena must be studied in a different way than physical phenomena: we understand language and other human activities by "*Verstehen*," or "understanding," as opposed to explanation by mathematical hypothesis. Husserl emphasized the role of *empathy* (*Einfühlung*) in understanding "others," and he took empathy as the key to our theory of culture or *Geist*. All these movements, from Hegel to Dilthey to Husserl, are at home in the tradition of continental philosophy, forming a background for later continental theorists from Martin Heidegger to Michel Foucault. Husserl's ontology has implications for this type of philosophy of mind as *Geist*. In the analytic tradition, meanwhile, theories of the relation of mind to social or cultural practices have been inspired often by the later work of Ludwig Wittgenstein, especially *Philosophical Investigations* (1953/2001), where Wittgenstein turns from logical theory to the "grammar" of ordinary language as shown in familiar "language games."

Still another approach to mind is that of *idealism*. There are very different types of idealism: George Berkeley's empiricist idealism, reducing bodies to sensory ideas in minds; Kant's transcendental idealism, appraising the ways in which things-as-they-appear are shaped by the mind's sensory and conceptual faculties; Hegel's social idealism, interpreting Mind's historical progression to self-realization. We return to issues of idealism and Husserl's "transcendental idealism" later in this chapter.

How exactly does Husserl's *ontology* frame the issues of mind, body, and culture? We have already laid the groundwork in mapping the architecture of his novel system of categories. We have explored his formal categories, with an eye to their role in logic or formal semantics. Here we turn to Husserl's conception of the material categories or regions of Nature, Consciousness, and Culture (*Geist*).

In Husserl's intricate ontology of essences we find a system of distinctions among different *types* of essence, governed by "laws of essence" that assay which properties an object may or must have if it falls under a given essence. Here is where Husserl's account of the three regions takes hold. Let us consider, succinctly, a Husserlian sketch of the three regions (drawing on basics in *Ideas* I and *Ideas* II):

1   Things under the essence *Nature* have properties including spatiotemoral location, material composition (as from electrons, protons, and so on), and causal relations. We are to appreciate these types of properties and their roles in the essence of material things. The various essences of objects in Nature we study in the *natural sciences* of physics, chemistry, biology, astronomy, and so on. Somewhat idiosyncratically, Husserl groups psychology with the natural sciences. His assumption is that (what he calls) psychology presupposes that psychic acts take place in a context of nature. Today we might consider "cognitive neuroscience" as a psychology tied into neurobiology, placing psycho-neural processes under Nature.

2   Experiences, acts of consciousness, fall under the essence
    Consciousness. Experiences have properties including the sensuous
    character of perception, featured in the "sensory data" (so-
    called "hyletic data") that are moments of perceptual
    experiences. Most important, our experiences are, in most
    instances, intentional, that is, directed toward objects of which
    we are thereby conscious. Moreover, all of our experiences are,
    by their regional essence, parts of a stream of consciousness, a
    stream with its distinctive form of unity, as one experience
    leads into another, generating a consciousness of the flow of
    time. We are to study acts of consciousness, just as we experi-
    ence them from the first-person point of view, in *phenomenology*.

3   Cultural objects and activities fall under the essence *Culture*
    (*Geist*, "Spirit"). We are all "persons." We are subject to moral
    obligations, such as truth-telling (*ceteris paribus*), helping
    others, and so on. We are members of social groups, ranging
    from our families to our ethnic sects to our political states.
    Our social activities include speaking with others, in our
    native tongue or in a learned foreign language, attending
    schools and earning degrees (such as a Ph.D.), acquiring citi-
    zenship, voting in elections, singing in choirs, obeying (or
    disobeying) traffic laws, competing with others in sports,
    exchanging ideas in the production of scientific or philosoph-
    ical theories, and much more. We are to study cultural objects
    and activities in the *cultural* or *social sciences*, in political science,
    economics, history, and so on.

What is most important, in Husserl's eyes, is to see how different
these properties are, the properties assayed in various theories
about (1) things in nature, (2) acts of consciousness, and (3)
cultural activities and their products. Objects of these three basic
types are so different in their properties, Husserl holds, that they
must fall under categorially distinct essences: thus, at the highest
level of generality, we find the regions Nature, Consciousness,
and Culture. Now, Husserl holds, objects in these different categories or regions must be studied in different ways. The methods
of the natural sciences include (very roughly) the techniques of

observation (from a third-person, "objective" standpoint), hypothesis formation and confirmation, and ultimately mathematical theory construction – producing, say, Newton's laws of motion or Einstein's general theory of relativity. By contrast, the methods of the cultural sciences include (in a gloss) observation and analysis of social structure and dynamics, especially the "well-observed" characterizations of our fellows in our home culture. The techniques of literary and aesthetic interpretation, or "hermeneutics," take their place here as well, as in today's studies in cultural criticism or humanistic "critical theory." By contrast, new methods of phenomenology are required in order properly to study our own conscious experiences, seeking their proper essence, including the structure of intentionality. In Chapters 5 and 6 we explore Husserl's proposals for the characterization and methodology of phenomenology.

Husserl vehemently resisted programs of reduction that he called "naturalism" and "historicism." His most sustained critique along these lines is the essay "Philosophy as Strict Science" (1911), which paves the way for his presentation of "transcendental" phenomenology in Ideas I (1913). In Husserl's view, naturalism seeks to reduce the essence of consciousness (and, for that matter, culture) to the essence of natural processes. If we do this, he holds, we simply lose the crucial properties of consciousness as such, notably the structure of intentionality, featuring the role of ideal meaning in directing consciousness toward its objects. Equally misguided, Husserl thinks, is historicism, which he understands as the program to reduce the essence of subjective experience to processes of human history. Such processes may include economic class struggle (in a Marxist analysis), mother–child dynamics including repression of childhood traumas (in a Freudian psychoanalysis), colonialist ideological exploitation (in a recent model), or a long-range historical teleology where Absolute Spirit achieves self-reflection at a certain point in European history (on a Hegelian model). Pure or transcendental phenomenology would avoid reduction in either a naturalist or a historicist direction. Husserl's transcendentalism, we might say, registers his rejection of the popular programs of either naturalism or historicism. However, the "ism" does not follow "transcendental" in Husserl's usage. (We would not want to echo the idiom of 19th-century American "transcendentalism," as Emerson, Thoreau, and Whitman sought a unity of consciousness with nature.)

Phenomenology is "pure" insofar as it studies experiences while considering only their properties that fall under the essence Consciousness, excluding consideration of their properties that fall under either the essence Nature or the essence Culture. Husserl's method of "bracketing" the natural world (and also the cultural world) is designed precisely to focus on those features of an experience that define it as consciousness, abstracting away from its features that define its place in nature or in culture. In Chapter 6 we delve into Husserl's technique of bracketing, or epoché. What makes phenomenology "transcendental," for Husserl, is its focus on what makes consciousness a consciousness *of* this or that object, especially the structure of ideal meaning or noema that presents that object *as* such-and-such.

We can now specify, in categorial terms, the relation between mind and body – and culture. In *Ideas* I (1913, §33ff.) Husserl explicitly holds that *the same object*, "I," has *diverse properties* falling under the essences Nature and Consciousness: properties that define me as a subject of consciousness, and properties that define me as a natural organism, a "body" in space–time with a complex composition of organs, molecules, and subatomic particles. In *Ideas* II (1912, throughout), we also find that the same object, "I," has properties falling under Culture, properties that define *me* as a person, a moral subject, and a social being. These themes are further appraised in the *Crisis* (1935–8), in connection with the structure of the "life-world." I am thus a perceiving-thinking-willing subject in consciousness, an embodied physical organism in nature, and a socially situated person in culture. As the *Crisis* further emphasized, in the everyday "life-world" I am all these things at once, an embodied, encultured, experiencing being.

Similarly, *the same event*, a psychic event I live through (say) as perception or volitional action, has diverse properties falling under Consciousness, Nature, and Culture. Qua act of consciousness, this event is subjectively experienced by me, is part of my stream of consciousness, is intentionally directed in a certain way, and so forth. Qua event in nature, this event is produced by neural activities in my brain in my human organism in a pattern of causal interactions with other natural processes. And qua event in culture, this event is (say) my seeing my university colleague or my act of speaking English to a friend.

In Husserl's ontology, then, the *entities* philosophy has distinguished as my mind, my body, and my cultural persona are not "substances" in the Aristotelian sense. Rather, they are importantly different aspects of one such "substance" called "I." In Husserl's ontology, these aspects are *moments* (dependent parts) of the individual or "substrate" that is me. These moments are *instances* of distinct *essences* falling under the distinct *regions* Nature, Consciousness, and Culture. Importantly, there are relations of *dependence* among such moments – that is how Husserl's doctrine of moments works. Thus, my moment of thinking about Husserl as I write this sentence is dependent – "supervenient" in today's idiom – on my moment of neural activity transpiring in a certain part of my brain. That same moment of thinking is, in a very different way, dependent on my having acquired a certain linguistic mastery over the language of Husserlian philosophy. This ontology of mind, body, and culture addresses issues of "mind" under vigorous discussion today – issues of the supervenience of mind on brain, the relative priority of mind over language (or vice versa), and much more. By distinguishing the formal and material essences that we have considered, Husserl's ontology allows a detailed and nuanced approach to the relations among minds, bodies, and cultures.

TRANSCENDENTAL IDEALISM

In the *Logical Investigations* (1900–1), influenced by Brentano and Bolzano, Husserl took the stance of a broadly Aristotelian *realism*: the world around us exists independently of us, things have their species and properties, and through perception and judgment we come to know the essence of things in the world. In his 1907 lectures published posthumously as *The Idea of Phenomenology* (1950/1970), it is commonly said, Husserl took a "transcendental turn," a turn toward *transcendental* philosophy, wherein we seek, in a broadly Kantian vein, the conditions of the possibility of our knowledge of the world, finding those conditions partly in the workings of our own mind. Then in *Ideas* I (1913) Husserl presented phenomenology in its mature form as "transcendental phenomenology," a discipline that is to study the essence of intentionality, or *"consciousness-of,"* and therewith the "constitution of objectivities of consciousness" (§86). Husserl did not there use the term "idealism," or the Kantian idiom "transcendental idealism." Yet his readers saw affinities with neo-Kantian doctrines of the day in German philosophy, and Husserl's assistants included in the index the entry "Idealism, phenomenological." By the time of the *Cartesian Meditations* (drafted in 1929), Husserl himself spoke of "the transcendental turn" (which he says Descartes failed to take), and he spoke of phenomenology as "a transcendental idealism" – partaking in the parlance of German philosophy with its reverence for Kant. But in a 1934 letter he wrote, "No ordinary 'realist' has ever been as realistic and concrete as I, the phenomenological 'idealist' (a word which by the way I no longer use)" (letter to Abbé Baudin, quoted in Føllesdal 1998). Evidently Husserl never found a name he liked for his position. At any rate, Husserl scholars have employed the term "transcendental idealism" for the stance of transcendental phenomenology in *Ideas* I and later works. Some say Husserl there abandoned the realism of the *Investigations* and leapt into a new form of idealism. Among his students and interpreters, realists think Husserl lost his mind to idealism, while Kantians think he came to his senses with a new form of transcendental idealism.

But what exactly was Husserl's position? The question "Realism or idealism or what?" is perhaps the thorniest branch of interpretation in Husserl scholarship. Most scholars read the early Husserl as a realist; some read the later Husserl as some type of idealist, while others argue for a continuing realism. Husserl generally expands rather than changes his views, consistently using previously established terms and formulations as his philosophical system continuously expands over the decades – quite in the spirit of a mathematician. (See Mohanty 1995 on the continuity in

Husserl's corpus.) The trick is how to understand those passages, most articulate in *Ideas* I (§§49ff.), where Husserl sounds like he is tending toward a new form of idealism. I shall describe a series of possible interpretations, indicating the views I myself find most fitting, and most interesting in their own right.

Realism with intentionality

Most of Husserl's corpus either espouses or assumes a basic realism: there are various types of objects in the world, bearing different types of essences, and there are various types of experiences in the world, in which we are conscious of objects of appropriate type through ideal meanings that represent such objects. Here is a doctrine of ontological realism joined with a semantic theory of intentionality, all fitting nicely with Husserl's categorial ontology already mapped out. (See Smith and McIntyre 1982; B. Smith 1982; Willard 1984; Drummond 1990; D. W. Smith 1995.)

Classical idealism

In the 18th century the British empiricist George Berkeley argued that material objects exist only in the mind. "To be is to be perceived," he wrote, "or to perceive": this tree exists only insofar as it is perceived, if not by a mind like me (or mine) here and now, then by God. Indeed, Berkeley argued, this tree, properly assayed, is nothing but a bundle of ideas in my mind, or in another mind. As an empiricist, Berkeley took the basic ideas (token ideas, not types of ideas) to be sensations of color, shape, and so on, from which other ideas, as that of the tree, are constructed. Now, Husserl adamantly insisted that his position was no subjective, Berkeleyan idealism (§55), and anyone who thought so had utterly failed to understand his transcendental phenomenology. Surely his differences from Berkeley support Husserl as he sharply distinguishes act, ideal content, and object of consciousness, and as he sharply separates essences under Nature and Consciousness: physical objects such as trees clearly do not reduce to "ideas," either sensory experiences or ideal concepts of trees. (Bell 1990 holds that Husserl embraced realism in his early works and moved into idealism in his later works. Philipse 1995 argues that Husserl is committed to a transcendental idealism that is ultimately Berkeleyan. A. D. Smith 2003 finds a distinctly classical form of idealism in Husserl's *Cartesian Meditations*.

Noematic idealism

As Husserl's account of intentionality develops in *Ideas* I, we find his mature conception of ideal intentional content, called noema or noematic sense. The "constitution" of a particular object is unfolded in a system of noemata, presenting the same object from different perspectives, with different properties, in different relationships, in different possible states of affairs, and so on. Thus, in Husserl's theory of noema and horizon (see Chapter 6 in this volume), to every possible object there corresponds a system of noematic senses that present the object in various ways. From the phenomenological standpoint, that is all we can say about the object in itself. Thus, on one interpretation, Husserl held that every object reduces – in "phenomenological reduction" – to a system of noemata. Call this doctrine *noematic idealism*. The "ideas" to which objects reduce are not concrete sensory experiences *à la* Berkeley, but rather ideal meanings *à la* Husserl, namely, noemata. Since the noema in an act of consciousness is characterized as "the object *as* perceived, or judged, or wished," noemata are an ideal form of what Kant called *phenomena*, or things-as-they-appear. Here, then, we find Husserl updating Kant by importing ideal meanings into a new form of neo-Kantian "transcendental idealism." (Gurwitsch 1964 develops just such a view, which he took as kindred to Husserl's phenomenology, and other Husserl interpreters similarly stress the notion of noemata as objects-as-intended.) The problem with this interpretation, however, is that Husserl says objects and their corresponding noemata are distinct in kind: the tree itself ("simpliciter") can burn away, but a noematic sense that correlates with the tree cannot burn at all, since a sense is not composed of matter and is not "real," or spatiotemporal (see *Ideas* I, §89). In

Chapter 6, we shall dig into the complexities of Husserl's account of the relation between noema and object.

Space–time idealism

Kant's doctrine of transcendental idealism, in the *Critique of Pure Reason* (1781/1787), holds that space and time are not properties of things in themselves, but rather forms of human intuition of space and time. What we know as spatiotemporal, physical objects, then, are defined by the forms of our own perceptual experience, and in that sense they are "transcendentally ideal" (but "empirically real" because perceived as in space–time). Now, Husserl was concerned with the mathematics of space and time, looking to the non-Euclidean geometries of his day. Husserl might have allowed, then, that things in nature are determined by (say) a Riemannian geometry describing a curved space–time, even though our everyday perceptions present things in a Euclidean geometry. When I see a tree, the-tree-as-perceived has – the tree is perceived *as* having – spatial properties that follow a Euclidean geometry. But the tree itself has spatial properties that follow instead a Riemannian geometry. So Husserl might hold that a tree exists and has its essence independently of my consciousness (contra Berkeley), but the *way* it appears in my everyday perception depends on my consciousness (*à la* Kant) – that is, the-tree-as-perceived depends on the form of my perceptual consciousness. In this model, the "space" of things *as* perceived is "transcendentally ideal." Furthermore, following out the argument in the *Crisis*, Husserl might say that our "mathematization" of nature in physics produces an idealization of space – say, a Riemannian physical geometry – that abstracts away from spatial things themselves, with which we are in touch in everyday life. Then the geometry of things in nature *as* judged in our mathematical physics is also "transcendentally ideal." From the details of Husserl's complex analyses, we might carve out such a quasi-Kantian idealism of space and time. (Compare Friedman 2001, including a revision of Kantian principles along these lines, and Ryckman 2005 on Weyl's partly

Husserlian conception of space–time in Einsteinian relativity theory.) But notice that the resulting Husserlian position on space–time would not be an idealism proper, according to which the world in general is reduced to ideas or to intentional contents. Moreover, Husserl resisted the Kantian idea of a *Ding an sich*, or thing in itself, beyond the reach of the intentional relation of cognition.

Intentional perspectivism

Husserl's ontology is robustly realist in positing objects of many types and essences of many types that are neither "in the mind" (composed of mental contents) nor dependent on mental activities for their existence. Such is the ontology outlined in the first chapter of *Ideas* I, regrouping results from *Logical Investigations*. Following on this ontology, as *Ideas* I unfolds, is a detailed analysis of intentionality. Every act of consciousness is directed via its ideal intentional content, or noema, toward an appropriate object in the world, if such an object exists. Some objects in the world around us are dependent on our intentional activities: the script unfolding on my computer screen as I now write is an artifact produced by my activity of composing this sentence; and the words I choose from the English language are themselves artifacts of complex human activity over several centuries. Other objects in the world around us are completely independent of our intentional activities, so far as we know: the formation of the tectonic plates on planet Earth do not owe their existence or their geologic essence to my thoughts about them, or to the scientific researches that discovered them. Now, regardless of the existence or essence of an object of a given type, and regardless of its dependence or independence, I cannot think of such an object or perceive it or otherwise "intend" it unless my experience has an appropriate meaning that semantically represents that object. This is how Husserl's basic theory of intentionality works. On one interpretation, then, the core doctrine in Husserl's transcendental idealism is this principle that intentionality is always directed *via an ideal, "transcendental" meaning*. In this way my intention of any object is dependent on the ideal content in my experience; if you will, consciousness of any object in the world essentially involves a specific *intentional perspective* on that object – whatever the ontological status of the object intended. It is tautological, on Husserl's theory, that consciousness is directed perspectivally. This perspectivism is arguably resonant with a broadly Kantian transcendental idealism, but there is no implication of an idealism that reduces spatiotemporal objects to their appearance in consciousness, or declares their spatiotemporality dependent on perceptual consciousness. So this perspectivism remains realist, amplifying the position of realism-with-intentionality. (See Smith and McIntyre 1982 and D. W. Smith 1995 on this perspectivist interpretation. Compare Føllesdal 1998, characterizing Husserl's position as an "idealism" of a new type – I prefer the term "perspectivism" – according to which our experience presents an independently existing, intersubjective world "constituted" in a concatenation of forms of consciousness or noemata. A perspectivist position of "internal realism" is defended, with nods to Husserl and Kant, in Putnam 1981, 1987.)

Universal experienceability

Husserl holds a related doctrine that carries his ontology a step further than the previous perspectivism. In *Ideas* I, Husserl says that every object is *experienceable* (*erfahrbar*) and so is never such that "consciousness and consciousness's I has nothing to do with it" (§47). That is, every object of whatever type is a possible object of consciousness, and indeed can in principle be experienced with evidence. Husserl returns to this point near the end of *Ideas* I: "In principle . . . there corresponds to *every 'truly existing' object the idea of a possible consciousness* in which the object is itself graspable *originally* [= intuitively] and thereby *completely adequately*" (§142, my translation). By "idea" (*Idee*) Husserl means a regulative ideal of reason (a Kantian notion), and he is discussing the equivalence of the ideal "truly existing object" and the ideal "[object] to be rationally posited." He soon turns to formal ontology (§§148ff.), so we see that the point here is that, according to *formal ontology*, every object in principle corresponds to a range of possible intentions and indeed cognitions of that same object (the same object "X" [§§131, 142). The quoted principle is an extension of Husserl's theory of horizon (§47). If an act of consciousness presents an object with certain properties, there is associated with the act a *horizon* of further possible acts presenting the same object (X) with other properties (details follow in Chapter 6). By extension, any object is potentially the object of a variety of possible acts of consciousness, indeed intuitive cognitions – that is, for a proper subject (not a frog, perhaps not a human either). Within such limits, every object is *potentially* experienceable, or knowable. Call this doctrine *universal experienceability*. (This doctrine is shared, in somewhat different forms, by many of Husserl's interpreters, such as Gurwitsch 1964; Føllesdal 1969/1982; Smith and McIntyre 1982; Drummond 1990.)

We may see this principle emerging from Husserl's high-level category scheme. To be an object of any type is to be situated in the formal or "logical" space of essences, that is, falling under essences of appropriate types. And the property of being so situated is part of the formal essence Object. But among the material essences is the region Consciousness. So every object of whatever type is formally situated in a "logical" space in relation to possible acts under the region Consciousness. Thus, part of the *essence* of any object, wherever it falls in the category scheme, is its formal relation to possible acts under the region Consciousness, including our own actual judgments as we put forth the category scheme itself. Moreover, Husserl holds, part of the essence of any object is its relation to possible "intuitions," that is, experiences with evidence appropriate to that object. This principle sounds like a generalization of the verificationist program, familiar in Viennese philosophy, holding that we can meaningfully talk about an object only if we could in principle gather perceptual evidence about it.

Dependence idealism

If Husserl turned toward a full-on idealism, the position to consider, given his system of categories, would feature dependence. There would be a theory about dependence relations between objects in the three regions of Consciousness, Nature, and Culture. Further, it might be held, no object in Nature or Culture can exist unless it stands in such relations to possible acts of consciousness, that is, every object in Nature or Culture depends on possible acts of consciousness. If Husserl held such a view, we might call it *dependence idealism*, set within his categorial ontology. But Husserl speaks of the "relative" rather than "dependent" status of natural objects, as we observe shortly.

Transcendental relativity

In 1915 Albert Einstein proposed the general theory of relativity, positing a non-Euclidean space–time where gravity is a geometric feature of the curvature of space–time. Working on the mathematics of relativity, Einstein consulted the mathematicians David Hilbert and Hermann Weyl. Hilbert was Husserl's colleague and friend at Göttingen, and Weyl was inspired by Husserl's phenomenology. Weyl's mathematical formulation of relativity theory was shaped explicitly by his conception of transcendental phenomenology. Here we find an interesting variant on transcendental idealism, motivated not by Kantian a priori considerations, nor by purely phenomenological considerations, but by empirical physics in a mathematical formulation informed by transcendental phenomenology. (See Ryckman 2005 for a detailed analysis of the relations between Einstein, Weyl, Hilbert, and Husserl, and a reconstruction of relativity theory within transcendental idealism.) If we read Husserl in the light of relativity theory, we might propose a distinctive form of ontology – call it *transcendental relativity theory* (as opposed to transcendental idealism). The central claim would be that there is a distinctive ontological relation between things in space–time and potential acts of consciousness. This relation is not a relation of dependence where consciousness brings things into being in space–time, but rather a contextual relationship (if I may put it so). Things in space–time exist together with temporal acts of consciousness, essentially linked in the formal or mathematical structure of the world. It is not our thinking that makes things so, that is, makes them situated in space–time and moving in gravitational grooves of space–time. Rather, consciousness is itself formally – Husserl might say "logically" – situated in such a world along with spatiotemporal, physical objects. There are not only *intentional relations* between consciousness and physical objects, and *causal relations* on occasion. There are also *contextual relations* between acts of consciousness and physical objects insofar as both types of object are situated in the formal space defined by the variety of essences Husserl distinguishes. Thus, every act of consciousness has the regional essence Consciousness, and so the essential structure of intentionality (as defined by phenomenology); while every physical object has the regional essence Nature, and so the essential structure of spatiotemporality (as defined by general relativity theory). Moreover, every physical object is "relative" to consciousness insofar as it is available for intentional relations to that object (this sounds broadly Kantian), while every experience is "relative" to space–time insofar as it is available for spatiotemporal relations to (say) appropriate neural events (this sounds broadly physicalist). Call this doctrine of formal ontology the *transcendental relativity of* objects in space–time. Physical objects are not "transcendentally ideal," their spatiotemporality dependent on perceptual consciousness. Rather, they are *transcendentally relative*, that is, their being in the world is defined in a formal relation to acts of consciousness bearing meanings that represent them. Such a view is an instructive extension of Husserl's texts.

With these interpretive possibilities in mind, let us look at Husserl's exact phrasing in *Ideas* I. In the chapter titled "The Region of Pure Consciousness" (§§47–55) we find:

> *Thus no real* [i.e. spatiotemporal, physical] *being is necessary for the being of consciousness itself* (in the widest sense of the stream of experience).

> *Immanent being* [i.e. the being of consciousness] *is thus without doubt absolute being in the sense that in principle nulla "re" indiget ead existendum* [it needs no "real being" to exist].

> On the other hand, the world of transcendent "res" [real beings]
> is throughout referred to [angewiesen] consciousness, and
> indeed not to a logically thought but to an actual [consciousness].
>
> (Ideas I, §49, my translation)

Accordingly, consciousness must be considered "in purity" as "a context of being [Seinszusammenhang] closed unto itself," as a "context of absolute being," whereas "the whole spatiotemporal world . . . is according to its sense merely intentional being, thus a being that has the merely secondary, relative sense of a being for a consciousness" (§49, my translation). What could be clearer? The being of consciousness is absolute, while the being of spatiotemporal, physical things is relative to consciousness! Here is a neo-Berkeleyan idealism! Yet Husserl concludes the chapter (in §55) with just the opposite claim. He says, "All real [spatiotemporal] unities are unities of sense," through the "sense-giving" of consciousness – which sounds like the good Bishop Berkeley updated. And then Husserl declares: "If anyone seeing our discussion objects that this means changing all the world into subjective illusion and throwing ourselves into the arms of a 'Berkeleyan idealism,' to this we can only reply that the sense of this discussion has not been grasped" (my translation).

Husserl is right. The line of argument in the chapter is quite different from a march into the arms of idealism. We need to bear in mind Husserl's doctrine of essence, including regions and categories, and we need to observe how he moves into the methodology of phenomenology in this chapter, concluding that "pure consciousness" is the proper field of the emerging discipline of phenomenology.

The chapter begins (§47) with the correlation of nature with consciousness: to every physical thing there correspond "manifolds of appearances" in perceptual consciousness and thus a horizon of possible perceptual experiences of that object, presenting it from different sides, in various lighting, and so on. A thing is a "thing of the surrounding world [Umwelt]," the world around it and around me, around us. (Compare §27 on the Umwelt, later called the Lebenswelt, or life-world.) Strikingly, Husserl says, "It lies in the essence that whatever is realiter [i.e. in space–time]" can "come to givenness," that is, can be experienced perceptually. That is, the essence of any physical thing entails that it can be experienced in a variety of "motivated" ways, generating a horizon of possible experiences correlated with the object. In this way the being of a physical object is *relative* to consciousness. My perception of a tree does not bring it into existence; nor does the tree itself reduce to subjective appearances in my experience. The tree is what it is, under the region Nature, not under the region Consciousness. But it stands in a relation of correspondence to a horizon of possible experiences under the region Consciousness.

Turning from physical things to acts of consciousness, Husserl argues (§49) that the *essence* of consciousness does not involve "real," spatiotemporal objects. Review the quotations just above, noting that necessities follow laws of essence. The essence of consciousness is, centrally, its being intentional, a consciousness-of- something (§§34–6). This property in itself does not require that an act of consciousness be a spatiotemporal event – even though in the "natural attitude" we recognize that my experiences occur in my human body (§§27ff.) and depend on the proper functioning of my brain. Nor does the essence of consciousness require that I am conscious of spatiotemporal things around me – even though, in the normal course of human experience in nature, I constantly see, hear, touch physical things around me in space–time. In the stream of experiences I typically enjoy, physical objects appear to me in a variety of "adumbrations" of shape, color, and so on. This structure of my consciousness is a feature of my normal range of experience in confronting things in nature. That structure is a contingent feature of my natural existence, but not an essential feature of consciousness per se, a necessary feature of every consciousness-of-something. In that respect, the being of consciousness is "absolute," that is, not relative to spatiotemporal reality, or indeed to anything else. (See §49 on normal connections of perceptual experience.)

Returning to the being of spatiotemporal, physical things (§55, as quoted), Husserl holds that the *sense* – not the essence, but the sense – of a physical thing entails that it is "for" consciousness, that its being is "relative" to consciousness, whose being is by contrast "absolute," not relative to anything else. But here Husserl has turned from the ontology of nature to the phenomenology of our perceptions of things in nature. The "annihilation of the world" that leaves a "residuum" of "pure" or "absolute" consciousness (§49) is not, as the phrasing may suggest, an ontological claim that the spatiotemporal world has been denied true existence. Rather, this dramatic phrase is an evocation of the methodology of epoché: we turn our attention from things in nature to our experiences of them, and to other types of experience. We do not deny the existence of physical objects; we do not reduce them ontologically to experiences or contents, but rather we analyze the unities of sense that correspond to them.

In Husserl's considered ontology, then, we find several of the principles we have already discussed: realism about the external world, coupled with intentional consciousness of things in space–time; intentional perspectivism, where all objects, including physical things, are experienced or "intended" through appropriate contents or senses; universal experienceability in principle; dependence on consciousness for some objects (artifacts), but not all (not all physical things); dependence of some aspects of spatiotemporal reality on the structure of our normal perceptions, namely, the way space and time appear in our experience, but not the form of space–time itself, that is, if our best physics is correct. However, we do not find, in Husserlian ontology, either classical idealism or wholesale dependence on consciousness.

Consider the formal ontological space defined by Husserl's scheme of categories or object types. Every object takes its place in this scheme of the world around us. We know that our own experiences take their place, under the region Consciousness. We know that physical things around us take their place, under the region Nature. We know that cultural objects (from pencils to governments) take their place, under the region Culture. We know that all objects are governed by formal essences including Individual, Property, State of Affairs, Number, and so on. What we learn from Husserl's discussions about the relations between objects in nature and acts of consciousness is that there are certain relations between natural objects and experiences. These relations – or "correlations" – should be seen as their own kind of formal relations; if you will, metacategorial relations. It is the status of these formal relations that make the mind–body problem so hard, and "transcendental idealism" so difficult to understand.

What of transcendental relativity? If Einstein's general theory of relativity is sustained, and if Husserl's categorial ontology is sustained, we may see physical relativity theory as an application in Nature of an ontological form we find in Consciousness cum Nature. (Think, as Husserl did, of pure geometry applied to things in nature.) All objects take their place in the formal structure of the world, and so objects are contextually related to objects in different regions, under different essences. Accordingly, consciousness and space–time are related in the formal context of the world, the *Umwelt*. Our task is to keep straight just where objects are in that structure, from physical things to intentional experiences to social interactions – including our collective theoretical discursions into these matters.

THE LIFE-WORLD, EVERYDAY ACTION, AND SOCIAL STRUCTURES

In *Ideas* I (1913), Husserl began his trek into pure phenomenology by observing the character of the *Umwelt*, the world around us, "the world of everyday life" (§27). In *Ideas* II (1912, drafted along with *Ideas* I), he expanded on the human body and its role in everyday actions, and on the social character of many things around us. These themes gained a sharp focus in the structure of the *Lebenswelt*, or life-world, as detailed in the *Crisis* (1935–8). These phenomena are richly discussed within the context of phenomenology: we experience physical objects around us not as purely spatiotemporal and material in composition, but as objects in the street or garden or kitchen, objects we deal with in practical and social activities like dining together or playing basketball together. Moreover, each of us experiences his or her own body not as a physical system of bones, organs, and organic chemistry, but as "my body." Husserl uses two words to distinguish these aspects of one's body (in *Ideas* II and in *Crisis*). My *physical body*, my body as physical object, he calls *Körper* (from the Latin "*corps*," from which English derives "corpse"); my *living body*, my body as I know and use it in everyday life, he calls *Leib* (the everyday German word, derived from "*leben*," the verb "to live"). Through *empathy* (*Einfühlung*), Husserl stresses, we experience "other I's," fellow subjects, fellow human beings, who act through their living bodies and join with us in social activities and institutions.

Now, drawing on Husserl's categorial ontology, we can construct an account of the *ontological structure* of objects, persons, actions, and institutions in the life-world, a structure coordinate with the phenomenological structure of meanings through which we experience such phenomena as in the life-world. The groundwork we have already laid.

"I" am a human being, living and acting and interacting with others, in the life-world. This being is a whole with various types of parts. Of course, I have arms, legs, head, and liver, "pieces" (independent parts) of my physical body. On Husserl's ontology, though, I have certain defining aspects or "moments" (dependent parts) that fall under the *distinct regions* Consciousness, Nature, and Culture. As a *subject* of intentional experience, I think, perceive, will, and so on, according to the essence Consciousness. As a *physical body*, I have a certain mass and height, electrochemical activity coursing through my brain, and so on, according to the essence Nature. And, as a *person* among "others," I interact socially with others in my community, subject to moral and legal principles, according to the essence Culture. These aspects – intentional, physical, and social – are united as *moments* of the individual I am. And these moments are bound together by *dependencies*, as my current thoughts depend on neural processes in my brain and on social forces in my cultural niche.

Generally, within the world around us, the life-world, there are relations among various types of objects in the world, relations that link objects under different regions. *Actions* in particular involve relations among objects under different regions. When I climb the stairs, or write with a pencil or hit a tennis ball with a tennis racket, my action is a complex whole with parts that include my volition or willing, my physical body's moving in response to my willing, and the effects of that movement on the stairs or the pencil or the racket's striking the ball. My volition is an event with a moment of intentionality, under the essence Consciousness. By contrast, my physical body is an object that moves in space–time, under the essence Nature. My living body, however, is a complex whole with moments including my volition and my physical body's movement. Within my living body there are dependencies: my body's movement is dependent on, caused by, my volition, while my volition is dependent on, "supervenient" on, neural events in my brain. Within the action there are also dependencies between my living body and nearby objects such as the stairs I climb, the pencil I write with, and the tennis ball I stroke with my racket. The essence Action, we might say, governs these dependencies as I "wield" my body in everyday actions such as climbing stairs, writing graphite marks with a pencil, or hitting tennis balls with my racket. All within the life-world.

The life-world is also a world of *social* or *cultural* activities. As a *professor*, I hold a position defined by the University of California – defined in a system of rules that are instituted by the State of California, but constrained by the Constitution of the United States of America. Thus, I am obligated to lecture and publish on philosophy, while I have freedom of speech, in what I say or write, within the limits of the Constitution. As *students* at the university, the people sitting before me as I lecture hold a position equally defined by the university. In our university work together, my students and I are all members of the university community; in this work, I lecture to students, they write essays for me to read, and so on. According to Husserlian ontology, these social activities fall under the essence Culture (*Geist*). My actions as I lecture fall under the essence Professorial Activities, while the actions of each student in the classroom fall under the essence Student Activities, all under the essence Culture. Now, these cultural activities of student and professor are themselves *actions*, complex wholes comprising *intentional* experiences of thinking and willing and *bodily* movements of speaking and writing and reading and their *social* effects on others in the lecture hall. My action of lecturing has moments falling under Consciousness and under Nature; my thinking and willing to speak fall under Consciousness, and my bodily movements (hands moving, lips and tongue moving, air flowing over them) fall under Nature, while my lecturing action, comprising these things and their social effects, falls under Culture. And, we know, there are *dependencies* among these things within the structure of my action. (Searle 1998 draws a contemporary account of similar structures, but grounds the whole system in naturalistic phenomena, arguing in effect that social reality depends on intentional states, which in turn depend on brains states, which depend on biochemistry and ultimately physics.)

The life-world, we conclude, is a complex whole comprising a wide variety of objects that fall variously under the regions Consciousness, Nature, and Culture, yet are connected by appropriate dependence relations – and other formal relations – between moments of these objects.

SUMMARY

Husserl developed a wide-ranging ontology that he integrated with his logic, his phenomenology, and his epistemology. A master of distinctions, Husserl crafted a system of ontological *categories* of importantly different types of object. Husserl's system of categories is underway in the *Logical Investigations* (1900–1) (as indicated in Chapter 3 of this volume). The system is refined and further organized in *Ideas* I (1913), where his ontology is used in his presentation of phenomenology.

Husserl distinguishes *essences* from concrete objects in time or space–time. Essences are ideal, nonspatiotemporal entities: species, properties, and relations – what Aristotle called universals – which may be instantiated in particulars. What is novel with Husserl, however, is his distinction between formal and material essences. *Formal essences* are ontological forms that correlate with logical forms: Individual, Property, State of Affairs, Number, and so on. Formal essences apply to objects with *material essences*, that is, essences that characterize substantive or material "regions of being," of which Husserl recognizes three: Nature, Consciousness, and Culture (*Geist*). The material essences of things in nature concern the structure of time, space, material composition, and causality; the material essences of acts of consciousness concern the structure of lived experience, especially intentionality; the material essences of cultural objects and institutions concern social activities of persons in communities. Clearly, the material essences of objects in these three regions are fundamentally different, yet the same formal essences apply to objects in these three material regions.

Husserl recognizes different types of ideal, nonspatiotemporal entities, including not only essences, but also numbers (and other mathematical entities) and meanings or senses. Like mathematics, logic and phenomenology also deal with ideal entities, for Husserl. Arithmetic studies numbers, in abstraction from their relation to groups of concrete objects (such as five crows on a tree limb). Logic studies propositions and their constituent concepts, in abstraction from their being thought in concrete acts of reasoning. And phenomenology studies experiences and their contents or "noemata," in abstraction, Husserl holds, from their being realized in concrete "psychological" acts in organisms in nature. Still, for Husserl ideal entities are instantiated in appropriate ways in concrete objects in the world.

Husserl emphasizes the ontology of *parts* and *wholes*. A distinction he often uses is that between independent parts, or *pieces*, and dependent parts, or *moments*. A piece of an object (say, a spoke in a bicycle wheel) can exist independently of the object, whereas a moment of an object (say, this particular instance of red in this flower) cannot exist unless that object exists. In Husserl's ontology, it is "moments" that tie ideal entities into the concrete world. Thus, the ideal property Red is realized in this rose insofar as a particular instance of Red is a moment of the petals of the flower. And the ideal content or sense of an experience of thinking such-and-such is realized in my current consciousness insofar as that content is a moment of my current act of consciousness.

Recent philosophy of mind has been focused on the mind–body problem, the issue of how mental states – especially conscious experiences such as seeing red or thinking that Aristotle was synoptic – are related to bodily states, especially brain states. Husserl's categorial ontology leads to an interesting approach to the mind–body problem. For Husserl, the same concrete experience of seeing or thinking falls under different material essences or regions. This event falls under the region Nature and also under the region Consciousness. For the same concrete event includes a moment that realizes a type of brain state and also a moment that realizes a type of conscious intentional experience.

Husserl's mature "transcendental" phenomenology is allied with an ontology of "transcendental idealism." Just what this doctrine entails is debatable. But one account holds that every object in the world, of whatever category, stands in a variety of potential relations to consciousness, that is, intentional relations in which the object is "intended" in different ways, through different contents or senses that prescribe different properties in that object.

FURTHER READING

Armstrong, D. M. 1989. *Universals: An Opinionated Introduction*. Boulder, Colorado: Westview Press. An appraisal of the ontology of universals.

———. 1997. *A World of States of Affairs*. Cambridge and New York: Cambridge University Press. A contemporary study of the ontology of states of affairs, a crucial notion in Husserl and his contemporaries.

———. 1999. *The Mind–Body Problem: An Opinionated Introduction*. Boulder, Colorado: Westview Press. An appraisal of the ontological issues that arise in the mind–body problem.

Chalmers, David J. 2002. *Philosophy of Mind: Classical and Contemporary Readings*. Oxford and New York: Oxford University Press. Readings in the philosophy of mind, featuring traditional and contemporary approaches to the mind–body problem.

Mulligan, Kevin. 1990. "Husserl on States of Affairs in the Logical Investigations". Epistemologia, special number on Logica e Ontologia, XII, 207 234, (Proceedings of 1987 Genoa conference on Logic and Ontology).

———. 2004. "Essence and Modality. The Quintessence of Husserl's Theory". In M. Siebel and M. Textor, editors, Semantik und Ontologie. Beiträge zur philosophischen Forschung. Frankfurt: Ontos Verlag, 387-418. http://www.unige.ch/lettres/philo/enseignants/km/doc/EssenceModalityQuintessence.pdf

Ryckman, Thomas. 2005. *The Reign of Relativity: Philosophy in Physics 1915–1925*. Oxford and New York: Oxford University Press. A study of the development of general relativity theory. Includes relations to Husserlian transcendental phenomenology.

Smith, Barry, ed. 1982. *Parts and Moments: Studies in Logic and Formal Ontology*. Munich and Vienna: Philosophia Verlag. Essays on issues of formal ontology, often informed by studies of Husserl's *Logical Investigations*.

———. 1994. *Austrian Philosophy: The Legacy of Franz Brentano*. Chicago and LaSalle, Illinois: Open Court. Studies of several philosophers influenced by Brentano, including ontological issues. Indicates the intellectual milieu in which Husserl came of age.

Smith, David Woodruff. 1995. "Mind and Body." In Barry Smith and David Woodruff Smith, eds. *The Cambridge Companion to Husserl*. Cambridge and New York: Cambridge University Press. A study of Husserl's categorial ontology and its implications for philosophy of mind, assessing aspects of the mind–body problem and including an interpretation of Husserl's transcendental idealism.

———. 2002. "Intentionality and Picturing: Early Husserl vis-à-vis Early Wittgenstein." In Terry Horgan, John Tienson, and Matjaz Potrc, eds. *Origins: The Common Sources of the Analytic and Phenomenological Traditions* (proceedings of the Spindel Conference 2001). *Southern Journal of Philosophy*, vol. XL, supplement 2002; published by the Department of Philosophy, the University of Memphis. A fictional dialogue between Husserl and Wittgenstein, bringing out their respective ontologies of states of affairs.

———. 2004. *Mind World: Essays in Phenomenology and Ontology*. Cambridge and New York: Cambridge University Press. Essays addressing phenomenological and ontological issues and their interrelations. Includes studies of several systems of ontological categories, including comparisons between Husserl and other figures.

Thomasson, Amie L. 1998. *Fiction and Metaphysics*. Cambridge and New York: Cambridge University Press. A study of the ontology of fictional objects, developing ontological views partly based in Ingarden and Husserl, notably the ontology of dependence.

Five

Phenomenology I

The new science of conscious experience

Husserl set out to establish phenomenology as a new discipline in philosophy and in science generally: a science of consciousness, distinct from psychology, from epistemology, and from other traditional fields of science and philosophy. Despite a century of practice and theory, however, the discipline remains poorly understood in many circles. Accordingly, we shall begin with an elementary account of the discipline, featuring a basic definition of the field of study and rather simple examples of what phenomenological analysis may look like. We then trace the development of Husserl's conception of phenomenology out of Brentano's idea of descriptive psychology, which Husserl integrated with Bolzano's vision of pure logic. Then we proceed to outline Husserl's analyses of the most basic structures of consciousness, including intentionality (consciousness-of-something), time-consciousness, spatial consciousness, and consciousness of oneself and others. In Chapter 6 we delve into more technical details of theory and method in Husserlian phenomenology, considering links to logical theory, ontology, and "transcendental" philosophy. These technical developments amplify Husserl's basic conception of phenomenology and frame his basic phenomenological analyses within a metatheory that defines Husserl's systematic philosophy as outlined in Chapter 2.

WHAT IS PHENOMENOLOGY?

Phenomenology is the study of consciousness as experienced from the first-person point of view. By etymology, phenomenology is the study of phenomena, in the root meaning of appearances; or, better, the ways things appear to us in our experience, the ways we experience things in the world around us. We practice phenomenology (with or without the name) whenever we pause in reflection and ask, "What do I see?," "How do I feel?," "What am I thinking?," "What do I intend to do?," answering in the first person, specifying the way I experience what I see, feel, think, and so on. We produce a phenomenological description of an experience as we declare, attending to our own experience, "I see that fishing boat in the fog," "I feel angry about what was just said," "I think that Husserl read Hume," "I intend to sweep the patio tomorrow." Phenomenology thus characterizes a given form of consciousness from the person's own subjective, first-person perspective. By contrast, neuroscience studies how consciousness is produced in a person's brain, characterizing his neural-mental state from an objective, third-person perspective. Thus, where a brain scan (an fMRI image) shows which parts of the brain are most active (burning glucose), a phenomenological description characterizes what the person is experiencing ("I see a fishing boat" or "I feel a pain in my left foot").

In a suggestive idiom we may say phenomenology studies *what it is like* to have a given form of experience. However, we must guard against misunderstanding. In recent philosophy of mind it has been argued that a physical account of brain activity fails to capture what it is like to feel pain or to see red. Accordingly, contemporary cognitive scientists and philosophers of mind often think of phenomenology as focused primarily or exclusively on the subjective qualities, or "qualia," of purely sensory experiences such as seeing red. However, Husserl did not look to sensory experiences and their qualia as the paradigm targets of phenomenological analysis. Indeed, Husserl took our perceptual experiences to have a conceptual content or meaning that presents things around us with a much richer character than mere sensation. And he took phenomenology to be concerned with the meaningful structures of experience far beyond pure sensation, addressing perception, imagination, desire, thought, and so on, as we engage the world around us.

If phenomenology studies our various types of experience, is phenomenology not a form of psychology? As we shall see, Husserl did conceive phenomenology as a development of what his teacher Franz Brentano called descriptive as opposed to genetic psychology. However, Husserl ultimately insisted that phenomenology be sharply distinguished from the natural science of psychology. Meaning is central to phenomenology: meaning is the significant content of conscious experience, which we ascribe in saying "what" a person sees or thinks or wishes. It is meaning that distinguishes nearly all of our experiences, and it is meaning that renders experience a consciousness "of" anything at all. Only through meaning, Husserl held, does consciousness present us with a world, an organized structure of things around us, including ourselves. But meaning, in abstraction from our lived experience, falls within the domain of study in logic: "pure logic," as Husserl put it. That part of logic that studies meaning has come to be called "semantics" (though this term was not yet established in Husserl's day). So phenomenology must in effect synthesize logic and psychology.

In his middle years Husserl came to champion phenomenology as a new science, distinct from the sciences of nature and indeed of culture, the natural and social sciences (as we call them today). In an essay titled "Philosophy as Strict Science" ("*Philosophie als strenge Wissenschaft*," 1910–11), Husserl argued at length against "naturalizing" consciousness in psychology or in physics – or, he would have added today, in neuroscience. By contrast, phenomenology was to be a new type of science:

> With [phenomenological investigation] we meet a science of whose extraordinary extent our contemporaries have as yet no concept; a science, it is true, of consciousness that is still not psychology; a phenomenology of consciousness as opposed to a natural science about consciousness.
>
> (Husserl 1910–11/ 1965: 91)

Husserl characterized phenomenology as a "transcendental" rather than "naturalistic" science, needing (as we shall see) quite different

methods of inquiry. What carries phenomenology beyond all
natural science, including psychology, for Husserl, is the central
role of meaning in experience. The study of meaning, in logic and
in phenomenology, does not proceed by empirical observation
and generalization along the lines familiar in physics, chemistry,
and so on.

Husserl sought to develop phenomenology into a systematic
discipline, a strict science, with a well-defined domain of study
and an effective methodology. Sciences like physics, chemistry,
and biology follow what we call the scientific method, in systematically recording observations (observations any scientist can
repeat) and analyzing them within a growing body of theory
consisting in hypotheses confirmed by observations (often
making essential use of mathematics). Phenomenology is different
from these natural sciences, however, in that the objects of
study – conscious experiences – are appraised from the perspective of the experiencer, the first-person or subjective point of
view. Here the scientist is both the studier and the studied, the
subject and the object of investigation. In that way, unlike physics
and other sciences, phenomenology is a first-person study. But, of
course, we all know that other people also experience states of
consciousness. In phenomenology, accordingly, our interest is not
in any particular experiences, mine or yours, but in the very
forms and structures of conscious experience: objective forms that
are realized in subjective experiences, be they yours or mine. The
objective phenomenological form of an experience includes the
meaning or sense that represents the object of consciousness as
experienced (from the subject's first-person perspective).

In Husserl's own words, phenomenology is the science of the
essence of consciousness (*Ideas* I, §34). What, briefly, is the
essence of consciousness? First, every experience, or act of
consciousness, is conscious: the subject experiences it, or is aware
of performing it. (Some mental states are not conscious; they are
not the concern of phenomenology.) Second, every act of
consciousness is a consciousness of something: in perception I see
such-and-such, in imagination I imagine such-and-such, in judgment I judge that such-and-such is the case, and so on. This

property of consciousness, its being of or about something, Husserl called intentionality. Thus, we say an experience is intentional, or directed (literally, "aimed") toward some object. We also say a mental state or act represents some object (an individual, an event, a state of affairs, or whatever), and so intentionality consists in this representational character.

In everyday language we say an action is intentional if done on purpose, with an intention. However, in Husserl's technical idiom, intentionality covers not only the way an intention or volition is aimed at doing something, but also the way a perception or thought or desire is aimed at some object, the object of perception, thought, or desire. So intentionality in Husserl's technical sense (the directedness of consciousness) includes as a special case what we mean by intentionality in the everyday sense (an action's being done on purpose, with an explicit intention or volition). Accordingly, Husserl adapts the verb "intend" so that we say a person "intends" an object in an act of consciousness, be it an act of perception, thought, or volition. Alternatively, we say the act "intends" the object. (Husserl coins "*intendieren*" as a technical term, also using "*meinen*" as in "*to mind*" something.)

To be more precise, Husserl allows (correctly) that some experiences are not intentional. When I feel dizzy or nauseous or anxious, my sensation is not of or about anything. But most of our experiences have more structure than that. Most of our experiences take the form of a consciousness-of-something, and all of our experiences in normal human life take their place in a structured, temporal stream of consciousness (to use William James' apt phrase). In any case, Husserl reserves the term "act" for those states or processes of consciousness that are intentional, a consciousness of something, and we shall follow this technical usage. Our acts of consciousness take their place, furthermore, within a matrix of habits (as James also stressed) including bodily skills and even habitual background ideas.

In Husserl's hands, then, phenomenology – the study of the essence of consciousness as lived – is centrally concerned with structures of intentionality: in perception, imagination, judgment, emotion, evaluation, volition, consciousness of time and space, experience of other people, and so on. So phenomenology is largely focused on how perception, thought, emotion, and action are directed toward things in the world, how things are "intended" in these forms of experience, and thus the meaning things have for us in different forms of experience. Husserl's full theory of intentionality comes into play, accordingly, as the center of the new science of phenomenology.

PHENOMENOLOGICAL DESCRIPTION

Before we address Husserl's detailed conception of the discipline of phenomenology, we need first to appreciate a minimalist form of phenomenology. "Plain" phenomenology (in Charles Siewert's phrase) would study forms of conscious experience, in relatively neutral terms, without commitment to the fancier reaches of theory in Husserl's philosophical system – or, for that matter, in competitor conceptions of phenomenology such as Martin Heidegger's. Today's philosophy of mind, adjoined with neuroscience and various models of mental representation (for example in perception), has come closer and closer to a basic conception of phenomenology, which would address consciousness in its own irreducible terms while holding that consciousness is somehow realized in the brain. (See Smith and Thomasson 2005.)

We practice phenomenology, most basically, when we give first-person descriptions of various types of conscious experience. Here are some elementary forms of such descriptions:

> I see that fishing boat on the edge of the fog bank rolling in on the Pacific.
> I hear that helicopter whirling overhead.
> I think that the whales are migrating south along the coast.
> I desire a warm cup of green tea.
> I feel exhilarated at the sound of the aria I hear being sung in the opera.
> I recall the look on her face – I can see it right now (in vivid memory).
> I imagine driving into the traffic at the Etoile roundabout in Paris.
> I intend to make that phone call in just a minute.

> I am walking briskly up the stairs to get to the noon meeting.
> I am hitting a spin serve to his backhand, springing upward with
> my legs.

Such characterizations of experiences we may call *phenomenological descriptions*. Each characterizes a particular act of consciousness from the subject's point of view. If carefully crafted, as the subject attends to his or her own experience, the description captures the essence of that type of experience. (Such descriptions belong to "pure" or "transcendental" phenomenology, Husserl specifies, when they are stripped of all presuppositions about the existence of the surrounding world of nature, in which, we normally assume, both our experiences and their objects occur. However, we leave the complexities of "transcendental" phenomenology for Chapter 6.)

In practice, phenomenologists develop much more elaborate accounts of experience, analyzing complex structures of consciousness and interpreting their roles and significance in our experience. However, it is important to recognize the basic domain of study that is indicated by such simple descriptions of experience. Here our understanding of mind begins, and it is only by abstracting from such elementary phenomenological descriptions that we begin to develop the science of phenomenology as Husserl advocated it.

Literature may describe a character's experience in a way that invites the reader to listen in, as it were, through a sort of deferred phenomenology. A form of phenomenological description winds its way through Marcel Proust's *In Search of Lost Time* (published in a series of volumes from 1913 until after Proust's death in 1922). The writer's perspective is that of a first-person recollection of his experiences, as if projecting himself in memory back into those experiences, in a reflection on their significance. The perspective is suggested by the original French title, *A La Recherche du temps perdu*: literally, if less poetically, "toward research of times lost," that is, a study of experiences lost in time, but here resurrected in a searching form of recollection. We are transported, as it were, through Proust's recollection into his own first-person perspective on living those experiences in times past. Here is a passage from the final volume, *Time Regained*:

I saw Gilberte coming across the room towards me. For me the marriage of Saint-Loup and the thoughts which filled my mind at that date – and which were still there, unchanged, this very morning – might have belonged to yesterday, so that I was astonished to see at her side a girl of about sixteen, whose tall figure was a measure of that distance which I had been reluctant to see. Time, colourless and inapprehensible Time, so that I was almost able to see it and touch it, had materialized itself in this girl, moulding her into a masterpiece, while correspondingly, on me, alas! It had merely done its work. And now Mlle de Saint-Loup was standing in front of me. She had deep-set piercing eyes, and a charming nose thrust slightly forward in the form of a beak and curved, perhaps not in the least like that of Swann but like Saint-Loup's. The soul of that particular Guermantes had fluttered away, but his charming head, as of a bird in flight, with its piercing eyes, had settled momentarily upon the shoulders of Mlle de Saint-Loup and the sight of it there aroused a train of memories and dreams in those who had known her father. . . . I thought her very beautiful: still rich in hopes full of laughter, formed from those very years which I myself had lost, she was like my own youth.

(Proust 1927/1999: 506–7)

The writer continues shortly after in a reflection on his role as writer of this narrative in which he is a first-person character:

I thought more modestly of my book [this book] and it would be inaccurate even to say that I thought of those who would read it as "my" readers. For it seemed to me that they would not be "my" readers but the readers of their own selves, my book being merely a sort of magnifying glass like those which the optician at Combray used to offer his customers – it would be my book, but with its help I would furnish them with the means of reading what lay inside themselves. So that I should not ask them to praise me or to censure me, but simply to tell me whether "it really is like that," I should ask them whether the words that they read within themselves are the same as those which I have written.

(Proust 1927/1999: 508)

Here we might hear echoes of Husserl's call for a description of the shareable essences of acts of consciousness, not merely a psychological description of one's own particular experiences. Proust's interest in our consciousness of time was shaped by the philosophy of Henri Bergson rather than that of Edmund Husserl. Interest in the structure and temporal flow of consciousness, however, ranged from Brentano in Vienna to Husserl in Germany to Bergson in Paris to William James in Cambridge, Massachusetts. Phenomenology by any other name is phenomenology.

In the 1930s, Jean-Paul Sartre wrote a novel called *Nausea* (1938). Written entirely in the first person, it explores the subject's sense of lost freedom and his recovery of his power over his life. Sartre had studied philosophy at the Sorbonne in Paris, and he had studied phenomenology in Berlin in 1933–4. This novel was the overture to his philosophy of existentialism, which took Paris (and the world) by storm as the Second World War ended. Early in the book the protagonist has from time to time suffered a strangely disorienting sensation he calls Nausea, a sensation he will later associate with his losing the power to give meaning to things. Here is a passage from *Nausea* describing this strange experience:

> When the patronne goes shopping her cousin replaces her at the bar. His name is Adolphe. I began looking at him as I sat down and I have kept on because I cannot turn my head. He is in shirt-sleeves, with purple suspenders; he has rolled the sleeves of his shirt above the elbows. The suspenders can hardly be seen against the blue shirt, they are all obliterated, buried in the blue, but it is a false humility; in fact, they will not let themselves be forgotten, they annoy me by their sheep-like stubbornness, as if, starting to become purple, they stopped somewhere along the way without giving up their pretensions. . . . Sometimes the blue which surrounds them slips over and covers them completely: I stay an instant without seeing them . . . His blue cotton shirt stands out joyfully against a chocolate-coloured wall. That too brings on the Nausea. The Nausea is not inside me: I feel it *out*

there in the wall, in the suspenders, everywhere around me. It
makes itself one with the café, I am the one who is within it.

                                          (Sartre 1938/1964: 19–20)

We do not normally experience such a de-structuring of our
visual experience. In fact, Sartre used mescaline to induce such an
experience, and in the novel he uses the quasi-hallucinatory experience itself as a metaphor for an existential loss of the sense of
self and of one's control over one's life (much as the protagonist
had lost control over his visual world). Clearly, the passage quoted
is offered as a phenomenological description of this type of experience, and the novel as a whole is a reflection on the significance
of one's sense of autonomy. The reader is drawn into the protagonist's point of view by empathy, by comprehending the
protagonist's fictional experience as if it were his or her own: thus
the first-person narrative. Husserl himself analyzed empathy (in
Ideas II) as an imaginative reproduction of the other's experience as
if one were living through it oneself. For our purposes, we note
Sartre's conception of the importance of giving meaning to ordinary objects around one. This theme is central to Husserl's theory
of intentionality: every experience represents its object only
through a specific formation of meaning, without which there can
be no coherent consciousness at all (as opposed to a kaleidoscopic
cacophony of sensations – blue or purple, there or where?).

Let us grant that we practice phenomenology in many guises,
as we find in Proust and in Sartre and already in everyday life. Yet
Husserl wanted to develop the practice of phenomenology into a
proper science. And to that end he developed a methodology
intended to ground the new science – much as Galileo and Newton
had developed the outlines of what we today call the empirical
scientific method. Husserl's method for phenomenology is a
special type of first-person reflection on experience in which we
develop phenomenological descriptions of key forms of consciousness. I am to "bracket" the question of the existence of the object I
am currently seeing (or desiring or thinking about), and so I am
to turn my attention instead to my *consciousness* of that object, to the
way I am experiencing it, proceeding to a phenomenological
description of this form of experience. This method, as we see in

Chapter 6, is keyed to Husserl's theory of intentionality, which is intertwined with his conception of logic and with the relation between consciousness and language (as explored in Chapter 3). Husserl's technique of bracketing is designed to turn my attention from the *objects* of my consciousness to my *consciousness* of those objects, to the way I experience those objects. There is no question of discarding the objects of my experience by this "bracketing" technique, as if I doubt their existence or even reduce them to my ideas of them. Rather, I retain my intentional relation to the world, but I turn my attention to the way in which my experience is directed toward the world, to objects just *as* I experience them. (See our detailed account of bracketing in Chapter 6.)

In some future time we might have a "virtual reality" machine that produces in one's brain any specified form of conscious experience. We could call this a *phenomenology* machine. (The objects of consciousness would be virtual, but the experiences would be real.) When I don such a headset, it causes appropriate neural activities to unfold in my brain and therewith I have an experience of a given type: I am conscious of this or that, I see various objects, feel various emotions, and experience myself performing various bodily actions as if of my own volition. Such a machine is the stuff of current science fiction, notably in the popular movie *The Matrix* (1999). If plugged into such an experience-inducing machine, I could then practice phenomenology in a new way. After experiencing a certain form of consciousness induced by the machine, I would then reflect on my experience with that form. I would not need to construct phenomenological descriptions in words (like those offered earlier). I could instead ask my fellow phenomenologists to don the headset and, at the right time, instruct them to attend to "that" form of experience. We then would proceed to develop theoretical models of the *structure* of that form of experience, much as a physicist develops theoretical models of an indicated form of physical process such as gravitation.

Lacking a phenomenology machine, we use another piece of technology: language! We ask our fellow phenomenologists to recall a more or less familiar form of experience as "lived" somewhere in one's life. We then reflect on that type of experience and construct a phenomenological description of that form of consciousness. If we had a "read-out" of the phenomenology machine, we could point to the articulation of that form of experience on the "tape" of the experience, the "tape" played in one's consciousness when one dons the headset. But without such a technology, we can only point to the articulation of a form of experience by constructing a piece of language that gives a phenomenological description of that form of experience. The examples previously offered are meant to indicate this articulation of consciousness within the limits of our extant language. Each phenomenological description awakens in the reader a sense of what that form of experience is like as lived.

To be sure, experience far outruns language. The word "red" can indicate the color of a rose, as we experience the hue, only if we know both the experience and the language. Given our prior range of experience and command of language, we can develop phenomenological descriptions along the lines we have seen above. Indeed, we have at our disposal some illuminating forms of language. On the formal side, we can study the logic of phenomenological descriptions, looking even to mathematical logic for studies of sentences like "I see that tree" or "I think that Freud suffered." On the literary or even poetic side, we can study the uses of language in descriptions of experience by Marcel Proust or Jean-Paul Sartre (as earlier). Or we can follow the quasi-poetic analyses of language used by Martin Heidegger in characterizing our everyday activities, or we can pursue the impressionistic accounts of bodily experience we find in Maurice Merleau-Ponty's analyses of perception. Both forms of language – the more formal or mathematical and the more literary or artistic – are reflected in Husserl's pursuit of phenomenology, as Husserl turned from mathematics to a philosophical theory of experience in everyday life.

In Chapter 3 we addressed Husserl's conception of logic, which frames his practice of phenomenology. In Investigation I of his *Logical Investigations* (1900–1) Husserl develops an account of the relation between language and experience. With suitable qualifications, he holds that language expresses the content or "sense"

(*Sinn*) of an underlying form of experience. This model of language *vis-à-vis* experience provides a foundation for the use of language as a tool of phenomenological analysis (as in the examples used earlier). Moreover, as we see in Chapter 6, Husserl's technical account of phenomenological method (whereby we are to turn from the *object* of my experience to my *consciousness* of that object) makes use of language in an essential way. There we see some logical theory at work. Meanwhile, we rely on our familiarity with both language and experience as we lay out a basic conception of the discipline of phenomenology (as in the earlier exercises).

THE EMERGENCE OF PHENOMENOLOGY AS A DISCIPLINE

The *Oxford English Dictionary* gives two definitions of phenomenology: "a. The science of phenomena as distinct from that of being (ontology). b. That division of any science which describes and classifies its phenomena." The second use lingers today but is not widespread, while the first usage pertains to the discipline articulated by Husserl.

The term "phenomenology," or the German "*Phänomenologie*," seems to have been introduced in 1637 by one Christoph Friedrich Oetinger, meaning the study of relations between things in the visible world (as opposed, presumably, to deeper spiritual reality). In the 18th century Johann Heinrich Lambert – a mathematician, physicist, and philosopher influenced by the reigning German philosopher Christian Wolff – characterized phenomenology as the theory of appearances fundamental to all empirical knowledge. The term was subsequently used, occasionally, by Immanuel Kant and then by the German idealists Johann Gottlieb Fichte and G. W. F. Hegel. However, it was not until late in the 19th century that the term began to take on the technical meaning in which Husserl used it. Franz Brentano in 1889 spoke of "descriptive psychology" or "descriptive phenomenology," and soon thereafter Husserl began developing his own, full-blown conception of phenomenology as a new philosophical discipline that would study consciousness, intentionality, and meaning.

In *Psychology from an Empirical Standpoint* (1874) Brentano distinguished genetic psychology from descriptive psychology. Genetic psychology is to study the causes or genesis of a given type of experience (fear of snakes caused by a childhood trauma, judgments about the habits of snakes drawn from perceptions of their behavior, and so on). By contrast, descriptive psychology is to study the various types of mental state as such: What is perception? What is emotion? What is judgment? Brentano held that descriptive psychology is prior to genetic psychology, since we cannot explain what caused a given type of experience until we have explicated what that type of experience is. A reader of Aristotle, Brentano brings to the science of psychology – taking shape in the late 19th century after two centuries of progress in physics and chemistry – the spirit of classification and analysis of basic types or species of things. This sort of analysis of psychological phenomena was the archetype of Husserl's conception of phenomenology.

Three of Brentano's students – Edmund Husserl, Kasimir Twardowski, and Alexius Meinong – radically extended Brentano's basic conception of the directedness of consciousness toward its objects. In *On the Content and Object of Presentation* (1894/1977), Twardowski sharply distinguished act, content, and object. Here we see the object of consciousness pulled clearly outside the act of consciousness: the intentional object is not, as in Brentano's model, somehow "in" the act of consciousness. In "On the Theory of Objects" (1904/1960), Meinong distinguished many types of objects "beyond being or nonbeing," every object a potential object of consciousness but an object in its own right. Here we see a further focus on the types of object available to consciousness. Husserl liked what he saw in these works, but he felt these models of intentionality still fell short. What was needed, in Husserl's eyes, was a deeper understanding of content and its relation to objects of various forms. This deeper conception of content – or meaning – Husserl drew from Bernard Bolzano's conception of logic. And meaning would prove to be the heart of Husserl's conception of phenomenology.

As Husserl refined the basic Brentanian conception of phenomenology, in his *Logical Investigations* (1900–1), he drew a careful distinction between the content and the object of an intentional experience. When I think of the founder of axiomatic geometry, the object of my thought is Euclid, whereas the content of my thought is the concept "the founder of axiomatic geometry." I can think of Euclid alternatively as "the most famous Greek geometer after Pythagoras." But then the object of my thought must be distinguished from the content of my thought, since different concepts can represent the same object. Now, where in the pantheon of human knowledge do we study such intentional contents in their own right – ideas, concepts, propositions? In *Theory of Science* (1837) Bernard Bolzano argued (against Kant) that we need to distinguish objective from subjective ideas or representations. Subjective representations (*Vorstellungen*) are what transpire in my mind or yours, literally a temporal part of my experience (realized in my brain). By contrast, objective representations are the contents that you and I can share when we think the same thought. When I think, "The founder of axiomatic geometry was Greek," and you think "The founder of axiomatic geometry was Greek," the content of my act of thinking is the same thing as the content of your act of thinking. Bolzano called this type of content a *proposition* (*Satz*). And, according to Bolzano (arguing against Kant), logic is the study of propositions and their component concepts – as opposed to the subjective events that transpire in your mind or mine. Husserl sought to extend Bolzano's conception of logic into his new science of phenomenology, concerned with contents of all type in appropriate forms of consciousness.

For Husserl, then, phenomenology is the descriptive, analytic study of types of consciousness (here extending Brentano), and this analysis will analyze, among other things, the objective contents of various types of experience (here extending Bolzano). These objective contents Husserl called *meanings* or *senses* (*Sinne*). Meanings are ideal entities, in the sense that different experiences (in your mind or in mine) may have the same content. Such meanings include what we may call percepts (how something looks), concepts (how something is conceived), images, thoughts or propositions, wishes, intentions, and so on. In addition to the ideal contents of various types of experience, phenomenology will study the ways in which experiences are united in a single person's stream of consciousness: as I see this, hear that, walk there, pick up that, intending to do such-and-such, feeling thus-and-so. Furthermore, phenomenology will study how we experience others, how our experience becomes intersubjective or social, how our experience relates to language and other social practices (from carpentry to government).

The discipline of phenomenology can be seen developing throughout the long and global history of philosophy, including the course of modern European philosophy from Descartes through Locke and Hume into Kant and later into Brentano. Husserl might be seen, thus, either as inventing a new science of phenomenology or as bringing the science into its own on the heels of Descartes, Kant, *et al.* As we dig into the works of these thinkers, however, we soon find important technical differences. Husserl did not begin with issues of skepticism, as did Descartes, Hume, and Kant. Descartes did not sharply separate mathematics from physics, as the disciplines were developing under his pen and other's pens, but by Husserl's day mathematics was seen as an application of pure logic, an abstract study awaiting application to the realm of space–time. Kant answered Hume's skepticism, while looking to Newton's physics, by proposing that space and time are defined by forms of human "intuition" (perception), so that our knowledge of physical phenomena in space–time has a kind of necessity in what Kant called synthetic a priori knowledge, a necessity that derives from the structure of the human mind. Husserl would have none of that. The world has its structure in itself, Husserl held, and our consciousness develops meanings through which we comprehend things in space and time. To be sure, we know things only as our concepts or meanings present them, but the objects in our world are distinguished from our concepts and percepts of them: so goes the structure of intentionality. And the relationships between our concepts or percepts and things in the world around us, well, that is the business of phenomenology: as it were, the logic or semantics of experience. Here Husserl's conception of logic enters his account of phenomenology. As Husserl's differences from his predecessors are drawn more sharply, then, his conception of phenomenology separates out from the related doctrines of epistemology and ontology he found in his predecessors, from Plato and Aristotle through Descartes, Hume, and Kant. In this way phenomenology emerged as its own discipline, a new science of consciousness and its intentionality.

HUSSERLIAN PHENOMENOLOGY: AN OUTLINE OF THE STRUCTURE OF CONSCIOUSNESS

In the practice of phenomenology Husserl developed remarkably detailed analyses of many of the most basic forms of consciousness. His results unfold in a sequence of books and posthumously published material, including lecture courses. If we gather together the main results (without noting specific texts), we find an outline of the overall structure of consciousness. This account of conscious experience we may sketch along the following lines, in a basic phenomenological description in the first person. (Note the rhetorical shift between plural and singular: as I describe my experience, our interest is in the forms of conscious experience that we all typically share.)

We are conscious in sensory perception of things around us in space and time. We see things, hear things, and touch things around us, things with qualities of color, shape, tone, and texture, things in spatial relation to each other and to us. And we see things happening around us, we hear melodies, we feel our own bodily movements as we run. So we are conscious in perception of events or processes that unfold over time, as well as enduring objects. As we perceive such things, we are at the same time typically involved in more or less deliberate activities in which we use our bodies in familiar ways, as we walk around and pick things up and employ them in our daily affairs. That is, we experience a variety of actions, volitional bodily actions, which are tied into our perceptions of objects and events around us. And our actions are normally infused with various emotions. Often we encounter and engage other people. We see other people, talk with them, build houses with them, and so on. We have emotions of love, hate, anger, joy, envy, and admiration. Throughout our acts or activities of consciousness, we are conscious of the passage of time, of experiencing and doing things over a period of time, things that transpire in time and are accompanied by a sense of time passing.

Thus I have retentions of my immediately past experiences, and also anticipations or "protentions" of my impending experiences, and a concurrent awareness of my current conscious experiences or activities, starting with my sensations in seeing, hearing, touching, and so on. My awareness of time depends on this formation of retentions, protentions, and inner awareness of my passing experience. In this form of awareness I am conscious simultaneously of the temporal flow of things in my environment and of the temporal flow of experiences in my stream of consciousness. In broad strokes, then, our consciousness presents us with things, including our experience, ourselves, and various things around us, including other people, all extant in space and time.

My overall experience consists in a stream of consciousness. This stream is temporally structured, and it is organized as a flow of "my" experiences. Moreover, the experiences in my stream are integrated in a coherent way, so that I have differing experiences of the same objects. For example, as I walk around this table I see and touch and even lean on the same table, that is, I am conscious of "the same" table in these different experiences of seeing, touching, and leaning upon the one object. That is, my experiences are intentionally structured so that "I" have these experiences and, further, so that certain groups of my experiences are all experiences of (directed toward) "the same" object. Without these basic forms of directedness from the same subject or "I" and variously toward the same object ("that" object), my consciousness would lack the coherence that is characteristic of my experience.

Within my unified stream of consciousness: I see and hear and touch things; I perform actions such as walking and talking and working with my hands; I talk and work with other people; I feel various emotions; I think about affairs of the day, affairs of state, and even philosophical matters. From this complex pattern of consciousness, my stream of experience, we may extract particular experiences and focus on them in phenomenological reflection, assessing what I see or feel or think or will in these experiences. Thus we consider a particular "act" of consciousness, reflecting on its content, or what I experience in that act of consciousness. Here we find the paradigmatic form of intentional experience, to which Husserl devotes much of his attention in his major works.

Among Husserl's most intriguing results, enriching his basic analysis of intentionality, are his detailed phenomenological analyses of our consciousness of time, of space, of embodiment, of self, of other persons, and of our surrounding "life-world" (*Lebenswelt*). The overall result is a rich analysis of the structure of consciousness, resonant with William James' monumental *Principles of Psychology* (1891), a work Husserl greatly admired. However, as we have emphasized, Husserl wanted to frame such "psychological" results within the emerging discipline of phenomenology, which was to be informed by Husserl's theory of intentionality, a theory of how the contents or meanings in our experience logically present or represent things in the world around us, things in space and time, among us, and so on. Husserl's specific analyses along these lines we sketch in the following sections.

INTENTIONALITY: THE CENTRAL FORM OF CONSCIOUSNESS

Husserl's theory of intentionality is the centerpiece of his account of phenomenology as the science of the essence of consciousness. The key concepts in the theory – the notions of act, content, and object of consciousness – are developed in Investigation V of the *Logical Investigations* (1900–1/2001). The theory is amplified further in *Ideas* I (1913/1969/1983). The details of the theory are laid out in Chapter 6 of this volume, addressing Husserl's famous concept of noema: the ideal content or sense in an experience, embodying "the object-*as*-intended." Here let us introduce the main outlines of Husserl's theory of intentionality, addressing the role of content or sense in consciousness and also the correlative "horizon" of consciousness.

Consider the experience I describe as follows:

> While playing a game of tennis, preparing to return my opponent's top-spin serve, I see this approaching yellow tennis ball, spinning heavily and streaking toward the corner of the service box on my backhand side.

My perceptual experience is a visual consciousness of the ball. What is the form of this relation of intentionality, this consciousness of the ball?

On Husserl's analysis, the intentional relation between act and object of consciousness has a structure that we may depict in the following schema:

background — subject – act – content → object) horizon.

INTENTIONAL RELATION

The same relationship we may depict in the familiar form of a cartoon, in Figure 5.1.

INTENTIONAL RELATION

Figure 5.1 The structure of intentionality

Within the structure of an intentional relation, on Husserl's model, we distinguish several elements:

1   The *act* of consciousness is an experience, in the example, a visual experience or perception. This experience is our chief concern, abstracted from the rich context in which it occurs, including my stream of consciousness, my playing a tennis match, my natural surroundings (the trees nearby, the declining sun), and my cultural environment (the tennis court, the practices defining the game of tennis). The act itself is a mental event or process; its object is something very different (in this case, a tennis ball), toward which the act is directed.

2   The *object* of my experience is, in this case, the ball spinning and moving in flight according to the laws of physics – that is, if there is such a thing out there, if I am not hallucinating.

3   The *subject* of the experience is the individual who has the experience: I, myself. (Husserl creates the noun "*das Ich*," adapted from the first-person pronoun "*ich*," for the subject, "I," but this everyday pronoun is often translated as "ego," lending an unintended air of mystery.)

4   A crucial part or aspect of the act is what we intuitively call its *content*, what philosophers call its intentional content. The content is specified by saying "what" I see (or think or imagine, and so on), describing what I see just as I see it. In this case the content of my experience is a concept or percept: "this tennis ball ... ." This content in my experience *prescribes* – presents or represents – the object of my perception. The content represents the object in a particular way, as a tennis ball served with spin to my backhand. The same object might be represented differently by a different content (say, if I mistake it, momentarily, for a yellow-jacket wasp flitting into my field of vision). But in the given experience the object is represented by the visual content "this tennis ball . . . ."

5   An act's content presupposes the subject's *background* of tacit understanding about what the content represents or prescribes: as Husserl says, the *implicit* meaning in the experience. In this case, my relevant background includes what I

know about balls and how to hit them, including my understanding of the behavior of tennis balls, the game of tennis,
common strategies in the game, my own bodily skills (how to
execute my backhand strokes), and so on.

6   This background constrains what I see so as to define a *horizon*
of open possibilities concerning the object I see. Thus, the
presented "tennis ball" cannot be an animated yellow being
about to unfurl its wings and fly off in an opposite direction
of its own free will – these possibilities are (in Husserl's
idiom) "unmotivated" in my experience, given the background of the content of the act.

7   These entities play their respective roles in the *intentional relation*
between act and object of consciousness. We may say the
content *prescribes* such-and-such an object, and if there is an
object that *satisfies* the content, then that is the object of
consciousness, the object *intended* in that act of consciousness.
If the content is satisfied, then the act is *intentionally related* to
that object. If the content is not satisfied, the act still has the
intentional character of being as if intentionally related to such an
object. (The preceding summary of Husserl's theory of intentionality follows the interpretation detailed in Smith and
McIntyre 1982.)

Husserl coins the verb "to intend" ("*intendieren,*" in German),
meaning that consciousness is aimed or directed at something in
this way. We may say an act *intends* an object, or alternatively we
say a subject *intends* an object in an experience (which intends that
object).

On Husserl's theory of intentionality, then, an act of consciousness, performed by a subject, is directed via its content toward an
appropriate object, if such exists, where this content rests on the
subject's background understanding of a horizon of meaning
about such objects. This structure of intentionality-via-content is
emphasized in the schema given earlier and alternatively in the
cartoon (Figure 5.1).

The content of an experience Husserl calls the *sense* (Sinn) or
meaning of the experience. The same term is used in logical theory,

by Husserl and his contemporary Gottlob Frege (the founder of modern logic). The analogy with language is apparent: as our speech carries a sense that represents something, so our thought or experience carries a sense that represents something. As Husserl linked phenomenology with logic, we may say that phenomenology turns to the semantics of experience as we analyze the sense or meaning of various types of experience, specifying how various meanings represent the objects of consciousness. When I think of "the victor at Jena" and later think of "the vanquished at Waterloo" (to use an example of Husserl's), I am thinking of the same object, Napoleon, but I am thinking of him in two different ways. The sense of my second thought is the concept "the military leader defeated at the Battle of Waterloo," while the sense of my first thought is the concept "the military leader victorious at the battle of Jena." These two concepts, or ways of thinking, represent or refer to the same individual, Napoleon. But Napoleon is not a proper part of my conscious experience, while the concept is: the concept is the content of my so thinking. Moreover, that content or meaning is semantically linked to other relevant meanings, for instance, in this case, the variety of concepts and propositions relevant to Napoleon, French political-military history, and so on. This complex of meaning defines the "horizon" of the object represented in my thinking about Napoleon.

TIME, SENSATION, AND THE STREAM OF CONSCIOUSNESS

After developing a phenomenological theory of intentionality and a phenomenological theory of knowledge in the *Logical Investigations* (1900–1/2001), Husserl dug into the structure of our consciousness of both time and space. Owing to his days in mathematics, Husserl had a recurring interest in the structure of time and space and our experience thereof. Indeed, theory of space and time was in the air in Husserl's day, as non-Euclidean geometry led into relativity theory and Albert Einstein's model of the curvature of space–time. Husserl's lectures on time-consciousness are gathered in a volume titled *On the Phenomenology of the Consciousness of Internal Time*

(1893–1917) (1966/1991, here called Time, 1991). His theory of the structure of time-consciousness developed prominently in lectures of the period 1905–10, the period when he was also developing his doctrine of meaning into the theory of "noema" elaborated in Ideas I (1913/1969/1983). In the same period Husserl pursued the structure of our consciousness of space and things in space. In the present section we summarize Husserl's analysis of time-consciousness, turning to consciousness of space in the next section.

Whereas acts such as seeing a tree or seeing a bird in flight have a meaning or content that specifies the object of perception, these acts themselves transpire within a basic stream of sensory experience. We are normally living through a flow of sensory experience that includes and synthesizes visual, auditory, tactile, olfactory, gustatory, and kinesthetic sensation. On Husserl's account, we do not normally experience pure sensations (feeling heat, seeing red, hearing middle C); rather, our sensory experience is normally structured by a sense of "what" we see, hear, touch, and so on. (I see that bird, hear that song, touch that rock) (Ideas I, §84). Yet we experience a temporally structured flow of sensory consciousness that is "animated" by meaningful conceptual apprehension. And that temporal flow of sensory consciousness plays a fundamental role in our experience of the world around us. In that temporal flow, as Husserl puts it, we are conscious of events flowing off in time in the world around us (the wave rolling onto the shore, the pelican swooping into the sea, the roaring sound of the surf, and so on). But in the same flowing experience we are also conscious of events flowing off in time in our own stream of experience. This doubly temporal structure of experience receives a detailed analysis in Husserl's lectures on time-consciousness. We turn to his analysis of time in that context.

Suppose (to adapt Husserl's central example) I am listening to a familiar melody, say, the Beatles' song "Yesterday." In the middle of the song I hear a note sung in the melody: Paul McCartney's voice singing the syllable "yes" at a certain pitch, supported by background instrumental accompaniment. This tone-syllable occurs in the middle of the phrase " . . . Oh, I be-lieve in yes-ter-day . . . ," lilting in the familiar melody. My continuous experience of hearing the song lasts about two minutes, as does the sound streaming from the stereo, but at the moment I am hearing a certain tone sung with a certain syllable. On Husserl's analysis, my auditory experience is a complex form of consciousness that ties into my just-past and just-coming phases of perception. Thus, I hear the present note; that is, I experience (as Husserl puts it) a *primal impression* of that syllable sung at that tone. At the same time, in the present phase of experience, I retain a sense of several immediately preceding notes or tone-syllables in the singing of the melody; that is, my present span of experience includes a series of *retentions* of past notes. These retentions retain, as it were, a portion of the song within my present moment of auditory consciousness. But these retentions do not reach back all the way to the beginning of the song. (Perhaps a Mozart can retain a long stretch of complex music, but I cannot.) Since the song is familiar to me, I also anticipate a portion of the song that is to follow the present tone (" . . . [yes]-ter-day. Why she had to go . . . "). That is, my present phase of experience, spanning about half a second, includes a series of *protentions* of future notes or tone-syllables. (Husserl coins the term "protention" in symmetry with the term "retention.") On Husserl's analysis, then, in hearing the song my present phase of perception is a complex form of consciousness comprising my present impression of the current note together with a series of present retentions of immediately past notes and a series of present protentions of immediately future notes. This passing phase of auditory experience – impression + retentions + protentions – is itself a part of the continuing experience that consists in my hearing the song over a period of some two minutes. Husserl depicted this complex temporal structure of a continuous hearing of a melody in a diagram similar to that in Figure 5.2. (Compare *Time*, 1991, §10.)

There is a "double intentionality" in this form of time-consciousness, Husserl finds (*Time*, 1991, §39). For I am conscious in retention of both the past tone and my past hearing of that tone; similarly for protention. The series of retentions in my current phase of perception thereby "constitutes" both the temporal

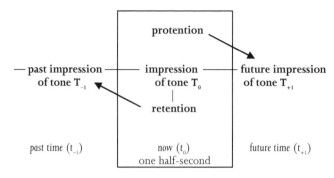

MY CURRENT PHASE OF PERCEPTION

IN MY CONTINUING HEARING OF THE MELODY

Figure 5.2 The structure of my consciousness of time

past of the melody I am hearing and the temporal past of my stream of consciousness in hearing the melody. And the series of protentions in my current phase of perception "constitutes" both the temporal future of the melody I am hearing and the temporal future of my stream of consciousness in hearing the song. My current impression of the current tone in the melody "constitutes" the presently occurring tone. But in my current impression there is no distinguishable intention of the impression itself. Rather, on Husserl's analysis, my present consciousness of my currently hearing the song consists in the unified structure of my current impression joined with my current retentions and protentions. My passing awareness of my flowing experience consists in this complex form of consciousness, in which I am conscious of the flowing melody and of my flowing experience of the melody.

The most basic form of "self-consciousness," in the sense that consciousness includes a consciousness-of-itself, is the form of time-consciousness. In the stretch of experience wherein I hear a fragment of a song, I am aware of my passing experience of the song's fragment precisely insofar as my experience is structured into the pattern of a current impression together with current retentions of just-past tones and current protentions of just-impending tones. In Husserl's analysis of the temporal structure of my sensory consciousness of a temporal process such as a song, then, we may see an analysis of my most basic form of awareness of my passing experience. Husserl characterizes this form of self-consciousness in dramatic terms:

> There is one, unique flow of consciousness in which both the unity of the tone in immanent time and the unity of the flow of consciousness itself become constituted at once. As shocking . . . as it may seem to say that the flow of consciousness constitutes its own unity, it is nonetheless the case that it does.
>
> (*Time*, 1991, §39)

Importantly, retention is not the same thing as a proper act of memory or recollection. (*Time*, 1991, §19.) A memory projects back into a former time; a recollection explicitly "re-lives" a prior experience, as when I recall a conversation I had last week. But the remembered or recollected experience is located well into the past. By contrast, the retained phase of perception is a proper part of the continuing perceptual experience in hearing the song, and the retention is itself a proper part of the current phase of the continuing perception. Similarly, protention is not the same thing as a proper act of anticipation. An act of anticipation projects forward into a future time, say, as I anticipate seeing an old friend next week. By contrast, a protention is a proper part of the current phase of my continuing perception, say, in hearing a song, and if the song continues as "protended" then the protended phase of perception is a subsequent part of the continuing perception.

The same form of continuing sensory experience of a continuing process would apply to other forms of perception. When I watch a pelican gliding above a long wave that is breaking near the ocean shore, in my current phase of experience I see the pelican flap its wings once. This visual impression is accompanied, in the present phase of experience, by retentions of having just seen the bird gliding along, and also by protentions of being just about to see the bird gliding along after flapping its wings. Husserl's example of hearing a melody is presumably a relatively simple form of experience. When we turn to vision, the temporal flow of events I see may be relatively complex. But of course a musical performance may also be complex. The point to stress is that every act of consciousness, even one whose content is quite complex, takes its place within the subject's continuing stream of consciousness. And the continuous flow of sensory experience forms a sort of familiar matrix within which intentional acts of consciousness unfold. That is, my familiar types of intentional acts of consciousness – hearing a crow caw, seeing a tree, thinking about Mozart, willingly jumping over that log on the path, and so on – take their place within my stream of consciousness, and that stream itself is structured fundamentally around a temporal flow of sensory experiences in which I am conscious of a temporal flow of events in the world around me.

In this sensory flow of experience, Husserl finds, our most basic consciousness of time is "constituted." Remarkably, Husserl holds, in this flow of experience both inner time and objective time are "constituted" (Time, 1991, §39). Inner time, phenomenological or subjective time, is the temporal structure of my conscious experience, whereas objective time is the temporal structure of the objects of consciousness comprising events transpiring around me (Time, 1991, §§1, 31, 32). Both forms of time are "constituted," according to Husserl, in the same form of consciousness. Thus, as I experience the sensory flux that is the normal state of consciousness, I am conscious of time in two coordinated phenomena. On the one hand, I am conscious of the temporal flow of things I sense, in hearing a melody, seeing a flying pelican, and so on. On the other hand, I am also conscious of the temporal flow of my own experience, as my sensory awareness of these things flows off in time even as the things I sense flow off in time. And yet the temporality of my consciousness is one structure, and the temporality of the song or the bird's flight is a distinct structure. As we know, the time of what I hear or see may diverge from the time in which I hear or see: I may seem to hear two notes at the same time, though they are played at slightly different times.

In Husserl's idiom, where consciousness intends an object, that object is said to be "constituted" in consciousness. The point is not that consciousness creates or constructs the object, but rather that in an experience there is a structure of meaning through which the object is experienced. This structure defines the "constitution" of the object *as* it is intended in the experience. We shall study Husserl's doctrine of constitution in detail in Chapter 6, using the theory of meaning and horizon. Husserl finds it nearly paradoxical that both objective and inner time should be "constituted" in the same flowing form of sensory experience. The air of paradox dissipates, however, if we remember that "constitution" is not bringing something into existence – as if consciousness must bootstrap itself into existence in time while simultaneously projecting into existence the song or bird's flight in time. Furthermore, the sense of paradox evaporates as we realize that the form of "constitution" of the temporal structure of consciousness is the form of awareness I have of my own passing experience.

Husserl factors temporal awareness into different levels of "constitution" in our consciousness of time and of objects occurring in time (*Time*, 1991, §§34ff.). First there is the flow of consciousness, which Husserl calls "time-constituting": consciousness already "constitutes" the flow of time within the flowing stream itself, that is, in virtue of the form of sensory impressions united with retentions of past impressions and protentions of future impressions. Here in the flow of sensory impressions the form of time is already "constituted." Yet there is more in the world than my stream of consciousness. Second, there are "manifolds of appearances": each sensible quality of an object can appear in different ways, for example as a square appears rectangular from an angle or a tone sounds different within a chord. The "manifold" of appearances of a quality in different possible perceptions "constitutes" that quality in an object. This "constitution" of the quality in a manifold of its appearances forms the next level of "constitution" of things in the world: the "constitution" of aspects of objects in nature. These appearances are themselves experienced in time, in possible phases of perception were I to look at a quality from different perspectives or hear a tone in different chords. Third, there are the material objects in nature themselves, which have a variety of properties, including sensible qualities that may appear differently from various perspectives. A material thing (*Ding*) is "constituted" in the various possible forms of experience that present it with various properties, including its sensible qualities. A material thing – a pelican over the ocean, a fragment of song, a wave crashing on the beach – is a being that persists in time. And my possible perceptions of a material thing intend or "constitute" the thing as something that persists or flows in time. Thus, on Husserl's analysis, my basic consciousness of the world around me "constitutes" in one swoop the complex relationship among objects, their appearances, and my flowing consciousness of objects with appearances. That is, my consciousness simultaneously (1) "constitutes" itself in time and (2) "constitutes" sensible qualities (of objects) occurring in time and (3) "constitutes" material objects themselves occurring in time, whether enduring objects such as a bird or ephemeral objects such as a wave.

In this way, Husserl's analysis shows, our world is structured in time, in the temporal flow of: (1) our flowing stream of consciousness; (2) our flowing sensory experiences presenting qualities with changing appearances in time; and (3) material objects or events flowing in time, material things of which we are conscious in sensory experience. Within this temporal matrix there occur, flowing in time, the intentional acts of consciousness of which we spoke in the previous section. Some of these acts are elementary sensory experiences of sensible qualities (the color of the bird, the sound of the tone in the song). Others of these acts are complex perceptions of objects or events (the pelican diving into the surf, the bar of "Yesterday" sung by Paul McCartney). Other acts are complex thoughts about mathematics or about philosophical concepts such as intentionality. All such acts, in any event, take place within the flow of the stream of consciousness.

SPACE, SPACE–TIME, AND MATERIAL THINGS

The familiar things around us occur in time – birds in flight, crashing surf, songs on the stereo, books lying on the table. Of course, these things also occur in space (as already indicated). Modern physics, with Albert Einstein, joins space and time together as space–time, as Husserl knew. Prior to theoretical physics, however, our everyday experience of familiar things already links their temporal and spatial characters: as I see that pelican gliding over the cresting surf, I experience it as a spatiotemporal thing in nature. Husserl devoted a full series of lectures to our experience of the spatial character of material things (objects and events), including the role of one's body in experience of material things. These lectures have been gathered under the title *Thing and Space: Lectures of 1907* (1973/1997, here cited as *Thing*, 1907). Husserl's analysis of the "constitution" of material things as spatiotemporal is detailed in these lectures, and the analysis recurs in later works, including, *inter alia*, *Ideas* I (1913), *Ideas* II (1912), and the *Crisis* (1935–8). This analysis adds important detail to the basic phenomenology of perception set out in Investigations V and VI of the *Logical Investigations* (1900–1). Notably, Husserl observes that we experience material things as related to our own body, through which we interact with objects. (Husserl contrasts the "living body," or *Leib*, with the inanimate "corporeal body," or *Körper*.) As I reach for this cup of coffee, I perceive it in relation to my body; I see it, I reach for it, I grasp it, always experiencing it as located in a spatial context centered on my body (sitting "over there," its bowl opening "upward," its handle pointing "leftward," all in relation to my bodily location and orientation). Again, as I see that raven flying by, I perceive the object as flying by me, over there in relation to my body, moving by me at a certain perceived distance from me, from my body as I turn my head and eyes in the direction of the cawing sound.

In the *Critique of Pure Reason* (1781/1787) Immanuel Kant argued that space and time are not objective properties of things in themselves, but rather "forms of intuition," that is, forms of things as they appear in human sensory cognition. For Kant, these forms are defined by "constitutive rules" that govern our sensory experience, constraining ways in which we can know things in space and time. Husserl's view is different, but he situates his account of the "constitution" of space and material things within the legacy of Kant's theory. Husserl sometimes referred to his lectures on space as "the Thing Lectures" and saw them as part of a planned "phenomenology and critique of reason" (*Thing*, 1907, Editor's introduction: xx). More directly relevant than Kantian philosophy of space and time, though also in Kant's wake, were the mathematical theories of space and number in Husserl's own time. Within the mathematical tradition Husserl had written his 1883 doctoral dissertation on the calculus and his 1886 *Habilitation* on number theory, reworked as his first book, *Philosophy of Arithmetic* (1891/2003). In that spirit, Husserl's analysis of the "constitution" of space took shape in the *Thing* lectures, building on his early mathematical work.

Husserl begins the *Thing* lectures with a distinction that shaped all of his later work: that between "the world of natural experience" and "the world of scientific theory" (*Thing*, 1907, §1). In the "natural" attitude in which we live our everyday lives, "an existing world stands before our eyes, a world that extends infinitely in space, that now is, previously was, and in the future will be" (p. 2). The world around us is thus spatial and temporal. We ourselves are the "centers of reference" for this world around us. "The environing objects [*Objekten*], with their properties, changes, and relations, are what they are for themselves, but they have a position relative to us, initially a spatio-temporal position and then also a 'spiritual' [= cultural] one" (p. 2). In this world we find objects such as birds, trees, and mountains. Furthermore, "In this same world I also find other I's [*andere Ich*]" (p. 3): other subjects, other people. So the world around us includes several kinds of spatiotemporal "things": rocks, plants, animals, and also things that are "spiritual" as well as physical, namely other people, hence also social groups and cultural artifacts such as books and houses. By contrast, the world of scientific theory includes bodies with mass, fields of gravity and electromagnetic force, and the form of space–time that physics posits – which Albert Einstein, in the very years Husserl was writing, argued has a structure different from the idealized Euclidean space that Newtonian physics had described. We today are in an even better position to appreciate the divergence between the world as we experience it in everyday life – the "life-world," or *Lebenswelt*, as Husserl would later call it in the *Crisis* (1935–8) – and the world as our contemporary physics describes it. This distinction sets the scene, then, for Husserl's detailed analysis of the structure of space as we experience spatiality in everyday perception and action.

The classical empiricists of the 18th, 19th, and 20th centuries held that what we fundamentally perceive are sensory qualities or "sense-data," such as patches of color or bits of sound. By contrast, Husserl's account of basic perception is much more complex. We see objects in motion, we hear songs, we touch tools, and so forth. When I see a bird in flight, my experience presents a complex phenomenon. The bird in flight looks different from different perspectives at different times. The shapes and colors that form the bird's appearance are qualities of the object, and these sensible qualities themselves may appear differently in different circumstances, from different angles or in different lighting. (A square looks rectangular from an angle, the red of an object looks different as the light changes, the tone in a song appears different when accompanied by other tones, and so on.) Accordingly, Husserl distinguishes three types of entity in the "constitution" of a material thing as given in perception:

1   the thing itself;
2   its *essence* (kinds, qualities, relations), notably including, where appropriate, (2ᵃ) its *sensible qualities* (some qualities are visible, others are not);
3   the *appearances* (Erscheinungen) or "adumbrations" (*Abschattungen*) of a sensible quality in a thing.

For example, the bird I see is an animate material thing in nature, having its existence and essence apart from my seeing it. The bird, a raven landing on the fence nearby, has properties including a distinctive shape and a bluish-black color in its feathers. This black in its feathers looks different as the sun suddenly fades (the bluish sheen is gone). All that complexity enters into what Husserl calls the "constitution" of the object as given in my experience. The preceding account of perception and its objects is succinctly gathered in *Ideas* I (1913, §43), drawing on details in the *Thing* lectures.

In the *Thing* lectures (*Thing*, 1907) Husserl elaborates the structure in the perceptual "constitution" of a thing and its spatial or spatiotemporal extension. Suppose I see a raven in flight, about to land on a fence. To begin phenomenological analysis, there is the "appearance" of the thing (Thing, 1907, §16), its raven-like shape from my perspective and its intense black from my view in the present light. The *appearance* of the thing is already "constituted" as a spatial entity, insofar as the perceived color-shape of the raven has a certain spatial, indeed spatiotemporal, extension: this spread of black in my current visual field (Thing, 1907, §§19–25). The appearance of the raven changes over time, as it flies in and lands on the fence, as it shifts its head around, as it lets out a cawing sound with its beak open. That is, the shape-appearance changes over this time period, and the black-appearance changes as the sun fades momentarily. Echoing Kant, Husserl groups these varying appearances as a "manifold [Mannigfaltigkeit] of appearances" (§§27ff.). Prior philosophers sought to reduce the material thing to a manifold of possible appearances: this view was called phenomenalism (not to be confused with phenomenology!). But Husserl by no means reduces the raven to its appearances. Rather, the appearances are appearances or adumbrations of certain qualities of the raven. The raven itself is distinct from its properties, and its properties may change over time – its size, weight, location, wing attitude, movement in flight. Moreover, the *sensible* qualities of the raven – its shape, color, attitude, and so on – are distinct from their appearances. Thus, I know that the shape and color I see in the raven may themselves appear differently were I to see the same bird from a different angle or in a changing light.

So the "constitution" of the raven in my experience begins with a manifold of appearances of its visible qualities, yet what I see is not simply the sensory appearances, but rather the *raven* as having various *properties*, including *sensible qualities* that exhibit such *appearances* as I see the bird from various sides, in various lighting, and so on. Indeed, the raven is intended as much more than a thing with perceivable qualities appearing in various ways. For, as I understand, the raven is an object with many further properties, including its biological species, its genealogical relations to other ravens, its past activities in the hills and trees in its habitat, and much more. As Husserl often says, the object is "transcendent" of what I have seen or touched or known of it so far; there is always more to come, more to the object (Thing, 1907, §33; Ideas I, 1913, §44). We may depict the basic structure in the "constitution" of the raven I now see in Figure 5.3.

EXPERIENCE: I see that raven, now there before me, before my body, as I turn my eyes, head, trunk toward it ...

Figure 5.3 Experience of a thing in space–time

MY BODY AND THINGS AROUND ME

Things around me I experience as located relative to my body, that is, in a spatial, a spatiotemporal, relation to my body, my "lived body" (Leib). For example, I see that raven over there, in front of my eyes, which are at the front of my head, which is atop my body, wherein my hands are to my right and left, with my trunk upright and my legs supporting me. Of course, these details of my embodiment are not thematic in my seeing the raven. Rather, this form of my embodiment – presupposed in seeing "that raven (before me, before my body, upright with respect to my body, and so on)" – is part of the background of my experience in seeing the raven. Specifically, this structure of my embodiment defines, as it were, the coordinate system of both my visual field and my kinesthetic field. Kinesthesis (or "kinaesthesis") is my sensation of my own bodily movement and attitude, that is, the placement and movement of my limbs, today called proprioception. As I turn to see the cawing raven, my kinesthetic sensation of moving my eyes, my head, my trunk, all this is integral to my visual experience of seeing the bird. As Husserl explicitly notes, my kinesthetic sensations of my body in motion (Thing, 1907, §§44ff.) are partly definitive of my visual field (§§48ff.). We may speak simply of my seeing that raven, but closer phenomenological description finds that "I see that raven, as I turn my head and my eyes in its direction." Husserl speaks thus of my "oculo-motor field" (§58): the object of my visual perception is located in a spatiotemporal field that is not merely visual, but is a visual-kinesthetic field of my current awareness. In the field are things I see; and in the field as well are my bodily movements as I turn my eyes toward what I see.

What I experience as *space* or *space–time*, then, is a structure in my current visual-kinesthetic field of consciousness. Moreover, this field also includes things as presented in my auditory sensibility, my tactile sensibility, and so on. In the right circumstance I may see a raven that I also hear and, if it were to alight on my outstretched hand, that I also feel on my hand and even, given its proximity, smell. Today's cognitive psychologists talk of the "binding" of these different sensory fields, as the brain unifies the influx of visual, auditory, tactile, proprioceptive-kinesthetic information. Bracketing the brain's underlying activity, Husserl's phenomenological analysis would characterize the *meaning* of my seeing the raven. On that analysis, the form of my experience is that of my perception of the raven before me, with its shape and color and cawing and movement appearing in certain ways, all this occurring in my current visual-motor-tactile-auditory-olfactory field of consciousness. Space–time as I experience it is part of the structure of such a field. And that field is defined in terms of relations to my body, to relevant parts of my body, which serves as the center of orientation in the field. The "constitution" of my own body – in my sensations of moving or moving my body (*Thing*, 1907, §83) – is thus central to the "constitution" of space and time and things around me in space and time (*Thing*, 1907, §73). (The role of my "lived body" [*Leib*] in my experience was elaborated in Husserl's subsequent works, *Ideas* II, 1912, and the *Crisis*, 1935–8.) This theme became central in the works of two subsequent phenomenologists: in Maurice Merleau-Ponty's *Phenomenology of Perception* (1945/2003) and Aron Gurwitsch's *The Field of Consciousness* (1964).

When I see that raven on the fence, I understand that I could move around it and see *the same* object from different perspectives (if only it won't fly off). Thus, the thing is "constituted" as the same object with changes in its qualities as perceived from different perspectives or in different perspectives (*Thing*, 1907, §79). This theme is emphasized in all of Husserl's main works. (See *Ideas* I, §§43, 131, 149.) In Husserl's idiom, the object of my perception is constituted as "the same" object intended in my different acts of perception, as I look at the same object, here and there, from different sides. Moreover, the object is "constituted" as "the same" object in a horizon of possible further perceptions. This picture is central to Husserl's theory of phenomenological constitution, elaborated in Chapter 6.

Our sense of space and of time interact in this pattern of constitution of "the same" object as given in different perceptions, actual and possible. Indeed, space and time are interconnected in our experience of material things. On the one hand, time is implicated in the constitution of objects in space; on the other hand, space is implicated in the constitution of objects in time. Specifically, the same object is constituted in my unfolding perceptual experience as I move around the object in space, as I move in time and as my experience unfolds in time. Thus, the raven is "before me now," before "my body," which persists through time in space and by means of which "I" move. Moreover, spatial objects are constituted as "the same" object which I could perceive in further experiences at different times. I could walk around the raven, or the raven could fly off and I would see it from different perspectives as it flies, all in time.

In the Thing lectures Husserl organizes his account of the "constitution" of space or spatiality, specifying some four levels of possible kinesthetic sensations of a given material thing (Thing, 1907, §73). First, there is the constitution of the "oculo-motor field" itself: the form of visual space, the field of what I can see before me, informed however by kinesthetic sensations of moving my eyes to see a given thing. Then there is a "linear manifold of approaching and receding": the field of possibilities for what I can see of a thing as I approach it or recede from it (in some line of bodily movement as in walking), or as it approaches and recedes from me. Furthermore, there is a "cyclical manifold of turning": the field of possibilities for what I can see of a thing as I turn my body toward or away from it (turning my trunk this way or that), in particular as I walk toward or around it. And finally there are combinations of these possibilities of sensory-motor consciousness of the same thing.

In Ideas I (1913) Husserl amplifies his account of the "constitution" of a material thing. There he develops his analysis of consciousness of the same object in different possible experiences, for example, possible perceptions of the same object from different perspectives (§§128–32). Then, closing the long course of the book, he appraises the "constitution" of material things in nature (§§148–53). Accordingly, we experience things – things are "constituted" in our experience – not only as things perceivable from various perspectives, presenting variable appearances, but also, of course, as objectively existing things with causal properties in the order of nature. Most of the properties of a material thing are, we understand, beyond our knowledge, "transcendent" of our current experience and outrunning the range of our cognitive abilities.

In his last phase of work, gathered in the Crisis (1935–8), Husserl returned to an important aspect of our experience and knowledge of things in nature. Our "constitution" of the essence of material things in mathematical physics develops a "mathematized" idealization of the spatial and spatiotemporal character of things around us. This idealization abstracts away from our familiar "life-world" level of understanding of things in nature. In particular, our mathematical descriptions of spatial movement abstract away from the role of our bodies in perceiving movements of objects in nature. Moreover, the physicist's description of nature abstracts away from another vital aspect of our everyday "constitution" of material things around us: their intersubjectivity.

SELF, OTHERS, AND INTERSUBJECTIVITY

I see around me other people, "other I's," other beings who are subjects with their own consciousness, who are fellow human organisms in nature, and who are "spiritual" (geistlich) persons in our common culture. Accordingly, when I see things around me in space–time, I understand these things to be "there for everyone," perceivable by others, utilizable by others, and so forth. And so the world around me is an intersubjective world, and this intersubjectivity is something I naturally experience as I gaze upon things or pick them up to use them or think about them.

In his 1912 manuscript published posthumously as Ideas II (1912/1952/1989), Husserl analyzed in detail different aspects of the self and correlative relations to others. On Husserl's account, "I" have importantly different aspects which distinguish me as subject of intentional experiences, as embodied subject or agent of actions, as natural organism, and as social being (in communities including my family, my nation, my university, and so on.). In Chapter 4 we considered the ontology of these different aspects of the self: there is one being, "I," who has properties that fall under three "regional" essences of Consciousness, Nature, and Culture. Here our concern is the phenomenology of experiences of self and other. Thus, I may experience *myself* as a subject, as a biological being, or as a cultural being. And I may experience others, other "I's," similarly. I may experience another as another subject (she sees what I see), as another "living body" or agent (he is walking toward the door), as another human organism (he appears to have hurt his foot), or as another person in my community (she is addressing our university Chancellor). And accordingly, living in a world with others, I may experience natural objects as beings linked to myself and others in virtue of our properties of intentional experience, embodiment, and social or cultural activity.

When I see that raven on the fence, I experience it as there for others also to see if they so look. In Husserl's terms, the object of my perception is "constituted" as "there for everyone." Specifically, the object is "constituted" as "the *intersubjectively identical physical thing*," and it is so constituted in "experience mediated by 'empathy'" (*Ideas* I, §151). Thus, the horizon of the object of my perception includes not only further aspects or properties of the same object that I could see if I moved around it, but also further possible aspects that others could see if they moved around it. In this way the object is "constituted" as an intersubjective thing. Husserl emphasizes the close tie between *objectivity* and *intersubjectivity* in this phenomenological feature of experience, beginning with everyday perception.

An object in my surroundings – the raven on the fence, the sailboat on the ocean – is *objective* in that it exists and is what it is regardless of whether I or anyone else is perceiving it, or thinking about it, or interacting with it. (Here we assume that Husserl is not an idealist, a point of disagreement among Husserl interpreters.) An object is *intersubjective*, however, insofar as it is available to intentional acts of consciousness by different subjects, by me and you and others. As Husserl says, the object is an "identical" object amid different possible acts directed toward it, "the pure X in abstraction from all predicates" (*Ideas* I, 1913, §131). But intersubjectivity consists in its being a pole of identity for acts by different subjects.

My experience of objects as intersubjective presupposes my consciousness of other subjects. How am I aware of others *as* others? Of course, I see other people. In my perception another is "constituted" as a material thing in nature, but not merely so. The other is "constituted" as an animate being, an animal in nature, but moreover as a fellow subject. According to Husserl, our primary form of experience of others, as others, is empathy (Einfühlung).

Surprisingly, the concept of empathy was not well developed until the early 20th century. In the 18th century David Hume had written of the importance of "sympathy" in ethical deliberations, but the term "empathy" had not yet entered the English language. In the 19th century German Romantics coined the term "Einfühlung" to mean feeling one's way into the emotional tone of a work of art such as a poem. Psychology was beginning to stake out its territory as a proper science, and the English word "empathy" seems to have been coined as a translation of the German technical term. In any event, Husserl developed an articulate phenomenology of empathy that builds on a phenomenology of embodiment.

In *Ideas* II (1912) Husserl appraised the "living body" (*Leib*) in rich detail (§§35–42; extending his results in the *Thing* lectures of 1907). My body is "constituted" in my experience in several different ways: (1) as the center of orientation for things around me in space–time; (2) as the unifying locus of my visual, tactual, kinesthetic, and other sensory fields; (3) as my "organ of will" and "free movement"; (4) as an object with its own peculiar "manifolds of appearance" through kinesthesis and through "wielding" my body as I move and act in the world; (5) and as "part of the causal nexus" of interactions among objects in nature. (I enter the causal order as I cause things to move by pushing on them via my body, and as things cause me to move by pushing on my body.) My experience of my body, structured in these ways, is integral then to my empathic experience of others (§§43–7). We experience animals in nature as "physical bodies" (*Körper*) with "appresented" (co-presented) "psychic lives." I see this dog, immediately and "intuitively," as a being that is a body animated with experiences of seeing and willing. And similarly, with empathy

I intuitively experience a fellow human being as a being that is
both bodily and psychic. So Husserl writes:

> It is only with empathy and the constant orientation . . . toward
> the psychic life which is appresented along with the other's living
> body and which is continually taken objectively, together with the
> body, that the closed unity, man, is constituted, and I transfer this
> unity subsequently to myself.
>
> (*Ideas* II, 1912/1989, §46, translation modified)

That is, in empathic experience I immediately see another human
being as a body with psychic experience, or rather as a bodily-
psychic being, that is, a "man." Remarkably, Husserl says I transfer
this sense of unity from the other to myself. So, Husserl finds, I
do not first put together my sense of my consciousness and my
sense of my body, and then transfer that composite sense to the
other; rather, I transfer the sense of body-psyche from the other to
myself. More aptly, Husserl will later say there is a "mutual
transfer of sense" between the other and myself (*Cartesian Meditations*,
1931, §51), whereby "the other is himself there before us 'in
person'" (§50). Notice the plural form "us" in this last remark:
the other "I" is intersubjectively before "us" – we are all in this
world together.

In *On the Problem of Empathy* (1916/1989), Edith Stein, Husserl's
student and assistant, presented a particularly sharp and succinct
analysis of empathy along the lines charted by Husserl. On Stein's
account, empathy consists, most basically, in a transfer of the sense
"I" between my own range of experience and the other's. Thus,
empathy is a form of "intuition" or direct experience of another
"I," an experience in which I immediately understand the other's
experience as if I myself were living through her experience.
When I see another person, then, the content of my seeing another
is in effect "another I" who sees "that object" as I would were I in
the other's place.

In *empathy*, then, I intuitively experience another "I." This is the
key to Husserl's analysis (note his mention of "other I's" in the
world, already cited from *Thing*, 1907). "Intuition" is a technical
term in Husserl's vocabulary, a part of his epistemology, to which

we turn in Chapter 7. Briefly, an intuition is an act in which an object is "itself" given with "evidence." In perception I am presented "this" object, given evidently. When I see another person, however, I am presented not merely "this" material thing, given evidently; rather, I am presented "she" or "you," or "this other [bodily-psychic] I." (For contemporary phenomenological studies, see D. W. Smith 1989: ch. 3 on empathy; and Zahavi 1999 on awareness of oneself and others.)

In Husserl's account, sharpened by Stein, the sense "I" is transferred from my own case to the other's (or vice versa). This form of experience Husserl calls "reproductive." In recollection my present consciousness presents reproductively what I previously experienced (in a prior phase of my stream of consciousness). In this form of reproductive memory, I re-live, as it were, my previous experience, but from a certain temporal distance. Similarly, in empathy my present consciousness presents reproductively what the other "I" experiences in her own case, but from a certain interpersonal distance. Thus, I "re-live," as it were, the other's experience, but from a certain distance, as I know the other is distinct from myself. In this way the "other I"'s experience is "constituted" empathically *as if* I were living through that form of experience within my own stream of consciousness. Or so goes the account of a vivid form of empathic experience. Typically, though, this transfer of sense is instinctive and seamless, without any sense of actively reliving the other's form of experience.

In point of ontology, the self is that being who experiences the acts within a unified stream of consciousness. In point of phenomenology, however, the intentional content or *sense* "I" encodes that unique mode of awareness in which I am aware of myself as "I" whereas another is aware of herself as "I." We know how the word "I" works; the sense "I" works similarly. In my stream of consciousness the sense "I" intentionally prescribes me; in your stream of consciousness the sense "I" prescribes you. In the background lies my understanding that I do not experience or live through your experiences, and you do not experience mine. Empathy emerges from that reciprocal understanding of the first-person form of consciousness.

In our running example, when I see that raven and see that you see it too, I immediately understand that you are seeing it somewhat as I might see it were I in your shoes, looking at it from your perspective. In this way, empathy grounds intersubjectivity, which adjoins objectivity in our "constitution" of the world around us.

THE LIFE-WORLD

From his earliest writings Husserl was concerned with the difference between things as we experience them in everyday life and the same things as we idealize their nature in mathematics. In geometry we idealize and "mathematize" shapes of everyday objects: the carpenter seeks a straight line in the edge of the board he is fashioning, but a perfectly straight line is an unrealizable ideal of Euclidean geometry, where a straight line is a series of points that never intersects itself or any other parallel line. In his last years of work, in 1935–8, Husserl worried about the effects of our "mathematization" of nature in physics. Our mathematical idealization of the properties of things in nature, of space and time and motion, carries us away from our everyday understanding of things as we see and touch and move among things in nature. Husserl's texts on these issues were gathered posthumously in *The Crisis of European Sciences and Transcendental Phenomenology* (1935–8/1954/1970, here cited as the *Crisis* 1935–8).

In the *Crisis* Husserl saw a crisis in European – and, we should say, global – culture, as our scientific conception of nature diverged from our everyday experience of the world, the "world of everyday life," the "life-world," or *Lebenswelt*. A kind of alienation has set in, whereby we view the essence of space–time and natural things and ultimately ourselves and our humanity in idealized mathematical terms that do not seem to connect with our everyday life. Relativity theory finds space–time curved in ways we do not recognize in everyday experience. Quantum mechanics finds a physical system distributed over a space of possible states that cannot be realized in our everyday affairs. Husserl was aware of the developments in mathematical physics in his era. Updating the natural scientific view since Husserl's day, however, we find the computer model of mental activity: intentional experience is modeled as software running on the neural circuitry of our brains, thereby "mathematizing" even our own subjective, first-person forms of consciousness. Sure enough, late-20th-century philosophy has been focused, almost obsessively, on the mind–body problem in this form: how can our subjective experience, bearing the phenomenal characters of "what it is like" to see and touch and desire and even think, be understood in terms of the mathematical algorithms that define computations allegedly carried out by our brains?

Husserl launched phenomenology as an extension of "pure logic," yet he carved out an account of how logic ties into the intentional contents of consciousness, in the long course of the *Logical Investigations* (1900–1). Later, in *Formal and Transcendental Logic* (1929), he returned to this part of what we may call the semantics of language cum experience. Logic must include not only the formal structures that modern mathematical logic defines (following Frege *et al.*), but also the "transcendental" structures of consciousness and its contents, which ultimately give meaning to the formal symbolic statements of mathematical logic ("mathematized" logic, we may say). In the *Crisis* (1935–8) Husserl extended this pattern of analysis from mathematical logic to mathematical physics. If mathematical logic *sans* intentionality cuts off the structures of meaning that are a part of logic writ large, the "crisis" in "the European sciences" stems from the way in which mathematical physics seems cut off from the structures of meaning that define space–time and motion as we know them in everyday life: the very phenomena to be explained (more deeply) by mathematical physics. The crisis of natural science, for Husserl, is the problem of understanding the ways in which mathematical physics is grounded in the life-world. Transcendental phenomenology is the discipline that offers a solution to the crisis, so Husserl urged.

Phenomenology is "transcendental" insofar as it studies the structures of meaning that characterize our experience. Husserl's phenomenology of our experience of time, space, material things, our selves and other people – outlined earlier – details a wide range of such phenomena. The solution of the "crisis" Husserl saw lies in integrating these phenomenological results with views of natural science, and indeed with contemporary cultural or social science, which also seeks to "mathematize" aspects of our psychological and sociological activities.

SUMMARY

Phenomenology is the study of consciousness from the first-person perspective: thus, we characterize different forms of experience, describing things just as we experience them, in perception, thought, imagination, emotion, desire, volition, and so on. Brentano distinguished descriptive psychology, or phenomenology, from genetic psychology: the former studies the types and characters of mental states, while the latter studies the causal genesis of mental states. Taking inspiration from Brentano, Husserl went on to develop phenomenology as a new and distinctive science. Husserl defined phenomenology, officially, as the *science of the essence of consciousness*. (We explored Husserl's theory of sciences in Chapter 3 and his ontology of essences, and the region of consciousness, in Chapter 4.) Typically, Husserl found, consciousness is a consciousness of something. That is, each act of consciousness is *intentional*, directed toward some object, a consciousness of that object. Accordingly, intentionality is the central structure in the essence of consciousness.

Husserl developed a detailed theory of the intentionality of consciousness. An *act* of consciousness is experienced by a *subject* and is directed toward an appropriate *object*. Crucially, the act carries a *content*, a sense that prescribes or presents an object as having various features. The act is directed toward, or *intends*, that object which the act's content prescribes. Further, what the content prescribes is constrained by a *horizon* of background meaning. *Intentionality* consists in this complex relation among subject, act, content, and object (if such object exists), constrained by horizon. Husserl's analysis of the structure of intentionality is the foundation of his new science of phenomenology. Husserl's conception of phenomenology, properly developed, reflects his conception of pure logic (where ideal meanings represent appropriate objects in the world, according to our reconstruction in Chapter 3).

Over the course of his career, Husserl analyzed, in considerable detail, basic structures of perception, judgment, action, consciousness of space, consciousness of time, awareness of one's own body and of oneself, empathic awareness of others, and much more. Of special significance is the structure of the life-world, our surrounding world as experienced in familiar activities of everyday life. Husserl's analyses of these diverse features of experience weave together an intricate account of the overall structure of consciousness – and thereby define the parameters of the new discipline of phenomenology.

Husserl's phenomenological analyses disclose the character of our world as essentially objective, subjective, and intersubjective. Thus, we experience a world of relations among the objective (the way things are spread out around us in time and space), the subjective (the way our own conscious experience flows off in relation to things around us), and the intersubjective (the way things are there for everyone amid our social activities in our common life-world).

FURTHER READING

Below are suggested texts that introduce phenomenology in a wide context, addressing the characterization of the discipline and the place of Husserl in its development.

Embree, Lester, Elizabeth A. Behnke, David Carr, J., Claude Evans, José Huertas-Jourda, Joseph J. Kokelmans, William R. McKenna, Algis Mickunas, Jitendra Nath Mohanty, Thomas M. Seebohm, and Richard M. Zaner, eds. 1997. *Encyclopedia of Phenomenology*. Dordrecht and Boston, Massachusetts: Kluwer Academic Publishers (now New York: Springer). A handbook of essays on many aspects of phenomenology and its history.

Moran, Dermot. 2000. *Introduction to Phenomenology*. London and New York: Routledge. A detailed overview of classic work in phenomenology, including a chapter on background in Brentano, four chapters on Husserl's work and life, and several chapters on later phenomenologists (Heidegger, Sartre, Merleau-Ponty) and broadly phenomenological continental philosophers (Gadamer, Arendt, Levinas, Derrida), all presented in historical context and chronological development.

Siewert, Charles. 1998. *The Significance of Consciousness.* Princeton: Princeton University Press. A study of consciousness in the tradition of analytic philosophy of mind, sympathetic to phenomenology in a minimalist form.

Smith, David Woodruff. 2003. "Phenomenology." Online at *The Stanford Encyclopedia of Philosophy* (Winter 2003 edition), Edward N. Zalta, ed. URL = http://plato.stanford.edu/archives/win2003/entries/phenomenology/. A basic introduction to phenomenology, its basic concepts, methods, and history.

Smith, David Woodruff, and Ronald McIntyre. 1982. *Husserl and Intentionality: A Study of Mind, Meaning, and Language.* Dordrecht and Boston, Massachusetts: D. Reidel Publishing Company (now New York: Springer). A study of Husserl's theory of intentionality, its background in Brentano and others, its role in phenomenology, and its development in relation to contemporary semantics.

Smith, David Woodruff, and Amie L. Thomasson, eds. 2005. *Phenomenology and Philosophy of Mind.* Oxford and New York: Oxford University Press. A collection of new essays on various aspects of phenomenology as a discipline and its role in contemporary philosophy of mind.

Sokolowski, Robert. 2000. *Introduction to Phenomenology.* Cambridge and New York: Cambridge University Press. An introduction to phenomenology, laying out Sokolowski's conception of the discipline, influenced by his interpretation of Husserl but without textual commentary.

Spiegelberg, Herbert. 1965. *The Phenomenological Movement: A Historical Introduction.* Second edition. Vols. 1 and 2. The Hague: Martinus Nijhoff. A two-volume history of the phenomenology, featuring studies of main figures and trends in the larger movement.

Zahavi, Dan. 1999. *Self-Awareness and Alterity: A Phenomenological Investigation.* Evanston, Illinois: Northwestern University Press. A contemporary phenomenological study of awareness of oneself and of others, hence of intersubjectivity.

——. 2003. *Husserl's Phenomenology.* Stanford, California: Stanford University Press. 2003. An overview of Husserl's transcendental phenomenology.

Six

Phenomenology II

Intentionality, method, and theory

The preceding chapter introduced Husserl's conception of the new science of phenomenology and outlined some of the main results in his analysis of the structure of consciousness. This chapter explores, in closer detail, the basic theory and methodology developed in Husserl's system of phenomenology. By practicing a special method of reflection on our experience, "bracketing" the question of the existence of the world we experience, Husserl explicates the structure of intentionality, wherein consciousness intends or represents an object in a certain way: through a given meaning or "noema," which takes its place in a "horizon" of meaning, in which the object is "constituted" in consciousness as having various possible properties. At the same time, Husserl uses that model of intentionality to explicate his method of reflection on the meaningful content of experience. Husserl's theory of intentionality – featuring structures of noema and horizon – distinguishes phenomenology, in his view, from empirical psychology. For Husserl, phenomenology is part "phenomena" and part "logic," and their integration is carried out in the details of his theory of intentionality. Our task now is to explain Husserl's revolutionary notions – intentionality, noema, horizon, constitution – in as simple a way as possible while laying out the key terms and their use in his articulation of phenomenology.

HUSSERL'S DEVELOPING CONCEPTION OF PHENOMENOLOGY

The conventional wisdom about Husserl's philosophical development sees a radical shift as Husserl moves from the *Logical Investigations* (1900–1) to *Ideas* I (1913), from his early period to his middle period and beyond. In the *Investigations* Husserl rejected 19th-century psychologism, which would reduce logic and mathematics, and other forms of knowledge, to contingent forms of human activity. Rather, Husserl held, philosophy should begin with a logic that studies ideal meanings, analyzing the relations of entailment among propositions and the semantic correlations of meanings with objects in the world, whereby propositions represent states of affairs in the world. Objective knowledge then supports propositions with appropriate evidence. And within these structures of meaning and knowledge, Husserl held, we find intentionality and thus phenomenology. In *Ideas* I, the conventional reading says, Husserl then took a radical "transcendental" turn. Phenomenology is no longer a step along the road from pure logic to objectivity of knowledge. Rather, phenomenology becomes the foundation of both logic and theory of knowledge, and of ontology as well. What we mean (logic), what we know (epistemology), and even what there is (ontology) are all defined within the structure of consciousness called intentionality. In the Kantian "transcendental" idiom, intentionality is the condition of the possibility of logic, epistemology, and ontology. For all meaning resides in consciousness, and the task of phenomenology is precisely to analyze the structures of meaning that we find in our conscious experiences of seeing, thinking, and willing. In this way, so the story goes, transcendental phenomenology provides a foundation for all of philosophy and indeed for all forms of understanding in philosophy, in the sciences, and in the arts.

What is missed in this conventional reading of Husserl, however, is the unity of Husserl's philosophy. This unity, explored in Chapter 2 of this volume, is laid out in the long course of argument in the *Logical Investigations*. Virtually all of that story remains in place in *Ideas* I. In the narrative line of *Ideas* I, Part One recapitulates and reorganizes basic principles of ontology largely charted in the *Investigations*, recast as the theory of fact and essence. These ontological principles are part of Husserl's conception of logic and its cognate ontology (detailed in the *Investigations*, reorganized here in launching *Ideas* I). Part Two then develops Husserl's mature account of the aims and methods of phenomenology, featuring the technique of "bracketing" the world in order to study "pure" consciousness. Part Three follows with Husserl's core distinctions among consciousness, sensation, intentionality, and the technical notions of "noesis" and "noema" (concrete experience and ideal meaning content). Finally, Part Four focuses on reason, evidence ("intuition"), and the objectivity of knowledge. This course of argument in *Ideas* I is broadly the same as that in the *Investigations*. Accordingly, the unity of Husserl's overall philosophical system remains in place – and continues to frame his work after *Ideas* I as well.

In *Ideas* I, important details of Husserl's system are either tacitly assumed or greatly compressed, including the lengthy accounts of logic itself, of how language expresses intentional content (philosophy of language), and of parts or "moments" (ontology). There are important revisions in the account of intentional content reconceived as *noema* (which we study in detail later in this chapter). As *Ideas* I unfolds, the focus is on Husserl's full account of phenomenology, its methods, and its core notion of noema. What is new is not a radical reduction of all the world to our ideas (patterns of noemata), but rather a very close account of how reflection on our experience explicates the intentionality of consciousness, revealing the contents of experiences and their role in directing consciousness toward objects in the world around us. This mature account of phenomenology presupposes principles of ontology and a broadly logical analysis of how meaning directs experience toward objects in the world.

We may hear strains of metaphysical idealism in *Ideas* I (§49), sung with the Kantian idiom of "transcendental idealism." Yet these idealist notes do not resonate with the rest of Husserl's philosophical system, wherein our thoughts are directed by objective meanings toward objective states of affairs in the world. Husserl often sought to incorporate into his own system major themes from other philosophers, including Brentano, Bolzano, Leibniz, Descartes, and Hume. Teaching in Germany in a period when neo-Kantian philosophy was prominent, Husserl wove into *Ideas* I Kantian themes of transcendental idealism. Yet Husserl's system differs from Kant's on important fundamentals of epistemology and ontology. We note these differences in passing, but here keep the focus on Husserl's "pure" phenomenology.

Our strategy in exploring Husserl's mature conception of phenomenology will be to trace the development of Husserl's account of method, his practice of that method, and his basic results in the unfolding theory of intentionality. In this path we shall follow Husserl through the highlights of *Ideas* I.

PHENOMENOLOGICAL METHODS

As an initial gloss, we may say that phenomenology studies the way we experience various forms of consciousness, characterizing "what it is like" to experience these states of consciousness. Some philosophers today think phenomenology addresses only what it is like to have sensory experiences, thereby describing the qualitative characters or sensory "qualia" of seeing red and the like. But Husserl's conception of phenomenology is far richer, and he was much exercised to develop a proper methodology for the new science of phenomenology.

The task of phenomenology, in Husserl's view, is to abstract the structure and content of an experience from the flow of consciousness, so that we may reflect on various forms of consciousness and their significance. In *Logical Investigations* (1900–1) Husserl developed the theoretical framework within which phenomenology was defined, featuring the intentionality of consciousness. Abstraction was a prominent theme in the *Investigations*, as Husserl addressed ideal meaning abstracted from uses of language, ideal species abstracted from concrete individuals, "moments" (dependent or "abstract" parts) abstracted from concrete wholes of which they are parts, and finally ideal intentional contents abstracted from "real" acts of consciousness. Subsequently, in Ideas I (1913), Husserl laid out an explicit methodology for phenomenology. The main technique he called "bracketing" or "parenthesizing" (Einklammerung). He sometimes declared this method his greatest achievement. Yet he felt the method was widely misunderstood by friend and foe alike.

Today, with the benefit of philosophical hindsight, we can define Husserl's methodology fairly simply, by using what we know about Husserl's theory of intentionality and related features of language appraised in Logical Investigations. In this recounting, Husserl's phenomenological method "brackets" the object of consciousness − and the surrounding world in general − in order to shift our focus on to the sense or meaning through which the object is experienced. Husserl then displays the sense by a "quotation" of the sense − much as linguistic quotation shifts our attention from what we are talking about to the words we are using to talk about it. In this way, we abstract meaningful content, or sense (Sinn), from our passing acts of consciousness. (This interpretation of Husserl's method, based on his theory of intentionality, is developed in Dreyfus 1982 and Smith and McIntyre 1982.)

Husserl's revolutionary technique of bracketing consists in a transformation (in the first person) from (1) my consciousness of that object to (2) my consciousness of that object. Husserl the mathematician would see this transformation as a mapping from the object of my experience to the experience itself: as it were,

$$B(E(o)) = E$$

where E is an experience that aims me toward o (glossed as a function E that assigns to me the object o if such exists), and B is a function that assigns to $E(o)$ the function E.

Of course, Husserl does not "mathematize" the transformation in this way, for that gloss would miss the important experiential aspect of the transformation. (In this spirit, Thomasson 2005 characterizes bracketing as a "cognitive transformation.")

Indeed, Husserl characterizes the technique of bracketing as a shift in *attitude*. In the "natural" attitude I see that tree across the way. Now I "bracket" the question of its existence. Thereby I focus on the *way* the object is presented in my seeing it, the sense it has for me in my visual experience, regardless of whether it exists. By this shift in attitude, I turn toward my consciousness-of-the-object through a modification of my intention of that object. Rather than peering "inward" to see what is transpiring in my mind, as classical introspectionist psychology may have seemed to suggest, I proceed, as it were, through the *object* of my experience to my *experience* of the object. That is, I turn toward a consciousness that I experience as consciousness-of-objects-in-the-world. (A characterization of phenomenological method as rooted in "outer observation" is developed in Thomasson 2005. A somewhat different take on the attitude shift is developed in Sokolowski 2000.)

Bracketing

In the "natural attitude," Husserl observes, we take for granted the existence of the world around us: that is, "I and my surrounding world [Umwelt]" (*Ideas* I, §27). As Husserl writes, "I am conscious of a world, endlessly spread out in space, endlessly becoming and having become in time. . . . Through seeing, touching, hearing, etc., . . . corporeal things in their respective spatial distribution are *for me simply there* . . . " (§27, my translation). The assumption that there is such a world, "out there" surrounding me, Husserl calls "the general thesis of the natural attitude." Suppose I place this thesis in brackets or parentheses (§§30–2). I do not deny the thesis, indeed I continue to accept it, but I do not make any use of it. Then as I look around me, I attend not to the presumably existing things of which I am conscious, but to my consciousness of them. I shift my attention from the *objects* of my consciousness to my *consciousness* of those objects. In this modified attitude, the phenomenological attitude, I practice phenomenology in a dedicated way: thus, I reflect on my consciousness of such-and-such things, regardless of whether such things exist in the world around me. Our goal in the practice of bracketing, Husserl declares (§33), is "*the winning of . . . a new region of being* [*Seinsregion*]," the region of "pure experiences," "pure consciousness," its pure "correlates of consciousness" (namely, meanings), and its "pure I."

Husserl's phenomenological method of *bracketing* can be elaborated as follows, in the first-person singular:

1   The general thesis of the natural attitude is the implicit thesis that there exists a world around me, in which I and my activities occur.
2   In order to shift my attention away from things in the world around me, I bracket, and so make no use of, the general thesis of the natural attitude.
3   I then attend to my consciousness of things in the world.
4   In this modified attitude toward the world, I give phenomenological descriptions of various types of experience just as I experience them.

Husserl also called this method *epoché* (§32), meaning that I abstain from positing the existence of the world I experience. (*Epoché* is a Greek word meaning to abstain, a word used by the ancient Greek skeptics.) Further, Husserl called the method "phenomenological reduction," speaking of "reductions" in the plural (§§56ff.), wherein I suspend specific theses about the existence of the world, including theses from the natural sciences, theology, even logic. Thus, in a pure description of my experience, I suspend what I know about physics, what I know about God, even what I know about logical inference.

Husserl insisted that in the attitude of epoché "I do *not* then *negate* this 'world', as though I were a sophist, I *do not doubt its existence* (*Dasein*), as though I were a skeptic" (§32, my translation). So phenomenological reduction is not ontological reduction, where the material world is reduced to ideas in the mind, as Berkeley had proposed. Nor is epoché a kind of epistemological reduction or retraction, where knowledge of the external world is reduced or withdrawn into knowledge of consciousness, as a Cartesian skeptic might have held. Yet it is not without reason that Husserl's readers heard echoes of Cartesian skepticism and Berkeleyan idealism in this talk of "bracketing" the world. At one place Husserl even spoke of a methodological "nullification" (*Vernichtung*) of the world (§49). Husserl had not chosen the best tactic for trying to explicate his phenomenological method. He might better have introduced his method by drawing on the foundations of phenomenology laid in the *Logical Investigations*, where phenomenology is to study the structure of consciousness, including the intentional contents or meanings that distinguish various types of experience.

Ascent to meaning

We can recast the account of phenomenological method in terms of the theory of intentionality:

1   My consciousness is usually a consciousness of something.
2   In order to shift my attention away from objects in the world around me, I bracket the thesis of the existence of the world including those objects.
3   I then attend to my consciousness of objects in the world.
4   In this modified attitude toward the world, I give phenomenological descriptions of various types of experience just as I experience them, where these descriptions characterize the contents or meanings of such experiences, presenting objects *as* experienced, regardless of whether the objects represented by these meanings exist.

In this account of phenomenological method we make use of Husserl's basic (ontological) theory of intentionality: an act of consciousness is intentionally directed via a meaning toward an object. Phenomenology studies the experience and its content or meaning, not the object represented by the meaning. Thus we ascend from our first-order experience of things in the world to our higher-order reflection on our ordinary experience and its meaning (somewhat as W. V. Quine spoke of a "semantic ascent" from language to talk about language).

This intentionality-based perspective on method does not, however, follow the pedagogical course of *Ideas* I. As Husserl began his account of method early in *Ideas* I (§§27ff.), he did not yet – in the course of argument in that book – have any theory of intentionality to use in characterizing method. This theory itself was to be developed through the practice of phenomenology, as the discipline would unfold in *Ideas* I. Thus, as he begins to practice phenomenology, Husserl is attending to consciousness as experienced (§33). And the basic character of consciousness, of each conscious experience, is to be a consciousness of something, to be intentional – here is the basic form of consciousness (§§33–6, 84). As his analysis of the structure of intentionality unfolds (§§84–5, 88–90, 128–31), Husserl appraises the way in which consciousness presents its object: in the first person, I see or imagine or think of or desire an object *as* thus-and-so. To characterize an experience phenomenologically, Husserl shows, we appraise the content or meaning of the experience and its role in presenting the object of consciousness as thus-and-so. Here we find Husserl practicing phenomenological method, and his ultimate characterization of what he is doing is telling: he is analyzing the *meaning* in an experience, as opposed to the corresponding object of the experience (§§88–90). Indeed, he is doing so by using a variation on a familiar logical device: quotation.

Meaning abstraction in phenomenological "quotation"

Suppose I am in my garden regarding a tree in springtime. I construct a phenomenological description of my act of perception:

> I see this blossoming Japanese plum tree.

If in phenomenological reflection I attend to my visual experience, practicing the method of phenomenological reduction, here is how I might characterize the results of my reflection – in Husserl's prose:

"In" the reduced perception (in the phenomenologically pure experience [*Erlebnis*]) we find, as belonging inextricably to its essence, the perceived as such, to be expressed as "material thing," "plant," "tree," "blossoming," and so forth. The *quotation marks* [*Anführungszeichen*] are obviously significant; they express that change in sign, the corresponding radical modification of the meaning of the words. The *tree simpliciter* [*schlechthin*], the thing in nature, is anything but [*ist nichts weniger als*] this *perceived tree as such*, which as perceptual sense [*Wahrnehmungssinn*] belongs inseparably to the perception. The tree *simpliciter* can burn up, be resolved into its chemical elements, etc. But the sense [*Sinn*] – the sense of *this* perception, something belonging necessarily to its essence – cannot burn up; it has no chemical elements, no forces, no real properties.

(*Ideas* I, §89, my translation)

So what I find in my experience through phenomenological reflection, Husserl says, is not the physical tree, but the sense "this blossoming Japanese plum tree": the content of my experience, carrying the way the tree is perceived, as opposed to the physical tree itself.

What is Husserl saying in this dense but revealing passage? Normally, in the natural attitude, I take it that in seeing a tree I am related to the tree in space and time: my visual experience is directed toward and, in my mind, partly caused by the tree spatiotemporally before me on the occasion of my experience. However, in the phenomenological attitude, I "reduce" the experience by bracketing the thesis of the existence of the world around me, including the actual physical tree before me. This is what Husserl means by "phenomenological reduction." What do I find in my experience through phenomenological analysis? Part of the essence of my "lived experience" (*Erlebnis*) is what Husserl calls the perceived tree as such, the tree *as perceived*, which Husserl says is the perceptual *sense* (*Sinn*) in the experience. Where the object of my perception, the tree itself, is a physical object that can burn up, the sense in my perception is something entirely different, something that cannot burn up and is not a physical object at all. Yet this sense of the object as perceived belongs "inseparably" to the perception, the perceptual experience. What my phenomenological description of my experience characterizes, then, is the sense in the experience, not the object of the experience. That is the point of bracketing: put in parentheses the presumed existence of the object, the tree that is presumably before me and affecting my eyes; attend instead to the meaning or sense through which that tree is represented in my experience. In this way I appreciate the intentionality of my perceptual experience.

In the passage previously quoted we should notice a very simple device that forms the heart of Husserl's method of bracketing: the device of quotation!

Suppose I say: "That is a plum tree." You ask: "What did you say?" I answer, quoting my own words: "I said: 'That is a plum tree.'" When I first said, "That is a plum tree," I was asserting that a certain plant is a plum tree. But when I quoted my assertion, reporting *what I said*, I was not asserting this fact: instead, I was reporting my words, and therewith the meaning of my words, that is, what I said. Quotation thus shifts my attention away from the tree, whose existence I assume, to my statement, to my words and so to the meaning of my sentence, the *sense* of my assertion. The shift to the phenomenological attitude, through the technique Husserl called bracketing, is similar to this shift. And, as we saw, Husserl uses precisely the device of quotation to effect the phenomenological shift away from the object of my consciousness to my *sense* of that object.

When I see that Japanese plum tree, my perception posits the tree with a certain arboreal type. That is, my experience is intentionally directed through the perceptual sense "that Japanese plum tree" toward a particular arboreal being, and my experience carries the attitude of positing the existence of what is represented through that sense, assuming the existence of the world around me. Now I shift my attention from the tree itself to my perceptual consciousness of the tree. In phenomenological description I report: "I see 'that Japanese plum tree'." In the phenomenological attitude I am not concerned with the existence of such a tree as I see, with the tree itself; I am concerned with my experience of seeing the tree. In my report I quote (as it were) the content or sense of my visual experience: "that Japanese plum tree." This *phenomenological quotation* (to give it a name) thus shifts my attention from the tree I am seeing to my visual experience of the tree, and specifically to the sense in my perception, the sense that presents or represents the tree itself in a certain way, the sense expressed by my words in quotation marks. I am thus reporting *what I see*, just as I see it: "that Japanese plum tree." In effect, I *quote* that content, my perceptual sense: my shifting regard moves from the object itself toward that content or meaning, moving straightway through the words to the sense they draw from my experience.

Normally, we quote *words*, whose sense we immediately grasp if the words are familiar. When we specify the words a person used, we are normally trying to specify, as exactly as his words allow, *what he said*, that is, the content or sense of his statement. Here, in the practice of phenomenology, I use the quoted words "that Japanese plum tree" to focus directly on sense, the noematic sense in my experience. In *phenomenological* or *noematic quotation*, then, we focus on the sense these words draw out from my experience. Noematic quotation thus moves straightway through words to the sense in the experience on which I am reflecting. If we use angle brackets in addition to the usual quotation marks, we can say the *sense* <that Japanese plum tree> is the noematic sense in my perceptual experience, the sense expressed (within the limits of language) by the *words* "that Japanese plum tree," words I so use in noematic quotation.

Husserl might have been wise to lay more emphasis on this technique of "phenomenological quotation," since "phenomeno-logical reduction" can sound like ontological reduction. He could then have stressed the connection to language, relying on his own prior account of the relation between language and experience. In the *Logical Investigations* Husserl had developed an extensive account of language, holding that the meaning (*Bedeutung*) of a sentence is the expressed sense (*Sinn*) of an appropriate underlying act of judgment. When we quote a sentence in a familiar language, we thus rely on the extant semantics of that language, which assigns it a certain meaning, which is a sense that may serve as the intentional content of an appropriate type of experience. We use two grammatical devices, then, which are familiar from everyday language: parentheses (for bracketing the object) and quotation marks (for quoting the content). Still, Husserl's focus is rightly on consciousness, on the shift from object to content of thought, rather than on the conventional signs that express these contents or senses. Indeed, much of what we see outruns our language.

In Chapter 3 we explored Husserl's outline of a logic or semantics, which defines correlations between expressions in a language, the meaning (*Bedeutung*) assigned them in the language, the corresponding sense (*Sinn*) in the underlying thought or experience intimated by the expression, and the object designated by the expression, which is also the object intended in the underlying act of thought or consciousness. Husserl assumes that the content or sense in an experience is expressible in language – that is, in principle and within certain limitations. These logical and linguistic doctrines afford a deeper account of how phenomenological quotation is related to the familiar form of verbal quotation wherein we quote a speaker's words and therewith bring out the meaning of those words. At present we rely, as above, on a tacit familiarity with these procedures, as Husserl unfolds his own special use of quotation in articulating the noema or noematic sense of a form of consciousness.

Husserl's method of bracketing was designed to effect a shift in attitude, from the ordinary, "natural" attitude to the phenomenological, "transcendental" attitude. Within the phenomenological attitude I am to describe my experience just as I experience it, and in that project of description or analysis I produce a noematic quotation that invokes or expresses the sense (*Sinn*) that is the content of the experience on which I am reflecting. Of course, I am using a piece of language to invoke that content (we do phenomenology in language), and I am using the linguistic device of quotation to "quote" that content. Now, the technique of bracketing is a negative trick: I do not make any use of the thesis of the existence of the world around me. But the technique of quotation is a positive trick: I focus on the content of the given experience and formulate (within the limits of language) an expression of that content. Clearly, Husserl's aim is the positive one of focusing on experience and its content. Bracketing is a preparation for this positive account of the content of an experience. And so, in phenomenological reflection, I turn my attention to the content of my experience, where my interest is not in what the content represents, or reaches in the world, but in how the content represents. (On the role of quotation in Husserl's phenomenological methodology, see Thomasson 2005; Smith and McIntyre 1982, the latter drawing on D. W. Smith 1970. A different take on quotation is developed in Sokolowski 2000 and Drummond 1990.)

The world in brackets

Despite Husserl's protestations, the method of bracketing has been misunderstood as a kind of denial of the world, of a piece with classical skepticism or idealism. We can now see how to correct that misconception. For the world is not lost or rejected in phenomenology, either in method or in ontology. Rather, the world enters "brackets" – phenomenological "quotation marks" – in order that we attend in reflection to our consciousness-of-the-world.

Consider the force of linguistic quotation. Read the following sentences in quotation (if you can):

"There's a squirrel in that plum tree."

"*Da ist ein Eichhörnchen auf dem Pflaumenbaum.*"

" 梅花樹上有隻松鼠 "

If you are fluent in English, you see the quoted English sentence already infused with meaning, that is, you immediately grasp *what it says* (with reference to the context of utterance), perhaps without noticing the words per se. Phenomenologically, it is as if you see through the words to what they mean: you see *what is said*, what is intended, the purported state of affairs that there's a squirrel in that plum tree. However, if you do not read German or Chinese, then you see, in the second and third quotations, only the German or Chinese symbols above, you do not see what is said with the symbols.

Now consider the force of phenomenological quotation. You consciously think that there is a squirrel in that plum tree. Now you turn your attention to your experience of so thinking:

> I think [as I now quote]: "There's a squirrel in that plum tree."

Reflecting on your experience, you see (comprehend) *what you think*, that is, you "quote" the content of your thought and straightway comprehend the intended state of affairs that there's a squirrel in that plum tree. Alternatively, in phenomenological reflection you form a phenomenological description of your act of thinking (including the thetic character of thinking):

> "I think that there's a squirrel in that plum tree."

If we use angle quotation marks – angle *brackets* – to specify phenomenological quotation, where it is not the words but the indicated experiential content that is "quoted," then we have this phenomenological quotation of the full content of your experience:

> <I think that there's a squirrel in that plum tree>.

The intended rodent appears thus within phenomenological brackets (literally, in our graphic scheme). The rodent does not leave the tree or the world; it merely recedes behind the now-foregrounded content. Nor does the cogitative experience leave the world; rather, that "psychological" process in the world is itself bracketed and so recedes behind its own now-foregrounded "transcendental" noematic content.

When I enter into phenomenological reflection in this way, turning to the structure of my acts of consciousness as I experience them, I do not lose the world as it enters the brackets (< . . .

>). Rather, in phenomenological reflection, I am turned toward the *way* the world is experienced in a given act of consciousness. I am turned thus toward the content or meaning in my experience. But this meaning is so familiar a part of my everyday experience of things in *the world* (trees, plums, squirrels) that I am turned in reflection toward the *meaning of such mundane things* (<there's a squirrel in that plum tree>).

So, for Husserl: Consciousness is a consciousness of things in the world around us. As we turn in reflection to the structure of consciousness as we experience it, we do not lose touch with the world of which we are conscious. Rather, we focus on the content through which we experience things in the world. And in phenomenological quotation, where the world appears to us in brackets (< ... >), we attend to meanings that we immediately understand as presenting putatively such things in the world, a world we do not thereby renounce.

There is something perhaps confusing about the perspective achieved in bracketing. We speak of the first-person perspective in experience, and we say phenomenology is to describe consciousness *as it is experienced* from the first-person point of view. When I see the plum tree, I intend that object in a certain way from my first-person perspective: I see it thus. Now, when in phenomenological reflection I turn toward the structure of my own experience, I describe its first-person structure: <I see that blossoming Japanese plum tree>, or, again, <I think that there's a squirrel in that plum tree>. But then I have stepped out of the original experience of seeing or thinking, and into a further experience directed upon the first. Is this new, "transcendental" perspective a third-person perspective? Well, it is the same subject − I − who has the original experience and who now reflects on that experience. In reflecting on the structure of the original experience as it is experienced by its subject (myself), I understand *what I experience* in that experience. More precisely, I abstract from that concrete experience its sharable noematic content: <I see that ... tree>. Understanding such content, with its intentional force, is the aim of phenomenology. I understand *what it would be* (= what it would *be like*) to have an experience with that content, that is, *as I would experience* it from that first-person perspective. Indeed, that is precisely the force of noematic quotation: I report what I would experience in an act of consciousness with the content <I see that blossoming Japanese plum tree>. As I form or read that description, I understand what it would be to experience such an act of consciousness.

REFLECTION VERSUS INTROSPECTION

It has been commonly thought that phenomenology proceeds by introspection. The gloss is tolerable if we understand introspection as an appropriate form of reflection on one's own ("inner") conscious experience: we begin with a familiar type of experience, whence reflection leads to phenomenological description and on to analysis of the content of the experience, including the way the content of consciousness prescribes a certain object. However, the term "introspection" may suggest an "inner" inspection of the contents of experience, which is certainly misleading. We should not think phenomenological reflection proceeds by a kind of mental periscope: put up the introspective periscope – a "phenomeno-scope" – and peer around inside your mind. Critics of the Cartesian "theater" of the mind often seem to have such a metaphor in mind. But Husserl did not think that way. Indeed, Husserl was very much concerned to distinguish phenomenology from the sort of introspectionist psychology that was current in his era.

In the late 19th century psychology was being developed as an empirical scientific discipline. The method of introspection had been used by Wundt and others to study the course of sensory experience. Brentano, however, sought to put psychology on the foundation of objective empirical investigation, by using some-thing like Aristotle's definition of essence, seeking to analyze the properties that define the essence of each type of psychic state: perception, judgment, emotion, and so on. In the *Logical Investigations*, we saw, Husserl sought to bring to the study of consciousness a kind of objectivity he found in logic. But how could we describe subjective experience in an objective manner?

Throughout his lifetime Husserl returned to this problem of method. His most famous methodology was the technique of bracketing presented in Ideas I. As we have seen, bracketing properly leads us to intentional content, through meaning quotation. But we do not simply peer at ideal meanings. Rather, we reflect upon their significance, their intentional force, their "semantic" power, as we reflect on the way they present objects in our own experience. Phenomenological analysis, then, leads from an appropriate description of a familiar type of experience to a focus on the content or noema of such an experience and then into an analysis of the intentional force of that content.

Reflection on meaning in language can serve as a reminder of just how complicated "reflection" can be. We begin with a familiar piece of language, then reflection on its meaning leads into semantical analysis. We understand the meaning, but analysis requires work. This work is not a matter of turning one's eyes inward to "see" the meaning. And phenomenological analysis, as we have seen, is similarly complex. Husserl likes to talk of "seeing" the way things are, in mathematics, in everyday life, and in phenomenology. His epistemology makes use of this extended notion of "seeing," as we find in Chapter 7. But we should already see (note the verb) that phenomenological reflection is not a matter of a different set of eyeballs, or of looking through a special "phenomeno-scope." (See Thomasson 2005 on the contrast between phenomenological analysis and introspection conceived as peering inward.)

EIDETIC ANALYSIS OF CONSCIOUSNESS

In Husserl's idiom phenomenology is an "eidetic" science since it studies the essence of consciousness. (Husserl is drawing on Plato's term "eidos," meaning the form of something.) As we saw, it is part of the essence of an experience to have a certain meaning as its content. But we must bear in mind that meaning and essence are not the same thing.

Husserl clearly distinguished meaning from essence, though his critics have often lost sight of the distinction. The essence (Wesen,

Eidos) of an entity (of whatever type) comprises the properties that make it "what" it is, that is, its species, qualities, and relations. The content of an experience comprises the meanings or sense that form "what" is experienced or intended in the act. But the essence of an object is part of the object, whereas the meaning in an experience of an object is part of the experience. If I see a tree, the content of my experience includes the sense (the concept or percept) "tree." The tree itself has the essence or species Tree, but that essence is not the same thing as the sense "tree." The species is instantiated in the tree (regardless of whether anyone is conscious of the object); the sense is entertained in my experience (regardless of whether there exists an object answering to the sense).

These distinctions between essence and sense belong to Husserl's ontology. According to Husserl's epistemology, however, we may have experiences and knowledge of both essences and meanings, but our comprehension of these entities is very different. The method of bracketing turns our regard from, say, a particular tree to a sense "tree." Essences such as the tree's essence are bracketed along with the natural objects that have these essences. Husserl holds that we can have "intuition" of essences as well as "intuition" of natural objects (as we consider in Chapter 7). But seeing a concrete tree (perceptual "intuition") is one type of experience, and "seeing" the essence Tree ("eidetic intuition" or insight) is quite a different type of experience. We grasp the essence Tree when we put together our knowledge of what a tree is like, what species, properties, and relations are typical of a tree. This is ultimately a matter of abstraction from observational knowledge we or others have acquired. But this type of cognition of essences is quite distinct from phenomenological reflection on a form of consciousness, effected by turning our attention from objects themselves to our consciousness of such objects. Thus, when Moritz Schlick, founder of the Vienna Circle of logical positivism, attacked Husserl's notion of eidetic intuition, it was a mistake to think this attack pulled the rug from under phenomenology. To this day, many are under the impression that phenomenology is a matter of "seeing essences." Let us clear away this confusion.

Phenomenology studies the *essence* of consciousness, and especially the essence of intentionality, the essence of consciousness-of-something (*Ideas* I, §34). In fancier terms, Husserl declares phenomenology "a descriptive eidetic theory of pure experience" (§75). It is often remarked, following Husserl, that phenomenology is an "eidetic" science. What does this mean?

Like biology or physics, phenomenology studies the "eidos" or essence – the characteristic properties and relations – of things in its domain of study. Botany studies individual trees only in order to develop laws about trees in general. The biologist's concern, while studying a given tree, is not that particular tree across the street, but the typical features of members of that species, the form of DNA of trees in that species, the species' place in evolutionary history, and so on. The arborist who is trimming that tree is interested in its particular form, but the biologist is interested in forms it shares with other trees. Similarly, phenomenology studies individual experiences only in order to develop laws about consciousness in general. The phenomenologist's interest is not in my experience just now as I see "that eucalyptus tree across the street," but rather in the structure of consciousness typical of visual perception – and more general forms of experience such as intentionality. In that spirit Husserl defined phenomenology as the science of the essence of consciousness. And, accordingly, phenomenological method involves an "eidetic" analysis of various forms and types of experience.

Husserl developed a detailed ontology of essences (*Wesen*) – ideal species, qualities, and relations – and a detailed epistemology of our knowledge or "intuition" of essences. Husserl's doctrine of intuition we take up in Chapter 7. At this point, however, we note the role of "essential insight" in Husserl's account of phenomenological method, not least because phenomenological reflection has sometimes been confused with "seeing essences."

When I see "that eucalyptus tree," the content or noematic sense of my experience is the perceptual sense "that eucalyptus tree." In phenomenological reflection I analyze the way in which that sense presents an object: the content "that . . . " (like the demonstrative pronoun used to express it) points out a certain object at a certain place now before me, and the conceptual content "eucalyptus tree" characterizes it as a certain kind of object. The way this perceptual sense works is typical of a simple form of visual experience. A phenomenological analysis of this type of experience characterizes the essence of such a visual experience, and that essence involves carrying the meaning found in this type of experience. Part of the task of phenomenology is then to analyze the intentional or semantic force of such meanings, that is, what and how they represent.

Let us be clear about what is, and what is not, analyzed in phenomenology. Phenomenology analyses the essence of the sample experience, which carries the sense "that eucalyptus tree"; phenomenology does not analyze the essence of the tree. What is the difference between the sense and the essence of the tree? (These entities are sometimes conflated.) The tree belongs to the biological species *Eucalyptus globulus*. That species – with its defining features including phenotypical characters and phylogenetic descent – is an essence analyzed in biology. By contrast, my experience belongs to the experiential species Seeing-A-Tree or (if only we spoke this way) *Perceptio arboretus*. That species of experience is analyzed in phenomenology, and part of the phenomenological analysis is specifying the intentional force of the sense "that eucalyptus tree." But the logical or phenomenological analysis of that meaning is no part of biology.

Following the methodology outlined, a phenomenological analysis or description of my visual experience (in the case at hand) will be something like: "I see that eucalyptus tree across the street." The noematic sense "that eucalyptus tree" is part of the intentional content of the experience so described. However, that noematic sense is not an essence of the tree: it is not a property instantiated in the tree, but rather a meaning that represents the tree. The predicative sense or concept "eucalyptus tree" semantically prescribes the property of being a eucalyptus tree, or, if you will, the essence *Eucalyptus globulus*. But the essence is "in" the tree in nature, a complex biological organism, while the sense is "in" my experience, a complex act of consciousness. The sense and essence are thus distinct entities. "Intuition" or "insight" about them is achieved in different ways, and is never, as Husserl's critics wrongly thought, simply "seeing" with special eyes for essence and sense, respectively. It is better, however, to suppress considerations of intuition until we tackle it head on in Chapter 7.

INTENTIONALITY VIA MEANING: THE DOCTRINE OF NOEMA

Meaning is the *medium* of intentionality, the medium in or through which we are conscious of something. Formally, ontologically, the intentional relation of act to object is mediated by a noema or noematic sense, the ideal content of the act of consciousness, which presents or prescribes the intended object in a certain way. But experientially, phenomenologically, our consciousness is propagated through meaning toward the object, so that I am visually conscious of that tree across the street, without being in any way aware of the meaning through which my consciousness is so directed. This is Husserl's basic story of intentionality.

In our pursuit of Husserl's philosophy we repeatedly encounter his basic theory of intentionality. In the *Logical Investigations* the structure of intentionality – the relation among act, content, and object – emerges in the context of his philosophical system as a whole. In *Ideas* I, however, the approach is to work from the first-person experience of "pure" consciousness to the structure of intentionality, drawing the necessary distinctions among act, object, noema (content), and ego as they emerge in phenomenological analyses of various elements of consciousness. Following Husserl's progress through *Ideas* I, applying his new phenomenological method, we can highlight his key results as follows.

When we bracket the thesis of the existence of the natural world around us, Husserl avers, we find ourselves turning in reflection to "pure" or "transcendental" consciousness (§33). Though our experience remains embedded in the surrounding world, we make no use of that relationship, including actual causal relations with things around us. Our concern, we then find, is with the essence of consciousness (§34), consciousness just as we experience it. Consciousness, we find, is almost always a consciousness of something. This property of experiences (Erlebnissen), "to be a consciousness of something," we call *intentionality* (Intentionalität) (§84). So we find that intentionality is the main theme of phenomenology, the *"pervasive phenomenological structure"* of consciousness (§84). Now, consciousness occurs not in isolation, but in a "stream of experience," or "stream of consciousness," a temporal structure with a characteristic unity (§84). The experiences in a unified stream of consciousness belong to a single "I" (Ich) or ego. Husserl adapts Descartes' term "cogito" for an occurring experience, while extending Brentano's metaphor of directedness: "In every occurrent cogito a radiating 'glance' is directed from the pure I [Ich] toward the 'object' of the respective consciousness-correlate [that is, content], toward the thing [Ding], the state of affairs [Sachverhalt], etc." (§84). Husserl reserves the technical term "act," or "act of consciousness," for this form of consciousness that is directed from an ego toward an object. ("Ding" is Husserl's term for material things in space and time. "Sachverhalt" is the term for states of affairs, or objects bearing properties or relations, a term widely used by Austrian philosophers, including Husserl and Wittgenstein.)

Our most ubiquitous forms of consciousness are perceptual experiences of seeing, hearing, touching things within the context of our everyday actions – regardless of whether those things we perceive actually exist, though we normally experience them as existing. Perception, we find, is both a sensuous and an intentional experience. A perceptual experience is a temporally extended mental process with two interdependent parts, "real" (reell) or temporal parts: a sensuous part or "moment," and an intentional part or "moment" (§85). The sensuous part he calls *hyle* (the Greek term for matter or stuff), and the intentional part he calls *morphe* (the Greek term for form). Husserl here adapts Aristotle's doctrine of matter-and-form: a bronze statue, Aristotle held, consists of a fusion of matter (bronze) with form (shape); similarly, Husserl holds that a visual experience consists of a fusion of sensation (matter) and interpretation or conceptualization (form).

In Husserl's ontology, "moments" are dependent parts, that is, parts that cannot exist apart from the whole of which they are parts; here, the sensuous and intentional parts of the visual experience cannot exist without each other, and so without the whole they form. Thus, I do not see a spread of blue broken by a bit of white; rather, I see that white sail (on a sailboat) amid the brilliant blue ocean. My sensuous visual experience of blue and white is at the same time an intentional visual experience of a sail on a boat on the ocean. Husserl calls this intentional part of the experience the *noetic moment* of the experience, or *noesis* (§85). He characterizes the noesis in an experience as the "'animating', *sense-giving* layer" (*"beseelende,"* sinngebende . . . *Schicht*) of the experience (§85). For an experience to be noetic is, by its essence, to harbor a "sense" (*Sinn*) on the ground of this sense-giving work (§88). The sense (*Sinn*) that is "given" to the object of perception is precisely the intentional *content* of which we have made much above.

In everyday life we are constantly experiencing perceptions of things around us, as we move among and act upon things near us, walking here and there, digging in the garden with a shovel, typing on the keys of a computer as words appear on the screen. But not every experience is a sensuous perceptual experience. When I am thinking "Husserl was influenced by Hume on the unity of consciousness," my current sensuous barrage of visual, auditory, and tactile experience is no part of my so thinking. My act of thought does not include a sensuous component. Even if I think with images, even images of words such as "Hume" or "unity," these images are not sensuous episodes. Yet my thinking does include a noetic component: if you will, my thinking is pure noesis. But noesis consists in the "sense-giving" function of consciousness.

With this noetic activity of consciousness Husserl introduces his famous notion of noema. The *noematic content* (*der noematische Gehalt*), or *noema*, of an act of consciousness is the ideal meaning structure correlated with the "real," or temporal, process of *noesis* in the act (§88). In Husserl's own words immediately following his introduction of the term "noema":

> Perception, for example, has its noema, at the most basic its per-
> ceptual sense, i.e., the *perceived as such*. Similarly, the respec-
> tive remembering has its *remembered as such*, just as its
> remembered, exactly how it is in its [being the] "meant"
> ["*Gemeintes*"], [the] "consciously grasped" ["*Bewusstes*"]; again,
> the judging has the judged as such, enjoying the enjoyed as
> such, and so forth. Generally, the noematic correlate, which here
> is called "sense" ["*Sinn*"] (in a very expanded meaning
> [*Bedeutung*]), is to be taken *exactly* as it lies "immanently" in the
> experience of perceiving, judging, enjoying; and so forth, that is,
> as it is demanded of us *when we inquire purely into this experi-
> ence itself.*

> (*Ideas* I, §88, my translation)

As is implied by Husserl's phrasing, the sense or noema belonging
to an experience is the ideal noematic content that presents an
object in a certain way, and the same object can be presented in
different ways through different structures of sense. To take an
example Husserl used elsewhere, suppose I am visiting a wax
museum. I see a woman waving at me on the stair. As I approach
her, I realize that "she" is a wax figure, a wax sculpture that looks
like a woman waving. The object I see is presented in very
different ways in my two visual experiences, where I first see
"that woman waving to me" and I then see "that wax figure." The
sense in the first perception is different and distinct from the sense
in the second perception. As Husserl puts it, they are so different
that my initial perception "explodes" and is followed by a very
different perception. To take another example Husserl used elsewhere: if I think of "the victor at Jena" and subsequently I think
of "the vanquished at Waterloo," then the same object, Napoleon,
is presented through two different noematic senses in these two
experiences. Both of these senses prescribe the same object,
Napoleon, but they designate Napoleon in different ways (*Logical
Investigations*, Investigation I, §12).

Here, in phenomenological reflection, we begin to appreciate
the structure of the *relation* of intentionality: how an experience is
directed toward an object of consciousness through a particular
noematic meaning or sense. In consciousness I am aware of an

object as it appears to me in that act, that is, as presented through a particular noematic sense. There lies the bottom line of phenomenology: we are conscious of things – we know or "intend" things – only *through* structures of sense that present or prescribe those things in particular ways. Yet we are not aware of the sense through which we experience an object until we step back from the experience and abstract its content. Only in phenomenological reflection do we thus become aware of the meanings through which we "intend" objects in the world around us.

In a Kantian idiom, we may say that meaning, or noematic sense, is the condition of the possibility of consciousness. It is only through noesis, and thus through a correlated noematic sense, that consciousness can be intentionally directed toward various things in the world around us. Husserl's full conception of this role of sense is explicated in relation to logical theory, according to the outlines of the *Logical Investigations*. We might say the logical view of meaning is an "outsider's view" of how meanings work, a view of the semantic relation between meanings of various form and the objects they represent – including propositions (meanings expressed in language by declarative sentences) and the states of affairs they represent. However, the phenomenological account of sense or noema in *Ideas* I gives us an "insider's view" of how meanings work to present the objects of consciousness, a phenomenological view from "inside" consciousness directed *through* meanings toward the objects as experienced.

The founder of contemporary logical semantic theory, Gottlob Frege (1848–1925), sharply distinguished the sense (*Sinn*) from the referent (*Bedeutung*) of an expression ("On *Sinn* and *Bedeutung*," 1892/1997). For example, Frege observed, the two expressions "the morning star" and "the evening star" both refer to the same object, Venus, but they have different meanings or sense and so refer to Venus in different ways. Each expression expresses a particular sense that determines a particular referent, but these two expressions refer to the same object by way of different senses. We may depict this model of reference via sense in Figure 6.1.

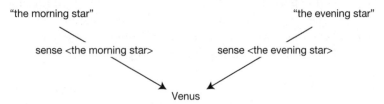

Figure 6.1 Reference via sense

Husserl and Frege shared this same basic model of linguistic representation: the relation of an expression to the object it represents is mediated by a sense. Frege laid out the details of how sense mediates reference by developing a systematic semantics correlating forms of expression with forms of object designated through appropriate forms of sense. Husserl sketched some examples of this semantic relationship, but dwelt instead on the details of what a sense is and how it relates to consciousness. (We addressed logical and linguistic matters in Chapter 3; here our concern is phenomenology, but it is wise to bear in mind the parallel structures of linguistic and mental representation.) As regards what kind of entity a sense is, the only thing Frege tells us is that a sense carries a "cognitive value" (*Erkenntiswert*) or "mode of presentation" (*Art des Gegebenseins*), that is, literally, a manner of being "given" in thought or experience. Husserl, on the other hand, went to great length to explicate what a sense (*Sinn*) is, how it is *experienced* and implicitly used in consciousness, focusing on its relation to an act of consciousness and its role in the intentional relation of act to object of consciousness, drawing distinctions that remain unexplicated in Frege. Husserl's model of the intentional relation we may depict in Figure 6.2, paralleling Figure 6.1:

Thus, when I think of "the morning star," my experience is directed via the sense <the morning star> toward the object Venus. The sense, we have seen, presents the object in a certain way, and so Husserl characterizes the sense as "the object as intended." If I were instead to think of "the evening star," my experience would be directed toward the same object, Venus, but by way of the sense <the evening star>.

This model of intentionality via sense – via noematic content – is central to the school of phenomenology called "West Coast" or

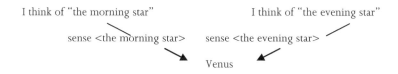

Figure 6.2 Intentionality via sense

"California" phenomenology (see Dreyfus 1982; Smith and McIntyre 1982). This model has sometimes has been dubbed the "Fregean" interpretation of Husserl's theory of intentionality. Just as linguistic reference is mediated by sense on Frege's theory of reference, so intentionality is mediated by sense on Husserl's theory of intentionality: thus the parallel structures just depicted. However, we might equally, or better, speak of the "Husserlian" interpretation of Frege's theory of reference, noting the same parallel structures. For it was Husserl rather than Frege who analyzed the role of sense in the intentional relation of an act of consciousness to its object, where a sense embodies a mode of presentation to consciousness. (Burge [2005] offers a corrective reading of Frege, arguing that for Frege sense is not intrinsically tied to linguistic meaning, which is social, but belongs to the realm of thoughts [*Gedanken*], which in themselves carry modes of presentation.)

We should recall that Husserl cited Bolzano, not Frege, as his chief inspiration in "pure" logic. Bolzano's distinction between objective and subjective ideas laid the groundwork for Husserl's distinction between noematic sense and noesis, where an act or noesis is intentionally directed via a noematic sense toward an appropriate object. While Frege did not address intentionality per se, Husserl addressed both linguistic reference and intentionality. For Husserl, a linguistic expression refers or "relates" to an object because it "intimates" a conscious experience of the object and so "expresses" the sense that is the content of that experience (see Chapter 3). In this way, Husserl held, linguistic reference via sense is itself founded on an underlying form of intentionality via sense. The key point here is that, for Husserl, *content* or *sense* plays a certain role in mediating intentionality, and sense plays a parallel

role in mediating linguistic reference (if you will, linguistic intentionality). You might say sense is the *medium* of intentionality:
consciousness propagates through sense toward its object. This
mediating role for sense is depicted in Figure 6.2. (There are,
however, important respects in which Husserl's theory of intentionality and reference diverges from a strictly Fregean theory. See
Smith and McIntyre 1982: chs. 5–8 on demonstrative and individ-
uative intentionality, on horizon and possible-worlds structure,
and on details of the form of a noematic sense and its relation to
the object intended. And see Beyer 2004 on singularity of intentionality and externalist features of intentionality in Husserl's
theory. We should note at this point that there are alternative
interpretations of Husserl's theory of intentionality and the role an
act's noema plays in the act's intentionality. We will sketch such
alternatives later, after exploring the details of Husserl's account of
the noema.)

Husserl's model of intentionality via sense, as here reconstructed, prompts three caveats. First, there is no question of a
"veil" of ideas or sense that stands between consciousness and its
object. Consciousness is a consciousness of its object, not of its
sense. Indeed, it is only in phenomenological reflection that I
become aware of the *sense* through which I am conscious of the *tree*
I see. This point is central to Husserl's methodology of bracketing.

Second, the "Fregean" reading of Husserl's model of intentionality should not be taken as "logicizing" phenomenology, that is,
reducing the study of consciousness to the study of logical structures, specifically propositions expressible in language by complete
sentences. (Welton characterizes the model as assuming "the restric-
tion of noematic content to Fregian-type propositions" [2000:
394].) In Frege's wake, logic-minded philosophers came to speak
of what Bertrand Russell called the "propositional attitudes":
believing that p, thinking that p, wishing that p, and so on. Jaakko
Hintikka (1962, 1969, 1975) addressed the logic of sentences
ascribing belief and perception, treating intentional attitudes
themselves as propositional in content: one believes that p, sees
that p, and so on. Again, John Searle (1983) held that intentional
content is propositional in form, even in perception. However,

Husserl did not hold that the noematic sense of every act is a proposition (*Satz*). Nor does the model of intentionality via sense assume this. When I see "this dog," the sense of my experience is a perceptual individual content, which prescribes an individual object. By contrast, when I see that "this dog is a bearded collie," the sense of my experience is a perceptual propositional content, which prescribes a state of affairs in my environment. And when I think that "this bearded collie likes to bounce," the sense of my act of thinking is a proposition. Ronald McIntyre and I (in Smith and McIntyre 1982) called an act like seeing "this dog" a *direct-object* act and an act like thinking that p a *propositional* act. Husserl himself called an experience like seeing "this dog" a *pre-predicative* experience, whereas seeing that "this dog is a bearded collie" is a *predicative* perception, and thinking that "this bearded collie likes to bounce" is also a predicative experience. A propositional act is thus one whose sense involves predication, whereas a pre-predicative experience is, for Husserl, attributive (seeing "this bouncing dog") rather than predicative (seeing that "this dog is bouncing").

A third caveat regards a chicken-or-egg problem. Where does intentionality enter the world, where does it all begin, in the act or in the sense? That is, which is the fundamental *bearer* of directedness? If an act is directed toward an object *because* the act's sense semantically prescribes that object, then it might seem that intentionality lies fundamentally in the sense rather than, as Husserl would seem to hold, in the act. (This problem for the mediator model of intentionality-via-sense is posed, in slightly different terms, in Drummond 1992: 99–100; see also his discussion of abstraction.) There is indeed a tendency in semantic theory to give meaning or sense the reins, and not without reason: it is concepts that represent, propositions that are true, and so on. Nonetheless, for Husserl, logic, and thus (what we today call) semantics, is grounded in intentionality: that is the thrust of the early *Logical Investigations* (1900–1) and the late *Formal and Transcendental Logic* (1929). So, for Husserl, it is because meaning resides in consciousness that meaning represents and so contributes its semantic force to acts of consciousness. Strictly speaking, it is only meaning-in-consciousness, or consciousness-with-meaning, that has intentional force – there is no chicken/egg choice.

Indeed, the answer to the chicken-or-egg problem lies in Husserl's account of the ontology of noema and noesis (see *Ideas* I, §§89, 98, discussed later in this chapter). Although the noema or noematic sense is an ideal entity (it cannot burn up, etc., per §89), Husserl says the noema is "in" the noesis in a unique way (per §98), as a "moment" or dependent part of the act of consciousness. Accordingly, Husserl might say the noematic sense in my perception of "this tree" is directed as it is *because* it is "in" this act of perception, and by the same token my perception is directed as it is because the noematic sense is "in" the act. In fact, when we turn in detail to how my perception is directed toward this object in my concrete surroundings, we find that the semantic force of the sense "this tree" depends on its occurrence in this particular experience in this particular context – only then does the sense, and by the same token the act, "intend" the object before me on that occasion. (This analysis of perceptual intentionality is developed in detail in D. W. Smith 1989. The analysis is not found in Husserl but is friendly to the spirit of Husserl's theory of intentionality as here reconstructed.)

NOEMATIC SENSE: "THE OBJECT AS INTENDED"

In Husserl's theory of intentionality, the noematic sense in an act of consciousness does the key work of presenting or prescribing the object intended in that act. How exactly does Husserl characterize the *sense* in an experience?

Let us revisit a passage quoted earlier:

> "In" the reduced perception (in the phenomenologically pure experience [*Erlebnis*]) we find, as belonging inextricably to its essence, the perceived as such, to be expressed as "material thing," "plant," "tree," "blossoming," and so forth. The *quotation marks* [*Anführungszeichen*] are obviously significant; they express

that change in sign, the corresponding radical modification of the meaning of the words. The *tree simpliciter* [*schlechthin*], the thing in nature, is anything but [*ist nichts weniger als*] this *perceived tree as such*, which as perceptual sense [*Wahrnehmungssinn*] belongs inseparably to the perception. The tree *simpliciter* can burn up, be resolved into its chemical elements, etc. But the sense [*Sinn*] – the sense of *this* perception, something belonging necessarily to its essence – cannot burn up; it has no chemical elements, no forces, no real properties.

(*Ideas* I, §89, my translation)

Husserl thus draws a crucial distinction between the object perceived and the object *as* perceived, also called the perceptual *sense*. These two entities are *categorially distinct*: they belong to distinct ontological categories. Specifically, the *tree* itself ("simpliciter") is a "thing in nature," a "real" object existing in space–time, something that "can burn up, be resolved into chemical elements, etc." By contrast, the *sense* of the perception "cannot burn up, it has . . . no real properties"; it is not a thing in nature, a "real" object in space–time. Rather, a sense (*Sinn*) is an ideal, nonspatiotemporal object, not a real, spatiotemporal object. (Recall Chapter 4 on categories and real versus ideal objects, and recall Chapter 3 on sense as ideal.)

Husserl here updates the notion of sense he developed in the *Logical Investigations*. Indeed, his terminology explicitly echoes that of the Investigations. Here, in *Ideas*, he distinguishes "the tree simpliciter" from "this perceived tree as such," that is, "the tree as perceived." This distinction is a special case of the distinction he drew in the *Logical Investigations* between the object which is intended and the object as intended. In Husserl's words:

In relation to the intentional content understood as object of the act [that is, as intentional object], the following are to be distinguished: the *object as it is intended*, and simpliciter the *object which* is intended [*der Gegenstand, so wie er intendiert is, und schlechthin der Gegenstand, welcher intendiert ist*].

(*Logical Investigations*, Investigation V, §17, my translation; see p. 113 of 1900/2001, vol. 2)

Note Husserl's use of the verb "to intend" (*intendieren*, in the German): in an act of consciousness I "intend" the object, or alternatively the act "intends" the object, and the object is "intended" in a certain way (*so wie*).

The distinction Husserl emphasizes, then, is that between the object intended and the *way* the object is intended. The way an object is intended in an act is encapsulated in the *sense* (*Sinn*) of the object in the experience, and that sense is the core of the *noema* or *intentional content* of the act. There are further components of the full noema (§§131–3), but here we focus on the sense that presents the object, which Husserl calls the "nucleus" (*Kern*) of the noema.

It is remarkable that in the two published English editions of *Ideas* I we find a pivotal sentence in the above passage translated to opposite effect:

> The *tree plain and simple*, the thing in nature, is as different as it
> can be from [*ist nichts weniger als*] this *perceived tree as such*.

(*Ideas* I, 1913/1931/1969, translation by W. R. Boyce Gibson)

> The *tree simpliciter*, the physical thing belonging to Nature, is
> nothing less than [*ist nichts weniger als*] this *perceived tree as
> perceived*.

(*Ideas* I, 1913/1991, translation by Fred Kersten)

My translation of the contested sentence (for immediate comparison) reads:

> The *tree simpliciter* [*schlechthin*], the thing in nature, is anything
> but [*ist nichts weniger als*] this *perceived tree as such*.

I translate "ist nichts weniger als" as "anything but" (following The New Cassell's German Dictionary, New York: Funk & Wagnalls Company, 1965). The nuances of the phrase are not easily captured. Yet Husserl's intent is clear. By "thing" (*Ding*) Husserl means an object in nature, in space–time; by "sense" (*Sinn*) he means an ideal content of conscious experience, which does not exist in space–time, in nature, but is "in" consciousness in a certain way. These cannot be numerically the same entity, since the tree can burn away but the sense "this tree" cannot burn away and is not even a physical object, a "real" object in nature. Indeed, these two entities belong to distinct ontological categories. The German phrase "*ist nichts weniger als*" translates literally as "is nothing less than." This phrase has led some Husserl interpreters to argue that in some manner the tree and the sense are one and the same entity – in direct contradiction to what Husserl writes in the next sentence. How should we understand Husserl's contested phrase?

Suppose a politician says, "A vote for my opponent is nothing less than a vote for nuclear war!" This does not mean that these two votes are one and the same thing; it means that the first type of vote approaches or leads toward the second in some important way. Similarly, in Husserl's German (an older idiom), the claim is not that the tree itself is numerically or ontologically identical with the tree-as-perceived, the sense "this tree"; rather, the claim is that the tree (the thing in nature) approaches or comes close to the sense in a particular way. Or better, we might say that, from the point of view of my experience, the tree-as-perceived is asymptotic to – approaching without touching – the tree itself. Indeed, the task of the sense in my experience is to intentionally approach the tree, without merging with the tree itself. Moreover, in perception – a form of direct cognition or "intuition" (*Anschauung*) – I experience the tree as "this tree itself" here before me in its "'bodily' selfhood" ("*leibhaftigen Selbstheit*": Ideas I, §3). Observing the quotation marks, we can specify the close relation between the sense "this tree itself" and the tree itself. Namely, the sense in my visual experience is intentionally or semantically related to the object: the sense presents or prescribes the tree itself and presents it as now here before me. Again, consider Husserl's use of quotation marks: the sense "this tree" semantically prescribes this tree now here before me, if there exists such a tree before me. However, the sense "in" my perceptual experience remains categorially distinct from the tree it prescribes. (See D. W. Smith 1989 for a further development of this type of contextual semantic relation in intentionality.)

To generalize: the noematic *sense* or *content* in an act of consciousness embodies the *way* the object is intended in the act, its intention "as such-and-such." The sense is distinct from the object of the act, but the sense presents – semantically prescribes – the object, presenting the object in a certain way. The act is a consciousness of that object which the sense prescribes, if such object exists. And so the intentional relation between act and object is semantically mediated by noematic sense, that is, the structure of the relation is:

act – noematic sense ("the object as intended") → object

if such object exists.

Husserl's idiom "the object as intended" has encouraged several different models of the noema and its role in intentionality. Husserl's idiom echoes Kant's "phenomena" or "things- as-they-appear," where natural objects are "phenomenal." Alternatively, Husserl sometimes speaks of the "intentional object" rather than the "intentional content" of an act. In the *Cartesian Meditations* (§§15–18) he speaks interchangeably of the "objective sense," the "intentional object," and the "*cogitatum qua cogitatum*" of an experience. These idioms echo traditional Medieval ontologies where objects exist "in *intentio*," suggesting that the noema be assimilated to the object itself. In the appendix at this chapter's end, we outline some alternative models of the noema and its role in intentionality. (See Dreyfus 1982 for the "Fregean" logical interpretation of Husserlian phenomenology, including Dagfinn Føllesdal's seminal article, and Mohanty 1982 for more on the Husserl–Frege connection. See Gurwitsch 1964 for the neo-phenomenalist, quasi-Kantian conception of phenomenology. See Drummond 1990 and Sokolowski 2000 for a realist theory of the "object as intended." See the Introduction to Smith and Smith 1995 for a brief contrast between such readings of Husserl.)

NOEMA = SENSE = OBJECT-AS-INTENDED

Why does Husserl talk about noematic content in such different terms: as "sense" and as "the object as intended"? Interpretations of Husserl have tended to divide over these idioms, choosing one or the other. The "logical" reading of Husserl focuses on the role of sense in representing objects of consciousness, looking to similarities between Husserl's phenomenological theory of intentionality via sense and the logical theory of linguistic reference via sense, notably in Frege's logical semantics. By contrast, the "phenomenal" reading of Husserl focuses on the experienced "appearance" of objects in consciousness, looking to similarities between Husserl's theory of intentionality and something like Kant's theory of "phenomena." Yet Husserl adamantly pressed both of these visions and their integration. How can we understand this Husserlian synthesis?

The idiom of *sense* plays well in the logical theory of representation, while the idiom of *objects-as-intended* plays well in the epistemic theory of representation. In the *Logical Investigations* (1900–1), I have urged, Husserl worked to integrate logical theory inspired by Bolzano with psychological theory inspired by Brentano. The idiom of "phenomena" has been common parlance in German-language philosophy since Kant. And indeed, when Husserl began his so-called "transcendental turn" in the 1907 lectures published as *The Idea of Phenomenology* (1950/1970), he emphasized the "phenomenon" as the focus of phenomenology, just as the term implies. In Kant's idiolect, "phenomena" are defined as "things-as-they-appear," which are distinct from "things-in-themselves." Husserl adapted this terminology, but within his own theory of intentionality: we experience phenomena, or objects-as-they-are-intended, objects *as* perceived, *as* imagined, *as* judged, *as* desired, and so on, which are distinct from the objects *which* are so intended. Husserl explicitly put these two idioms together: the sense = the "object as intended." To renounce either idiom is to miss Husserl's synthesis, and our aim here is to show how the two idioms work together in Husserl's system. We quoted Husserl in full where he explicitly assimilates the two idioms, noting his theoretical use of quotation marks in phenomenological "quotation." This device of sense-quotation is itself adapted from logic, indicating the synthesis of the logical with the experiential.

As noted, Frege himself, chief architect of the new logic, characterized a sense (*Sinn*) as carrying a "way of being given" (*Art des Gegebenseins*). That has to mean: given in consciousness. What a sense *does* is determine or prescribe an object of reference; what a sense *is* is a form of consciousness of an object, embodying the way an object is known or intended in consciousness. Frege also says a sense includes a "cognitive value" (*Erkenntniswert*). (Both "*Art des Gegebenseins*" and "*Erkenntniswert*" appear in the early pages of "On Sense and Reference" (1892/1997), and he says no more about the connection between sense and cognition or consciousness.) Frege is searching for an account of sense that would be developed only later, in Husserl's work. There is no theoretical opposition, then, between these claims about sense, its representing an object and its embodying the way an object is cognized. The two claims address the same point at different *levels* of language or experience: the *experiential* level (I experience an object as thus-and-so), and the *metaexperiential* level (the sense of my experience prescribes the object of my experience). These two levels are the "object" level of experience (I intend the *object* as thus-and-so), and the "reflection" level of experience (I reflect on my *experience*, which presents the object as thus-and-so). This distinction applies in logic and in phenomenology. Quotation is the logical device that moves from referring to an object to referring to an expression; noematic quotation is the phenomenological device that moves from intending an object to reflecting on a noema that presents the object.

When we abstract the noematic sense from an experience and talk about it in our phenomenological theory of intentionality, or alternatively in our logical theory of ideal meaning, we ascend to a higher level of language, focusing on the sense as a certain kind of entity. In a logician's turn of phrase, we practice semantic ascent, moving from our experience to our language about our experience, as we reflect on the content of our experience, "quoting" the noematic content. Similarly, in logic we practice semantic ascent as we ascend from our use of words to our logical or semantic talk *about* those words, quoting the words and assessing what and how they represent. Remember that in *Logical*

Investigations Husserl worked his way from "pure logic" into "pure phenomenology" over the long course of narrative in that work. In *Ideas* I, however, Husserl emphasized the methodology of our study of "pure" consciousness. There he wanted us to *experience* noematic sense, and then to talk about it in phenomenological description. Husserl's method of phenomenological reduction and quotation was designed to shift our attention from the objects we experience to the ways we experience these objects: thus from this *tree* I see to this tree *as I see* it – from this tree to "this tree." When I characterize the sense as "the tree as I see it," in effect I project myself as if back into the experience upon which I am reflecting. This process is akin to empathizing with my own experience, attending to it in a reflective or "transcendental" attitude. Thus, when I reflect on my own experience, I take two positions with respect to my experience: I am the subject of the experience on which I reflect, and I am the observer or analyst of that same experience. In the first attitude I take an "insider's" position, and in the second attitude I take an "outsider's" position, in full cognizance that I am at once both insider and outsider. Husserl does not describe his method in these terms, but hindsight allows such a view of phenomenological reflection.

A similar methodological situation arises in logic. In the 1930s the great logician Alfred Tarski (1901–83) developed what he called a semantic conception of truth (see Tarski 1944/2001 – by the way, Tarski knew something of Husserl and the theory of intentionality). Tarski's theory of truth entailed, for a simple sentence of English, the canonical form of truth-conditions expressed as follows:

"Snow is white" is true (in English) if and only if snow is white.

As speakers of English, we recognize two occurrences of the same sentence. On the left it appears in quotation marks, where it is used to name a sentence, the very sentence used between the quotation marks. On the right it is used again, this time to specify the conditions under which the named sentence would be true. In Husserlian terms, if I say the above, I take a semantic ascent to quote the sentence and then go on to say it would be true under the conditions I assert as I repeat the sentence without quotation. When I quote the sentence, I focus on the words and at the same time their meaning, the proposition expressed by the sentence. However, when I use the sentence the second time, I "intend" a certain state of affairs, without focusing on the sentence or proposition I am using to represent that very state of affairs. Central to Tarski's logical-semantic theory of truth was his distinction between two levels of language that seem to merge in everyday language: the language I use in the right side of the equivalence just given, and the language I use in the left side. The sentence I quote belongs to the "object" language, whose semantics is at issue; the sentence I use on the right belongs to the "metalanguage" in which I state the semantics or truth-conditions for the sentence on the left. As a speaker of English, I use and understand the same sentence in two occurrences. In a Husserlian framework we might say: as a phenomenologist appraising my use of language, I distinguish two attitudes or positions, namely, my "transcendental" reflection on the sentence (in saying "'Snow is white', is true if and only if snow is white") and my "mundane" attitude toward the state of affairs that snow is white. (For the record, Tarski himself presented a mathematical system modeling truth without ontological commitment to either propositions or states of affairs. By contrast, Husserl's account of intentionality, say, where I think that snow is white, would hold that my thought is true just in case the content of my thought, the proposition expressible by "Snow is white," successfully represents the state of affairs that snow is white.) (See the essays in Lynch 2001 on theories of truth, including theories of the role of quotation in the Tarski schema.)

To return to Husserl's idiom: The state of affairs itself, that snow is white, is one thing, while the sense or proposition "snow is white" is another thing. The close connection between them is semantic: that proposition represents or semantically prescribes that state of affairs. The state of affairs itself could also be represented in different terms, say, in the proposition "A quantity of H_2O below 0 degrees Celsius reflects a full spectrum of sunlight on Earth." So the way the state of affairs is intended in my saying, "Snow is white," is reflected in the sense "snow is white," but not in the sense expressed by the longer sentence quoted before the preceding period. Notice that I have just referred to that sense in two ways: as the sense; and as the state of affairs *as intended* through that sense. Only the latter way invites me into the quoted sentence, into the way I intend the state of affairs as I say, "Snow is white." When I reflect on the *way* I intend the state of affairs in so speaking, I adopt a "metalanguage" attitude toward the experience, as distinct from an "object-language" attitude toward the state of affairs itself.

THE ONTOLOGY OF NOESIS AND NOEMA

Exactly what type of entities are noesis and noema, according to Husserl's ontology?

After introducing the distinction in *Ideas* I, Husserl proceeds to an intricate account of the ontology of noesis and noema, addressing their basic types and their modes of being. In this account Husserl assumes the notion of "moment" that he had developed in the third of the *Logical Investigations* (Investigation III, §17). A *moment* is defined as a dependent or "abstract" part of a given whole: the moment is an entity that is a part of the whole but cannot exist apart from the whole. Here Husserl draws on an idea that began with Aristotle. A piece of paper is white, but the paper is a concrete individual, while whiteness itself is an ideal species, or "universal." So far, we have something like Plato's distinction between a particular and a "form" (*eidos*) or property it exemplifies. But Aristotle held that *this white* in this paper is particular to the paper, a particularized quality that could not exist unless the paper existed. Husserl's version of this doctrine holds that this white is an individual that is an instance of the ideal species White but is a moment, or dependent part, of the piece of paper. With this neo-Aristotelian doctrine in hand, we turn to Husserl's account of the ontology of noesis and noema.

An experience, or act of consciousness, is a lived mental process. How this process relates to neural processes in the brain – the classical mind–body problem – is beyond the purview of phenomenology. But within the scope of phenomenology we can say that an experience is a "real" (*reell*) or temporal process. (Husserl uses the German "*reell*" to mean occurring in time.) And, of course, we can say it is a mental or "psychic" process, that is, as Brentano emphasized, a process of consciousness, a process the subject lives through with a certain "inner" awareness of the process, a process that is typically intentional (see *Logical Investigations*, Investigation V, §§1–8).

A perceptual experience, we saw, has two parts: a sensuous moment and a noetic moment (*Ideas* I, §85). The sensuous moment, comprising sensous "data" (*Data*) or sensory "material(s)" (*Stoffe*), gives the experience its sensuous character; the noetic moment gives the experience its intentional character, "giving" it the noema or noematic sense that presents the object of consciousness. These two parts of the experience, sensation and noesis, do not occur independently: they cannot occur apart from the whole experience, or apart from each other, as, say, I see "this red-leafed Japanese plum tree." In an experience of pure thinking, we noted, there is no sensuous part, there is only the noesis.

Husserl speaks often of the correlation between noesis and noema, but these are importantly different types of entity. Amplifying the distinction between noesis and noema (*Ideas* I, §97), Husserl says the sensuous and noetic moments in a perception are "real" (*reell*) moments of the experience, while the noematic moment is a "non-real" (*nichtreell*) moment of the experience. Here Husserl introduces a thoroughly novel ontology of content. In *Logical Investigations* (Investigation V), he had spent a lot of ink in marking out different notions of "content," or different uses of the term. His own account there distinguished "real" and "ideal" or "intentional" content. In *Ideas* I we find his fully developed account of this distinction.

The sensation and noesis in an experience are "real," temporal components of a perceptual experience. Correlated with the noesis in an experience (whether or not the noesis is joined by sensation) is a noema. Staying with the case of perception, we know the noematic sense – the tree as perceived, "this Japanese plum tree" – is not something in nature, in space–time. (This point is explained in the passage we quoted from §89.) Now (§97) we are told the noema is not "real," not in time, not in the temporal flow of consciousness. This means the noema is an "ideal" entity. Moreover, Husserl calls the noema a moment of the experience. Both noesis and noema are moments, dependent parts, of the experience: contents of the experience, entities that are "in" the experience insofar as they are dependent parts of the experience. But the noesis is a real, temporal part, while the noema is a nonreal, nontemporal part. How can an ideal, nontemporal meaning be a moment of a real, temporal experience?

It is striking that Husserl calls the meaning itself – as opposed to the noesis with which it is correlated – a moment of the experience. For Husserl is said to join Frege and Lotze in Platonizing meanings, taking meanings to be ideal entities set apart from real processes. True, Platonic forms are supposed to be ideal species, and in *Logical Investigations* (Investigations II and V), Husserl took meanings to be ideal species or types of intentional experiences. By the time of *Ideas* I, Husserl had concluded that meanings are not a kind of species, but their own kind of ideal entity (§128): sense (*Sinn*), aligning more with Frege on *Sinn* than with Plato on *eidos*. Husserl keeps both species and meanings in his ontology, but treats them as distinct kinds of ideal entity. Indeed, Husserl says, it is part of the essence (= species) of an experience to include in the experience a sense or noema (*Ideas* I, §88).

The noema is "in" the experience in a unique way. In Husserl's words:

> [T]he real experience-unity of hyletic and noetic component pieces [*Bestandstücke*] is totally different from the unity of noematic component pieces "consciously grasped in" them. . . . That which is "*transcendentally constituted*" "through" the noetic functions "on the ground" of the material [sensuous] experiences is indeed a "given" [object] and . . . an *evidently* given [object]; but it belongs to the experience even in a wholly different sense than the real and therewith authentic constituents of the experience.
>
> (*Ideas* I, §97, my translation)

Both noesis and noema, then, are components – and in that sense "contents" – of the experience, but they are contained in it in wholly different ways.

Husserl then expands on the "mode of being" of the noema (§98). If we turn our attention from the real components of an experience to the noema, say, the seen tree as such, we find:

> That which is given in this attentive regard is now indeed itself, logically speaking, an object, but a thoroughly *dependent* [*unselbständiger*] [object]. Its *esse* consists exclusively in its "*percipi*" – except that this proposition applies in nothing like its Berkeleyan sense, here the *esse* does not contain the *percipi* as a real component piece.
>
> (*Ideas* I, §98, my translation)

This provocative passage is meant to clarify the special mode of being of the noema, the tree-as-perceived, as opposed to both the mode of being of the actual tree and the mode of being of the "real" components of the experience of seeing the tree. Husserl's claim is that the noematic sense in the perception is *dependent* on the experience: the noema is a moment, or dependent part, of the experience. Yet the noema is not a "real" component of the experience. We might think of a "real" entity as a dependent part of an experience, existing in the experience. But how should we think of an ideal, nontemporal entity as a dependent part of an experience? How can a nontemporal entity be any kind of component of a temporal entity?

The answer lies in Husserl's original notion of moment. The ideal form White exists "in" this white paper insofar as this white in this paper instantiates the form White. Similarly, the ideal sense "this Japanese plum tree" exists "in" this perceptual experience insofar as this noesis of seeing "this . . . tree" is correlated with the sense "this . . . tree." So noematic meanings are ideal entities that are realized in temporal experiences in a way parallel to the way ideal species are realized in temporal objects, yet meanings are realized in such a way that they are *experienced* in temporal experiences. Here is the novelty in Husserl's ontology of meaning.

Berkeley held that a material object exists only insofar as it is perceived; in his famous slogan, to be is to be perceived, or *esse est percipi*. Husserl echoes Berkeley's quip not for the tree itself, but for the tree-as-perceived, the noematic sense of the tree. And then Husserl adds that the being of the perceived is not, as for Berkeley, a real perceptual component. If "the perceived" is the tree-as-perceived, its mode of being is that of the noema, not that of the perceptual experience. And the mode of being of the noema, Husserl holds, is that of an ideal meaning's being a moment or dependent part of the experience. This mode of being is unique to meanings: only meanings exist in precisely this way!

Husserl's doctrine of noema should be seen as his developed explication of the idea behind Brentano's notion of an object's existing "intentionally" "in" consciousness. Brentano had revived the Medieval notion of "*intentio*," with his claim that every mental phenomenon includes an object intentionally within it. It has never been clear how to understand Brentano's claim. Does the object exist in the mind as opposed to reality? Is this a version of idealism, like Berkeley's or like Kant's? If not, what ontological status is this mode of being that Brentano calls "existing in mind"? In Husserl's discussion we have an articulate answer to these questions: for an object to exist "in" consciousness is for "the object *as* intended" – a noematic sense prescribing the object – to be a moment of the experience.

Now, meanings are studied in logic or philosophy of logic, and logician-philosophers like Husserl, Frege, and Bolzano are called "Platonists" when they say that logic is about ideal meanings – propositions and their constituent concepts – taken as objective entities that exist but are not in space–time. Are such meanings not like Plato's "forms" or "ideas" (*eidos*), residing outside the real world in a Platonic heaven? Interestingly, Husserl explicitly resisted the charges of Platonism that were leveled against his *Logical Investigations*.

In the opening part of *Ideas* I, before turning to phenomenology, Husserl addressed the ontology of ideal entities or essences. As "Platonizing realists," he said, we make statements about ideal entities, treating them formally as objects having properties. But we avoid a false "Platonistic hypostasizing" because we sharply separate "objects" and "real actualities," that is, things in spatiotemporal actuality (*reale Wirklichkeit*) (§22). The category Object is a category of formal ontology: anything at all is an object. With this doctrine in mind, after he has presented his account of noematic sense, Husserl says that the noema belonging to an act of consciousness is a unique kind of objective entity (*eigenartige Gegenständlichkeit*) (§128). For Husserl, then, a noema is a type of ideal entity *sui generis*. Noemata are not species, numbers, sets, and so on; they are *meanings*, ideal entities that enter into temporal experiences in a particular way. For Husserl, meanings are objects, all right, as Bolzano and Frege insisted. But that does not imply an existence in a far-away heaven of Platonic ideas. Rather, for Husserl, ideal meanings are "in" temporally real experiences: they are ideal moments of lived experiences. Indeed, phenomenological reflection puts us in touch with ideal meanings: I know a meaning as "the object as intended" in my experience.

THE STRUCTURE OF A NOEMA

Noema = thetic content + sense

In the *Logical Investigations* (Investigation V, §§20–1), Husserl says the "intentional essence" of an act of consciousness is a union of two aspects called the "quality" and "matter" of the act. The *matter* is what is intended as intended, and the *quality* is the attitude taken toward it, namely, perceiving, imagining, or judging, and so on. Every act has both of these aspects. In *Ideas* I, Husserl holds, further, that the essence of an act involves a certain ideal intentional content called noema. Husserl factors the noema of an act into two components of meaning called "sense" and "thetic" "ways of givenness" (§§130, 132, 133). The *sense* (*Sinn*) prescribes the intended object as intended, say, "this blossoming plum tree"; this noema component corresponds to the act's matter. The *thetic* content specifies the way the object so presented is "posited," say, in an attitude of seeing as opposed to hearing or imagining or desiring; this noema component corresponds to the act's quality. In Husserl's new terminology, the thetic or positing character of an experience consists of the act's general species, say, seeing, wishing, thinking, judging, valuing, or willing, together with modifying characters such as clarity, attentiveness, intuitiveness or evidentness, probability, and degree of "doxic" commitment (§§99–117). So the noema of any act is a structured meaning formed from a sense and a thetic content that modifies the sense. The act's noesis thus combines moments of quality and matter, which in turn carry noema components of thetic content and sense, respectively.

The full structure of an act's noema is shown quite naturally by example. Consider the types of experience we describe as follows:

> I see this blossoming plum tree.
> I see the look of perplexity on my student's face.
> I hear that cawing crow.
> I think that Husserl admired Bolzano.
> I judge that a thunderstorm is brewing.
> I wish that it would rain.
> I imagine that a soft rain is falling on the roof.
> I desire some dark chocolate ice cream.
> I value loyalty in a friend.

In these simple phenomenological descriptions, the verb reports the thetic character of the act described, while the direct-object phrase reports the noematic sense of the act. As our descriptions indicate, the sense in an experience can be rather complex, formed from concepts that come together in the form of, say, the sense "this blossoming plum tree" or "a soft rain is falling on the roof." In a fuller description, adverbs may modify the verb, ascribing further structure in the thetic character of an experience. For example:

> I hear rather faintly that cawing sound of a crow in the distance.
> I wish fervently that it would rain.
> I see clearly and attentively the face of that perplexed student.

These adverbial phrases qualify the thetic character of the act described, whereas phrases in the direct-object phrase qualify the object as intended.

Given Husserl's account of noematic meaning and meaning quotation, we can schematize the structure of an act's noema, in such cases, as follows:

NOEMA

"(THETIC CONTENT) + (SENSE CONTENT)"

"(I see clearly) (that speeding sports coupe rounding the bend on the highway ahead)."

"(I judge intuitively) (that those thunderclouds carry hail)."

A systematic analysis of these structures of meaning in a noema, and their semantic correlation with acts and their objects, would define a "pure logic" of consciousness, as foretold in the Prolegomena of the *Logical Investigations*. Given the theoretical foundations of logic and the theory of intentionality, Husserl unfolds pieces of such a logic of noemata over the course of *Ideas* I. After introducing consciousness and its intentionality, he distinguishes noesis and noema. When he introduces the noema, he notes that the noematic sense is the nucleus of the noema (§§88–90, 130), indicating there is more to the structure of a noema. By and by, he marks out distinctions of thetic character, extending thetic character from the central example of perception to wishing, judging, liking, valuing, and willing or volition, and elaborating on the degrees of conviction an experience may hold or lack (§§99–117). These distinctions are "logical" distinctions within the form of a noema. Given these distinctions, he focuses on the typical form of the sense in a full noema.

Noematic sense = "object (X)" + "predicates"

When I approach an object, say, a tree on a hill, I see it from one side. As I walk closer, I see it again from a different viewpoint. As

I sit under it awhile, I see it from still another perspective, looking up at its gnarly limbs. Through this extended course of experience, I repeatedly see "the same" object, sometimes continuously as I walk, other times interruptedly as I look here and there, but always my perceptions of the tree intend "the same" object. Similarly, when I think repeatedly of the same individual, say, when I think that Plato studied mathematics, then I think that Plato admired Socrates, then I think that Plato focused his philosophy on ideal forms such as The Good, throughout these varied acts of thinking, my experiences are thoughts about "the same" individual.

In order to capture this structure of experience, wherein we are conscious of "the same" object in different ways in different acts, Husserl analyzed a basic form of noematic sense. In any noema, Husserl held (*Ideas* I, §131), we distinguish within the noematic sense two basic components: a sense of the "object" intended and a sense of the various "predicates" attributed that same object. As Husserl writes:

> [In] *noematic description* of the meant [*das Vermeinte*] as such . . . the identical intentional "object" is evidently separated from the changing and variable "predicates." It is separated out *as central noematic moment*: the "*object*" ["*Gegenstand*"], the "object" ["*Objekt*"], the "*identical*," the "determinable subject of its possible predicates" – *the pure X in abstraction from all predicates* – and it is separated *from* these predicates, or more exactly, from the predicate-noemas.
>
> (*Ideas* I, §131, my translation)

That is, in a phenomenological description of an experience we distinguish within the noematic sense ("the meant as such") two components of sense: the "object" and "its predicates." Here are two types of meaning within the sense that prescribes the object of consciousness. (There are surely other forms of sense, but Husserl emphasizes this paradigmatic form, so let us stay with this paradigm.)

When I am conscious of an object, then, the noematic sense of my experience divides into two components: the "X" content prescribes the object "simpliciter," while the accompanying "predicate-senses" prescribe various properties the object is intended as having (*Ideas* I, §131). In Husserl's idiom, the "determinable X" presents the object itself, which is "determined" or qualified by the properties presented by the predicate-senses. Husserl's paradigm is that of seeing a particular object, which is seen as having a variety of properties and is expected to have still further properties. Consider the experience whose form we have described repeatedly:

> I see this blossoming plum tree.

The sense of the act described here factors into two components: "this," which designates a particular object before me ("X"); and the predicate-senses "tree," "plum," and "blossoming" (configured together as "blossoming plum tree"). There is much to say about the way these types of sense work.

Surely this form of noematic sense is only the beginning of a logic, or formal phenomenology, of consciousness. More complex forms follow, implicitly, where Husserl discusses forms of judgment (explicitly the domain of logical theory), evaluation, imagination, time-consciousness, consciousness of other persons in empathy, and so on. We might begin to amplify Husserl's above-mentioned analysis by looking to the forms of experience we describe using proper names ("Husserl"), demonstrative pronouns ("this"), and definite descriptions ("the so-and-so") – forms of language that have been analyzed extensively in philosophy of language, years after Husserl wrote. We cannot fail to notice the variable "X," used by Husserl the former mathematician familiar with the new Fregean logic of quantifier expressions ("some object x is such that x is a tree").

Demonstrative pronouns are based in perception, as Husserl explicitly argued (*Logical Investigations*, Investigation I, §26; Investigation VI, §5). Thus, in our description of seeing a tree, the content ascribed by "this" functions to single out the object itself in the context of vision, without calling upon its properties: this demonstrative sense introduces an X type of sense. Alternatively, consider the experience described as follows:

> I think that Husserl appreciated the apple tree in his garden.

Here the proper name "Husserl" singles out a particular object, the man himself, to which the predicative content attributes a horticultural sensibility. Proper names refer directly, without calling upon specific properties of the individual named. This linguistic feature has been much explored since Husserl's day, but was noted by Husserl (*Logical Investigations*, Investigation I, §16, noting John Stuart Mill's view of names as non-connotative). By contrast with names and demonstratives, a definite description singles out its referent by appeal to properties of the referent. Thus consider the experience described so:

> I surmise that the burglar entered the house by the back window.

Here the noematic sense "the burglar" does not function like an X-type sense. Rather, it prescribes whatever individual burglarized the house (in the case under investigation). This sense introduces an individual "X" into my deliberations, about whom I continue to speculate, but the sense "the burglar" works differently than a sense "John Q. Thief" or "that man climbing through the window."

To capture the way in which different acts are directed toward the same object through noemata involving different predicate-senses, we might form a phenomenological description as follows:

> There is an object x such that I see that x is a California live oak tree and I see that x is leaning downhill and I see that on this side x has a broken limb and I think that x was struck by lightning and I judge that x is 100 years old and I like the look of the admirable arching boughs on x.

The variable "x" we use here to track the identity of the object as it is intended in a sequence of acts of perception, thought, judgment, and aesthetic evaluation. By contrast, we use the predicates "California live oak," "leaning," "was struck by lightning," "100 years old," and "admirable" to ascribe different properties of the object as it is intended in the various acts. In this phenomenological description of a complex of co-directed acts, we describe acts whose noemata include the same X but different predicate-senses.

Suffice it to say the several types of noematic sense we have been considering work differently. The important result in Husserl's analysis of sense as "X + predicates" is the way in which our experiences track the same object through different acts of consciousness. For the work of an "X" sense is precisely to prescribe the same object in various acts. As I walk around the tree, turning away from it, returning my gaze to it, I see "the same" object "X," regarded from different perspectives, with different properties visible from different sides. My varying experiences thus present the same object with different properties, and the X-sense prescribes that particular object, while adjoined predicate-senses prescribe different properties of that identical object.

THE HORIZON OF EXPERIENCE AND IMPLICIT BACKGROUND MEANING

A vital part of Husserl's phenomenology is his account of the "horizon" of what we experience. When I approach a tree, seeing it from different perspectives, as I gaze upon it at this moment from this one side, there is more to the content of my current experience than a simple percept or visual meaning such as "this tree" (infused with sensory content) or even "this blossoming plum tree" or "this sturdy live oak tree." Part of our implicit understanding of things in nature is a sense of what Husserl called their "transcendence": there is always more to come, more to any given thing than what we see in a given experience, certainly more than what I see of this tree from this one side. A fuller form of phenomenological description of my visual experience (ascribing an X in the complex noematic sense) might be:

> I see this object *x* which is such that *x* is a tree and *x* is a Japanese plum and *x* is blossoming now on the side facing me and *x* will bear plums in another month . . . and so forth.

As Husserl remarks, "The 'and so forth' is an . . . absolutely indispensable moment in the thing-noema" (Ideas I, §149). This element of meaning, "and so forth," prescribes what Husserl calls a horizon (Horizont) of the object as intended in the experience, a range of "indeterminacy" about the object, that is, a structure of possibilities for the same object ("x") that are left open or undetermined by the act's noematic content, including what the perceived object might look like from the back side (compare Ideas I, §44, quoted later).

Seeing the tree at this moment, I expect that if I walk further around the tree I will see more branches of a similar kind, with blossoms on that side too. My expectations about the object constrain what I see in my current perception of the tree. Constrained by my background understanding, my perception leaves open a horizon of possibilities about the same object. This range of possibilities is defined by the noematic sense in my experience together with the content of my implicit – often vague and indefinite – background ideas about such objects, including beliefs, expectations, and practices. Thus we may define the horizon of an act of consciousness as the range of possibilities for the intended object that are left open by the act's noematic sense together with relevant background ideas that are implicit or presupposed in the core sense. These possibilities are possible states of affairs in which the intended object has further properties compatible with what is prescribed by the act's sense constrained by its background presuppositions. We may also speak of the horizon of further possible experiences of the same object, experiences whose noemata prescribe the same object with further properties compatible with what is prescribed by the original act's noematic sense together with its implicit presuppositions. Or we may speak of the horizon of further noemata or senses that prescribe the same object with further properties allowed by the act's noematic sense together with implicit presuppositions. (A detailed reconstruction of Husserl's notion of horizon is developed in Smith and McIntyre 1982: ch. 5.)

The possibilities left open in an experience must be compatible with the conceptual content of the experience. For example, given my concept of a tree, the object I see, as perceived, will presumably have bark but cannot bark like a dog. Within the range of conceptual possibilities, however, the possibilities left open in my experience must be "motivated," not "empty," possibilities. Consider an example Husserl uses (*Ideas* I, §140). As I walk into an unfamiliar room, I see a desk across the room. I do not count the number of legs on the desk, which are mostly out of view; I merely see "that desk." How many legs can "that desk" have, the object as intended in my perception? Given my long familiarity with desks, it very likely has four legs. It might have six or even eight legs if it is unusually ornate (like the one in my own office), but it cannot in any likelihood have ten legs: that possibility is not motivated by my prior experience with desks. Motivated possibilities are precisely those to which I would assign a reasonable probability given my past experience (*Logical Investigations*, Investigation I, §§2–3; *Ideas* I, §140).

The notion of horizon is introduced quite early in Husserl's road map of phenomenology in *Ideas* I, as horizon is tied into noematic sense even before the noema is explicated:

> A thing [*Ding*: material thing] is necessarily given in mere "ways of appearing" [that is, from one side], and necessarily there is thereby a *nucleus of "what is actually presented"* surrounded in apprehension by a *horizon* [*Horizont*] of nongenuine [*uneigentlich*] *"co-givenness"* and more or less vague *indeterminacy*. And the sense [*Sinn*] of this indeterminacy is once again predelineated [*vorgezeichnet*] through the general sense of the perceived thing in general and as such, respectively, through the general essence of this type of perception that we call thing-perception. The indeterminacy . . . *points forward* to possible manifolds of perception [*Wahrnehmungsmannigfaltigkeiten*] that, continuously merging with one another, close together into a unity of perception in which the continuously enduring thing in ever new series of adumbrations [*Abschattungsreihen*] shows again and again new "sides" ["*Seiten*"].

> (*Ideas* I, §44, my translation)

So a material thing can appear from only one side at a time, but we understand that further aspects or "adumbrations" of the same object can appear from different perspectives. This understanding is part of the (noematic) *sense* of the perception of a thing. Thus, the sense in the experience "predelineates" a *horizon* of indeterminacy about the object, a range of properties left open for the same object. And this range of possibilities left open for the object "point forward to" a *manifold* of perceptions in which the same object would be presented from new sides. That which is given inattentively Husserl calls "backgound" (*Hintergrund*) (*Ideas* I, §35) or a "horizon of inattentive background" (§83). Modes of attentiveness belong to the "ways of givenness" in an experience (§92), which are reflected in the thetic part of the act's noema (§§130–3). "Every perception has . . . its background of perception," which entails potential "positings" in further perceptions (§113).

As the structure of the noema is explicated in *Ideas* I (§§128–33), the noematic sense in a perception accordingly predelineates the horizon of the object as perceived. Whence the meaning "and so forth" is an essential component in the noema of a perception of a thing (§149). That component of sense specifically opens up a horizon of possibilities for the object intended. And corresponding to that horizon of possibilities is a manifold of possible perceptions that fill in the properties of the object in ways compatible with the act's noema together with expectations or background ideas about that type of object. This "manifold" of noemata defines "all possible 'subjective ways of appearing', in which [the thing perceived] can be noematically constituted as identical" (§135). Thus Husserl writes:

[T]o every thing and ultimately to the whole thing-world with one space and one time [that is, nature] there correspond the manifolds of possible noetic events, the possible experiences of single individuals and of individuals in community that relate to it, experiences that as parallels to the previously treated noematic manifolds have in their essence itself the peculiarity according to sense and proposition [*Sinn* und *Satz*] to relate to this thing-world. In them there thus come the relevant manifolds of hyletic

> data belonging with "apprehensions," thetic act-characters,
> etc. . . . The unity of the thing stands over against an infinite,
> ideal manifold of noetic experiences of a wholly determined
> essential content . . . , all therein united in being consciousness
> of "the same" thing.
>
> (*Ideas* I, §135, my translation)

Corresponding to the manifold of possible perceptions associated with a given act of perception, then, is a manifold of noemata, joined with a manifold of possible sensory ("hyletic") data that would support or "fulfill" noeses with such noemata. And corresponding to that manifold of noemata is a manifold of possibilities prescribed by these noemata in these possible perceptions. A note on terminology: the German term *"Satz"* is the traditional term for a *proposition*, that is, what is posited – proposed or asserted – in a declarative sentence or in a judgment. Husserl takes this term from Bolzano but widens it: a *Sinn* includes the way an object is presented, while a *Satz* adds a positing character such as judging, perceiving, desiring, and so on. Thus we understand a *Satz* as a "position" or "proposition" held on an object presented through a *Sinn*.

Amplifying the notion of horizon in his relatively late work *Cartesian Meditations* (1931), Husserl writes:

> We can *ask any horizon what* "*lies in it*," we can *explicate* or
> unfold it, and "*uncover*" the potentialities of conscious life at a
> particular time. Precisely thereby we uncover the objective sense
> [*Sinn*] implicitly meant, though never with more than a certain
> degree of foreshadowing, in the actual cogito. This sense, the
> *cogitatum qua cogitatum* [the cogitated qua cogitated], is never
> present [*vorstellig*: presented] as a finished given [object]; it
> becomes "clarified" only through explication of the given horizon
> and the new horizons continuously awakened.
>
> (*Cartesian Meditations*, §19, my translation)

The emphasis here is on meaning that is *implicit* rather than explicit in an experience. Interestingly, such meaning is never fully accessible to the subject, never fully "presented" in consciousness. The meaning implicit in an experience we may call *background* meaning.

Though Husserl does not say so, this range of meaning lies in the background of the experience, presupposed by and so implicit in the core of meaning in the act's noematic sense. Indeed, we may argue along Husserlian lines, the manifold of *meanings* that are implicit in an act's noema are part of the *horizon* of the object as intended. (Such a view is developed in the essay "Background Ideas" in my *Mind World* [D. W. Smith 2004].)

The term "horizon" appears regularly and saliently in Husserl's many works, with varied uses, always highly suggestive. As the passages quoted indicate, Husserl's account of horizon appeals to his notion of "manifold" (*Mannigfaltigkeit*), adapted from non-Euclidean geometries under development in his day and featured in the *Prolegomena to Pure Logic*, launching the *Logical Investigations*. We may think of a manifold as a structured multiplicity. The German term is often translated simply as "multiplicity," but this translation misses the structure Husserl has in mind: a manifold consists of "many" things "folded" together in a certain way. (We explored Husserl's notion of manifold in Chapter 3.) If now we reconstruct an ordered account of Husserl's theory of horizon, organizing and extending what we find in such passages as we have quoted, then the story might run as follows.

In *Principles of Psychology* (1891) William James observed that what we see is surrounded by a "fringe" of things to which we are not attending. Husserl broadens this notion – radically. (The first English translation of Husserl's *Ideas* I, by W. R. Boyce Gibson, translates "*Horizont*" as "fringe," an allusion to James.) Accordingly, the horizon of an object as seen includes background objects, where the object is in the focus of attention and the surrounding objects are in the background of inattention, the periphery or margin of attention. The 1930s Gestalt psychologists (with influence from Husserl) held that perception has a general form of Figure/ Ground or Object/Background ("*Gestalt*" means form or figure). In our example above, the noema of my perception of a tree prescribes an object, "this tree," against a background of surrounding objects, where the tree is presented attentively and the surrounding objects are presented inattentively, "dimly" and "indeterminately." Part of the background of the object as perceived, then, is the spatial distribution of objects nearby. One of those objects is my own body. My left hand appears in my visual field as I shield my eyes from the sun, and that hand is part of the background of the tree I see. What I see, as seen, forms my visual field. But part of the horizon of the tree I see is my body, not merely my hand as I see it framing my view of this tree, but my whole "living" body. I take this tree to have a back side, and I take my hand to belong to my full body, most of which I do not see (and, for the most part, never will). In fact, my body serves as an "origin" of the spatial organization of my surroundings, my "surrounding world" (*Umwelt*). The Cartesian coordinate system can be seen as an abstraction from this phenomenological structure wherein all objects in my surrounding world, notably those I now see before me, are oriented with respect to my own body: not a single point (a zero point $<0, 0, 0>$ for the three axes), but a structured living body featuring my head and feet (defining "up"/"down"), my hands (defining "left"/"right"), and my face and back (defining "front"/"back"). Another part of the background of what I see is not spatial, but temporal. The temporal flow of events is part of the horizon of this tree as I see it. The limbs are moving slightly in the breeze, moving in time. The tree as perceived is spread out in space and also in time: things in nature are experienced as spatiotemporal things. Furthermore, my memory, short and long term, is tied into my current perception. I see this tree swaying in the breeze, the same tree I saw a moment ago while walking up the hill, the same tree I expect to see a moment hence as I walk further. My seeing "this tree . . . " carries my retention of what I just saw and my "protention" of what I shall presumably soon see; what I just saw and what I am about to see of the tree are part of the horizon of this tree in my perception. And further in the background of what I currently see lies what I happen to remember about the tree from a previous encounter. And further in the horizon lies my own stream of consciousness, for my current perception takes its place in a temporal flow of experiences of which I am aware in my consciousness of "internal" time, in the flow of my own experiences. That is, in the horizon of the object as I see it are both the flow of events in the surrounding world and the flow of events in my stream of consciousness as I see the object. Still further in the background of what I see are the significances or meanings, the noematic senses, relevant to "this tree" and further items of sense in the horizon of meaning associated with my perception. Implicit background meanings themselves lie in the horizon of what I see as I so experience it.

A good part of the preceding account of horizon is expounded in modified terminology in the writings of two phenomenologists who were greatly influenced by Husserl: in Maurice Merleau-Ponty's *Phenomenology of Perception* (1945/2003), and in Aron Gurwitsch's *The Field of Consciousness* (1964) and *Marginal Consciousness* (1985). Both Merleau-Ponty and Gurwitsch drew explicitly on the work of Gestalt psychologists who conducted experiments in the 1930s.

By the 1960s a cousin to Husserl's notion of horizon developed within modal logic, in Jaakko Hintikka's logic of knowledge, belief, and perception: as it were, a mathematical logic for locutions like "S knows/believes/perceives that p," that is, a logic for attributions of intentionality. In Hintikka's logical scheme for attributions of perception:

> "S perceives that *p*" is true in the actual world if and only if, for every perceptually possible world compatible with what S perceives in the actual world, in that possible world it is the case that *p*.

If we transpose this equivalence directly into the Husserlian language of intentionality, we might say:

> In the actual world W* S perceives that *p* if and only if in every perceptually possible world compatible with what S in W* now perceives, in that alternative world it is the case that *p*.

Corresponding to the given perception, then, there is a manifold of *possible worlds* – perceptually possible states of affairs or courses of events – compatible with what S perceives in that perception. These possibilities feature the object of perception in further possible situations, with further possible properties and relations, always compatible with what S perceives. This structure of possibilities makes up what Husserl called the horizon of that perception. (See Smith and McIntyre 1982 for the full story of how Husserl's model of horizon is reflected in Hintikka's model of possible worlds.)

There is a historical development of logical ideas leading from Husserl to Hintikka, with stops at Carnap and Tarski along the way. The outlines of that story are sketched in Chapter 5, where we looked into the conceptual foundations of phenomenology in relation to logic.

ONTOLOGY IN PHENOMENOLOGY

Pure phenomenology, we might well assume, appraises structures of consciousness (including noema and horizon) without making use of metaphysical or ontological commitments. "To the facts of experience alone!" might be the mantra, echoing Husserl's prescription "To the things [Sache] themselves!" In this assumption we hear strains of the Kantian doctrine that we can know things only as they appear, and neo-Kantian ideas were in the air as Husserl wrote *Ideas* I. That is to say, we are to describe and analyze consciousness without any forays into further analyses of the transcendent reality toward which consciousness is as-if directed. In strict Husserlian terms, pure phenomenology is to study consciousness in abstraction from the world of nature and also from the world of culture, addressing the essence of consciousness while bracketing the essence of nature and the essence of culture. The substantive or "material" ontologies of nature and culture are thus to play no role in the results of pure phenomenology – any more than they would in pure mathematics (which might later be applied to systems of nature or culture).

Nonetheless, phenomenology makes use of certain kinds of ontological principles. The distinction between concrete objects and their essences is an ontological distinction, and Husserl assumes this distinction when he says phenomenology is to study the essences of concrete acts of consciousness. So, despite talk of bracketing the question of the existence of "the world," phenomenology is not supposed to eschew all ontology. Indeed, as we noted earlier, *Ideas* I begins with an outline of fundamental ontology, starting with the distinction between "fact" (concrete object) and essence. As the course of analysis proceeds, Husserl draws the distinction between noesis and noema, which is again an ontological distinction: noemata are ideal meanings, whereas noeses are concrete moments of acts of consciousness. Furthermore, although an act's noema is an ideal entity, Husserl holds that the noema is a moment of the act, an ideal moment with a unique "mode of being": here again Husserl makes an ontological claim. In the practice of phenomenology, then, Husserl makes use of certain ontological claims concerning objects, essences, meanings, and parts or moments. These claims belong to what Husserl called "formal" ontology as opposed to "material" ontology (or ontologies), as we explained in Chapter 4. And Husserl uses principles of formal ontology as he pursues the material ontology of consciousness through phenomenological analysis. (Briefly, formal ontology applies within various material ontologies; for instance, the object/essence distinction applies within the ontologies of nature, culture, and consciousness – as Husserl parses these disciplines.)

We spoke in Chapter 5 of a minimalist form of phenomenology. It is important to keep this core phenomenology in mind. At the minimal level of analysis in phenomenology, we should remain as neutral as possible about matters of ontology. But Husserl is concerned also to develop a proper philosophy of phenomenology, a metatheory that would appraise, *inter alia*, how consciousness, with its phenomenological structure, fits into the world, with its ontological structure. As his development of phenomenology proceeds, then, Husserl lays out analyses of various structures of consciousness, including perception, spatiotemporal awareness, self-awareness, other-awareness, and so on, observing relevant forms of intentionality in these types of consciousness. But he also lays out principles of ontology to explicate what consciousness and its intentionality are all about: consciousness of something consists in an intentional relation among subject, act, noema, and object; an act's noema is an ideal meaning correlated with a noesis; the noesis is a concrete moment of the act; the noema in the act prescribes an object in a certain way; the noema predelineates a horizon of open possibilities for the object; and so on. But Husserl also finds within consciousness commitments to various ontological claims, to which we turn now.

As Husserl's analyses of noematic structure proceed, he finds ontological presuppositions within certain structures of sense. Specifically, the phenomenological distinction between the two types of sense, "object" and "property," corresponds to a presupposed ontological distinction between the two types of entity, Object and Property. According to Husserl's analysis, I *experience* this difference in what I see: I see "this *object* with these *properties*." In my experience, then, I assume a distinction between the thing I see and the properties I see it as having, and this distinction is manifest in the structure of the noematic sense in my visual experience. The point is not that these technical terms from ontology are wafting through my consciousness; rather, our use of such terms in *phenomenological description* ascribes appropriate structures to the experience itself.

Specifically, in phenomenological description Husserl factors predicate-senses themselves into different senses that carry presuppositions about the ontology of the intended world around us. Here is how Husserl unpacks some of these presuppositions:

> [T]o [an act's] noema there belongs an "objectivity" – in quotation marks – with a certain noematic composition, which becomes explicated in . . . *a description of the "meant [vermeinten] objective just as it is meant"* . . . To it there are applied formal-ontological expressions such as "object," "property," "state of affairs"; material-ontological expressions such as "thing," "figure," "cause"; material determinations such as "rough," "hard," "colored" – all have their quotation marks, thus the noematically modified sense.
>
> (*Ideas* I, §130, my translation)

We recall the significance of the quotation marks: we are talking about items of sense, not what they designate in the world.

As we saw in Chapter 4, Husserl distinguishes formal and material ontology. Formal ontological categories include Object, Property, and State of Affairs – these categories apply to objects in any domain, whether physical objects, numerical objects, musical objects, or whatever. By contrast, material or regional ontological categories apply to objects in a specific domain or region, such as Nature, Culture, Consciousness. Thus, a tree is a thing in nature, a thing with spatiotemporal properties. More specifically, it has a certain shape or geometrical figure, and it stands in causal relations (as when the wind blows its branches around). It has particular properties or "determinations," such as being rough on its bark, hard to a certain degree, and colored with a certain shade in its leaves. These properties fall under its regional essence as part of nature. But the tree is, more abstractly, an object rather than a property. And it has an array of properties (including those just cited). The tree and its properties form states of affairs consisting in the tree having specific properties. Those features of the tree are, in Husserl's terms, formal rather than material. These distinctions among types of properties belong to ontology, but we are currently concerned with phenomenology.

In the passage just quoted, then, Husserl finds that our *experience* of objects presents objects with such distinguishable features as those just mentioned: properties that fall under formal and material categories. We do not use this technical jargon of ontology in our everyday lives; nor do we explicitly draw these distinctions as we see a tree with blossoms on its boughs. Yet, in phenomenological analysis, Husserl claims, we find such distinctions at work as we see or think about or act upon familiar things in the world around us. To see a tree, Husserl holds, is an experience with a structured noema that can be analyzed as a meaning that presupposes such distinctions. To be sure, the analysis or explication of an act's meaning, its noema together with its horizon of implicit meaning, requires all that goes into phenomenological reflection: as I see "this tree . . . ," the full range of meaning in my experience does not stare me in the face (as does the tree). The meaning in an experience requires considered explication, much as meaning in language requires careful interpretation beyond, say, what a sentence wears on its sleeve, as it were. Under phenomenological analysis, Husserl finds, a simple experience such as my perception of a tree reveals implicit commitment to ontological distinctions concerning what I see and its relation to the world around me.

Not least among the implicit, presupposed distinctions concerning things we encounter in everyday life is the elementary distinction between the *same* object and its varying properties. This phenomenological structure, "object *x* + properties P, Q, . . . ," is the basis of Husserl's rich account of the horizon of an experience. The distinction of object-identity amid property-variation is a distinction of formal ontology, presupposed in the phenomenological structure of horizon. However, as Husserl fleshes out the horizon of a typical perception of an object, he traces out ways in which the noematic sense of a perception draws upon background presuppositions about the material as well as the formal ontology of objects in nature.

Thus, having outlined how the sense of a thing in nature (say, a tree) carries commitment to formal-ontological features such as "object" and "property" (*Ideas* I, §§130, 148), Husserl then addresses the material ontology presupposed in the sense of a natural thing:

> The thing is given in its ideal essence as a *res temporalis*, in the *necessary "form"* of *time*. . . . The thing is furthermore according to its idea a *res extensa*; it is e.g. in spatial respect [a thing] of endlessly manifold changes in form. . . . The thing is finally a *res materialis*; it is a *substantial* unity, as such a unity of *causalities*.
>
> (*Ideas* I, §149, my translation)

That is, the sense of a thing in nature presents it as a temporal, a spatial, and a causal object. These aspects belong to the material or "regional" ontology of any object in nature. And, Husserl finds, the very idea or sense of a natural object presents it as having properties of these three basic types.

In the preceding ways, we find phenomenology drawing on ontology. The noematic sense of an object in nature, Husserl says, presents the object as having a specific ontological structure: formally, as being an object bearing properties (species, qualities, relations); and materially, as being an object with temporal location, with spatial extension, and with causal relations to other things in nature. All this structure belongs to what Husserl calls the "constitution" of the object in consciousness.

In the closing sections of *Ideas* I (§§150ff.) Husserl gives his most focused account of "constitution." What is most difficult to understand in this discussion is the relation between phenomenology and ontology. It may sound as if Husserl is advancing from phenomenology (we *experience* objects as having certain ontological structures) to ontology (objects have certain ontological structures *because* we so experience them – our experience *makes* them so). That is, it may sound as if consciousness *produces* the objects around us, bringing them into existence and giving them their essences, creating and constructing objects in nature (in space and time), other subjects in their streams of consciousness, and other persons in culture. On such a view, my perceptual experience would project "this tree" into being: "Let there be this tree, on a hillside, with a raven perched on a front branch" – and so the tree on the hill with the raven would come to be. In such an ontology "I" would be the *deus ex machina* who leaps in to sustain the world. This doctrine of constitution would be a radical form of idealism. But that is not what we find in Husserl when we look at the details. Rather, Husserl's conception of the constitution of the world is an extension of what he called pure logic in the Prolegomena in the *Logical Investigations*. In the Prolegomena, Husserl proposed a systematic correlation between structures of meaning and structures of object represented by appropriate meanings. In *Ideas* I, Husserl proposes a systematic correlation between structures of noemata and structures of intended objects. In both cases, in logic and in phenomenology, the correlations involve an application of Husserl's early notion of manifold drawn from mathematics.

(In Chapter 4 we considered whether Husserl was a metaphysical idealist of some sort. In *Ideas* I [§49], he says the being of the world is "relative" to consciousness. And in *Cartesian Meditations* he struggles to defuse the worry of "transcendental solipsism." Nonetheless, metaphysical idealism and solipsism do not fit with Husserl's philosophical system.)

THE CONSTITUTION OF OBJECTS IN THE WORLD

Immediately after introducing the notion of intentionality in *Ideas* I (§84), Husserl declares that the greatest problems of phenomenology are "the *functional problems*, or those of the '*constitution* [*Konstitution*] of *objectivities of consciousness*'" (§86). "Function" in this sense, as opposed to the mathematical sense, Husserl writes, is "grounded in the pure *essence* of noesis. Consciousness is precisely consciousness 'of' something, it is its essence to harbor 'sense' ['*Sinn*']." That is, the function of intentionality is precisely that of "constituting" an object through (noematic) sense.

Husserl's theory of constitution is a theory of the *structure* of intentionality – a complex structure. Simply put: an object is *constituted* in an act of consciousness insofar as the object is intended *as* such-and-such, where the structure of the act's noematic sense is correlated systematically with the structure of the intended object and its essence, that is, the structure of "the object as intended." If you will, the meaning content of the act projects a certain structure in the projected object, and so the object-as-intended is constituted with the projected structure. Briefly, the structural correlation is that mapped in our prior discussion of the structure of intentionality via noema (cum horizon):

act – noematic sense <object X with properties P> → [object X with properties P]

where this intentional relation is conditioned by a horizon of further possible experiences of the same object.

If the act's content is satisfied, then the object exists and is so structured – in the world, at the terminus of the act's "ray" of intentionality. In short, "constitution" is just structured intentionality. The word "constitution" literally means putting things in place together: "co-institution." Intentionality puts in place a certain object with certain properties; intentionality, if successful, puts an object with properties in its place in relation to the act. (The angle brackets above express noema quotation. The square brackets represent an objective structure in the world; they do not represent Husserlian "brackets," though the point might be made by reading them in that way.)

More fully stated, in terms of Husserl's full theory of noema and horizon:

> An object X is *constituted* in an act A of consciousness if and only if:
>
> (1) act A intends "object X with properties P," where A has a noema with sense <object X with properties P> , that sense prescribes object X with properties P in the actual world W, and if the sense is satisfied in W, then object X with properties P is the object intended by act A in the actual world W; and
>
> (2) corresponding to act A is a horizon of possible acts A* . . . , where A* intends "object X with properties P*," where
>
> A* has a noema with sense <object X with properties P*> ,
>
> that sense prescribes object X with properties P* in possible world W*,
>
> and if the sense is satisfied in W*, then object X with properties P* is the object intended by act A* in world W*;
>
> where X's bearing properties P* in W* is compatible with X's bearing properties P in W, that is, the "determinations" of X intended in the horizon act A* are compatible with what is left open and motivated by the noematic sense in act A.

Constitution then consists in this pattern of intentionality, this structure of what is intended in A together with the acts in the horizon of A. The act-horizon of A is a manifold of possible further experiences of the same object. The noema-horizon of A is a manifold of further noemata which prescribe the same object with further possible properties of the object, properties compatible with and motivated by what is prescribed by the noema of A itself. And the object-horizon of A is a manifold of possible states of affairs in which the same object has further properties compatible with those prescribed by the noema of A. This complex structure correlating manifolds of acts, noemata, and possible states of affairs forms the *constitution* of the intended object in consciousness. This complex structure is displayed in Figure 6.3.

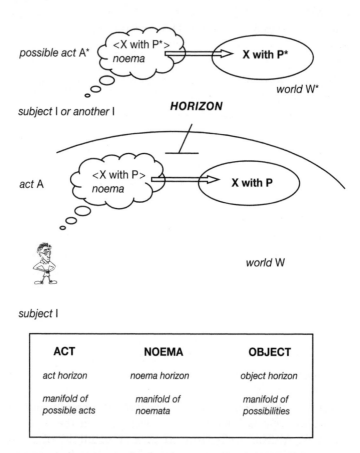

THE STRUCTURE OF CONSTITUTION

Figure 6.3 The constitution of an object in consciousness

The *formal* structure of constitution, as so depicted, is detailed in Husserl's theory of noema and horizon. The *material* structure of constitution for a thing in nature is specified in Husserl's account of the ontological presuppositions carried in an act's noema: presuppositions of formal ontological distinctions, in the concepts of "object" and "property"; and presuppositions of material ontological distinctions, in the concepts of "temporal," "spatial," and "causal" aspects of a "thing in nature."

Here we fold the formal/material distinction back into the structure of constitution, as opposed to the structure of either a noema ("this object that is a tree in nature") or the intended object itself (this object that is a tree in nature).

In Husserl's doctrine of constitution we may hear echoes of Kant's transcendental idealism. Husserl's explicit analysis of constitution is found in the closing sections of *Ideas* I: in Part Four, "Reason and Actuality," comprising chapter 1, "The Noematic Sense and the Relation to the Object," chapter 2, "Phenomenology of Reason," and chapter 3, " . . . Problems of the Theory of Reason." Here is Husserl's phenomenological critique of reason, echoing while implicitly correcting Kant's *Critique of Pure Reason* (1781/1787). Kant did not use the term "constitution" (*Konstitution*), but he did speak of "constitutive" (*konstitutiv*) principles governing or defining any possible experience of objects, and he spoke directly of the "construction" (*Konstruktion*) of concepts in geometry (p. 633) and so in effect of our perceptual "construction" of objects such as triangles in Euclidean space. Kant famously argued that space is not an objective structure of things-in-themselves, but rather a "form of intuition" in our perception of things as spatial and so a structure of things-as-they-appear. Husserl's analysis of space and time and perception of spatiotemporal things does not say that we "construct" things in space and time; rather, we implicitly construct the *meanings* through which we experience things in space–time. Though Husserl in his own way covers many important Kantian themes (sensation and conception, representation, awareness of space and time, and so on), Husserl's driving concerns were different from Kant's (Kant sought to overcome Humean skepticism, avoid metaphysics, and explain how synthetic a priori knowledge is possible in geometry and physics). Moreover, Husserl's milieu was very different. The new form of logic was taking shape around him, and with it the discipline that would become known as semantics in 20th-century logic. Husserl was very much aware of the relevant developments in mathematics and logic, and his account of the structure of intentionality, in the account of constitution, is in effect a logical semantics of consciousness.

APPENDIX: ALTERNATIVE MODELS OF NOEMA

Husserl characterized an act's noema as both "sense" and "the object as intended." This dual characterization has led scholars to interpret, or develop, his theory of noema in divergent ways. Some four interpretations have been prominent, each developing a distinct model of the noema and its role in intentionality. Each can be seen as a further development of core ideas in Husserl. A comparison will be illuminating and will set off our own interpretation by contrast with alternatives.

The intentional object model

Husserl sometimes speaks of the "intentional object" correlated with an act of consciousness: as in *Cartesian Meditations* (1931/1960), where he speaks of the "intentional object" or "*cogitatum qua cogitatum*" (§§15–16), which is "in" consciousness as "objective sense" (§18). So "intentional object" is another term for the noematic sense or object-as-intended. An *intentional object*, we may say, is an object that exists in an intentional relation to an act of consciousness. This notion echoes the original Scholastic doctrine, revived by Brentano, where an object is said to exist "in" an *intentio*. But this idea might be developed in various ways. Husserl's Polish student Roman Ingarden elaborated the notion of an "intentional objectivity" as a "purely intentional object" (see Ingarden 1965/1973, §20: 117ff., and note his prior discussion of linguistic meaning, resonant with our earlier discussion). Ingarden puts forth his own conception of intentional objects as a modification or extension of Husserl's conception of noemata

(p. 117, footnote 84, citing *Ideas* I). In Ingarden's ontology, a "purely intentional" object is "created" by an act of consciousness, whereas an "also intentional object," or extra-intentional object, exists autonomously and happens to be the "target of an intention" – that is, if there is such an object in addition to the purely intentional object. Yet both are "transcendent" of acts of consciousness, that is, they are objects distinct from consciousness and not literally a part of any act of consciousness. For example, when I see that eucalyptus tree over there, my experience produces a purely intentional object "that eucalyptus tree over there [with a certain appearance]," but the tree itself that stands across the street from me (as it were, looking back at me) exists in space–time independently of my seeing it, and so is an also-intentional object. By contrast, the fantastical gnarly-armed tree I am currently imagining (while reading a Dr. Seuss story) does not exist in space–time but is a purely intentional object, and there is no further also-intentional object that my intention reaches. Since Ingarden objected to Husserl's transcendental idealism (Ingarden 1975), pressing a realist ontology himself, we may note that Ingarden's ontology would posit both ordinary objects like trees and purely intentional objects like fictional trees as objects with distinct *modes of existence* in the world. Fictional objects, for Ingarden, exist in the world, but they are purely intentional objects created, like works of art, by acts of consciousness. The intentional object model differs from the mediating-sense model we have developed in this chapter by pulling "sense," as it were, out of the ray of intention and pressing it into the existential status of the object intended. (Other theories of intentional objects were elaborated by Husserl's contemporaries Alexius Meinong and Kasimier Twardowski, and indeed Husserl began his explicit work on intentionality with a 1894 essay titled "Intentional Objects" in the collection Husserl 1994: 345–87).

The neo-phenomenalist model

When I see an object such as a tree, Husserl stressed, I see it as a tree visible from this one side in this morning light, but I can also see the same object from different sides in different lighting. Accordingly, there is a system of noemata that reflect the various ways in which the same object can be perceived: the tree as seen in one act of perception, the tree as seen in a further act of perception as I walk around it and look at its back side, and so on. Husserl's collaborator Aron Gurwitsch proposed to identify the object itself with this corresponding system of noemata. "[W]e may define the *appearance of a thing as the thing itself as given in a particular one-sided manner of presentation* . . . ," where "the thing itself proves to be the all-inclusive systematic grouping of its appearances" (Gurwitsch 1964: 184; details follow on pp. 220ff.). These "appearances," Gurwitsch holds (p. 185), are what Husserl called noemata, where a noema is an "object as it is intended" as distinguished from the "object itself." So on Gurwitsch's ontology, a thing like a tree is identified with a system of noemata each of which consists in the tree itself as intended from a different perspective. Gurwitsch's use of the term "appearances" reflects the Kantian notion of phenomena or "things-as-they-appear," but Gurwitsch is extending Husserl's notion of noemata or "objects-as-intended." Nineteenth-century phenomenalism identified a material thing with an array of sensory appearances. In effect, Gurwitsch transforms classical phenomenalism into a doctrine that might be called noematic phenomenalism or noematic idealism (see Chapter 4 in this volume). This doctrine offers a neo-phenomenalist ontology of the "intentional object," where the intended object itself resolves into a system of noemata, whence each noema is a part of the object. This neo-phenomenalist model of noema differs from our mediating-sense model (developed in this chapter) in that the neo-phenomenalist noema is part of the structure of the *object* rather than the *content* of the act.

The mediating-sense model

The noema is not something at the terminus of the ray of intention, but rather something internal to the ray of intention: the ideal content of experience; as it were, the medium of intention. The noema is distinct from the object of the act of consciousness, we have stressed. Moreover, the noema is not a part of the *object* itself (as on the prior two models). Rather, the noema is part of the *intention* reaching toward the object. Specifically, the noema is the *content* of the act, that "in" the act which embodies the *way* the act is directed toward the object, if such object exists. The content is "in" the act, being a "moment" of the act (as we saw in the section titled "Noematic sense: 'the object as intended'"), and thereby *mediates* the intentional relation between the act and the object (if such object exist). This structure of the intentional relation we articulate accordingly in our model of mediating sense:

act – noematic sense ("the object as intended") → object

When Husserl calls the noema a "sense," this appellation ties into the logical theory of reference via sense. But what is a sense? It is something that plays this role of mediating intentionality because it embodies the *way* the object is intended. This model of the noema is sometimes called the "California" or "West Coast" view of the noema, and it is key to the so-called "Fregean" model of intentionality. (It is elaborated in Føllesdal 1969/1982; Dreyfus 1982; Smith and McIntyre 1982; and a similar view is developed in Mohanty 1982, writing from a different geography.)

The bracketed object model

In the natural or mundane attitude, I see a tree across the street. By contrast, Husserl holds, in the phenomenological or transcendental attitude, I see that same tree but I "bracket" the question of its existence. Thereby, in reflection, I become aware of the tree not in itself, but merely as I see it. The noema, the object *as* it is intended, thus comes into view in reflection, and only in reflection. Accordingly, one might say the noema of my perception is the "bracketed" object, the perceived object itself shorn of its presumed status as existing in the surrounding natural world: the noema is the object "transcendentally viewed." This conception of the noema – sometimes cast as an "East Coast" alternative to the "West Coast" view of the noema just elaborated – has been developed by Robert Sokolowski and John Drummond (see Sokolowski 2000; Drummond 1990, drawing on earlier writing of Sokolowski). On this conception, the noema of an act of consciousness is not ontologically distinct from the object of an act, but is "somehow identical" with the object. How? The noema is "the object transcendentally considered," "the objective correlate [of an act] precisely as it is being looked at from the transcendental attitude" (Sokolowski 2000: 59; the point is amplified on pp. 185–97). Thus, "The object, the sense, and the noema are the same differently considered. In the natural attitude, we are turned to the object *simpliciter*. . . . Only in the reflective attitude, however, do we focus on the object as a sense" (Drummond 1990: 59). Furthermore, since the same object can be intended in different ways, from different sides or aspects, the object is itself "an identity presented in a manifold of appearances" (Drummond 1990: 151, drawing on Sokolowski's notion of identities in manifolds, as in Sokolowski 2000: 27ff., 59). This manifold of appearances is the horizon structure we have studied.

So what exactly is a noema on this model? At one level, we are told, to talk of an act's noema is to talk of act's *object*, albeit "noematically," "transcendentally," even "philosophically," and so the noema is not an entity at all and not an entity that mediates the intentional relation of act to object (Sokolowski 2000: 59–60, 185–97, 222–3, in explicit contrast to the "West Coast" model depicted.) However, in Husserl's categorial ontology (see Chapter 4 in this volume), anything is an entity, even an object-as-transcendentally-viewed. So what type of entity is that? We are told that: the noema = the object as intended = the object as transcendentally viewed. There are problems with this equation. What comes into view in transcendental phenomenological reflection is the object-as-intended, but now we seem to have the (object-as-intended)-as-transcendentally-viewed: the original act intends the object X as F, and now the reflective act intends (X-as-F) as T, so the original act's noema is X-as-F and the reflection's noema is (X-as-F)-as-T. That cannot be right, so perhaps the phrase "object as transcendentally viewed" is misleading. The aim of the account is to say that phenomenological reflection remains tied somehow to the object of consciousness, the object itself. Yes, the object itself in *relation to* the act of consciousness. But here we seem to have lost the declared goal of phenomenology, which is to turn toward *consciousness* with its noematic content, rather than toward the object itself. Recall Husserl's use of noematic quotation (in the section on "Phenomenological methods" earlier in this chapter). If Kurt says "Plato rules," and we say "Kurt said, quote, 'Plato rules,'" the point of our quotation is not to talk about Plato "in the linguistic attitude," but to turn our regard to the *words* Kurt used to talk about Plato (and also thereby to their sense). Similarly, the point of a noematic quotation "Plato rules" is to turn our regard from the subject's thinking that Plato rules to the *sense* "Plato rules," which embodies the way Plato is intended in that act of thinking. The aim is not to consider Plato noncommittally, bracketing his existence, but to reflect on one's *consciousness* of Plato and its *sense*. Thus, we start with an intention of an object via a sense, and then – by noematic quotation – we move (back up the ray of intention) from the object represented through the sense in our experience to the sense that represents that object. (Compare Thomasson 2005, arguing – by drawing on Wilfrid Sellars together with Husserl – that to talk noncommittally of how a red object looks produces a description of one's sensory experience of red, the red-appearance of the object.)

The key point for this model, then, is that the noema is assimilated to the *object* of consciousness, rather than to a mediating content that embodies the *way* the object is intended. Turning to ontology, on this model: first, the noema is identified with the *bracketed* object; second, that object is an "identity in a manifold of appearances." Now, it is infelicitous to say two things are identical ("somehow") – phenomenology does not require that we revise number theory so that $2 = 1$. So it would be better to say, not that the noema is identical with the object, but that the noema is the object itself *restricted* to the presented aspect and *shorn* of its presumed existence. Then, we could say, the *bracketed object* model holds: where an act A intends an object X as having a feature F_1,

(1) the object of the act is X, and the noema of the act is $X\text{-as-}F_1$, where X may or may not exist and X may or may not really be F_1, and (2) X is a pole of identity in the system $\{X\text{-as-}F_1, X\text{-as-}F_2, X\text{-as-}F_3, \ldots\}$, where F_i are purported features of X as intended in alternative acts directed toward X from different perspectives. This model, so developed, is a variation on the intentional object approach to intentionality. It is akin to Meinong's "object theory" and to Hector-Neri Castañeda's "guise theory." For Meinong, an object itself is "beyond" being or nonbeing, an "incomplete" object is an object limited to certain properties, and acts of consciousness are directed toward incomplete objects and only indirectly thereby toward complete objects. Similarly, for Castañeda, an object is composed of "guises," complexes of properties, and our thoughts are directed toward guises, which are components of objects themselves. (See Smith and McIntyre 1982 on the distinction between object theories and content theories of intentionality. See Meinong 1904/1960 and D. W. Smith 1975 on Meinongian objects vis-à-vis intentionality. See Castañeda's presentation in Tomberlin 1986: 91–137; and D. W. Smith 1986 on Castañeda's guise theory.)

Retrospective on these models of the noema

The mediating-sense model of noema places the noema in the intentional "ray" emanating from an act of consciousness toward an object. On this model, the noema or sense of an act is an abstraction of the *way* the act is directed. By contrast, the other three models of noema place the noema somehow within the object toward which the intentional ray is directed. Husserl's talk of the "intentional object" reflects a traditional Medieval ontology, and his talk of the "object as intended" echoes a Kantian idiom. These ways of talking seem to lead toward some form of "objectual" understanding of the noema of an act. However, Husserl's background in logical and mathematical theory (observed in Chapters 1–3) leads toward the "logical" or "semantic" conception of the noema as an ideal sense that mediates intentionality. That interpretation, which we have just expounded, places Husserl squarely in the context within which he wrote, within what Alberto Coffa has called "the semantic tradition" of the late 19th and early 20th centuries (see Coffa 1991). Husserl's basic theory of intentionality via ideal content emerges in the texts we have dissected. This theory could be extended consistently to allow that an object of consciousness is an object whose being is merely possible existence (say, in various possible situations or worlds), or merely intentional existence, or even "bracketable" existence. Some of Husserl's language suggests ontological variations along such lines: he speaks, as noted, of "intentional objects," and he speaks of "possible worlds." (See Smith and McIntyre 1982 on the role of possible worlds in a Husserlian, or perhaps neo-Husserlian, theory of intentionality.) Even if Husserl's ontology includes intentional or possible entities, it already includes ideal meanings, which direct consciousness toward objects, be they actual or possible or merely intentional. Alas, we shall not be able to pursue such variations on Husserlian themes here.

SUMMARY

Husserl's conception of phenomenology emerged, in *Logical Investigations* (1900–1), with his theory of intentionality as the central structure of consciousness. By the time of *Ideas* I (1913) he had extended that theory and developed a distinctive method by which phenomenological reflection would proceed. Husserl's mature "transcendental" phenomenology featured the method of "bracketing," the notions of "noema" and "horizon," and a complex account of the "constitution" of objects in consciousness. The essence of consciousness is unfolded through this phenomenological analysis.

The new method of phenomenology is called "phenomenological reduction" or phenomenological "bracketing." In the everyday "natural" attitude, we assume the existence of things around us in space and time, in nature. In order to shift into the "transcendental" attitude of "pure" phenomenology, I "bracket" – make no use of – this general thesis of the natural attitude. Thereby I restrict my attention to my experience per se, to the structure of "pure" consciousness. Each act of consciousness, we then see, consists in a "noetic" process or "noesis" (fulfilled with sensory "hyle" in the case of perception); and correlated with this noesis is a "noema." The noesis is the intentional part (moment) of the act of consciousness, a process that occurs in time. The correlated noema is an ideal content or sense, which does not occur in time, but which presents or prescribes the object of consciousness The noema is characterized, alternatively, as the object-as-intended: the object of consciousness just *as* it is experienced or intended in that act. The object intended through this sense may or may not exist and, as in the case of seeing a tree nearby, may or may not actually occur in space–time (as assumed in the natural attitude). Yet the act intends this object even if no such object exists. By describing this object just as it is experienced, then, I describe my *consciousness* of the object, characterizing its own form of intentionality, featuring the relevant noema. Further reflection reveals a "horizon" of further possibilities regarding the object of the act. These possibilities are "predelineated" by the noematic content of the act, prescribed by a horizon of further noemata presenting the same object with further possible features.

Intentionality, we see in phenomenological reflection, consists in this structure of consciousness, wherein an act is directed toward an object via a noema constrained by a horizon of further possible significances. In Husserl's "transcendental" idiom, an object is said to be "constituted" in consciousness insofar as it is intended as having certain features and as possibly having a variety of further features, that is, insofar as it is so characterized by a given noema and correlated horizon of meaning.

With this enhanced account of intentionality and the constitution of objects in consciousness, Husserl presents his conception of phenomenology as transcendental. The more minimal conception of phenomenology is thereby elaborated within an extended theory of intentionality and a particular conception of transcendental philosophy. Husserl's conception of logical semantics is here put to work in the foundations of phenomenology. By the same token, Husserl's conception of phenomenology is put to work in the foundations of logical semantics. Ideal sense or meaning is now explicated as noematic intentional content, with all its force in the flow of consciousness.

FURTHER READING

Coffa, J. Alberto. 1991. *The Semantic Tradition from Kant to Carnap: To the Vienna Station.* Edited by Linda Wessels. Cambridge and New York: Cambridge University Press. A study of the historical development of semantics from the 19th century forward, indicating Husserl's place in the tradition.

Dreyfus, Hubert L., ed. 1982. *Husserl, Intentionality and Cognitive Science.* In collaboration with Harrison Hall. Cambridge, Massachusetts: MIT Press. A collection of essays addressing the semantic core of Husserl's theory of intentionality and its relation to contemporary cognitive science and the representational theory of mind, including Dagfinn Føllesdal's seminal 1969 article "Husserl's Notion of Noema."

Drummond, John J. 1990. *Husserlian Intentionality and Non-Foundational Realism: Noema and Object.* Dordrecht and Boston, Massachusetts: Kluwer Academic Publishers (now New York: Springer). A study of Husserl's theory of intentionality and noema, defending a partly different interpretation of noema than that in Smith and McIntyre (1982) and Dreyfus (1982).

Drummond, John J., and Lester Embree, eds. 1992. *The Phenomenology of the Noema.* Dordrecht and Boston, Massachusetts: Kluwer Academic Publishers (now New York: Springer). Studies of Husserl's theory of the noema.

Dummett, Michael. 1993. *Origins of Analytical Philosophy.* Cambridge, Massachusetts: Harvard University Press. A study of the roles of Frege and Husserl in the development of the tradition of analytic philosophy, addressing issues of intentionality, sense, and reference, and the relative priority of mind and language.

Friedman, Michael. 1999. *Reconsidering Logical Positivism.* Cambridge and New York: Cambridge University Press. A study of Carnap's logical empiricism and its historical background, including Husserl's phenomenology and the concept of "constitution."

Hill, Clair Ortiz, and Guillermo E. Rosado Haddock. 2000. *Husserl or Frege? Meaning, Objectivity, and Mathematics.* Chicago and LaSalle, Illinois: Open Court. Studies of relations between Husserl, Frege, and others.

Mohanty, J. N. 1982. *Husserl and Frege.* Bloomington: Indiana University Press. A study of the historical and conceptual relations between Husserl's theory of intentionality and Frege's semantic ideas.

Richardson, Alan W. 1998. *Carnap's Construction of the World: The Aufbau and the Emergence of Logical Empiricism.* Cambridge and New York: Cambridge University

Press. A study of Carnap's logical empiricism, including his conception of "constitution" and its relation to Husserlian phenomenology.

Ryckman, Thomas. 2005. *The Reign of Relativity: Philosophy in Physics 1915–1925.* Oxford and New York: Oxford University Press. A study of general relativity theory, addressing Husserl's transcendental phenomenology in relation to Weyl's mathematical formulation of Einstein's theory.

Smith, David Woodruff. 1995. "Mind and Body." In B. Smith and D. W. Smith, eds. *The Cambridge Companion to Husserl.* Cambridge and New York: Cambridge University Press. A study of Husserl's ontology, including Husserl's conception of formal and material ontology, relating the theory of intentionality to contemporary philosophy of mind.

Smith, David Woodruff, and Ronald McIntyre. 1982. *Husserl and Intentionality: A Study of Mind, Meaning, and Language.* Dordrecht and Boston, Massachusetts: D. Reidel Publishing Company (now New York: Springer). A book-length study of Husserl's theory of intentionality, meaning, and horizon, including relations to contemporary logical or semantic theory.

Thomasson, Amie L. 2005. "First-Person Knowledge in Phenomenology." In David Woodruff Smith and Amie L. Thomasson, eds. *Phenomenology and Philosophy of Mind.* Oxford and New York: Oxford University Press. A contemporary account of phenomenological method, explicating Husserl's method by contrasting it with inner observation and comparing it instead with uses of quotation.

Tieszen, Richard. 2005. *Phenomenology, Logic, and the Philosophy of Mathematics.* Cambridge and New York: Cambridge University Press. Studies of Husserlian phenomenology in relation to philosophy of logic and mathematics.

Seven

Epistemology

Beyond rationalism, empiricism, and Kantianism

The preceding two chapters studied Husserl's conception of phenomenology, the science of the essence of consciousness. Husserl's approach to the theory of knowledge moves through his conception of phenomenology. In the *Logical Investigations* (1900–1) and again in *Ideas* I (1913), Husserl develops a phenomenological theory of knowledge. Early modern philosophy explored the roles of reason and sensory experience in the foundations of our knowledge, looking toward the emerging sciences, especially physics, in which both mathematics and empirical observation were key. Husserl returns to these classical epistemological issues, armed with the results of his explorations in phenomenology. In this chapter we pursue Husserl's phenomenological theory of knowledge, considering its place in his overall system of philosophy.

HUSSERL'S PLACE IN EPISTEMOLOGY

Epistemology is the theory of knowledge. What counts as knowledge, philosophers ask? Is knowledge justified true belief, as Plato considered, or something more? What do we know? What are the grounds or evidence for the knowledge we have? Is our knowledge founded primarily in perception (observation), or in reason (logic and mathematics), or in a combination of observing and reasoning? Is our knowledge derived from the authority of experts, or the practical wisdom of elders, or the spiritual wisdom gained in revelation or meditation? Is modern science the model of knowledge most expertly drawn? To what extent is our current knowledge dependent on the developments of science? What is the status of our everyday knowledge, which we take for granted as we go about our daily affairs?

Pursued since the dawn of philosophy, epistemology achieved its modern form, and arguably came into its own, in the 17th century, as philosophers began reflecting on the methods of modern science at its inception. In his *Meditations on First Philosophy* (1641), René Descartes – mathematician, physicist, philosopher – reasoned that all of our knowledge must be founded on reason, if our knowledge is to be truly certain. His model was mathematics. Remember that it was Descartes who invented analytic or algebraic geometry ("Cartesian" geometry), which was to lead into the calculus and higher mathematics, all used extensively in modern physics from Isaac Newton on down. *Rationalism* thus pressed the case for reason as the basis of knowledge, as Gottfried Willhelm von Leibniz, Baruch Spinoza, and others followed on Descartes' heels.

Early in the 18th century, John Locke, George Berkeley, and David Hume argued, contrary to rationalism, that all of our knowledge is founded ultimately on sensory perception. Reason builds on the testimony of the senses, without which we would have nothing to reason about and no knowledge whatsoever about the world around us. *Empiricism* thus pressed the case for sensory experience as the basis of knowledge.

If we look to modern science as a paradigm of organized knowledge, we see a clear path of empirical investigation, where perceptual observation leads through complex reasoning into well-supported, often mathematical *theories* in physics, chemistry, biology, neuroscience, psychology, and so on. Empirical science follows *inductive* reasoning from *observations* of particular events to generalizations and ultimately into mathematical theories like Newton's law of gravity. But empirical science also follows *deductive* reasoning as in axiomatic geometry and higher mathematics, which are applied to observations in, say, Newton's mathematical theory of gravity. What we call the *scientific method* today is thus a synthesis of empiricist and rationalist aspirations.

By the late 18th century, Immanuel Kant was already trying to reconcile the rationalist and empiricist sides of our knowledge of the world, with Newtonian physics on his mind. In his Critique of Pure Reason (1781/1787), Kant's "critical" or "transcendental" philosophy sought the necessary conditions of the possibility of our knowledge. On Kant's analysis, our knowledge is essentially conditioned by the structure of our own minds. Human cognition is the product, specifically, of an application of concepts to sensations, producing "intuition" of things in the world, not as they are in themselves but as they appear. Concepts bring order to the barrage of sensory stimuli, as the mind applies basic concepts or "categories of the understanding" (noted in Chapter 4 of this volume) to the "manifold of sensibility," the barrage of unstructured sensory data awaiting conceptualization as, say, I see this tree with green leaves below white clouds dotting the blue sky.

In the 19th century, before Husserl came on the scene, Bernard Bolzano's Theory of Science (1837) reinvigorated the rationalist side of knowledge in his theory of theories as systems of ideal propositions; on the empiricist side, Bolzano recognized singular "intuitions" of individual objects. Then Franz Brentano's Psychology from an Empirical Standpoint (1874) elaborated an empiricist view enriched with the intentional structure of experience. The seeds were sown for a new kind of theory of knowledge. Drawing on Bolzano and Brentano, Husserl developed phenomenology, as his conception of "pure logic" led into the theory of intentionality, a theory of evidence, and therewith a phenomenological theory of knowledge.

By now you will have guessed that we have already seen key ingredients of Husserl's theory of knowledge. The Logical Investigations (1900–1) begins, in the Prolegomena, with a "theory of science," a vision of systematic, objective knowledge that coheres as a body of propositions concerning a field of objects. Systematic knowledge begins, however, in more elementary experiences of perception or other forms of "intuition." Accordingly, the Logical Investigations culminates in the book-length Investigation VI, titled "Elements of a Phenomenological Explication of Knowledge." What makes Husserl's theory of knowledge phenomenological is his analysis of the structures of experience that form knowledge. On Husserl's account, knowledge is the product of two essential forms of experience: the intentional and the "intuitive" or evidential characters of experience – if you will, the rational and empirical "moments" of cognitive experience. Both intentionality and intuition play their roles in making knowledge possible: intentionality offers *representation* of things in the world ("that eucalyptus tree by the roadside"), while intuition provides *evidence* of the existence of such things ("I *see* that eucalyptus tree by the roadside"). Husserl characterizes intuition (*Anschauung*) as an experience in which an object is given "itself" with "intuitive fullness," or "self-evidence," as in seeing an object as opposed to merely thinking of it. Under intuition, however, Husserl includes not only sensory perception, in seeing physical objects (or hearing, touching, smelling, tasting things), but also "seeing" or having "insight" about essences or essential truths, and indeed "seeing" or having "insight" about meanings or intentional contents. Investigation V details the structure of intentionality, and then Investigation VI explores the role of intuition and intuitional meaning (*Anschauungssinn*) in the formation of knowledge. While Husserl's focus is on sensory perception as the paradigm of intuition, his account is generalized to allow for the intuitive evidence we experience in eidetic insight into the essences of objects and phenomenological insight into the essence of consciousness.

Husserl's account of knowledge continues in *Ideas* I (1913), with a sharper account of the relation between sensation and meaning in perception (§§84, 89–90). At the end of that book, after his mature account of phenomenology and intentionality is in place, after he has analyzed structures of both judgment and perception, Husserl turns to the "phenomenology of reason" – a phrase echoing Kant's "critique of reason." In that context, he explicates the conditions of the possibility of knowledge in terms of the phenomenology of "intuition" along with intentionality. In the *Cartesian Meditations* (1931), Husserl gives more organization to his theory of intuition, distinguishing several types of "evidence" in intuitive experience. In notes collected as *Experience and Judgment* (1939/1948/1973), Husserl explores further the structure of sensory "experience" (*Erfahrung*, as opposed to *Erlebnis*, or "lived-experience"), and its role in supporting judgment, distinguishing perceptual judgment from perception itself: here is the first step toward knowledge, in the transition from seeing an object to seeing that the object is thus-and-so. Finally, in the Crisis (1935–8), Husserl elaborates on the role that everyday experience plays in our knowledge of the world around us, including our scientific knowledge, as we inherit a great deal of background knowledge from our surrounding culture. Husserl's phenomenology sidesteps skepticism by assaying the kinds of evidence that are possible in grounding our beliefs about the world, and by explicating the way our knowledge depends on everyday "life-world" experience. Here is a very different response to skepticism than anything in Descartes, Hume, Kant, et al.

OUTLINES OF HUSSERL'S PHENOMENOLOGICAL THEORY OF KNOWLEDGE

Knowledge is not itself an act of consciousness. Rather, it is the accumulation of *beliefs* (states, not acts, of mind) formed through appropriate acts of *judgment* in the face of *intuitive evidence*, especially as we see things and reason and judge about them. As Husserl puts it in the *Crisis* (1935–8), our knowledge – from everyday knowledge to disciplinary knowledge in the sciences – lies in beliefs that are the "sediment" of prior intentional acts, most often those of our forebears. Think of our knowledge in geometry or carpentry or shipbuilding (or indeed philosophy). Assuming an ontology of intentional contents, *what we know* – our store of knowledge, if you will – consists in an accumulation of *propositions* supported by *evidence*, that is, propositions that are the contents of past judgments supported by perceptual observations or other intuitive experiences.

In Husserl's theory of knowledge, we find both rationalist and empiricist motifs. On the rationalist side, we observe three important strands of theory. First, there is Husserl's theory of *logic* as the theory of theories, stressing the rational order of a systematic body of knowledge, or "science," in a given theory such as geometry, physics, or psychology. Here we find a traditional form of *rational insight*. Second, there is Husserl's theory of *representation* or *intentionality*, analyzing how various concepts or meanings, in language or in acts of consciousness, prescribe or represent appropriate objects in the world. Here we find the theory and use of *phenomenological insight*, in understanding the intentional force of the noematic sense in a given experience: if you will, "seeing" meaning and its intentional force. Third, there is Husserl's theory and use of *essential insight*, or *Wesenserschauung*, literally looking at or observing essences. In Chapter 3 we addressed logic, theories, meaning, and representation, while in Chapters 5 and 6 we addressed meaning, intentionality, and methods for explicating the intentional force of meaning in our experience (by the technique of bracketing). In Chapter 4 we surveyed the many types of essence (formal and material) that Husserl distinguished, noting his practice of *Wesenserschauung*, or seeing essences. It remains, among other things, to explore further the phenomenon of *Wesenserschauung* as Husserl characterized it, here within the context of his theory of knowledge. It's not so mysterious as it sounds: abstraction is something we do all the time, as we recognize similar features or forms in different concrete objects or events.

On the empiricist side of Husserl's epistemology, we find that, for Husserl, our *knowledge of things in nature* is founded on *sensory perception*; just as the empiricists said. However, on Husserl's phenomenological analysis, a perceptual experience is rarely (as some empiricists have held) a pure sensation of a sensible quality such as red. Rather, an act of perception (as in seeing a tree) is a fusion of sensation and conceptualization ("hyletic" sensory data and "noetic" interpretation: per *Ideas* I, §85). Indeed, sensation seldom occurs without that conceptualization whereby meaning is given to the incoming barrage of sensory data. Here Husserl modifies the empiricist story along lines drawn by Kant.

Kant's theory of knowledge sought to answer Hume's skepticism (among other things), as Kant distinguished *phenomena* and *noumena*, or things-as-they-appear and things-in-themselves, showing how we might know things as they appear but not things as they are in themselves. As we saw in Chapter 6, Husserl radically extends the notion of "phenomena" as "noemata," or things-as-intended, taking the form of ideal intentional meanings.

But Husserl rejected the Kantian notion of a *Ding an sich*, or thing-in-itself beyond the reach of empirical cognition. Despite flirtation with what looks like a form of Kantian transcendental idealism, Husserl developed a very different theory of the structure of cognition. On Husserl's analysis, perception proceeds through a noema (presenting "the tree *as* perceived") and thereby *reaches* the existing thing itself ("the tree simpliciter"), provided the perceptual noema is *intuitively* supported or "fulfilled" by appropriate sensory data. Of course, the proper theory of intentionality was not yet available to Kant or to other epistemologists prior to Husserl's work in the wake of Bolzano and Brentano.

Husserl's theory of knowledge, then, moved beyond classical rationalist, empiricist, and Kantian models in several fundamental ways.

1   Unlike his predecessors, Husserl developed an articulate *theory of intentionality*, a theory of how meaning directs experience toward various things in the world. He used that theory in the analysis of both perception and empirical judgment based on perception, hence empirical knowledge of nature.
2   In Husserl's epistemology, we employ *eidetic intuition or essential insight* (*Wesenserschauung*), as we abstract and explicate the essence of various objects. Here Husserl goes beyond traditional empiricism, but also beyond a logic-centered rationalism, as his critics quickly saw. (Moritz Schlick, founding the Vienna Circle in the 1920s, explicitly attacked Husserl's notion of *Wesenserschauung*.)
3   In Husserl's epistemology, our knowledge of conscious experience depends on our own direct, subjective experience of consciousness. We can explicate the intentional structure of consciousness, and focus on the meanings contained in our experiences, Husserl proposed, through *phenomenological reflection* on our own experience, which we pursue by the technique of bracketing (see Chapter 6). Descartes, Hume, and Kant were all practicing rudimentary phenomenology in their diverse accounts of cognitive experience (in perception, reason, judgment), but Husserl insists that his predecessors had not yet

mastered the practice of what we may call *phenomenological* or *transcendental* intuition, the source of properly phenomenological knowledge of consciousness.

4 Further, our knowledge of *other people's experience*, and of *cultural* objects (tools, artifacts, institutions, values), depends on our *empathy* with other people in various cultural activities. In Husserl's epistemology, empathy provides a kind of deferred direct evidence of others' experiences, as I can often "see" what another is feeling or thinking – though my knowledge of others is far from infallible.

5 In Husserl's epistemology, we explicate "formal" essences – Number, Individual, State of Affairs, and so on – through *categorial intuition* (as observed in Chapter 4). Correlatively, we intuit *logical forms* in propositions. Thus, in a special type of eidetic intuition, we "see" formal structures of objects in the world, structures that are semantically correlated with logical structures of meaning, reflecting our logical concepts of quantity, individual, state of affairs, and so on.

This kind of insight into formal ontological structure is perhaps the most radical and unfamiliar method in Husserl's toolkit. Yet it seems to be practiced on a daily basis by mathematicians, albeit without explicit ontology and epistemology. Or so the former mathematician named Husserl held as he launched his philosophy in the Prolegomena to the *Logical Investigations*.

Husserl's doctrine of intuition can be seen as a radical extension of empiricism, sweeping rationalism and empiricism together in a wide notion of intuition. Husserl remarks:

> If "*positivism*" means so much as the absolutely presupposition-free grounding of all sciences on the "positive," that is, what is to be grasped originarily [*originär*: "originally," i.e. intuitively], then *we* are the genuine positivists. In fact, we let *no* authority shrink the right to recognize all kinds of intuition as equally valuable sources for the justification for knowledge – also not through the authority of "modern natural science."
>
> (*Ideas* I, §20, my translation)

Empiricism becomes positivism when the model of knowledge is that achieved in the "positive" sciences, the natural sciences. For classical empiricists or positivists, only sensory perception provides basic justification for knowledge. By contrast, Husserl widens the notion of intuition to include not only perceptual intuition, but also eidetic intuition and phenomenological intuition.

As we explore the details of Husserl's theory of knowledge, we stress two themes: systematic theory and intuition. Through complex phenomenological analyses, Husserl explicates the structure of many, quite different forms of intuition, in which an object of appropriate type is given in a direct, evident, intuitive way.

Husserl does not assemble his theory of knowledge in one neat package. Rather, the elements of the theory are developed in various texts. We can map out a structure in his theory of knowledge, however, if we take his categorial ontology as a guide (drawing on Chapter 4). Accordingly, we shall structure his theory of knowledge as coordinate with his ontology. Different types of object in the world are known in different ways, but our knowledge of a given type of object always consists in propositions "sedimented" from past judgments supported by appropriate intuitive experiences.

INTUITION AS EVIDENT EXPERIENCE

In everyday English, we say someone has intuitions about impending events, or about other people, sensing their motives. In contemporary philosophy, we explicate our intuitions or intuitive beliefs about, for example, ethical principles or what counts as really knowing something. In logic, we consult our intuitions about which forms of inference are valid. In Husserl's idiom, however, "intuition" is a technical term with a special role in his phenomenology.

In Medieval Scholastic philosophy, the term "*cognitio intuitiva*" was introduced to mean direct cognition of something, as in visual perception. Subsequently, in the German philosophical tradition, "*Anschauung*" takes the place of the Medieval Latin term, and is translated into English as "intuition." "*Anschauung*" literally means looking at something. Intuition provides direct knowledge of an object, without inference from other judgments. Thus, intuition provides basic knowledge, from which further inferences can be drawn. Visual perception is the paradigm of intuition, as when I see that tree. From that point on, however, theories of intuition vary. For Kant, intuition is a sensory-conceptual representation of a phenomenon. For Bolzano, intuition is a singular representation of an object. For Husserl, intuition covers a range of *self-evident* forms of experience, beginning with seeing a physical object before one.

In his phenomenological description of intuition, Husserl says that in a visual experience – such as seeing or touching a tree – the object is given "originarily" (*originär*) in its "'bodily' selfhood" (*"leibhaftigen" Selbstheit*) (*Ideas* I, §3). This "originary" character (a neologism) refers to the origin of knowledge in self-evident observation. What of the further characterization? It is natural to say that in sensory perception the object is experienced as "itself" "bodily" present; this is to say, I experience the tree itself in an embodied relation to me, that is, a causal relation to me. Think of the experience of touching a tree. Yet Husserl extends this characterization to all kinds of intuition, specifically to *essential insight* (*Wesenserschauung*), insight about an essence such as triangularity or treehood – or any of the types of essence we met in Chapter 4. In emphatic prose, Husserl writes:

> The essence (eidos) is a new kind of object. As the given of individual or empirical [*erfahrenden*] intuition is an individual object, so the given of essential insight [*Wesenserschauung*] is a pure essence.

> Here there lies before us not a merely external analogy, but a radical commonality. *Essential insight is still intuition* [*Anschauung*], as the eidetic object is still an object. . . . Empirical intuition, specifically sense experience [*Erfahrung*], is consciousness of an individual object, and as intuitive "brings it to givenness," as perception . . . brings consciousness to grasp the object "originarily," in its "*bodily*" selfhood [*originär, in seiner*

"leibbhaftigen" Selbstheit]. In exactly the same way essential insight is consciousness of something, an "object," a something toward which its glance is directed, and what in it is "itself given" ["*selbst gegeben*"].

(Ideas I, §3, my translation)

Even objects dealt with in formal logic, he adds, "subjects of possibly true predications," can be grasped in "bodily selfhood." Strong stuff! Husserl's doctrine of essential insight, correlated with his doctrine of essence, met with stiff resistance, but Husserl insisted he had been badly misunderstood. As we explore the notion of intuition, we shall find that the practice of essential insight is not so bizarre as Husserl's rhetoric may suggest.

The heart of intuition, for Husserl, is "evidence" (Evidenz), that is, self-evidence. In Logical Investigations, he says an intuition is a "fulfilled" presentation of its object, that is, evidentially fulfilled, as a hypothesis or expectation might be fulfilled by observations. In Ideas I, he says that in intuition an object is given "originarily," that is, with originating evidence, which provides the justification of knowledge. In Cartesian Meditations, he elaborates on types of "evidence." As we shall see, Husserl distinguishes a variety of kinds or grades of evidence, often speaking of what is more or less "adequate" evidence. In English, we take evidence to be the claims offered in support of another claim or proposition: the witness saw the suspect leave by the back door, a damning piece of evidence. However, in Husserl's technical usage (playing off the English), *evidence*, or *evidentness*, is a phenomenological character of an experience. If I merely think, hypothetically, that the suspect left by the back door, my thought carries no evidence; but if I actually see him leave by the back door, my seeing this event is an evident observation. Indeed, the observation is self-evident, that is, its evidentness does not rest on inference from any other experiences or judgments. Intuitiveness consists in this character of self-evidentness.

On Husserl's analysis, an act of perception includes both a sensory moment and a noetic or meaning-giving moment (Ideas I, §85). In virtue of the sensory aspect, the experience is an *evident* presentation or intention of its object. We might say the sensory element "fulfills" the noetic or intentional element, and so "fulfills" the meaning in the experience, whence the experience has the character of intuitive "fullness" (compare *Ideas* I, §136). The intuitive "fullness" of an act of perception is this character of being evident, self-evident. In every intentional experience an object is "given," that is, intended, and intended *as* such-and-such. But in intuition the object is "given" with evidence or fulfillment, that is, it is given intuitively, self-evidently, as thus-and-so. Investigation VI of the *Logical Investigations* works over this notion of intuitive fullness in great detail, emphasizing the fusion of the interpretive and intuitive components of an experience of intuition. This analysis carries over, with simplification, into *Ideas* I in the model sketched earlier.

Now let us turn to the noematic sense of a perception, the intuitive-perceptual sense presenting "the object as seen." In perception, Husserl says, the object is intended or given "itself." This means, I take it, that the experience is a "direct" presentation of the object. As Husserl explicitly observes, we use demonstrative pronouns when we express the content of a perception or perceptual judgment. We naturally say, as in the phenomenological descriptions developed in prior chapters, "I see *that* black bird" or "I see that *that* is a black bird" (to use Husserl's example). And the demonstrative pronoun "that" refers, Husserl says, "directly" rather than "attributively." Just as the perception refers or intends directly rather than attributively, presenting "that . . . " rather than, say, "the object that is a black bird, about twelve inches high, making a sharp cawing sound, about fifteen feet in front of DWS at noon on 1 August 2005" (see *Logical Investigations*, Investigation I, §26; Investigation VI, §§4–5.) Decades later, philosophers of language would study how a demonstrative works as opposed to a description. Thus, a definite description, such as "the author of *Waverly*," refers by appeal to a property or cluster of properties unique to the referent (having authored the *Waverly* novels), whereas the demonstrative pronoun "that," on a certain occasion of utterance, refers by appeal to the *presence* of the object before the speaker, often pointing at the object. When Husserl says the object is given "itself" or in its "'bodily' selfhood," we can understand this best by considering how a demonstrative works. In seeing or indeed touching "that," my experience presents the object itself, directly, and does so by virtue of its presence before me – my experience is *pointing* at the object right before me. The intuitive presentation of "that" object is then normally joined by a predicative presentation, thus, a visual presentation of "that black bird."

From today's perspective, I propose, we can see in Husserl's account three distinguishing features of perception that qualify it as intuition: (1) The *thetic character* of a perception includes the character of intuitiveness, or evidentness, that is, intuitive fullness; (2) the *noematic sense* of a perception includes the demonstrative sense "this," which presents the object directly, not attributively; (3) the conditions of reference or successful intention include the intended object's being *present* to the subject, that is, bodily present, located before the subject in space–time. (See D. W. Smith 1989 for an analysis, in my own terms, of several forms of "acquaintance," what Husserl called intuition, elaborating similar phenomenological structures of "demonstrative" or "indexical" forms of experience.)

These phenomenological features of perception are specific to sensory intentional experience in a spatiotemporal setting. Other types of intuition, such as grasping an essence, will have to be described differently, yet so as to qualify as an intuitive presentation of an object "itself."

ESSENTIAL INSIGHT THROUGH IMAGINATIVE VARIATION

"Seeing" or "looking at" essences – *Wesenserschauung* – may sound like a magical intellectual faculty. I send my mental periscope high into the Platonic heaven of eidos, I peer around, I "see" the essence Triangle, and I describe what I "see." I "see" that, by essence, a triangle is a figure formed by three intersecting straight lines, which meet in angles of various possible size, where the sum of the three interior angles is 180°. Or I "see" the essence Tree, not any concrete tree, but the ideal form Tree. I "see" that, by essence, a tree has a trunk, roots, a number of branches, with

branches of branches, where leaves or needles appear at the ends
of the smallest branches. Or I "see" the essence Consciousness,
whereby I "see" that, by essence, an act of consciousness is intentional, carries a meaning or noema that aims toward some object,
and is experienced by a subject. But now I retract my eidetic
periscope, I open my physical eyes, and over here I *see* a triangle
painted on a canvas, while over there I *see* a tree. . . . But wait!
Nothing like this picture of *essential insight* emerges as we read the
details of Husserl's account of intuitive insight about the nature or
essence of a triangle, a tree, an act of consciousness.

   Ideas I (1913), we noted, opens with Husserl's account of
essence (*Wesen*) and essence-insight (*Wesenserschauung*). This account
is an amplified version of a piece of theory laid out (in a lengthy
polemic) in the *Logical Investigations* (1900–1), where Husserl talks
not of essence and essence-insight, but of "ideal species" and
"abstraction" of species from concrete instances (Investigation II),
and finally of "intuition" of ideal objects (Investigation VI). These
terms suggest something more familiar than do "essences" and
"seeing essences" – familiar, if not quite prosaic.

   In *Ideas* I, Husserl coined a cluster of terms in his effort to
characterize, phenomenologically, what we are calling (in translation) essential insight. He spoke of observation of essences
(*Wesenserschauung*), knowledge or acquaintance of essences
(*Wesenserkenntnis*), grasping of essences (*Wesenserfassung*), description
of essences (*Wesensbeschreibung*), positing of essences (*Wesenssetzung*),
and science of essences (*Wesenswissenschaft*) (see the index of the
German edition). The term that achieved salience for some readers
was *Wesenserschauung*, which sounds like "seeing essences." But
other of his terms are equally suitable, especially *Wesenserfassung*,
"grasping essences." Though we speak naturally of insight, we
also speak naturally of grasping the nature (essence) of something –
or, switching to another type of ideal object, grasping an idea or
concept or meaning. What does Husserl's prior account of these
things look like?

   Investigation II of the *Logical Investigations* is titled "The Ideal Unity
of the Species and Modern Theories of Abstraction." Husserl
sketches his own view and expounds it by contrast with nominalist

views he rejects in the empiricists Locke, Berkeley, Hume, and Mill. Here we cannot do justice to Husserl's argument over some 80 pages, but we can extract his key results: an ontological theory of universals as ideal objects, and an epistemological theory of abstraction whereby we know universals.

As we noted in Chapter 4, Husserl's theory of ideal species, later called essences or eidos, is a realist theory of what traditionally are called universals, that is, kinds, properties, relations – and, for Husserl, "formal" objects or ontological "forms" (see also Chapter 3 of this volume). Husserl argues at length against nominalism, the view that when we consider the members of a species there is no further object that is the species, there is only the name (perhaps a mental name or concept) we use to group the individual objects. By contrast, Husserl holds, positively, that species are objective, *ideal* objects, shareable by concrete things in space–time but not themselves spatiotemporal. Above all, Husserl insists on the objective existence of species, arguing that we cannot avoid positing them. He seems to include numbers, sets, and other mathematical objects under ideal species. Also (in Investigation I), he takes senses or meanings to be ideal species of acts of consciousness (later, in *Ideas* I, he takes senses to be their own type of ideal objects, as we saw in Chapter 6). Husserl's discussion of species is interwoven with discussion of modern theories of abstraction, in a critique of views of Locke, Berkeley, and Hume. He is particularly attentive to Hume, in a chapter called "Phenomenological Study of Hume's Theory of Abstraction."

Take a ripe tomato. Husserl argues that we must distinguish the species Red, the instance of Red that is a moment of the object (here, the tomato), and the object itself. The species does not reduce to the collected objects that are red, or to the collected instances of Red (moments) in those objects. Nor does it reduce to an idea of the red in the object (as when I see the object as red), or to the meaning or concept of red, or to the expression "red." Husserl criticizes the empiricists and nominalists for failing to recognize and distinguish these diverse entities. For Husserl, then, ideal species are not unfamiliar objects, though we must be careful to distinguish them from related objects of distinct ontological types.

How do we know species? Husserl approaches this question through a critique of empiricist notions of abstraction, focusing on Hume's theory of abstraction. For Hume, roughly, when we look at the tomato we recognize its resemblance to other red objects, and focus our attention on the resemblance. Thereby we abstract the species Red (or, for Hume, the idea of red) from a group of red things whose resemblance we recognize. Hume was on the right track, Husserl thought, but did not draw the required distinctions, and so did not offer an adequate phenomenology of grasping species. Husserl's own theory of our abstraction of species assumes the relevant distinctions. On Husserl's theory of intuition of species, then, I grasp the species Red by considering in imagination the similarities among various red objects, each bearing its own instance of Red. By abstraction from a variety of possible instances of Red in various objects, I grasp intuitively the species Red itself. This account of species abstraction, or intuition of ideal species, Husserl extends in *Ideas* I.

In *Ideas* I, Husserl characterizes the method of *eidetic variation*. In order to grasp the essence Red, I practice a form of imagination or "free phantasy." I imagine varied instances of Red, imagining objects whose colors vary from Red (shading toward Blue or Yellow), and by abstraction I grasp the essence that is shared by those objects I imagine as red. Or consider the essence Triangle. I imagine varying shapes and judge which ones are triangles. From this imaginary group I abstract those features that I judge to be shared by triangles of varying type. In this way I generate the insight – I come to "see" – that, by essence, a triangle has three straight-line sides which form interior angles that sum to 180°. Or take the essence Tree. I imagine a variety of objects. If the object has no trunk, no limbs, no roots, I judge that it is not a tree. And so I judge intuitively, I come to "see," that, by essence, a tree has a trunk, roots, branches, and so on. My judgments are supported by intuitive evidence – today we speak of "pattern recognition." This sense of evidence qualifies the experience as intuitive.

In *Ideas* I, Husserl introduces this method of grasping essences in "free phantasy" immediately after introducing essential insight:

> The eidos [*Eidos*], the *pure essence* [*Wesen*], can be exemplified
> intuitively in the givenness of empirical experience
> [*Erfahrungsgebenenheiten*], in such [givenness] of perception,
> memory, and so forth, but equally as well *also in the givenness of*
> *mere phantasy* [*Phantasiegegebenheiten*]. Hence, in order to
> grasp an essence itself and *originarily*, we can set out from corre-
> sponding empirical intuitions, *but just as well also from non-*
> *empirical, non-existence-grasping, moreover "merely imaginative"*
> *intuitions* [*"bloss einbildenden" Anschauungen*].
>
> (*Ideas* I, §4, my translation)

Furthermore, Husserl holds that knowledge of essences does not
in itself depend on any knowledge of facts (§4). This is a tricky
point. Obviously, our ability to imagine objects under the relevant
essence normally begins in actual experience of such objects.
Husserl's claim must then be that once we have acquired knowledge of facts about objects under an essence, when we move on to
grasp the essence itself, with the relevant sort of intuitiveness,
then we may use phantasy or imagination alone. Our grasping the
essence depends on our varying instances of the essence in imagination. The source of intuitive support that is relevant to grasping
the essence, Husserl holds, comes from these experiences of imagination. To bolster his claim, Husserl refers to the geometer at
work: it is through imagining possible instances of triangularity,
not seeing actual triangles, that the geometer achieves insight
about the essence of triangles. Later, turning to the essence of
consciousness (§70), Husserl allows, interestingly, that phenomenological reflection can proceed by phantasy, reflecting on imagined
acts of consciousness, just as well as on actual acts.

There are, however, grades of intuition of essences. As I develop
my grasp of an essence, my intuitive knowledge of it expands. Yet
most essences can be known only partially, and so not "adequately."
Specifically, Husserl says, "the essence 'Thing' [i.e. Material Thing
in Nature] is originarily given, but . . . this givenness can in principle be no adequate [givenness]" (*Ideas* I, §149, my translation).
Since our knowledge of things in the region Nature is empirical,
we do not follow "free phantasy" alone as we develop our intuitive grasp of essences under nature, such as the essence Tree. We

see and touch trees in everyday life, observing many features of trees around us; our botanist colleagues study trees in detail, as biologists expand our theories of photosynthesis, cellular activity, and much more; and evolutionary biologists expand our theories of how trees emerged on planet Earth. As our knowledge of various aspects of trees expands, our *intuitive* comprehension of what it is to be a tree expands. Where does imagination play in our intuitive grasp of, say, the essence Eucalyptus? Well, as we organize our extant knowledge about eucalyptus trees (drawn from perception and inference), we imagine varying properties, concluding that some properties are characteristic of eucalyptus and others are not, given our actual observations of such trees. Our observations lead us to conclude, as we vary characteristics in imagination, that individual trees may vary somewhat from the norm.

Thus, we must handle with care Husserl's insistence that imagination alone provides intuitive support for grasping such an essence. In this respect, Husserl's claim for free phantasy can be misleading. Clearly he assumes that we acquire knowledge about trees, and thus about the essence Tree, through perception. After we have acquired such empirical knowledge, we use "free phantasy" to sort out the structure of the essence Tree. But we could not, realistically, investigate the essence Tree by pure imagination alone.

However, in mathematical theories, where Husserl began his intellectual life, a "pure" mathematical theory is indeed produced, with intuitive support, in a system of axioms and theorems, by imagining how a "world" characterized by the theory would look. But a "material" ontology concerns objects we know by means other than pure imagination. Husserl's account of essences in the material regions of Nature, Consciousness, and Culture is not limited to insight gained from pure imagination.

Clearly, we are integrating Husserl's account of eidetic variation with his account of systematic theory construction. Intuition of essences is, then, not a simple, single experience of suddenly "seeing" how things are. It is, rather, an experience of grasping, with intuitive evidence, how things are, *given* prior experiences and background beliefs, many of which are part of our collective development of knowledge about objects falling under a certain essence.

VARIETIES OF INTUITION OR EVIDENCE

Husserl's phenomenology of intuition is wider than we have seen so far, addressing quite a variety of experiences he classed as intuition. However, true to form, Husserl never collected these diverse results. I shall try to organize his results, as I understand them, drawing on fragments of theory scattered over works including *Logical Investigations* (1900–1), *Time-Consciousness* (1905–17), *Thing and Space* (1907), *Ideas* I (1913) and *Ideas* II (1912), and *Cartesian Meditations* (1931).

Intuitions, for Husserl, divide into two basic kinds: originary and reproductive. We have considered only originary intuitions so far. *Originary* intuitions, as the term suggests, serve as origins of knowledge. *Reproductive* intuitions, instead, reproduce forms of experience found in originary intuitions, and some serve as a sort of deferred origin of knowledge.

Originary intuitions include experiences of perception, essential insight, and phenomenological insight. Each of these types of experience presents its object in an originary, self-evident way. Perception presents things in nature, essential insight presents essences, and phenomenological insight presents acts of consciousness and their contents.

Reproductive intuitions include experiences of recollection, imagination, and empathy. Recollection (a special form of memory) presents past events, "reproducing" what I earlier perceived, or what I have earlier judged on the basis of perceptual evidence. Imagination presents possible objects or events, "reproducing" what I might see or judge (depending on the type of object imagined). Empathy presents another's experience "as if" one were experiencing it oneself. In this sense empathy "reproduces" in my experience the type of experience I take another to have. Husserl has a great deal to say about each of these types of experience, but we must rest content with a brief sketch of their role in epistemology.

We have indicated the roles of perception, judgment, and inference in knowledge formation. Memory too plays an obviously essential role in our knowledge: just consider the impact of memory incapacitation that follows brain damage or deterioration as in Alzheimer's. If Husserl is right about the role of imagination in essential insight, then we also rely on imagination insofar as we know the nature or essence of a type of object, say, a eucalyptus tree. We do not often phantasize explicitly about a tree in order to judge that it is a eucalyptus. But we understand that it would not be a eucalyptus if it dropped its long, grayish-green leaves and sprouted long evergreen needles, or if it sent roots down to the ground like those of a banyan tree, or if it blossomed with red roses. Imagination proposes these "unmotivated" possibilities, which our intuitive judgment quickly rejects. Husserl's theory of horizon (elaborated in Chapter 6) implies that our knowledge about familiar types of objects, such as a eucalyptus tree, depends on this capacity for imagination.

Particularly interesting is the role of empathy in our knowledge of others. When I see the sadness in another's face, I do not see her sadness in the way I see her furrowed eyebrows. I see – "physically," as it were – the shape of her eyebrows. But when I see – immediately, evidently, intuitively – that she is sad, my experience is empathic. In a very articulate form of empathy, I place myself imaginatively in the other's place, so that in imagination I experience what she is actually experiencing. The English word "empathy" entered our vocabulary as a translation of the late-19th-century German term "Einfühlung," literally feeling one's way into another's experience. Originally the term was used in literary criticism for feeling one's way into the emotional tone of a poem. The term then migrated into the nascent discipline of psychology. For social theorists including Wilhelm Dilthey, whom Husserl knew, the social or cultural sciences rely on empathy to develop an understanding (*Verstehen*) that is quite different from the kind of understanding achieved in physics. At any rate, Husserl picked up on the phenomenon of empathy and found in empathy a basic source of our knowledge about others. (*Ideas* II analyzes empathy. Stein (1916/1989) sharpens the phenomenology of empathy along Husserlian lines.)

Husserl defines intuition, we saw, as an *evident* experience of something "*itself.*" But Husserl distinguishes three importantly different grades of evidence: mere subjective certainty, adequacy or completeness of evidence, and apodicticity or indubitability. Perhaps the best account of these is in the *Cartesian Meditations* (1931). "Any evidence is a grasping of something itself . . . , with full certainty of its being, a certainty that accordingly excludes every doubt" (§6). Thus (in the first person): an evident experience is *certain* if I do not doubt the existence of the object posited in the experience. "Adequate evidence" is the ideal of perfection, as opposed to "*imperfection*" or "*incompleteness*, a one-sidedness . . . [in] 'experience' with *unfulfilled components*" (§6). Thus, an evident experience is *adequate* if I am intuitively given all aspects of its object, that is, all aspects of the intended object are presented evidently (as least certainly) – there is nothing further to be known about the object, there are no "hidden sides" to be ascertained. "An *apodictic* evidence, however, is not merely certainty of the [states of affairs] evident in it; rather it . . . [is] *at the same time the absolute unimaginableness* (inconceivability) *of their non-being*" (§6). That is, an evident experience is *apodictic* if I cannot doubt the existence and properties of the object presented in the experience, I cannot imagine their non-being (in the face of this experience). The *Cartesian Meditations* begin with Husserl's critique of Descartes' famous quest for "absolute certainty" in the *Meditations* (1641), and accordingly Husserl finds, phenomenologically, more types of evidence and more varieties of evident experience than Descartes had considered. Husserl will find that perception is certain but inadequate and dubitable, while phenomenological reflection is apodictic but inadequate, as we note later in this chapter.

Sensory perception is certain, but inadequate and nonapodictic. In the clear light of day, when I see that eucalyptus tree, I do not doubt what I see. But there are many aspects of the tree that are not presented, evidently, in my current experience: the back side of the tree I cannot see, its history and future are not presented in my current perception, and the intricacies of its biology are not presented in this perception. So my perception is far from "adequate," in Husserl's sense. Nor is perception apodictic. As skeptics ancient and modern have long stressed, no matter how vivid this perception, I can doubt its deliverance on grounds that I could be dreaming. Or, to go with Descartes' "evil genie" argument, it is at least possible, so far as I know, that there is an evil demon who is causing this perception to appear in my mind though there is no tree before me. In a contemporary version of the argument, my perception could be produced, so far as I know, by someone manipulating the neural firings in my brain. Well, to this extent, I *could* doubt what I now see, that there is a eucalyptus tree with a certain appearance as presented in my current visual experience – this much is at least conceivable, so my experience is not apodictic.

As noted earlier, Husserl finds that our intuitions or intuitive judgments about "material" *essences* of things in nature are not adequate (*Ideas* I, §149). Not only are perceptions of individual things inadequate and dubitable, but insight about the *essences* of things in nature is also inadequate and dubitable. There is always more to learn about the essence of a natural kind such as Eucalyptus. If natural sciences are about essences under the region Nature, as Husserl holds, then of course all natural sciences are based in intuitive judgments that are not "adequate" in Husserl's sense: there is always more to learn about the essence of any natural kind. And in principle further evidence about natural essences could prompt revision of what we claim to know about them. Further, our intuitive judgments about cultural objects, and so about the essences of cultural phenomena, are also, obviously, not adequate. There is always more to discern about, say, the nature of our institutions, from national governments to universities to libraries and so on. Nor are such things known apodictically; we could doubt what we know about such institutions.

In *Ideas* I, Husserl crystallizes the phenomenology of evidence and adequacy in these terms:

> To every *region and category* of purported object there corre-
> sponds phenomenologically not only a *fundamental kind of*

senses (Sinnen), moreover *propositions (Sätzen),* but also a *fundamental kind of originarily giving consciousness* of such sense and, belonging to it, a *fundamental type of originary evidence (Evidenz)* . . .

Every such evidence – the word understood in our extended sense – is either *adequate,* in principle not to be further "strengthened" or "weakened," thus without graduality of a weight; or it is *inadequate* and therewith *capable of increase or decrease.*

(Ideas I, §138, my translation)

According to its sense, or posited sense (proposition, in Husserl's special sense of the term), Husserl notes, a "thing" in nature can be given in perception only with inadequate evidence (§138). This principle lies behind the structure of the horizon of, say, seeing a tree (compare Chapter 6 on horizon). The inadequacy of perception even allows such radical revision, with further experience, that my perception can "explode" (§138), so that the sense in my experience now prescribes something very different, say, not a tree at all, but a soldier moving forward with arboreal camouflage.

Finally, what kind of evidence is there in the experience of *phenomenological reflection?* In *Cartesian Meditations,* Husserl recapitulates the way epoché, or "bracketing" the objective world, leads phenomenological reflection to "transcendental subjectivity" (§8). Descartes was on the right track with "I think, therefore I am," Husserl finds, . . . yet Descartes failed to make "the transcendental turn" because he believed that he had "rescued a little tag-end of the world" (§10), namely, the "pure ego", the being who thinks, from which Descartes claimed he could ultimately deduce the existence of the rest of the world. Husserl goes on to distinguish the "pure" or "transcendental" I, pure subject of experience, from "I, this man," with "a psychic life in the world" (§11). The distinction is not between distinct objects called "I," but between distinct aspects or moments (instancing distinct essences) of the one object, I: my experiencing is one aspect or moment of me, my bodily shape is quite another, and the method of bracketing allows me to focus on my conscious experience as such. (See Chapter 6 on bracketing and Chapter 4 on the ontology of aspects or moments.) Practicing "transcendental" reduction, or bracketing, I reflect on my current consciousness. In this reflection, Husserl holds, I have *apodictic* evidence of my current experience ("I think") and of my being ("I am"). Thus, "the sense of the indubitability with which the ego becomes given in transcendental reduction [= bracketing] actually conforms to the concept of apodicticity we explicated earlier" (§9), that is, the unimaginableness of my non-being, when I am having a conscious experience. In this Descartes was indeed correct, Husserl finds, provided we recognize the relevant distinctions of evidence. However, my phenomenological evidence of my experience is *not adequate*, for my memory of my past experiences in my stream of consciousness is not adequate (§9). There is more to my stream of consciousness than my current experience, of which I have apodictic evidence.

We depart the arena of evidence by noting an issue in grasping essences. Most essences, it would seem, are complex and can be grasped only inadequately (there is always more to know) and nonapodictically (further evidence may prompt revision). These limitations would seem to apply to essences of various types of experience, even though a concrete experience does not have hidden sides like a physical object – I live through the whole experience on which I reflect. The limits on our knowledge of most essences are indicated by Husserl's concern with "'definite' manifolds." For, if our knowledge of a given essence is ideally expressed in an axiomatic theory about the field of objects exemplifying the essence (a "manifold," recall, is the form of a field of knowledge), then for many or most essences we cannot expect complete knowledge (capturing a "definite" manifold). (Compare *Ideas* I, §72, on definite manifolds, and then §§73–5 on phenomenology as "descriptive theory of the essence of pure experiences.") In the 1930s Kurt Gödel would produce his incompleteness theorems, to the effect that no theory rich enough to express arithmetic can be complete (that is, there are propositions in the theory that are true but cannot be derived from axioms in the theory). Gödel's results, though directed at certain mathematical theories, are likely symptomatic of the limits of our knowledge of most essences, including essences of acts of consciousness.

SYSTEMATIC KNOWLEDGE IN THE SCIENCES

In Husserl's day the term "science" (*Wissenschaft*) meant any systematic body of theory or knowledge about a given domain of objects. In today's idiom, "the sciences" include physics, chemistry, biology, neuroscience, psychology, sociology, and so on. But in the wide sense of the term found in Bolzano and Husserl, more abstract disciplines also count as "sciences": geometry, arithmetic, algebra, logic, and even ontology, epistemology, and phenomenology count as sciences when practiced systematically. Philosophy itself Husserl held to be a "strict science" when practiced appropriately. Accordingly, Husserl's theory of knowledge begins, in the *Logical Investigations*, with the theory of *theories*, or sciences in this wide sense.

Knowledge in a systematic *theory* takes the ideal form, for Husserl, of a system of propositions unified in two ways: (1) they represent and characterize objects in a given domain or field and (2) they hang together deductively, ideally forming an axiomatic theory like geometry. Here is the model of knowledge sketched in the Prolegomena of the *Logical Investigations* (see Chapter 3 in this volume). However, what makes a theory a body of *knowledge*, rather than a theory of merely possible objects of some type, is the way its propositions are supported by *evidence*, thus by intuition in Husserl's sense. The full course of the *Investigations* was required to formulate, in Investigation VI, a theory of knowledge, where "intuitive" or "evident" intentional experience transforms a mere theory into a body of knowledge.

Which comes first, ontology or epistemology? To say what exists, we must *know* what exists; to say what we know, we must say what *exists* to be known. The answer to this "chicken-or-egg" problem lies in Husserl's theory of dependence: dependence can run in two directions at once. In Husserl's philosophical system, then, ontology and epistemology are interdependent. So let us use Husserl's ontology (Chapter 4) to help sort out his epistemology. Broadly, the essences or types of object Husserl distinguishes are isolated by essential insight or abstraction. So, as Husserl develops his ontology of formal and material essences, he is practicing his epistemology of essential intuition or abstraction.

Basically, Husserl holds that knowledge consists in beliefs "sedimented" from appropriate judgments supported by intuitive experiences. Let us apply this theory to our knowledge of objects in certain domains. Specifically, let us look a bit more closely at what Husserl would count as systematic knowledge of objects in the three "regions" of Nature, Consciousness, and Culture.

Our knowledge about objects and events in *Nature* begins with sensory perception, perceptual intuition. We form perceptual judgments about things we see, hear, touch, and so on, and we draw inferences to form further judgments. Thus, I see that tree, I visually judge that that is a tree, I infer and so judge that it is a juniper tree, given its similarity to other trees that people have told me are junipers. Here we are working at the level of everyday knowledge, often guided by what many others have learned. The natural sciences – physics, chemistry, biology – proceed from such everyday knowledge. Scientists carefully observe the behavior of physical objects and events, and form hypotheses of a more abstract character, often using mathematics to characterize the essence of the relevant phenomena. And so, over the long haul, we or the experts accumulate a systematic body of theory supported by observational evidence. Philosophy of science studies the details of this methodology in the special sciences, notably physics. Husserl's epistemology emphasizes the process of abstraction whereby we characterize the *essence* of things in nature. For Husserl, the process by which we accrue scientific knowledge is a complex form of coming to grasp the essence of, say, gravity, electromagnetic attraction, or the neuronal storage of information in human memory. Each particular theory in natural science articulates the essence of a given domain: Newton's theory of gravity describes the essence of attraction between massed bodies; Einstein's general theory of relativity describes the essence of space–time; Freud's theory of repression describes the dynamic by which conscious ideas are pressed into the unconscious; and so on. Practicing scientists will not describe their work in Husserl's terms, but Husserl will articulate what natural scientists do according to Husserl's *theory* of scientific knowledge. (Yes, that epistemological theory is a theory, according to Husserl's Bolzanoesque theory of theories.)

Now, our knowledge about experiences in *Consciousness* is quite different. As we considered in Chapters 5 and 6, Husserl offered a complex theory of our knowledge of consciousness. We "live" our own subjective experiences, or acts of consciousness. We observe that our experiences are typically intentional, a consciousness of something. If we bracket the question of the existence of the objects of our experience, then we turn our attention to the experiences and their contents or meaning. We then reflect on the essence of these experiences, and so on their meanings, considering what their meanings purport to represent. As practicing phenomenologists, "scientists" of consciousness, we thus develop a theory of the structure of consciousness, supported by the intuitive evidence of our experiencing various acts of consciousness and reflecting on them. In this way we abstract and describe or analyze the essence of consciousness. If natural science breaks down into the more special sciences of nature, phenomenology – the science of consciousness as experienced – breaks down into more special phenomenological sciences: the theory of perception, the theory of judgment, the theory of emotion, the theory of consciousness of time, the theory of consciousness of space, the theory of "intersubjectivity," and so on. As we noted earlier, Husserl allowed that our intuitive evidence of the structure of consciousness is, as Descartes proposed, apodictic, albeit in a sense refined by Husserl's phenomenology of grades of evidence.

Our knowledge of cultural objects is quite different. Artifacts, institutions, laws, and social organizations are objects in *Culture*. What they are, their essence, depends on social or collective activities. Our knowledge of cultural objects depends on how we understand what others in our culture think, desire, and will. This level of cognition begins in *empathy*, or *Einfühlung*, literally feeling my way into the other's experience. As we grow up within a culture, we learn a language, we learn everyday behaviors ("manners"), we learn informal rules (when to speak or bow, when not to), we learn formal laws (drive on the right side of the road, walk on the right side of the sidewalk when encountering other walkers), and so on. What we learn – our *knowledge of culture* – derives from others and is learned from others. Take a very simple example. I see an object, and I perceptually judge that it is a fork, something to eat with, especially useful in handling solid foods. How do I know it is a fork? Clearly, this item of knowledge is "sedimented" from the activities of my forebears, and I learned this item in my very early years. In Husserlian terms, I "saw" that forks are used for eating, and so I abstracted the essence of forks from my observations of *others* using them to eat. These observations depend on an elementary knowledge of what others are doing and trying to do, a comprehension Husserl would describe as empathy with intentional acts of others. Here is a special type of "seeing," insight into the experience of others: "I see [empathically] that she wants to use that fork to eat." Without this empathic knowledge of others' experience, I cannot have the simple experience of seeing something *as a fork*, and thus have the knowledge that this object is a fork. Complex cultural objects include social organizations such as families, communities, professions, or nations, and ultimately cultural events or processes such as the history of the Roman Empire or the Ming Dynasty. As we develop a systematic theory about, say, culinary tools or empires, our knowledge of culture divides into the special *cultural or social sciences*: sociology, anthropology, history, cultural criticism in the arts, and so on. In Husserl's epistemology, each cultural theory involves intuitive evidence from empathy but proceeds to abstract the essence of some domain of cultural objects or activities. Thus, we find, say, the theory of the historical development of eating utensils, the "social contract" theory of modern states, the Marxist theory of capitalist exploitation, the theory of *laissez-faire* economics, the theory of postmodern architecture, or what have you. (*Ideas* II, 1912, focuses on empathy, including consciousness of my or another's "living body" as opposed to "physical body."

The *Crisis*, 1935–8, extends Husserl's account of the life-world, which is "there for everyone" and includes cultural phenomena dependent on empathy.)

For Husserl, we saw in Chapter 4, the sciences indicated above develop "material" ontologies. That is, they characterize the "material" essences of objects in domains falling under the regional essences Nature, Consciousness, and Culture. These sciences are constrained, in Husserl's system, by a *formal ontology* characterizing such "formal" essences as Individual, Property or Essence, State of Affairs, Number, Manifold, and so on. For Husserl, forms or formal essences define "formal" objects, including numbers, essences, states of affairs, and so on. The special formal sciences, including arithmetic, logic, and so on, develop more specific areas of formal ontology. These formal sciences are grounded in intuition of formal essences. If we return to Husserl's categorial ontology, distinguishing such formal essences as Individual, Property, State of Affairs, Number, Manifold, and so forth, as mapped out in Chapter 4, we find that the ground of these categorial distinctions lies in working intuitively with case studies from which we are to abstract these formal essences and recognize distinctions among them. These intuitive observations are systematized in the category scheme we assembled in Chapter 4. In Husserl's epistemology, these observations are themselves produced by practicing essential insight.

THE LIFE-WORLD, SCIENCE, AND BACKGROUND KNOWLEDGE

Husserl's notion of the life-world marks an important and novel contribution to epistemology. All of our knowledge depends, in a specific way, on our everyday background knowledge of things in what Husserl calls "the surrounding world of everyday life," the *Lebenswelt* or "life-world." This principle has consequences for our specialized knowledge in the sciences, and arguably it blocks the rise of skepticism.

Husserl outlines the notion of *Umwelt*, my surrounding world, in *Ideas* I (1913) and *Ideas* II (1912). A few years later he adapts the term *Lebenswelt*, borrowed from the social theorist Georg Simmel. Ultimately, he puts the notion to extended use in the *Crisis* (1935– 8), the posthumous volume fully titled *Crisis of European Sciences and Transcendental Phenomenology*. Husserl's epistemological concern in the *Crisis* is the way in which mathematical physics depends on the life-world. He is concerned to avoid the loss of meaning that he sees resulting from the "mathematization" of nature, which idealizes and abstracts away from our basic knowledge of things in everyday life.

Now, the life-world is not an ontological structure, a domain distinct from, say, the natural causal order. There is only one *world*, which includes literally everything. Rather, the life-world is a *phenomenological* structure: it is the world *as* experienced in everyday life. That is, the life-world is not a distinct domain of objects, but a range of noematic *sense*, embracing the types of sense presenting objects as we experience them in everyday life. Hence, Husserl speaks of our understanding "ruling as constitutive of the always already developed and always further developing meaning-configuration 'intuitively given surrounding world'" (*Crisis*, §28). The *Umwelt*, the *Lebenswelt*, is thus a structure of meaning, and it includes the idea of intuitive givenness. (Recall Husserl's doctrine of constitution and horizon, explored in Chapter 6.)

Husserl launches his conception of transcendental phenomenology, in *Ideas* I, with the opening salvo: "I am conscious of a world, endlessly spread out in space, endlessly becoming and become in time" (*Ideas* I, §27). This world, he explains, is "continuously present [*vorhanden*]," and "[t]hereby this world is for me not there as a mere *fact-world* [*Sachenwelt*], but in the same immediacy as *value-world, goods-world, practical world* [*Wertewelt, Güterweld, praktische Welt*]" (§27, my translation). "This world," Husserl writes, is "*the world in which I find myself and which is at the same time my surrounding world* [*Umwelt*]" (§28). All of my experience takes place in this world, my *Umwelt*, and all objects of my consciousness I experience as residing in my *Umwelt*. Notice that this structure is defined indexically or ostensively as "my" world and "my surrounding world." Thus, I experience objects as objective matters of fact, but also, in many cases, as bearing value and as part of my practical activities. For instance, I see the clouds gathering on the horizon (a matter of fact), but I also see the beautiful sunset (a matter of value), and I also see and grasp and wield this shovel as I dig in the garden (a practical affair). Whatever the essence of these things may be (in Husserl's categorial ontology), the ways in which I experience them, through the indicated noematic sense, define their place in my *Umwelt*. Even ideal objects, viz. essences and meanings, are appropriately related to objects in my *Umwelt*, being essences or meanings of things in my surrounding world.

The *Crisis* weaves a fascinating, complex tale, from which we here draw only a fragment. Husserl proposes a diagnosis of a cultural problem stemming from modern physics, an intellectual crisis in "the European sciences." Starting with Galileo, Husserl avers, modern physics has "mathematized" the essence of nature (§9), increasingly idealized and abstracted from the ordinary things around us. Relativity theory and even quantum mechanics were already launched in Husserl's day. Husserl refers to Newton, Planck, and Einstein at the outset (§1), and later to Einstein and Michelson (§34b). Moreover, general relativity theory was given a mathematical formulation by Hermann Weyl, who drew inspiration from Husserl's transcendental phenomenology (see Ryckman 2005). There is nothing wrong with this mathematical modeling of nature, for Husserl the lapsed mathematician: physics is a great achievement, well founded on intuitive evidence. The problem is rather a lacuna in our epistemology, in our phenomenological theory of knowledge in mathematical physics. We have lost track of the phenomenological link between our knowledge in physics (§9) and our intuitive experience of things in our "surrounding world of life" (§§28ff.).

We might put the "crisis" in this way, assuming the full range of Husserl's system (appraised in prior chapters). Our experts in physics have developed a mathematical theory (a system of propositions) about the essence of space–time and thus of physical objects and events occurring in space–time. In everyday life, of course, we do not experience familiar objects as having the mathematized essence posited in our judgments in physics. We experience things as "that tree," "that falling apple" (indicative of gravity), "those lines of refracted light" (observed in the experiment of quantum mechanics where an electron beam is split into two). The perceptual observations that serve as empirical evidence for our physical theories are themselves, in Husserlian analysis, experiences of objects as they appear in our familiar Umwelt. The objects we so observe are not experienced, in these perceptions, as having the mathematized essences posited in our theories. In our theoretical judgments, however, we posit objects as having just these mathematized essences – and not as having the essences posited in our everyday perceptions. There are, accordingly, two distinct ranges of meaning that represent things in nature: the meanings in our theoretical judgments in physics, and the meanings in our everyday life-world experiences, including the perceptions that serve as observational evidence for our theoretical judgments. And these two ranges of meaning represent objects as having two distinct ranges of essence. Enter the crisis: we really do not understand how things in nature can have both of these very different essences, or how the everyday world – including ourselves and our surroundings – finds its place in mathematized nature. As Husserl remarks, pointedly, "Since the intuitively given surrounding world, this merely subjective realm, is forgotten in scientific investigation, the working subject is himself forgotten" (Crisis, "The Vienna Lecture," Appendix I: 295). As Martin Heidegger might have put it, in the practice of science we have "forgotten" the meaning of the being of the everyday. (Husserl's Crisis may have been prompted partly by Heidegger's Being and Time [1927/1962], though the Crisis draws on the phenomenology of Ideas I [1913] and Ideas II [1912].) Physicists and philosophers of physics have worried long over the disconnection between our everyday image of the natural world and our theoretical constructs in relativity theory and quantum mechanics. With Husserl's theory of the life-world, set in the context of his phenomenology, ontology, and epistemology, we find a particularly astute formulation of the problem.

The gap between theory and experience is felt not only in the empirical science of physics. Already in ancient times, Husserl finds, geometry moved away from its "origin" in everyday perception and, for that matter, carpentry (see Crisis, "The Origin of Geometry," Appendix VI). "We are constantly conscious of the world . . . as the horizon of our life," Husserl writes, and we are "coconscious of the men on our external horizon in each case as 'others.' . . . It is precisely to this horizon of civilization that common language belongs" (p. 358). Euclidean geometry was developed by others in ancient times, and the written results guide us today. Indeed, we cannot do mathematics without the aid of a symbolic language, much less pass it on to others. When the Pythagorean theorem was written down, the original knowledge became passive, "sedimented," awaiting reactivation through reading and thus thinking through the theorem and its proof, intuitively. As Husserl writes:

> Accordingly, then, the writing-down effects a transformation of the original mode of being of the meaning-structure, [e.g.] within the geometrical sphere of self-evidence, of the geometrical structure which is put into words. It becomes sedimented, so to speak. But the reader can make it self-evident again, can reactivate the self-evidence.
>
> (*Crisis*, 1935-8: 360)

In reading geometry, then, we become intuitively aware of the content of a theorem, but we are also dimly aware of its historical origin. "Making geometry self-evident, then, whether one is clear about this or not, is the disclosure of its historical tradition." (Crisis, 1935-8: 371)

In Husserlian terms, the origin of an idea, say, in geometry – in history, in civilization, in culture – is "predelineated" in the meaning-content of the idea. And so, the historical origin of the idea lies in the horizon of our experience in practicing geometry. This historical element of meaning, Husserl notes, plays a neglected role in epistemology: "Certainly the historical backward reference has not occurred to anyone; certainly theory of knowledge has never been seen as a peculiarly historical task" (p. 370). Husserl is emphasizing not merely the fact of the history of geometry – its development in a language, a civilization, a cultural formation – but also its role in knowledge itself. As we explicate the Pythagorean theorem, making it self-evident to us as we read and think, we are reactivating the "sedimented" theoretical knowledge established with intuitive evidence by Euclid *et al.* This reactivation is part of the phenomenology of practicing geometry. Still prior to the early geometers' theorizing, however, lay the practical activities of building things with boards featuring straight lines. A technique of measuring, Husserl notes,

> is always already there, . . . pregiven to the philosopher who did not yet know geometry but who should be conceivable as its inventor. As a philosopher proceeding from the practical . . . to the theoretical world-view . . . , he has the finitely known and unknown spaces and times as finite elements within the horizon of an open infinity.
>
> (*Crisis*, 1935-8: 376)

And so, in geometry as in physics, our theory rests on the intellectual labors of others and this work depends on practical, everyday activities such as, for geometry, making and measuring straight lines on boards with which to build cabinets or houses.

A general epistemological principle is emerging: all of our knowledge, from everyday perceptual judgments to theoretical judgments in geometry and in physics, depends on a *background* of implicit knowledge about the world around us. This background consists largely of what others have learned in theory and practice before us, a background that spreads outward in horizon from our knowledge of "my surrounding world." This background takes the form of my implicit sense of the life-world, my *Umwelt*. As Husserl puts it, the life-world is characterized by "presuppositions," forms or constructs of sense (*Sinnesgestalten, Sinnesgebilde*), which are "anonymous" in origin yet serve as "*one* single ground [*Grund*]" of all the sciences, of all knowledge (*Crisis*, §29). Thus, my *Umwelt* is defined by a complex horizon of meaning that represents possibilities for familiar things in my surroundings. This range of meaning conditions my knowledge of everything, beginning with my knowledge of things around me. And most of this knowledge, embodied in the relevant range of meaning, is drawn from a long tradition or history of knowledge established long ago by others. That knowledge is extant, "sedimented," in my culture, carried forward in language and other social practices, without which we could not develop further knowledge in everyday life or in the special sciences. Without which that is, our knowledge *depends* (ontologically) on this background sense of our surrounding world. (See D. W. Smith 2004: ch. 5, for my own, Husserl-friendly account of the background.)

In this way, Husserl's phenomenological theory of knowledge is extended in his phenomenological analysis of the sense of the life-world and its role as a ground of knowledge.

BEYOND SKEPTICISM

Classical epistemology was often a response to the problem of skepticism, the challenge that we can never really know, with certainty, what we claim to know about the world around us. Husserl was not much concerned with skepticism, presumably because his phenomenology of evidence portrays a more realistic account of knowledge than the target of classical skepticisms. In any event, Husserl's theory of the dependence of knowledge on life-world experience arguably undercuts the force of skepticism.

Quite simply, if all of our knowledge depends on our sense of things in the life-world, then the skeptic's challenge cannot get off the ground. How can I be *absolutely certain*, the skeptic asks, that there are birds and trees and other people in my surroundings? How can I be certain, moving onward, of the observations on which scientific knowledge is based, and how then can science be certain? How can I be certain of the theorems of geometry? And so on. The Husserlian answer is: I cannot even frame these questions without *presupposing* that my surrounding world is of a certain character and structure. Philosophers from David Hume back to the ancients observed that skepticism may be compelling in the philosopher's study but cannot be practiced on the streets. If Husserl's phenomenology is right, however, the skeptic cannot press his case even in the study, for the *sense* of the *Umwelt* cannot be suspended even in the quietude of the study.

But doesn't Husserl's method of bracketing or epoché precisely put out of play the everyday assumption that the world around me exists, the "general thesis of the natural [everyday] standpoint"? (Compare *Ideas* I, §§30–2.) How can my sense of the life-world then remain in play as we proceed with transcendental phenomeno-logical analysis of experience? Well, after introducing the notion of the life-world, Husserl presses his method of epoché (*Crisis*, §§35–49). He now proposes a variation on the method, a step-by-step procedure that he thinks will avoid a misleading "Cartesian" form of epoché (where we move in one step from everyday acceptance of the world to reflection upon experience). We shall not go into these procedures on this occasion. The point to note is Husserl's result: *phenomenological* analysis (following appropriate procedures) finds that every intentional experience has a noematic sense that predelineates a horizon emanating from my implicit, presupposed sense of "my surrounding world."

The skeptic can pretend that this sense of *Umwelt* is not there, or is something we must abstain from accepting until we have certainty of it – which, the skeptic charges, we will never have. (Recall that the Greek term "*epoché*" is drawn from the ancient skeptics, meaning to abstain from belief.) But this move by the skeptic is a move in bad faith. Careful phenomenological analysis, Husserl finds, reveals an implicit back-reference to "my *Umwelt*," a presupposition we are unable, in good faith, to deny. In the prac-tice of phenomenology, I turn from my experience of things in the world around me to my reflection on experience. I then analyze the *meaning* or noematic sense in a given form of experi-ence. And I find, as a result of phenomenological analysis, that this meaning is linked with my sense of the life-world, a *meaning*-structure that is always with me. The skeptic is in the same boat, and his/her skepticism founders on the ground of the life-world. Even as s/he questions this meaning-structure, s/he presupposes it – or so the counter-skeptical argument goes.

(A related line of argument about our background claims and practices can be drawn from Ludwig Wittgenstein's *On Certainty*

[1949–51/1972]. Compare Searle 1983: ch. 5 on "the background"; and D. W. Smith 2004: ch. 5 on "background ideas," including practices, extant in our culture. Compare Friedman 2001 on relativized a priori assumptions in our knowledge of space–time. Friedman's line of argument indicates, I would argue, how we can change our fundamental background assumptions, but only while keeping our ship of everyday life-world knowledge afloat.)

SUMMARY

Husserl developed a phenomenological theory of knowledge featuring an account of systematic knowledge forming a proper theory, an analysis of various forms of "intuition" (*Anschauung*) or "evidence" (*Evidenz*), and an account of the role of the life-world in the formation of knowledge. Husserl's epistemology thereby synthesized and transcended prior epistemological paradigms of rationalism, empiricism, and Kantianism, extending his phenomenological theory of intentionality into a theory of knowledge.

For Husserl, knowledge is formed in acts of rational judgment supported by evident or intuitive experience, that is, intuition. Systematic knowledge in the particular sciences takes the form of a theory, a system of propositions that characterize a particular domain of objects and are bound together by deductive consequence and (where appropriate) probabilistic "motivation" (according to Husserl's account of "pure" logic). But the propositions in a theory count as knowledge only when judged with the support of evidence, or intuitive "fulfillment," which comes in experiences such as perception.

On Husserl's analysis, intuition consists in an intentional act of consciousness that has a thetic character of intuitiveness or "evidence": that is, intuition consists in a self-evident intention of an object (or state of affairs). Sensory perception is the paradigm of intuition. Thus, a visual perception is a fusion of intentional and sensory components in the experience, a fusion of noesis and hyletic or sensory "data." Thanks to its sensory component, a visual intention of an object is evident, or intuitively "fulfilled." Here we see the rational and empirical aspects of knowledge, in the conceptual and sensory aspects of an experience, say, in seeing a eucalyptus tree and visually judging that there is such a tree at a certain place.

While perception is the paradigm of intuition, Husserl recognizes several distinct types of intuitive experience, including sensory perception, essential insight, categorial insight, and phenomenological insight. He talks of "seeing" in all these cases, but these forms of experience are quite different, as his analyses show.

Essential insight (*Wesenserschauung*), or eidetic intuition, consists in "seeing" something concerning a particular essence, say, "seeing" that a triangle has three interior angles or "seeing" that a tree normally has branches. For Husserl, eidetic variation in imagination leads to such insight. Thus, I consider a variety of putative examples of, say, a triangle or a tree, and in reflection I vary the putative properties of these objects. Thereby I come to "see" that by its essence a triangle has three interior angles (otherwise it is not a triangle), or that by its essence a tree normally has branches. By such imaginative variation, I come to "see" the similarities between relevant instances of the essence in question, that of a triangle or that of a tree. (Today we call this pattern recognition.) "Categorial" intuition, for Husserl, consists in "seeing" something concerning an ontological category (a formal essence), especially the ontological form State of Affairs. When I judge that a state of affairs obtains, say, where I judge that that tree is a eucalyptus, I "see," categorically, that the object and its species are joined into the state of affairs that this object is of that species. Logical and mathematical intuitions turn, similarly, on "seeing" aspects of logical and mathematical form.

An important type of intuition for Husserl is phenomenological intuition, or insight about the structure of consciousness. The technique of bracketing turns my attention from objects in the surrounding world to the structure of my consciousness of such objects. Then, in eidetic variation, I reflect on a particular form of consciousness, say, seeing a eucalyptus tree, considering its intentional essence, which can be shared by this experience and others.

Thereby I come to appreciate the structure of such an experience: I "see" that consciousness is, in this case, a consciousness of something, a sensory-intentional experience, a visual presentation of "that eucalyptus tree," and so on. Knowledge in phenomenology is formed through this practice of eidetic phenomenological intuition or reflection. Here we see Husserl's epistemology folding back on his phenomenology.

On Husserl's analysis, then, evidence is formed in various ways for judgments about different kinds of things. In mathematics, logic, physics, biology, psychology, or phenomenology, we proceed from appropriate types of intuitive experience. Through reasoned theory-formation, we build up knowledge about the types of object presented through such intuitive experience. As we reason further about objects in a given domain (numbers, logical proofs, gravitational forces, evolving species, intentional experiences), we rely on rational insight about reasoning, which may itself be made the theme of rational insight in pure logic. In this way, Husserl's epistemology is interdependent with his phenomenology, his ontology, and his logic.

For Husserl, all of our knowledge, in various domains, depends in certain ways on our everyday experience of the surrounding world, the life-world. Mathematical sciences abstract away from features of things in the world as we know them in everyday life. This "mathematizing" of things in nature can be problematic, Husserl argued in the Crisis (1935–8), as we lose touch with our familiar world, which includes ourselves and our own experience. To appreciate the ways in which the special sciences depend on our everyday forms of experience is thus to tie the sciences of mathematics, logic, physics, biology, and psychology (today, we would add neuroscience) into the structure of our own experience, a structure we come to know through the practice of phenomenology.

FURTHER READING

Fisette, Denis. 2003. *Husserl's Logical Investigations Reconsidered*. Dordrecht and Boston, Massachusetts: Kluwer Academic Publishers (now New York:

Springer). Contemporary essays on the *Logical Investigations*, several of which address epistemological issues.

Friedman, Michael. 1999. *Reconsidering Logical Positivism*. Cambridge and New York: Cambridge University Press. A study of Carnap's logical empiricism or logical positivism, indicating relations to Husserl's transcendental phenomenology.

——. 2001. *Dynamics of Reason*. Stanford, California: CSLI Publications. A revised Kantian epistemology of "relativized" synthetic a priori knowledge of space–time, considering Einstein's theory of the geometry of space–time, allowing for relations to phenomenology.

Mulligan, Kevin. 1995. "Perception". In B. Smith and D. W. Smith, editors, *The Cambridge Companion to Husserl*, Cambridge and New York: Cambridge University Press, pp. 168–238.

Nelson, Alan, ed. 2005. *A Companion to Rationalism*. Oxford: Blackwell Publishing. Introductory essays on rationalism.

Richardson, Alan W. 1998. *Carnap's Construction of the World: The Aufbau and the Emergence of Logical Empiricism*. Cambridge and New York: Cambridge University Press. A study of Carnap's logical empiricism and its historical background, including the role of Husserl's phenomenology.

Roy, Jean-Michel. 2004. "Carnap's Husserlian Reading of the *Aufbau*." In Steve Awodey and Carsten Klein, eds. *Carnap Brought Home: The View from Jena*. Chicago and LaSalle, Illinois: Open Court. A study of Carnap's logical empiricism in relation to Husserl's transcendental phenomenology.

Ryckman, Thomas. 2005. *The Reign of Relativity: Philosophy in Physics 1915–1925*. Oxford and New York: Oxford University Press. A study in the philosophy of relativity theory, addressing our knowledge of space–time and including relations to Husserlian transcendental phenomenology.

——. 2006. "Husserl and Carnap." In Richard Creath and Michael Friedman, eds. *The Cambridge Companion to Carnap*. Cambridge and New York: Cambridge University Press. A study of the relations between Husserl and Carnap on the "constitution" of the world and the role of elementary experience in the formation of knowledge.

Smith, A. D. 2003. *Husserl and the Cartesian Meditations*. (Series: Routledge Guidebook to Philosophy). London and New York: Routledge. A study of Husserl's *Cartesian Meditations*, developing the Cartesian side of Husserl in that work and drawing a strong idealism from the work.

Smith, David Woodruff. 2005a. "Rationalism in the Phenomenological Tradition." In Alan Nelson, ed. *A Companion to Rationalism*. Oxford: Blackwell. A study of rationalist elements in Husserl's phenomenology and in other phenomenologists' work.

Willard, Dallas. 1984. *Logic and the Objectivity of Knowledge*. Athens, Ohio: Ohio University Press. A study of principles of epistemology, drawing on Husserlian views in the *Logical Investigations*.

———. 1995. "Knowledge." In B. Smith and D. W. Smith, eds. *The Cambridge Companion to Husserl*. Cambridge and New York: Cambridge University Press. A study of Husserl's theory of knowledge.

Wittgenstein, Ludwig. 1949–51/1972. *On Certainty*. Edited by G. E. M. Anscombe and G. H. von Wright. Translated by Denis Paul and G. E. M. Anscombe. New York: Harper Torchbooks, Harper & Row. First published by Basil Blackwell, 1969, from notebooks written in German during 1949–51. Wittgenstein's last work, developing a critique of skepticism, reflecting on G. E. Moore's refutation of skepticism ("Here is a hand," of that I am certain). Wittgenstein's account of background practices and propositions is similar to Husserl's prior account of the life-world and its role in grounding everyday knowledge.

Eight

Ethics

Values founded in experience

In previous chapters we studied Husserl's account of fundamental structures of consciousness and their correlation, in intentionality, with fundamental structures of things in the world. For Husserl, we thereby "constitute" various types of object in various forms of experience. Our experience forms knowledge of objects and of facts when our judgments are based in evident or intuitive experience. However, we "constitute" objects not only as having factual properties (species, spatiotemporal location, and so on), but also as having values. And we "constitute" actions as having moral values. In this chapter we consider Husserl's views on the nature of values, including their place in our experience and in the world. We focus on Husserl's ideas about ethics, addressing the phenomenological and ontological foundations of values in general and moral values in particular, and considering the place of Husserl's views on ethics in his overall philosophical system. On some points Husserl's ethical views are less explicit than his views on other matters, so we shall be involved in a project of reconstruction. Ultimately, we shall consider the implications of Husserlian views for contemporary "constructivist" approaches to ethics – in which values are somehow constructed in activities of will or reason.

HUSSERL IDEAS ON ETHICS AND VALUE THEORY

Husserl frequently writes in passing about values, about our experience of values amid things in the life-world. But what exactly are Husserl's views on ethics and the nature of values? What role do these views play in his philosophical system of logic, ontology, phenomenology, epistemology, ethics, and so on?

We have studied Husserl as one of the great systematic philosophers, along with Aristotle and Kant (and others). While Aristotle and Kant each developed a well-known ethical theory, with an associated political theory, Husserl is not widely known for contributions to ethical or political theory. Yet he lectured extensively, over a period of many years, on ethics and foundational issues about the nature of values. Texts of some of his lectures are gathered in a posthumous volume titled, in English translation, *Lectures on Ethics and Value Theory* 1908–1914 (Husserl 1908–14/1988, in German with no English translation yet). In his primary writings, Husserl addresses the character of normative disciplines, including ethics, already in the Prolegomena of the *Logical Investigations* (1900–1) (§§14–16), whence he argues that logic is not a normative discipline (concerning how we should reason). In later works, he addresses values and moral phenomena amidst phenomenological analyses of perception, action, personhood, intersubjectivity, and culture: in *Ideas* I (1913), *Ideas* II (1912), and the *Crisis* (1935–8). Accordingly, Husserl's philosophical system explicitly appraises the nature of values and their role in our experience and in the world overall. Thus, his conception of the life-world includes values, his account of the region Culture (*Geist*) addresses interpersonal interactions and morality, and his lectures on ethics assess the objectivity of values and their place in phenomenology and in formal ontology. Indeed, his phenomenological analysis of our "constitution" of things in the world around us – linking objectivity, subjectivity, and intersubjectivity (as emphasized in Chapter 9) – applies to values as well as "facts" (non-normative "objectivities"). Furthermore, his account of empathy – how we experience others – has important implications for both ethical and political theory. Husserl also wrote a great deal about aesthetics, drawing on his phenomenology of perception, empathy, and varieties of aesthetic experience. We'll focus here, in any event, on ethics and the nature of values. Our task is to reconstruct, in a systematic way, Husserl's views on values and ethics, bearing in mind his overall philosophical system and his penchant for system-building. (Melle 2002 presents an illuminating account of Husserl's views on ethics in different periods of Husserl's career. Further studies of phenomenology and ethics, looking to Husserlian phenomenology, are found in Mandelbaum 1955; Embree *et al.* 1997; Drummond and Embree 2002; and Mensch 2003. Husserl's views on aesthetics appear in Husserliana XXIII (*Intersubjectivität* I). On the phenomenology of aesthetic experience in film, applying Husserlian theory to cinematic representation, see Casebier 1991. On aesthetic theory of literature, assessing the role of intentionality in relation to author and reader, see Thomasson 1998, developing views with roots in Husserl and Ingarden.)

Ethics is the theory (or account) of how we should live, the theory of right and wrong action, moral obligation or duty, moral and human rights, good and bad character, and so on. Philosophers sometimes divide ethics into normative ethics and metaethics. *Normative* ethics addresses norms that specify which actions are right, wrong, obligatory, prohibited, and so on: such norms as the Bible's Ten Commandments ("Do not steal," "Honor your father and your mother," ...), or the Golden Rule ("Do unto others as you would have them do unto you"), or the Buddha's Eightfold Path ("Practice compassion by following the eight ways of Right Views, Right Intent, Right Conduct, ... "). By contrast, *metaethics* studies the nature of ethics itself. "*Meta*" means "with" in Greek; hence metaethics is a discipline cognate to ethics, as metalogic is cognate to logic. (We can also say, with Aristotelian philosophy, that metaphysics is cognate to physics; unfortunately, a narrow and polemical use of the term has also developed, where "metaphysics" exceeds the bounds of natural science and empirical knowledge.) Metaethics may analyze moral *discourse*, considering what we mean by terms such as "good" or "right" or "obligatory"; or it may analyze our *concepts* of what is good or right or obligatory; or in a more Platonic vein it may study the ideal forms or *essences* of Good or Right or Obligation. The *status* of moral values may be considered one type of metaethical question: is there a fundamental divide between facts and values – where do values fit into the order of the world? Moreover, the *foundations* or *origins* of values would fall under some conceptions of metaethics – and there lie our concerns. Husserl himself speaks of foundations of normative disciplines, and so of normative propositions, contrasting foundational principles of ethics (say, Kant's categorical imperative, "Act only on a maxim you could will to become a universal law") with principles of "normative ethics" ("A soldier should be brave") (*Logical Investigations*, Prolegomena, §14). Thus, we ask where values come from: are values objective features of the world (as Plato held)? Or are moral precepts products of God's will (as are the Ten Commandments, literally handed down to Moses)? Or do ethical values come into being only through our acts of willing in appropriate ways (as Kant and Sartre held)? Or do values emerge only with our collective agreement (as social contract theories of political values hold, following Hobbes and Rousseau)?

Husserl's discussions of ethics center largely on foundational theories about values, rather than on specific norms ("Do not lie," "Love your neighbor"). Our concern, accordingly, is to sketch Husserl's account of the foundations of ethics, including the essence of values, their place in the world, their relation to non-normative properties of things, and their relation to various forms of intentional experience, especially choosing or willing a course of action. Given Husserl's system of phenomenology, ontology, logic, and so on, his conception of the foundations of ethics, or of moral values, will be distinctive. Given Husserl's conception of "foundation" in the sense of *Fundierung* or ontological dependence, and given his conception of "constitution," a Husserlian conception of the foundations of ethics or of ethical norms will not be on the same page as what we might draw from prior models of the foundations of morality. Looking toward relevant models, however, we shall consider the implications of Husserlian ideas for contemporary "constructivist" ethical and political theories, according to which values are constructed as we desire, deliberate, and will. Husserl's phenomenological analysis of "constitution," I believe, can serve to clarify and deepen this "constructivist" approach to the foundations of ethical imperatives. (For discussions of Husserl's views in relation to classical themes in ethics, see three essays in Drummond and Embree 2002: Melle 2002 on Husserl's views on ethics and values, Drummond on Aristotelian ethics vis-à-vis phenomenology, and Crowell on Kantian ethics vis-à-vis phenomenology. Kant's ethics, or metaethics, is stated succinctly in Kant 1785/1959, a text relevant to our present study. The literature on ethics per se is huge, but for our purposes the reader might well see the studies in Rawls 2000, where one of the great ethical-political theorists of our time reflects on key issues in the history of ethics. Korsgaard 1996 pursues the foundations of moral value, or what makes moral claims normative, in the character of the will, reflecting on Kantian principles and on the political theory in Rawls 1971/1999, restated in Rawls 2001.)

What, then, are Husserl's particular views on ethics? Where Plato held that values are objective forms defining The Good itself, Husserl addressed the objectivity of ethics by analogy with the objectivity of logic. The goodness of a person, the rightness of an action, or the justice of a decision – such values are objective, in that they are there to be agreed upon by everyone in the right circumstances. And yet values, like other properties of things, are "constituted" in our experience: notably, in our willing to do the good or right thing and to do so for good reasons and motives. In that way, values are inherently related to subjective experience. And still, values are intersubjectively accessible, and we are accountable for the values we "constitute."

HUSSERL'S IDEAS ON ETHICS AND VALUE THEORY

When philosophers seek foundations for ethics or for moral values, what exactly are they seeking? Indeed, what is meant by "foundations" in ethical matters? The answers are by no means clear, and would seem to vary across different ethical theories. For the Platonist, moral values are founded in objective ideals; for the utilitarian, in the balance of pleasure over pain; for the Kantian, in a basic principle, the categorical imperative; for a certain theological view, in the will of God, say, as passed down in the Ten Commandments. As we shall consider, Husserl would seem to approach the question of foundations with a distinctive conception of foundation: recall his conception of "founding" (Fundierung), or ontological dependence. How is this notion applied or modified to deal with values? Initially, as we shall see, Husserl holds that values in a given domain are founded in what he calls a "ground norm" (Grundnorm). Our task is to try to ferret out Husserl's distinctive conception of foundation in relation to moral values.

Husserl addresses the foundations of ethics early in the Logical Investigations (1900–1). In the Prolegomena to Pure Logic (§§14–16), he outlines a theory of "normative sciences," including systems of ethics, and their relation to "theoretical sciences." Recall that, for Husserl, pure logic is the theory of theories or sciences (Prolegomena, §§62–72), where pure logic as a theoretical discipline is contrasted with logic as a "practical" or normative study of how we ought to reason (see Chapter 3 in this volume). Husserl has his eye on ethics, then, already in his early study of logic, on the way to his conception of phenomenology.

A normative discipline or science, Husserl says, propounds principles about what is "good" or "should be" in a given domain – evaluations such as "A soldier should be brave," or alternatively "A good soldier is brave" (Prolegomena, §14). More specifically, a system of ethics deals with what is morally good, or what one morally should or ought to do. Again, a political system specifies what sort of political organization for a society is good or just, or how things should be in a body politic. And an aesthetics concerns what is good in art, literature, architecture, or what things should be like in art, and so on. Now, Husserl holds that "each normative . . . discipline . . . presupposes one or more theoretical disciplines as its foundation or fundament [Fundament], in the sense, namely, that it must have a theoretical content free from all normativizing [Normierung]" (§16, my translation). In a prosaic example (not in Husserl's text), the normative proposition "This is a good knife" presupposes the theoretical proposition "This is a knife," and the normative proposition "A good knife is sharp" presupposes propositions in the theory of knives, such as "A knife has a blade." Again, the normative claim "A soldier should be brave" presupposes theoretical claims about soldering, such as "A soldier follows orders," "A soldier uses weapons," and so forth. Husserl thus assumes that an object's having a value-property

depends on its having non-evaluative properties: as other philosophers would later say, goodness "supervenes" on natural
properties. But Husserl goes on to a more interesting doctrine
about the foundation of values.

A normative science ascribes value-properties, or norms, to
objects in a given domain (for soldiers, being a good or bad
soldier) – typically including comparative evaluations of better or
worse. The norms for a domain, Husserl says, form "a closed
group." For this group of norms, Husserl holds, there is a most
basic norm, a "ground norm" (Grundnorm), that governs the relevant features carrying value. The ground norm for a domain,
Husserl holds, is not strictly "normative," but rather "defines" the
value-range for that domain. In Husserl's opaque but intriguing
formulation:

> The constitutive contents of positive and relative value-predicates
> [for objects in a given sphere] are so to speak the measuring
> units [*messenden Einheiten*], according to which we measure
> objects of the relevant sphere.

> The totality of these norms [for a given domain or sphere of
> objects] obviously forms a closed group determined through fun-
> damental valuation. The normative proposition which places a
> general ordering on the objects in the sphere, that they shall suf-
> fice to the greatest possible extent for the constitutive features of
> the positive value-predicates, has marked out a position in every
> group of norms belonging together, and can be indicated as the
> *ground norm* [*Grundnorm*]. This role is played, e.g., by the cate-
> gorical imperative in the group of normative propositions which
> make up Kant's ethics, as [it is] by the principle of the "greatest
> possible happiness of the greatest possible number" in the ethics
> of the utilitarians.

> The ground norm is the correlate of the definition of "good" and
> "better" in the sense in question. It tells us on what ground
> (ground value) all normativizing must be conducted, and does not
> therefore present a normative proposition in the authentic sense.

> The relationship of the ground norm to the authentically normative
> propositions is analogous to that between the so-called defini-
> tions of the number-series and the theorems – always referred
> back to these – about numerical relations in arithmetic. One could
> also here indicate the ground norm as a "definition" of the stan-
> dard concept of good – e.g. of the morally good – wherewith the
> ordinary logical concept of definition would be left aside.
>
> (Prolegomena, §14, my translation)

Evidently, Husserl conceives ground norms as a special type of
formal measures that define membership in a group of substantive
or *material* norms for a domain or sphere of objects – much as
formal essences (Individual, Property, State of Affairs) define
forms of objects in a material domain (Nature, Consciousness,
Culture). (Recall Chapter 4 on formal and material essences.)
Thus, the *ground norm* for a group of norms, for objects in a given
domain, places those norms in that group, thereby defining relevant *values* carried by objects in the domain. The norms for a
domain of objects are in this way *founded* on or by the ground
norm. The ground norm is *formal* in the sense that it applies to all
norms in that domain (though not to norms in other domains).
Strictly speaking, ground norms are not themselves "normative,"
as they do not ascribe substantive values, but instead form "a
'definition' of the standard concept of good" – a "definition" of
"normativity" for values ascribed in "authentically normative
propositions." Accordingly, in the quotation just given, Husserl
first speaks of the ground norm as the "normative proposition"
that grounds the norms or "value-predicates" in a given sphere;
but then, speaking more strictly, he says the ground norm, the
grounding proposition, does not "present a normative proposition in the authentic sense."

"Norms" are values (corresponding to "value-predicates"), and
values are of many types. Looking to ethical theory, notice how
Husserl separates Kantian ethics and utilitarian ethics. In Husserl's
view, these ethical systems define different types of moral values.
We are not looking at competing theories of the foundations of
the same moral values: we are looking at distinct spheres of
norms, distinct because they are grounded in different "ground
norms." What is "good" because it brings pleasure or well-being,

and so is morally praiseworthy, is quite different from what is "good" because it is willed in the correct way, and so is morally obligatory. Indeed, contemporary ethical theories often worry about how to define the appropriate range of moral predications ("good," "evil," "obligatory," "permissible," "impermissible," and so on). But how, in Husserl's approach, are we to conceive of the foundations of moral values, whichever sphere of values we address?

As the above passage suggests, Kantian ethics is a useful case study for Husserl's conception of what would count as the foundations of ethics or of moral values (even though Husserl is critical of Kantian ethics in the end). In the *Foundations of the Metaphysics of Morals* (1785/1959), Kant famously argued that moral principles have a "foundation" in a single basic principle he called the *categorical imperative*: "Act only on that maxim by which you can at the same time will that it should become a universal law." We commonly ask, "What if everyone did this?," but Kant elaborates that test in more articulate terms. For Kant, the foundation of moral evaluation for any particular action lies in the way that the agent's *will* – guided by *practical reason* about what to do – is constrained by this basic principle. Suppose I tell a lie in order to gain a sum of money. My action is effected through my will to lie in order to gain money, that is, I will to act in accord with the maxim "I should lie if I seek to gain money." This "hypothetical" imperative or maxim guides my action, as I reason that I will now tell a lie since it will bring me remuneration. According to Kant, this action is morally wrong because it fails the test of the categorical imperative: I could not rationally will that the maxim guiding my will become a universal law, that is, a principle that anyone else could justifiably follow in similar pursuit of money. How, then, would the foundation of Kantian ethics be developed in terms of Husserl's theory of normativity?

Kantian ethics is a normative science, in Husserl's sense. The domain of this normative science is the sphere of rational human actions performed by will. An action is morally good, according to Kantian ethics, just in case it is performed in accord with a good will. And, for Kant, a good will is a volition formed in accord with the categorical imperative "Act only on that maxim. . . . " On

Husserl's theory of the foundation of moral values, then, the categorical imperative propounds the *ground norm* of Kantian ethics. But this proposition, "Act only on that maxim . . . ," is not strictly normative. It is not itself a normative proposition, saying what one should or should not do – even though Kant formulates it, misleadingly, as an imperative. Rather, it constrains, or "defines," and so serves to generate genuinely normative propositions such as "Do not lie" or "Treat your neighbor with kindness." We might say the categorical imperative is a *metanormative* or *metaethical* proposition: a proposition that itself *defines the norms* asserted in properly normative ethical propositions such as "Do not lie" or "Treat your neighbor with kindness." But what sort of "definition" is this?

What is the analogy Husserl draws with "definition" in arithmetic? Suppose the natural numbers (1, 2, 3, 4, . . .) are defined as follows:

1 is a number.

If n is a number, then $n + 1$ is a number.

This is not a logical construct or dictionary definition ("A bachelor is an unmarried adult male"), but rather a formula that generates the natural numbers by applying a criterion, indeed, a metric: being greater by 1. Similarly, Husserl holds, the categorical imperative in Kantian ethics serves as a founding "measure" that defines normativity for moral propositions. Similarly, staying with the metric metaphor, we might say the standard meter stick in Paris (in the old days of international standards) is not itself measured as one meter long, but rather serves as a measure – a "measuring unit" (in Husserl's phrase) – that generates measurements of length in meters: being so many lengths of the standard stick. Accordingly, we may say the categorical imperative is a *metanormative* or *metaethical* proposition, playing off the post-Husserlian conception of metaethics in the sense of a theory of the foundations of ethics.

A further analogy, I suggest, lies with post-Husserlian metalogic. Following Tarski's semantic conception of truth (Tarski 1944/2001), logicians formulate a truth definition along the following lines (for, here, a language L including, inter alia, the conjunctive words "and," "or," "not"):

> (T) A sentence Σ (in language L) is true if and only if –, where, for appropriate elementary forms of sentence Σ (in L): "*s* and T" is true if and only if "*S*" is true and "T" is true. "*S* or T" is true if and only if either "*S*" is true or "T" is true. "It is not the case that S" is true if and only if "*S*" is not true. And so on.

A full Tarskian "definition" of truth for a language (L), following the schema T, depends on the specified syntax of the language in question. The point to observe here is that this "definition" serves to constrain, in a metalogical *semantics* for the language, the *rules of inference* in the language, for instance, the rule called Modus Ponens: "If P then Q. P. Therefore, Q." The truth definition thus affords a semantic *foundation* for the *validity* of such logical rules of inference. In this way, if you will, the truth definition forms a complex *ground proposition* (compare: "ground norm") for a given system of logic with a specified language. Where the rules of inference are logical, the truth definition is *metalogical* (compare: metanormative). Indeed, Tarski held that the truth of sentences in a given language must be formulated in a further language called the *metalanguage* of the first language. If we carry the analogy over to ethics, then we would say the categorical imperative is the *metaethical* foundation of Kantian ethics, formulated in a metalanguage for moral discourse. Thus, in a Husserlian metaethics, as I am conceiving it with an eye to Tarskian metalogic, we would give a *normativity definition* using a ground norm that defines moral values, and in the case of Kantian ethics the categorical imperative would play this role. What would such a "definition" of moral values look like?

Let us formulate the Kantian ground norm K – a variation on the Kantian categorical imperative – as follows:

(K) An action A by a person S in circumstance C is morally good
or right
if and only if, in doing A in C,
S wills to do A in C and at the same time
S could reasonably (with practical consistency) will that
anyone else wills to do a similar action in a similar circumstance.

Here in schema K is a normativity definition for actions performed
within the relevant domain of values, that is, moral values
pertaining to actions performed by human beings – volitional
subjects who are embodied agents – whose will is autonomous
and rational and subject to standards of practical consistency. My
telling the truth in circumstance C is morally good precisely
because my action meets the normativity conditions: I will to
tell the truth in C and I could reasonably will that anyone else will
to tell the truth in conditions similar to C. Strictly speaking, then,
the ground norm K is stated in a language formally distinct from
that of the normative ethical proposition "It is morally good or
right that I tell the truth in circumstance C." Whereas the normative language speaks of values of actions, the normativity
definition K does not speak of these values themselves, but rather
of what constrains the obtaining of these values, what "grounds"
these values where carried by a particular action. And it is this
grounding that morally justifies the particular action. To be strictly
Kantian, the circumstance C involves the agent's aim as expressed
in a hypothetical imperative, "I should do A if I want to achieve
effect E." But further consequences of A than E might be included
in C if relevant to the moral evaluation. For instance, in
assessing Kant's argument against lying, philosophers often insist
on the relevance of further consequences – would telling the lie
save someone's life? Of course, a utilitarian ethics would formulate a very different normativity definition, where the conditions
of moral worth involve not the agent's will, but the actual overall
consequences of the action. Notice also, following the comparison with a truth definition, that a definition of moral worth,
along these lines, would need to map out the relevant features
of moral evaluation – as it were, the "syntax" of moral human
life.

To be clear, in the analogy between metaethics and metalogic, we were not yet addressing normativity in logic. As the *Prolegomena to Pure Logic* proceeds, Husserl distinguishes pure logic from practical logic. Practical logic is a normative discipline, saying, "One should reason in accord with Modus Ponens"; such norms concern how one should reason, where the domain of objects so normed is the set of acts of reasoning. By contrast, pure logic is a theoretical discipline, saying Modus Ponens characterizes an objectively valid form of entailment among ideal propositions. Pure logic thus provides a *foundation* for practical logic. But this is a step beyond the way in which a semantic truth definition provides a foundation for syntactic rules of inference in a logical language. The structure of syntax and semantics for a language together form a *theoretical* foundation for a *normative* practical system of logic concerning how one should reason. And, similarly, Husserl holds, the foundations of ethics form a theoretical discipline that grounds the normative discipline of a practical ethics that says, for example, "One should not lie." That theoretical discipline is a metaethical theory that offers a definition of normativity for ethics. Unlike the case of logic, however, the norms "defined" in the metaethical theory are just that: norms, that is, values that guide the will in action, and so arise in *practical* or *normative* ethics.

Given Husserl's account of the foundations of ethics, we now see that Husserl offers an explicit theory of the "source of normativity" (to borrow the currently fashionable term used in Korsgaard 1996). In Husserl's own words: "The ground norm (or the ground value, the final end) determines, as we saw, the unity of a [normative] discipline; it is also that which introduces into all normative propositions the thought of normativity [*Normierung*, normativizing]" (Prolegomena, §16, my translation). Husserl's picture of the foundations of ethics is amplified in texts where he writes focally on ethics – in the *Ethics* lectures, to which we now turn. As we consider later on, Husserl's conception of the foundations of moral values also involves a further type of foundation in the "constitution" of values in consciousness – but that part of the Husserlian story must here wait in the wings.

PURE ETHICS, THE OBJECTIVITY OF VALUES, AND THE PHENOMENOLOGY OF WILL

Husserl gives his full attention to ethics in lecture courses. Some of these lectures are gathered in the volume *Lectures on Ethics and Value Theory: 1908–1914* (*Vorlesungen über Ethik und Wertlehre*, 1908–14/1988, available only in German). The core of Husserl's theory of ethics, I submit, is the confluence of three themes: values are objective, yet values are "constituted" in acts of will, and moral values address others. Here we see, in Husserl's approach to ethics, his integration of objectivity, subjectivity, and intersubjectivity.

In the *Ethics* lectures, Husserl distinguishes "pure" ethics from ethics as a "practical art" propounding specific ethical norms such as "Do not steal," "Treat every person as an end, not a means," and so on. For Husserl, *pure* ethics is a theoretical study of the foundations or "origins" of normative ethical judgments. Husserl's ethical theory would take its place in his overall philosophical system, tying into his views in logic, ontology, phenomenology, and epistemology (recall Chapter 2). Indeed, Husserl's conception of pure *logic* shapes his conception of pure *ethics*. As he distinguishes pure logic from logic as a practical art where we develop specific rules of inference, so he distinguishes pure ethics from practical ethics where we craft specific ethical maxims (such as "Do not lie"). Husserl's *phenomenology* finds values all around us. For our experience regularly presents us with objects as bearing various types of value, for instance as we experience a gorgeous sunset, a beautiful poem, a sleek and responsive automobile, a wicked act of violence, a malicious look in another's eye. True to form, Husserl also addresses the *ontology* of values. For Husserl, values are objective features of things, but features of a unique type, features with their own categorial niche in the world: the category Value. (Recall Chapter 4 on categories.) Moral values, in particular, depend on the structure of will, emotion, practical reason, and interpersonal experience. So moral values are objective features of actions, but these values arguably depend on proper activities of will in connection with emotion and reason. Husserl's account of *intersubjectivity* in the life-world also has implications for ethics and politics, as many values reflect our empathic experience of others. We should keep in mind Husserl's formal/material distinction, which he puts to work in logic, ontology, and phenomenology. Accordingly, we may see the distinction between pure and practical ethics as that between the "formal" and "material" aspects of moral value. If we judge "One should not lie," that material practical norm is judged in accordance with the proper form of moral judgment. Thus, a Kantian pure ethics would hold that this judgment is valid just in case one could will that the substantive norm or maxim "Do not lie" be universalized: this is a formal constraint on the will in that it applies to any action in any material circumstance. Though Husserl was ultimately critical of Kant (for failing to give emotion, especially love, a proper role in ethics; see Melle 2002), the example of Kantian ethics illustrates Husserl's approach to grounding values somehow in ideal forms of experience.

In addressing the objectivity of values, Husserl's *Ethics* lectures echo his vision of logic in the *Logical Investigations*. Thus, the *Ethics* begins with an appraisal of the "parallelism between logic and ethics" (Part A, §§1–8). Here is Husserl's metatheory of ethics, following the lines of his metatheory of logic, immediately citing (Part A, §1) his *Investigations* and *Ideas* I. Logic was often treated incorrectly (for instance by Mill) as a practical art (*Kunst*), whereas "pure logic" is to be a theoretical discipline, studying ideal propositions along with correlated formal ontological structures (Part A, §1). Similarly, Husserl holds, ethics was often treated as a practical art, and accordingly as a purely normative discipline. This was the stance of "ethical empiricism," expressed in the views of a succession of British moral theorists, including Hume and Mill. Here lies "psychologism," in ethics as in logic. But ethics should be developed, Husserl holds, as a "pure" and a priori *theoretical* discipline guiding the normative discipline. (On the history of such empiricist ethical views in relation to Husserlian phenomenology, see Willard and Smith 1997.)

Thus, Husserl writes:

> So therefore in analogy with pure logic and pure arithmetic the idea of a pure ethic next offers itself. On the opposite side stands

ethical empiricism, as psychologism or biologism; everything which the a priorist takes an interest in as pure principle [ethical empiricism] moves into the peculiarities of human nature and human emotional and volitional life, and in further consequence [ethical empiricism] lets ethics be looked on and valued only as a technology leaning upon psychology and biology.

(*Lectures on Ethics and Value Theory*, Part A, §2, my translation)

Husserl proceeds to argue at some length against skepticisms about a priori values, promoting instead the "absolutism" (Part A, §2) of a "pure" ethics. As the lectures unfold, Husserl sketches the ideal of a "formal axiology" and then a "formal practique [Praktik]," that is, a formal theory of good (axiology) and a formal theory of practice.

A formal axiology will take the standpoint of "objectivism" or "idealism," against that of the "relativist, sometimes psychologistic, sometimes anthropologistic and biologistic skepticism" (Part A, §11b). That is, formal axiology assumes the "objectivity of values" (Part A, §11b title) or ideals (thus "idealism" in one sense). In accord with Husserl's conception of formal ontology, these formal theories will carve out a place in formal ontology for the "pure" forms Good and Practice (Part A, §§5, 9–12, 18–21). That is, if we reconstruct a Husserlian category scheme as in Chapter 4, we will place the ideal formal essences Good and Practice, and also Right, in appropriate niches in the category scheme. Under the category Property we would add Value as a formal essence, subsuming Good and Right. Under Good would fall the concrete instances or "moments" of goodness in objects of appropriate type (say, the particular goodness in a good knife, a good idea, a good person); under Right would fall instances or "moments" of right actions (say, in a concrete action of helping a neighbor, telling the truth at a courtroom trial, and so on). And under Intentionality we would place Practice, subsuming particular types of activity such as Walking, Writing, Speaking, and so on: under Practice, then, fall instances of volitional action such as concrete acts of walking, writing, speaking, and so on. Since pure ethics is the a priori theory of right action and good character, we would then analyze connections between the essences Right and

Good. We would specify what it is about an action that makes it right – its contribution to a good character (as Aristotle observed), its good consequences (as Mill held), its being performed with a good will properly formed (as Kant urged), and so on. In Husserlian ontology, the rightness of an action would *depend* onto-logically on such features of the action. (Compare the role of dependence in the ontology of mind, as reconstructed in Chapter 4.)

With these elements of a *formal ontology of values* under his belt, Husserl turns to the relevant phenomenology, the "phenomenology of the will" (*Lectures on Ethics and Value Theory*, Part A, §§13–17). He distinguishes several types of volitional act, indicating there are still others. Whereas an act of wishing concerns what might be, an act of will is "actualizing" (Part A, §14), willing to bring something about. Some acts of will are decisions about the future, while others, those on which Husserl focuses, are acts of willingly treating or "handling" things (*Handlungswille*) (Part A, §15). These latter acts of will occur in everyday volitional activities that involve using one's body, as in walking, hitting a ball with a stick or a racket, playing a piano, and so on. Here we see the link to the living body (*Leib*) and the life-world (*Lebenswelt*). On Husserl's phenomenology, we experience objects in our surrounding world as having values, we experience our own acts of will and, through empathy, others' acts of will, and we ascribe values to volitional actions. These are the phenomena to which ethics pertains. For Husserl, the point of opposing "psychologism" or "biologism" in "pure" ethical theory is that moral values depend not on the contingencies of human experience in acts of valuing, willing, and so on, but on the *ideal* structure of these intentional activities. Phenomenology studies the correlation between concrete acts of consciousness and their ideal content. Thus, the phenomenology of will studies the corre-lation between concrete acts of will and their ideal content. As pure logic studies ideal *propositions* (declarative propositions such as "2 + 3 = 5," "Aristotle is synoptic"), pure ethics studies ideal *values* founded in ideal forms of will: we might say, ideal *volitions* or "normative propositions" (imperative propositions such as "Do such-and-such," "Tell the truth"), as opposed to "factual" proposi-tions ("Aristotle is synoptic," "2 + 3 = 5"). Here the phenomenology of will draws on Husserl's theory of ideal contents, and the foundations of ethics are tied into this range of phenomenology.

Husserl's systematic approach to philosophy is apparent, then, in his approach to the foundations of ethics. His vision of pure logic outlines what we today call a philosophical metalogic, and this vision of pure logic guides Husserl's vision of pure ethics. As we might say today, Husserl's vision of the foundations of ethics is a philosophical *metaethics*, wherein pure or formal principles (ground norms) constrain applied or material ethical principles in any normative ethical theory. Since normative ethical propositions ("Do such-and-such") apply to willed actions, the foundations of ethics are tied into the phenomenology of will and of volitional action. Further, for Husserl, phenomenology is shaped by a categorial ontology, itself reflected in Husserl's account of pure logic. Knowledge in ethics, we may infer, also follows the path to objective knowledge in a phenomenological moral epistemology, where evident or intuitive experience guides our well-formed judgment about what it is morally right or obligatory to do. (Recall Chapter 7 on intuitive evidence.)

THE "CONSTITUTION" OF MORAL VALUES IN RELATION TO WILL, REASON, AND LOVE

What makes an action morally good or right or obligatory? – what is at issue in this question? We have so far focused on Husserl's account of the *metaethical* foundation of moral values in "ground norms" like the Kantian categorical imperative. Now, within such *formal* constraints delimiting or "defining" moral values, we look into the *phenomenological* foundation of values, in substantive or "material" conditions in the "constitution" of values in our experience. In what ways, for Husserl, are moral values intended and thereby "constituted" in appropriate forms of consciousness? Alternatively, what is the "origin" of moral values in our experience, in the structure of their "constitution"? What role does the "constitution" of an action and of its value play in ethical theory, for Husserl? In light of the phenomenology of action and values, how does Husserl respond to the more familiar lines of normative ethics? I do not expect explicit or finished answers to these questions within Husserl's framework (given the texts I know), but I hope to explore these issues in a Husserlian framework, drawing on a variety of relevant themes discussed by Husserl.

So, we ask, in what *forms of experience*, with what *forms of meaning*, are actions and their moral values "constituted"? I may *judge* that I should tell the truth about such-and-such in a given circumstance. Or I may *reason* to the conclusion that it would be right or obligatory for me to tell the truth. Or I may *will* that I now (rightfully) tell the truth. I may *want* to rightfully tell the truth, or I may *feel* morally compelled to tell the truth. In these varied acts of consciousness, I intend my *action* of truth-telling *as* having moral worth. The *value* of my action is "constituted" in a manifold of such possible forms of experience in which my action is intended as having said moral worth. (Recall our account in Chapter 6 of Husserl's theory of constitution.) Central to that manifold is my intending or *willing* to so act, specifically where I now act out of so willing.

At one level, to will is already to value. When I act in such-and-such a way, I enact or execute my will to so act. And in willing to so act, I posit value in that action. Thus, the content of my willing is already an imperative, a norm, "Do such-and-such." Indeed, this primordial structure of value in willing is reflected in the etymology of the words "will" and "value": the root "*wal*" derives from "*wield*" in Old English and Germanic forms meaning to rule. Now, moral theory holds that there are standards or grounds – norms – that constrain the values propounded in willing. But that is already to say that value arises through volition that meets some standard. Here, at any rate, is the beginning of a theory of the phenomenological foundation of moral value. (On the etymology of "value" in the root "*wal*", see *The American Heritage Dictionary of the English Language*. New York: Houghton Mifflin Company, 1992, Indo-European Roots Appendix.)

On one reading of Husserl's transcendental idealism, consciousness brings the world into being. On our reading of Husserl's ontology, however, the "constitution" of a tree in my act of visual experience does not bring into being either the tree itself or its spatiotemporal-causal properties in nature. (Recall

Chapter 4 on transcendental idealism.) Yet if "factual" objects like trees and their properties are not intentional artifacts, values may yet be. Beauty is in the eye of the beholder, so it is said. But if aesthetic values are a subjective matter of taste, moral values are not simply "aesthetic" values. Most ethical theories, that is, seek some kind of objectivity for moral values. And yet, on some "constructivist" approaches to ethics, *moral values* are objective but are nonetheless brought into being precisely through acts of consciousness, specifically through *willing* or through practical *reasoning* – two constructivist models inspired by Kantian ethical theory. Husserl's phenomenology may serve to underwrite such a position, as we shall come to see. (As we proceed, I shall leave scare quotes around the term "constitution," or the cognate verb "constitute," reminding us that this is a technical idiom, one whose exact force we are in the process of explicating in regard to the "constitution" of values. Shorn of the reminder, the term too easily slips into meaning the way something is built, not the way it is intended.)

Think of how the "constitution" of values would arise for Husserl, in light of his overall philosophical system. Husserl's objectivism of values is resonant with a Platonic ethics focused on the form of The Good, though Husserl does not place ideal forms in a Platonic heaven (as we saw in Chapter 4). But there is more to Husserl's position on moral values. Virtue ethics, often associated with Aristotle, focuses on the way a particular act reflects and contributes to the agent's character, comprising his moral *virtues* (or vices). As we move into the period of modern philosophy, however, the locus of moral worth moves into the realm of consciousness. Humean "sentimentalist" ethics focuses on the role of *feeling* in grounding moral values, especially the feeling of sympathy for others. Utilitarian or consequentialist ethics, championed by Jeremy Bentham and John Stuart Mill, focuses on the consequences of an action for *pleasure* and *pain*, where a right action promotes the greatest good, specifically in the balance of total pleasure over total pain produced. By contrast, Kantian ethics focuses on the way the will operates in an action, where a right action issues from a will that exercises "practical reason" properly, that is, willing an action so that one could will that others will in the same way (to paraphrase Kant's categorical imperative). Now, with phenomenology at hand, Husserl specifically addresses these issues: in the *Lectures on Ethics and Value Theory* (Parts B, C, and Supplementary Texts). Particularly relevant to Husserl's approach to ethics is his critique of Kantian ethics (Supplementary Texts, Number 3).

Consider, then, the *value* or *norm* propounded in the moral principle "One should not lie" or "Do not lie" – a ubiquitous principle of human conduct. How is this value "constituted" in appropriate ranges of our experience, and how would that issue play in Husserl's critique of traditional moral theories? For a Platonic ethics, this principle is simply an ideal objective value, written into the order of the world. But Husserl would want to say how that value is tied into our conscious intentional experience; veracious speech does not simply instantiate that value, but intentionally enacts it, perhaps motivated by an appreciation of the value of truth-telling. For an Aristotelian virtue ethics, this principle is manifest in its practice as a part of a virtuous person's moral character – a good person does not lie (at least, other things being equal). But Husserl would want to know how this value is at work in and motivating one's occurrent actions of truth-telling. For a Humean sentimentalist ethics, this principle is an expression of sympathy for others – I should not lie because my lying would hurt others, with whom I naturally sympathize. Today (as already in Husserl's day, but not yet in Hume's), we speak of empathy as distinct from sympathy. Accordingly, we might say it is wrong for me to lie to another because I would not like the action were I in the other's shoes. Empathy plays a prominent role in the structure of the life-world, on Husserl's analysis, and so we might expect Husserl to press an empathy-based ethics. Yet Husserl resists a Humean "feeling"-based ethics (*Gefühlsethik*) (*Lectures on Ethics and Value Theory*, Part A, §2). My judgment that I should not lie is not properly formed, Husserl seems to hold, by reasoning from merely "psychologistic" considerations of my feelings of empathy or sympathy for others. Again, Husserl rejects a utilitarian ethics, whereby lying is wrong because its consequences produce more pain than pleasure. For Husserl, ethical norms such as "Do not lie" are not properly "constituted" as flowing from such merely "psychologistic" or "biologistic" contingencies – even where I judge that I ought to seek to produce more pleasure than pain in the world.

A Kantian ethics holds that lying is wrong because the maxim "Lie [to gain money]" does not rationally accord with the categorical imperative. Yet Husserl also resists a reason-based or "understanding"-based ethics (*Verstandesethik*) (*Lectures on Ethics and Value Theory*, Part A, §2). When I reason and so judge that I should not lie, what makes my proposed action wrong, Husserl seems to think, involves more than my rational capacity to apply the categorical imperative. From a Husserlian perspective, however, what is interesting in the Kantian approach is that it is precisely the form of the will that grounds the morality of an action. For the Kantian, an action is right just in case it is performed through – in Husserlian terms – an *act of will* that is formed in a certain way, namely, in accord with a line of potential reasoning that the given maxim could be universalized without practical contradiction. Thus, for Kant, the morality of an action is grounded solely in the agent's potential exercise of reason – practical reason – in choosing and so willing what to do. And there's the rub for Kant's critics. Human feeling, one's concern or compassion for others, plays no role in making an action moral. In his later years Husserl echoes such critics, explicitly arguing that love plays a central role in the foundation of ethics, in the conditions of will that render an action moral (see Melle 2002: 241ff.).

But in what ways does the will bring moral authority with it? A moral value is not an inert "fact." Rather, it is a norm governing our actions. Indeed, it is experienced precisely as a value that affects us, that moves us to action, that lays a claim on us to act in a certain way. The phenomenology of will and of experiencing moral value must explicate this sense of moral force. Normative ethics will be founded somehow in this aspect of moral phenomenology.

Husserl's approach to normative ethics might be gleaned from an account of his evolving moral philosophy. The editor of Husserl's *Lectures on Ethics and Value Theory*, Ulrich Melle, has constructed an overview of Husserl's views on ethics in different periods (Melle 2002). Husserl's earliest views (as we have already noted) concerned formal axiology and formal "practique," formal principles about the good and about practice or action. Subsequently, Husserl criticized "empiricist" ethics, including Hume's ethics of feeling or sentiment, utilitarian ethics, and Kantian rationalist ethics. Husserl's criticisms of these traditional options, I take it, move along these lines: sentimentalist ethics loses the objectivity of moral values; utilitarian ethics offers a technique for calculating pleasure and pain but loses the locus of subjectivity in the will and its formation and motivation; and Kantian ethics excludes compassion for others, hence proper intersubjectivity, in the name of practical reason. More particularly, Husserl criticized Kant's categorical imperative, seeking a more fundamental, still formal principle of value theory. Accordingly, Husserl pressed an alternative "categorical imperative" adapted from Brentano (Melle 2002: 236): evidently, Husserl's "ground norm" (per our earlier discussion). This principle Husserl glossed as "The better is the enemy of the good": that is, "Do the better" or, in Brentano's formulation, "Do the best that is attainable." This formal principle of value theory and practice theory (compare today's game theory) is to provide a very basic foundation for ethics. This principle may sound like the utilitarian principle "Do what has the better consequences." But, no, Husserl sees his ground norm as purely *formal*, so that what counts as the better action is to be determined by further *material* considerations. Those considerations are: for the Kantian, how the will operates (rationally, following Kant's own categorical imperative); for the utilitarian, how the action results (in causing pleasure and pain); for the sentimentalist, how the agent feels about others. Where, by Husserl's lights, are the proper material foundations for *moral* values? An abiding traditional answer is: in love, in compassion for others. As Husserl continued to lecture on ethics in later years, he emphasized the role of love in moral evaluation.

On Melle's reconstruction, Husserl distinguished "objective values" from "values of love" (Melle 2002: 244). Objective values are, for example, values perceived in objects, as when I see a beautiful sunset over Catalina or the handsome cathedral at Chartres.

Such values are passively "constituted" in a receptive way in perception. By contrast, "values of love" are actively "constituted" or given through "love of subject." A subject or "I" is a special type of object (in the wide sense of formal ontology), that is, a being that plays the *role of subject* in an act of consciousness. I "constitute" other subjects through empathy, and love of others presupposes empathy. (Recall that empathy is a recurring theme for Husserl in *Ideas* II and in the *Crisis*.) Moral values, then, are values of love. These values are "constituted" – and *practiced* – in acts of will concerning others, as I act through volition in relation to others. So, for Husserl, moral values are founded at one level in the *formal* principle he calls a "categorical imperative" ("Do the better"). But at a different level, Husserl holds, moral values are founded in a *material* principle of love. That is, a basic substantive moral principle is "Love your neighbor as yourself" (as phrased in Christian moral doctrine) or equivalently "Practice compassion for others" (so phrased in Buddhist moral doctrine). This principle presupposes the "constitution" of others as other *subjects,* fellow *persons* in our *intersubjective* world. For Husserl, recall, the region of Culture or *Geist,* the intersubjective or social world, is the domain of community and therewith of morality. For Kant, practical reason alone determines how the will is to operate in a morally correct way – compassion does not play a direct role in Kantian ethics, to the dismay of Kant's critics, including Husserl. For Husserl, we infer, practical reason is *motivated* by considerations of love for others, when the will operates in a morally correct way. Thus, the early Husserl emphasized the formal structure of values in practice, and the later Husserl stressed the material structure of values in actions that express love or compassion for others. The task remains for a well-developed normative ethics to detail how practical reason is to work and how compassion is to motivate.

ONTOLOGICAL FOUNDATIONS OF MORAL VALUES?

We have been developing a composite picture of Husserl's ethical theory, a theory of the *foundations* of moral values. For Husserl, moral values are "defined" in one way in the *formal* principle "Do the better." This principle is Husserl's "ground norm" for the sphere of moral values in human actions, a principle "defining" the formal bounds of practical norms (such as "Do not lie" or "Tell the truth"). Instructively, the Kantian principle "Act on a maxim you could will be to universal" might be seen as further "defining" the better action as one performed in accord with that principle of will (such an action is better than any other). But Husserl is not a Kantian. The better action, for Husserl, is further "defined" by principles specifying the way the agent's will operates in relation to both practical reason and love or compassion for others. So, as I understand Husserl's ethical theory, the *moral worth* of an action − its being morally good or right or obligatory − is *founded* in two different levels of structure in the action:

1 its *formal* structure of "doing the better" − a form that applies to all valuable actions; and
2 its *material* structure of willing in relation to both practical reasoning and feeling compassion for others − a form that is realized in a concrete action insofar as the will is appropriately guided by reason and compassion in the case at hand.

These structures are, respectively, the formal and material foundations of the action's moral worth. Notice that we have descended from the principles or propositions that characterize these structures to the *structures* themselves: there lie the foundations of moral value, that is, those structures in the world which make an action morally good or right or obligatory. And how does the "constitution" of value unfold in that intentional structure of action? In a given case, my action's worth is "constituted" in the way I will to act in light of my *reasoning* about what to do and my *feeling* compassion for others. On Husserl's theory, then, the moral worth of an action is founded in the way the action and its value are "constituted" in the agent's willing so to act.

When we think of the foundations of moral judgments or of the moral value of an action, we think of that on the basis of which an action is morally *justified*. Thus, in the considerations above, we considered what principles "define" or determine the moral value of an action: these principles *justify* the action, morally.

Similarly, when we look to the foundations of belief, we look to those experiences that provide evidence for the belief, thus to the evident propositions that justify the believed proposition, epistemologically. When Husserl speaks of "foundation," however, he usually has in mind *ontological* foundation, or *Fundierung*.

Can we find the "foundations" of moral value in ontological structures? The very idea sounds wrongheaded, unless we are working in a properly Platonic ethics (where ethical norms are Forms realized in actions). Isn't morality about how we behave – rather than how the world is at some basic level? But wait. In Husserl's wake, Heidegger aligned phenomenology with "fundamental ontology," where phenomenology seeks not merely forms of consciousness, but more fundamentally our "modes of being," where intentionality is grounded in the form of "transcendence," which is more fundamental ontologically than the subject–object or act–object structure that Husserl analyzed. (See Heidegger 1927/1982 on modes of being and transcendence.) And writing in the wake of both Husserl and Heidegger, Sartre took consciousness to have its own mode of being called "being-for-itself," within which, Sartre held, consciousness produces value when one wills or chooses. (See Sartre 1943/1956 on the being of values.) We shall explore this notion later. The point at present is to see how such an idea might work within a Husserlian framework: would it make sense to think of the foundations of moral values as *ontological*?

Well, for Husserl, values occur in the world, and they have their own categorial niche. As we learned in Chapter 4, very different things – "objects" in the widest formal sense – are fundamentally different in their essence and in the mode of their being. Some objects are temporal, some are spatial or spatiotemporal, some are ideal (numbers, meanings), some are conscious (experiences), some are social (greetings), and some – values – *are normative*. Accordingly, we might say the *being* of the moral value of an action – the action's *being* of value, the "moment" of value occurring in the action (as a dependent part of the action) – is what is founded: given Husserl's conception of foundation. Thus, where Kant sought the "foundations of the metaphysics of morals," Husserl sought, we gather, the foundations of the being of morals.

On the Husserlian model we have constructed, an action's being moral is founded or dependent on the structure of the agent's volition, that is, the way the will is formed in relation to reason and compassion.

Husserl's use of ontology in pure ethics would parallel his use of ontology in pure logic. What makes logic objective, for Husserl, is its study of ideal forms of meaning. Thus, pure logic studies ideal propositions, their forms, their logical ("consequence") relations to other propositions, and their semantic correlations to the objects and states of affairs they represent. Similarly, for Husserl, what makes ethics objective is its study of ideal forms of action, notably forms of volition – according to our earlier account. Accordingly, pure ethics studies those ideal forms of meaning that are the noematic contents of volition in action. An action is a form of embodied movement effected through a volition, that is, an act of conscious willing to do such-and-such. This volition has a "real" content, or noesis, and a corresponding ideal content, or noema: an ideal meaning of the form "I hereby will to do such-and-such." An act's noema is instantiated "in" the act's noesis. The action is (partly) "constituted" in this volition, a volitional noesis carrying a volitional noema. What is distinctive of an act of volition, however, is that the real-time occurrence of my willing *causes* my movement, *executing* my action (to whatever degree of success). Also distinctive of volition is the form of the noema: <I hereby will to do A>, where the thetic component is <will> and the sense component is the imperative or normative proposition <Do A> or, in an alternative version, <I hereby do A>. Here is an application of Husserl's theory of noesis and noema to the case of volition and action; here is a Husserlian ontology of volition and action. (See D. W. Smith 2004: ch. 4 for a relevant model of volition and causation in action.)

Now, in pure ethics, an ethical appraisal of the action will assess the noematic content of the volition. Where the volition is a conclusion of a process of practical reasoning, the volition presupposes that reasoning. And where the volition and its background reasoning are motivated by the agent's compassion for others, the volition presupposes that compassion. Then the corresponding ideal meanings come into play: the volition's noematic sense <Do A> presupposes the reasoning content and is "motivated" by the emotional content. These relations among noematic contents of volition, reasoning, and compassion are analogous to the logical relations that may hold among factual propositions. For Husserl, then, pure ethics studies such ideal contents of volition. Given that part of a Husserlian ontology of action and volition, we add our reconstruction of a Husserlian ethics. What makes an action morally good or right or obligatory, we gathered, is the complex structure of the agent's volition in relation to practical reason and compassion. That structure, we now observe, is itself formed from ideal forms or meanings of volition. In that way, for Husserl, what makes an action moral is defined in terms of the ontology of action and volition and the way the moral value is "defined" and founded by the two levels of structure mapped earlier.

A further point of ontology arises in Husserl's account of the life-world. An action occurs in the social sphere of the life-world, which for Husserl belongs to the material region of Culture (Geist). How are moral values "constituted" for actions, in the life-world?

THE PLACE OF VALUES IN THE LIFE-WORLD

The foundations of ethics in Husserl's philosophy appear in some detail, but with little explicit discussion of ethics, in Book Two of Ideas, Ideas II, initially drafted in 1912 along with Book One, though Husserl never released Book Two for publication. As we saw in Chapter 4 of this volume, Ideas I outlined a categorial ontology in which formal essences such as Individual, Property, Number, and so on apply to objects falling under the three regions, or highest material essences, Nature, Consciousness, and Culture or Spirit (Geist). As we saw in Chapter 6, the "constitution" of an object consists in the correlation of a manifold of meanings with a manifold of properties of that same object. Ideas II, subtitled Phenomenological Investigations Concerning Constitution, includes much of Husserl's most detailed analyses of the "constitution" of objects in the three regions (see §§50–61).

Husserl's story in *Ideas* II includes the following highlights regarding the three material regions:

1 Objects in *Nature* are intended as occurring in space and time and in causal relations. "Animalia" in Nature are intended as "psychic" beings whose minds "animate" their "living bodies." We humans are such animals in nature. Moreover, we intend a human being as an animated living body (*Leib*), alternatively an embodied subject. Thus, I move my body intentionally, by my acts of will. But the relation between my willing movement and my movement is a relation of "motivation," Husserl holds, not causation. Moreover, the sense of a human being, the sense "I as man," rests on empathy. I intend others as human beings by virtue of empathy, but I also intend myself as a human being by virtue of empathy, since I understand the movement of my own body in the same way as I understand the movement of another's body. Since Husserl is analyzing a structure of constitution, this is a claim about noematic sense, not about the "real" psychological processes carrying such sense.

2 We know that objects in the region *Consciousness*, acts of consciousness, are intentional, carry meaning, and so intend others in various regions. Thus, the essence Animal, or specifically Human Being ("Man," *Mensch*), depends on the essence of intentionality, and even on the specific essence of empathic experience of an "other I."

3 The cultural or "spiritual" world, the world of objects in the region *Culture*, is "constituted" with several crucial features.

(a) A *person* (*Person*) is the "center of a surrounding world (*Umwelt*)" (§50). A person is by essence not merely an embodied subject, a "human I," but also a *social* and so intersubjective being. This *Umwelt* is a world that is *my* and *our* world.

(b) We experience many objects in our common *Umwelt* through "acts of valuing" (§50), and thus objects with *value* properties ("pleasant," "beautiful") surround us.

(c) Furthermore, we experience persons as members of a *moral* community. So the cultural world is a moral realm.

Of the moral aspect of action, Husserl writes:

> Morally-practically, I treat a human being [*Mensch*] as a mere thing [*Sache*] if I do not take him as a moral [= morally relevant] person [*Person*], as a member of a moral association of persons, in which a moral world is constituted. Likewise, I do not treat a human being as a subject of rights if I do not take him as a member of the community of rights, to which we both belong, but take him as mere thing [*Sache*], as lacking in rights as a mere [material] thing [*Ding*].
>
> (*Ideas* II, §51, my translation)

Thus, the moral world, our communal world of moral values and rights, is "constituted" as I treat human beings in appropriate ways. Clearly, Husserl here means human rights in the deepest sense of the Enlightenment tradition.

Here is the core of a Husserlian approach to ethical and political theory. Values are objective properties of persons and personal actions, which occur in our *Umwelt*, our *Lebenswelt*, and they are so "constituted" in our "moral-practical" experiences, in our perceptions and judgments of human beings as persons, and in our actions wherein we treat human beings as members of our moral and political world. Central to our experience in the moral-political *Umwelt* is the role of empathy in taking and treating relevant objects as not merely natural objects, not merely pure subjects ("I" and "other I"), not merely embodied subjects or animated bodies, but *persons*, members of a moral and political community. On Husserl's analysis, our moral and political experience carries meaning that characterizes objects *as* persons (phenomenology). And, for Husserl, if our experience of persons is veridical, then the relevant objects in the world around us have objective *value properties* such as being good, useful, moral, right, just, and so on (ontology).

On Husserl's analysis, the life-world plays a key role in the structure of intentionality – in the horizon of everyday experience – and a basic role in grounding knowledge. (See Chapter 6 on horizon and Chapter 7 on the life-world's role in the formation of knowledge.) The term *"Lebenswelt"* is prominent in Husserl's last work in the *Crisis* (1935–8). However, this notion is sharply presented already at the beginning of Husserl's presentation of phenomenology in *Ideas* I (1913) and amplified in *Ideas* II (1912). In *Ideas* I (§28) Husserl speaks simply of the *Umwelt*, my and our "surrounding world" of everyday life. Husserl writes pointedly of my experience of things in this world: "this world is for me not there as a mere *fact-world* [*Sachenwelt*], but in the same immediacy as *value-world, goods-world, practical world* [*Wertewelt, Güterweld, praktische Welt*]" (§27, my translation, quoted in Chapter 7 of this volume).

Here we see the traditional distinction between fact and value, but the distinction is applied here to things *as* we experience them in our surrounding world. Objects, such as bicycles or stoves, are intended as having *values*, as being *good* things, as being *practical* things we use in our activities. Further, actions are intended as *right* or *wrong*, and people are intended as being of *good* or *bad* character. Given Husserl's theory of intentionality, the contents or meanings in our everyday experiences thus prescribe values in objects, persons, or actions in the world around us. In this way, the *value-structure* of objects, persons, and actions in the life-world is "constituted" in our experience of things in our surrounding life-world. (Recall our account of the "constitution" of objects in Chapter 6.)

In the *Crisis* (1935–8), Husserl develops a lengthy account of the ways in which all intentionality is rooted in the life-world. Our "constitution" of nature in mathematical physics, in particular, is founded on our background sense of spatiotemporal objects as we experience them in everyday life. This argument in the *Crisis* has implications for the constitution of values, as well as the constitution of "factual" properties such as spatiotemporal location, movement, and causality. If we "constitute" moral values in intentional activities of will, reason, and love (as considered earlier), then, following out the line of argument in the *Crisis*, our constitution of values – in such activities – is *founded* on our familiar activities in the life-world, including our engagement with others in our moral community. Thus, values play two roles in our constitution of values in the life-world. First, values are features of the *objects* of our experience: we experience objects around us (including persons and actions) *as* having values – *just as* we encounter them in our surrounding life-world. Second, values are features in our surrounding life-world, that is, values are already part of the *context in which* we experience, encounter, and deal with objects: more precisely put, the life-world, carrying values, is the *ground or background* of our experience of all things, including our experience of things as having values. If you will, our *evaluation of* things around us is itself founded, partly, on our background *sense of values* that surround us. (Recall our account of "horizon" in Chapter 6.)

ENLIGHTENMENT VALUES IN CRISIS

Why be moral? Why be rational? Why be compassionate? These are perhaps the most trying questions in moral philosophy. Husserl approaches these questions, obliquely, during his last phase of work, posthumously published in the *Crisis of the European Sciences and Transcendental Phenomenology* (1935–8).

Husserl does not pose these questions explicitly in the Crisis, nor does he attempt to answer them directly, yet the implications of the Crisis bear on exactly these questions. In 1930s Germany there was a sense of "crisis" about meaning or values. Nietzsche had trenchantly traced the origins of 19th-century "nihilism" – the loss of meaning, the collapse of values in "master" and "slave" moralities – while outlining the long history or "genealogy" of the very concept of morality, from biblical times unto the close of the 19th century. This was the aim of Nietzsche's "polemic" against "morality" in *On the Genealogy of Morality* (1887/1998), interrogating "the value of values," even "the *value* of compassion and of the morality of compassion." Nietzschean historical "genealogy" took on a new form in Heidegger's *Being and Time* (1927/1962). In that work, moreover, Heidegger pressed his revisionist conception of phenomenology, an "existential" form of phenomenology (as it would come to be known) as against Husserl's "transcendental" phenomenology. In particular, Heidegger emphasized the historical-cultural background of our sense (*Sinn*) of being in the world. In that historical context, Husserl came to address the "crisis" of values and of meaning that was articulated by existential thinkers from Kierkegaard and Nietzsche to Heidegger. Husserl clearly felt the "crisis" was a threat to his form of phenomenology as the ideal form of philosophy, a threat indeed to the very form of rationality that Husserl took as constitutive of "European humanity" – a threat to reason itself, scientific and philosophical, the highest value of the European Enlightenment. Reason was also, with Kant, the foundation of ethics, that is, practical reason following the categorical imperative. Suppose we are right in our prior sketch of the outlines of a Husserlian ethics, where the foundation of moral values lies in their "constitution" through a proper integration of will, practical reason, and love or compassion. Now bear in mind the moral-political climate in which Husserl wrote the manuscript of the Crisis. Hitler had come to power in 1933, Nazi gangs were burning books, Jews were the scapegoat of choice, Heidegger in 1934 had enforced Nazi regulations that locked Husserl out of the university on account of his Jewish origin. The moral and political implications of the Crisis were left implicit, an existential choice by its author. What, Husserl asked, was the source of the "crisis" of meaning, of "European humanity," of the "European sciences," and of the phenomenological movement itself? On Husserl's diagnosis: the "crisis" is at bottom the loss of the true meaning of rationality, and so the true value of rationality.

As we have observed along the course of our narrative in previous chapters, the salient theme of the Crisis is a reformulation of the context and methods of transcendental phenomenology. Husserl's new take on transcendental phenomenology is cast in a historical form, developing what Nietzsche would call a "genealogy" of the form of rationality in "theoretical," especially mathematical, science. (Husserl nowhere mentions Nietzsche, but the emphasis on "historicity" is central to Heidegger's conception of phenomenology.) In the Crisis, Husserl argues that in "mathematizing" nature, mathematical physics, from Galileo to Einstein, has lost touch with our background experience of nature in our everyday experience. Thus, the mathematical conception of space–time, gravity, and so on is an abstraction from our experience of spatiotemporal objects and events as they appear in our "life-world." Our scientific judgments are thus founded on our everyday perceptions and judgments about things in the world around us. As we abstract away from our everyday experience, however, we lose the full sense of spatiotemporal-causal phenomena in nature. Ultimately, Husserl implies, we lose our sense of ourselves – in the full and proper phenomenological theory of sense and its role in intentionality and so in the "constitution" of nature. It is not a long step, then, to a loss of compassion for others and for ourselves. We have lost touch with our life-world experience of *values*, values based in compassion for others and in our basic sense of human rights. What else could explain what was happening in Husserl's *Umwelt*?

In 1935 Husserl delivered a lecture to the Vienna Cultural Society titled "Philosophy and the Crisis of European Humanity." This text served as prolegomena to the work that became the *Crisis*, and it is reprinted as "The Vienna Lecture" in an Appendix to the main text of the *Crisis*. Existential philosophy, we noted, was much in the air, notably through Heidegger's existential variety of phenomenology. Existentialism downplayed the importance of reason and elevated the role of emotion and will. At the same time, Nazi politics in Germany were openly dismissive of rationality. Against this background, Husserl took a lofty attitude in championing rationality. Husserl emphasized the origins of the "theoretical" attitude in the ancient Greek thinkers who, Husserl argued, invented the ideals of "philosophy" and "science" in the proper development of "theory." The Renaissance reinvigorated the Greek ideals of reason in the 14th century, and the Enlightenment elaborated modern rationality in the 17th and 18th centuries. Here were the roots of modern philosophy, embodying the pure ideal of reason. But the great success of modern mathematical science, Husserl argued, has pulled us away from our foundational experience in the life-world. Addressing the existential *Zeitgeist*, Husserl poses a challenge:

> Is it not the case that what we have presented here [as a defense of rationality] is something rather inappropriate to our time, an attempt to rescue the honor of rationalism, of "enlightenment," of

an intellectualism which loses itself in theories alienated from the
world, with its necessary evil consequences of a superficial lust
for erudition and an intellectualistic snobbism?

(*Crisis*, 1935–8, "The Vienna Lecture": 289)

And do not these words resonate once again in the 21st century?

If Husserl found worry in the "mathematization" of nature, in
the *Crisis* his point was not that mathematical physics is a bad
thing, but rather that we have lost track of its place in our overall
"constitution" of the world. Thus, the *Crisis* spells out a new,
stage-by-stage methodology for transcendental phenomenology.
First, we are to bracket the world as presented in mathematical
terms, leaving us with the life-world, which is the ground of our
mathematical theorizing. Then, appreciating these two levels of
meaning in our "constitution" of the surrounding world, we are
to bracket the world as experienced in our everyday life, that is,
the life-world. Only then are we in a position to reflect on the
"pure" structure of consciousness, practicing transcendental
phenomenology. Where does rationality fit in this program?

Here is how Husserl appraised the status of rationality in "The
Vienna Lecture":

Mathematical natural science is a wonderful technique for making
inductions with an efficiency, a degree of probability, a precision,
and a computability that were simply unimaginable in earlier
times. As an accomplishment it is a triumph of the human spirit.
As for the rationality of its methods and theories, however, it is a
thoroughly relative one [that is, relative to the subjective activities
of pure consciousness]. It even presupposes a fundamental
approach that is itself totally lacking in rationality. Since the intuitively given surrounding world [*Umwelt*], this merely subjective
realm, is forgotten in scientific investigation, the working subject
is himself forgotten; the scientist does not become a subject of
investigation. (Accordingly, from this standpoint, the rationality of
the exact sciences is of a piece with the rationality of the
Egyptian pyramids.)

(*Crisis*, 1935–8: 295)

This attitude informs Husserl's extended program in the *Crisis*. If we put the subject back into the world "constituted" through proper rationality, if we tie rationality back into the subject, what do we find? In *Formal and Transcendental Logic* (1929), Husserl had argued that "formal logic" must be founded on "transcendental logic," which is founded on intentionality theory: meaning, expressed in formal symbols, is sense carried in acts of "pure" or "transcendental" consciousness. How, then, are *values* carried in acts of consciousness? A detailed account of the "constitution" of moral values in acts of consciousness that are themselves enacted in the life-world where values surround us – this *phenomenology* of values would restore rationality to its proper foundations. Such a view, at any rate, seems to be at work in Husserl's concerns in the *Crisis*.

TOWARD A HUSSERLIAN "CONSTRUCTIVIST" – "CONSTITUTIONALIST" – ETHICS

How might we develop more fully a Husserlian approach to ethical theory grounded in phenomenology? One important line of development is along the lines of a "constructivist" approach to ethical and political theory – an approach that has been unfolding recently in the writings of John Rawls, T. M. Scanlon, and Christine Korsgaard. On this view, moral as well as political values are "constructed" by appropriate activities of will or reason, individual or collective (as the case may require). More precisely, in Husserlian terms, values are "constituted," as we have considered above. Within the classical phenomenological movement, this approach to values, partly framed by Husserl's program of phenomenology, is seen in the work of Jean-Paul Sartre.

In *Being and Nothingness* (1943/1956) Sartre elaborated a "phenomenological ontology," amidst which he framed an explicit "ontology" of values. On Sartre's account, we *create* our values as we *choose* or *will* what we are to do: values are, if you will, artifacts of intentionality, of volition. Sartre's philosophy was focused on our human being, or "existence" (adapting Heidegger's use of that term) – whence Sartre's well-known "existentialism." According to Sartre, we are radically free, wholly responsible for our actions, which are born entirely of our free choice or will: we are "condemned" to freedom, with no further excuse. But we are not simply choosing freely to follow one or another *extant* value, a value that is already out there in the world, an "a priori" value, as Sartre put it. Rather, it is wholly within the activity of conscious choice that values are born into the world.

In Sartre's phenomenological ontology, everything we deal with is a "phenomenon" appearing in consciousness, that is, an object of intentionality, an object imbued with meaning – so a phenomenon, for Sartre, is an intentional object, for which Sartre occasionally uses the Husserlian term "noema." Behind the phenomenon, however, is "being in itself," which on rare occasions appears, as it were, through cracks in the phenomenal world. Now, for Sartre, *values* appear in the phenomenal world: this action is "to be done," "desirable," "good" or "right" – its value appears insofar as it is chosen or willed in the exercise of freedom. Interestingly, Sartre finds, a value – an object or situation with value – appears as a "lack," an absence in being, what is not yet existent but is desired and chosen to be realized. Such is "the being of value." What is important for our purposes, in Sartre's scheme, is the ontology of values: values enter the world in "phenomena" of consciousness – their being is, we might say, that of intentional artifacts. (See Sartre 1943/1956: 133–46, a section titled "The For-Itself and the Being of Values." Consciousness is "for-itself," or self-conscious, "consciousness (of) itself" in Sartre's idiom, whereas a mere object like a stone is "in-itself," with no consciousness and so no self-consciousness.)

In his popular essay, "Existentialism Is a Humanism" (1945/1956), Sartre encapsulated – more directly and more succinctly – his theory of ethical values:

> I declare that freedom, in respect of concrete circumstances, can
> have no other end and aim but itself; and when once a man has
> seen that values depend upon himself, in that state of forsaken-
> ness he can will only one thing, and that is freedom as the foun-
> dation of all values. . . . [W]hen I recognize, as entirely authentic,
> that man is a being whose existence precedes his essence [i.e.

his moral essence], and that he is a free being who cannot, in any circumstances, but will his freedom, at the same time I realize that I cannot [in good faith] not will the freedom of others.

(Sartre 1945/1956: 365–6)

Sartre summarizes his existential doctrine in the slogan "Existence precedes essence," holding that we have no "human nature" or moral essence prior to our existing, that is, prior to our acting. Hence, we each "make" our self. But, more than that, we each *create* our own *values* in acting, in freely willing to do such-and-such. When Sartre speaks of the "foundation" of values, he means an ontological, a phenomenological-ontological, foundation. This notion of foundation derives from Husserl's notion of "founding" (*Fundierung*), or ontological dependence, and from Heidegger's kindred notion of "fundamental ontology" emphasizing our "being" (*Sein*) as opposed to the "beings" (*Seienden*) we deal with. Thus, our acts of choice or will bring values into being: values *depend for their being* on our willing. For example, the value of being truthful depends or is founded, in my own case, on my willing to be truthful – my act of willing to act in accord with the maxim "Be truthful." Here, I submit, is the foundational principle – the "ground norm" (in Husserl's idiom) – of Sartre's ethics:

I create a value when I will in good faith with respect to freedom, my own and others.

Alternatively, the "categorical imperative" of Sartre's ethics is:

Act so as to will freedom, your own and every other's.

There is resonance with the biblical "Do unto others as you would have them do unto you," as well as the Kantian "Act on a maxim you could will that everyone follow" (to simplify Kant's formula). However, the will plays a special, "constitutive" role in Sartrean phenomenological ontology.

In these formulations, from Kant to Sartre, the words "will" and "could will" center ethics on the activity of will. Sartre declares freedom "the foundation of all values," echoing the ideals of the

Enlightenment. These ideals Kant had crafted into an ethical ideal in his categorical imperative, and these ideals inform modern European social-political theory as well. What is striking in Sartre's vision, however, is the place of freedom of will and hence values in a *phenomenological ontology*. Values are *founded* in "acts" of will, which are enacted in embodied actions. For Sartre, acts of will both *are* free (in point of ontology) and are *experienced* as free (in point of phenomenology). And in the free exercise of will, for Sartre, values are "constituted" and enacted and thereby brought into being – and hence founded, in a Husserlian sense. To create a value, an authentic value, however, Sartre holds, we must will in good faith, and that means, at bottom, recognizing our own freedom and also others' in the very act of willing. The condition of willing freedom in good faith is crucial, because – as Sartre emphasizes in *Being and Nothingness* (Part One: ch. 2) – we often will in "bad faith," partially deceiving ourselves by treating ourselves or others as less than free.

Sartre's ethics is sometimes called "voluntarist," meaning that values are determined by the will, ultimately by willing freedom as one wills to act thus-and-so (see Olafson 1967; on the history of voluntarism in early modern moral philosophy, see Schneewind 1998). For a Sartrean, however, the point is not that an action is good or moral simply because the subject or agent wills it – where, instead of God's will determining moral value, the agent's will does so. Rather, it is the *way* in which the will is formed, in the subject's own process of willing, that grounds moral value. This feature also informs more recent "constructivist" approaches to ethics.

In *The Sources of Normativity* (1996), Christine Korsgaard poses the question "What is the 'source' of normativity in ethics?" – where "ethical standards are *normative*" in that they "make claims on us; they command, oblige, recommend, or guide" (p. 8). "When we seek a philosophical *foundation* for morality", Korsgaard writes, "[w]e are asking what *justifies* the claims that morality makes on us" (pp. 9–10, emphasis added). Appraising "what makes morality normative," Korsgaard distinguishes "voluntarism" from "the appeal to autonomy." Of the latter approach she writes:

> This kind of argument [from autonomy] is found in Kant and con-
> temporary Kantian constructivists, especially John Rawls.
> Kantians believe that the source of the normativity of moral
> claims must be found in the agent's own will, in particular in the
> fact that the laws of morality are the laws of the agent's own will
> and that its claims are ones she is prepared to make on herself.
> The capacity for self-conscious reflection about our own actions
> confers on us a kind of authority over ourselves, and it is this
> authority which gives normativity to moral claims.
>
> (Korsgaard 1996: 19–20)

Korsgaard subsequently (pp. 90–130) argues for a "constructivist" account of the source or foundation of morality. *Constructivism*, in this broadly Kantian sense, holds that we construct moral values. What legitimizes the values we so construct – the "source" or "foundation" of these values – is the *way* we construct them: strictly, the procedure we follow is coming to endorse a specific value (say, "Be truthful" or "Do not lie"). Much as a society must follow appropriate procedures in setting out its laws or its political constitution, as Rawls argued at length (Rawls 1993), so an individual must follow appropriate procedures in setting out a "law" for herself, a maxim guiding her action. Accordingly, Korsgaard urges a "procedural" rather than "substantive" (Platonic) realism of moral values: "values are constructed by a procedure, the procedure of making laws for ourselves" (Korsgaard 1996: 112). Korsgaard summarizes her analysis as follows:

> I have offered an account of the source of normativity. I have argued
> that human consciousness has a reflective structure that sets us
> normative problems. It is because of this that we require reasons
> for action, a conception of the right and the good. To act from such a
> conception is in turn to have a practical conception of your iden-
> tity, a conception under which you value yourself and find your life
> to be worth living and your actions to be worth undertaking. That
> conception is normative for you. . . . And that [conception of your iden-
> tity] is not merely a contingent conception of your identity, which you
> have constructed or chosen for yourself, or could conceivably reject.
>
> (Korsgaard 1996: 122–3)

This account of the source of normativity is broadly Kantian, as
Korsgaard avers. But it is also, more precisely, Sartrean – though
Korsgaard mentions neither Sartre nor phenomenology. On
Korsgaard's neo-Rawlsian–Kantian analysis, what makes a moral
claim normative is the way in which consciousness *constructs a reason*
for acting (so far Kantian) that corroborates the subject's conception of her *identity* (enter Sartrean) and affirms the *worth* of the
action in contributing to her life (here the Sartrean theme takes
center-stage). In the first person: the action I choose or will gains
value only in light of my reflection on the significance of the
intended action in relation to my sense of my own personal identity or "self" (as Sartre put it). So, on this conception, my will is
autonomous in that (1) I will *freely*, on the basis of appropriate reason
and (2) thereby I construct a *law* or norm for myself (and anyone
else in similar circumstances, per Kant and Sartre). In Kantian terms,
my will is *self*-legislating, self-*norming*. In Sartrean terms, my will is
self-*constituting* and indeed "*self*"-constituting.

What exactly is the sense in which the "source" of normativity
lies in my will? A sharp answer flows from Husserl's theory of the
foundation of moral values (as reconstructed earlier): the *normativity* of an ethical norm – whence its moral claim on the subject
(agent) – is founded in the way the will is formed in relation to
love and reason. Specifically, normativity is founded on both a
formal and a material structure in the conscious intentional activity
of willing in relation to reason and compassion: the norm itself is
"constituted" in that pattern of intentional activity. The autonomy
theory entails that moral value is actively created in such a pattern
of willing. In neo-Husserlian terms, values are thus *intentional artifacts* of willing in an appropriate way. Roman Ingarden, writing in
Husserl's wake, carefully analyzed ways in which artworks are
ontologically dependent, or founded, on intentional acts of
consciousness (see Ingarden 1961/1989; Thomasson 1998). The
present Sartrean–Kantian autonomy model can be explicated in
such phenomenological-ontological terms: moral values are
"constituted" and thereby ontologically founded in appropriate
activities of will – in relation to reason and compassion, for Husserl.
Here is where Husserl's system of ontology and phenomenology
takes hold, in giving an analysis of foundation in the relevant sense.

There is really nothing like this in the moral theories of Plato, Aristotle, Hume, Kant, Mill, and others.

Is this Husserlian theory of the foundation of moral values, then, "constructivist" in the currently evolving sense? We might point to two relevant paradigms of the "construction" of values. One is the theory of social contracts, which Rawls developed in detail on the heels of Enlightenment political theory (Rousseau, Hobbes). The other is the theory of "constitution," developed by Husserl and elaborated, in his own terms, by Carnap. In the lineage of Rawls' political theory, a political system is held to be just or fair just in case it is constructed as if through a quite specific form of agreement. If all of us in the system were in the "original position" where we did not know who would be rich or poor, influential or not, and so on (we are working behind this "veil of ignorance," in Rawls' terms), would we agree to the principles that define our system – say, principles like those of the Constitution of the United States of America? The fundamental principle or "ground norm" of a theory of political justice along these lines would be (in terms of our present discussion): "Construct the principles of a political constitution as if we were all agreeing on the principles while in the original position of ignorance." In an analogous ethical system, our moral principles would be constructed by following a method more Kantian. The fundamental principle or "ground norm" of a "constructivist" Kantian theory of moral correctness would be: "Construct the maxim of your current will as if you did not know who would be affected" – whence Kant's categorial imperative, "Act on a maxim you could will that anyone would follow." T. M. Scanlon has considered a parallel structure between the "construction" of a proof in mathematics and the "construction" of the justification (compare proof) of the moral worth of an action (Scanlon 2005; see also Scanlon 1998; James forthcoming). Interestingly, Scanlon nods to Carnap's notion of the "construction" of knowledge in a given domain, here thinking of mathematics. But Carnap's notion of "construction" is an adaptation of the Husserlian notion of "constitution" – as noted, Carnap's German term of art is "*Konstitution*," not "*Konstruction*" (the term "*Aufbau*," literally "build-up," occurs only in the title of the *Aufbau*). So we are back to Husserl's conception of "constitution": values are "constituted" in appropriately formed acts of will in relation to compassion and reason.

For Husserl, "constitution" is not literally construction. Rather, there is a tracing back to foundations, to the relevant forms of meaning and the acts of consciousness carrying such meaning. The "constitution" of a particular ethical value, then, consists in the way that value, or norm, is *intended* in an act of will that involves a proper regard for compassion in a proper form of practical reasoning about what to do in the given circumstance. Given Husserl's articulate account of "constitution," we can see that, for Husserl, moral values are objective, "there for everyone," thus intersubjective, even as values are intended in subjective acts of will. In this way, Husserl's theory of constitution entails a distinctive approach to ethics – and similarly, though we have not turned in that direction, to political theory.

SUMMARY

Husserl's views on ethics and the nature of values are arguably less well developed than his more familiar views on logic, ontology, phenomenology, epistemology. Still, his ideas on ethics frame a novel account of the foundations of moral values. His conception of pure ethics, a specific conception of metaethics, outlined a novel notion of ground norms that frame a *definition of normativity* for a domain of values. His critique of traditional ethical theories – from Humean sentimentalist to Kantian rationalist to Millian utilitarian ethics – joins familiar critical themes, but gives these a unique force when framed by his conception of pure ethics. Framed by the formal principle "Do the better," moral values are constituted in acts of will formed in relation to practical reason respecting love for others. This account of the "constitution" of moral values extends Husserl's phenomenology and coordinate ontology, looking to values as they appear in our surrounding life-world.

Perhaps most significant, however, is the way in which Husserl approached ethical theory. Husserl held that moral values are *objective*, yet they are "constituted" in certain forms of *subjective* consciousness, and they take their place in our *intersubjective* world of everyday life.

Ultimately, Husserl's ethical doctrines take their place in his overall system. There is an ethical motivation for the rationalism of his conception of logic and its role in the foundations of knowledge. Phenomenology itself, Husserl's brainchild, carries ethical implications for human knowledge and its implications for social and political life, as Husserl argues in the *Crisis*. The role of ontology and phenomenology is apparent in our reconstruction of Husserl's metaethics. Husserl's distinction between the formal and the material guides his conception of pure ethics, while the "constitution" of values depends on his account of the existence and "constitution" of objects in general, now applied to value objects in particular.

FURTHER READING

Drummond, John J. 2001. "Ethics." In Steven Crowell, Lester Embree, and Samuel J. Julian, eds. *The Reach of Reflection: Issues for Phenomenology's Second Century*. Center for Advanced Research in Phenomenology, Inc. Electronically published at www.electronpress.com. An overview of ethical theories viewed from a phenomenological perspective.

Drummond, John J., and Lester Embree, eds. 2002. *Phenomenological Approaches to Moral Philosophy: A Handbook*. Dordrecht and Boston, Massachusetts: Kluwer Academic Publishers (now New York: Springer). Studies of phenomenology's implications for ethics.

Dummett, Michael. 1993. *Origins of Analytical Philosophy*. Cambridge, Massachusetts: Harvard University Press. A study of Frege and Husserl at the origins of the analytic tradition, emphasizing the role of language in the methodology of analytic philosophy.

James, Aaron. Forthcoming. "Constructivism about Practical Reasons." *Philosophy and Phenomenological Research*. A study of constructivist ethics focused on the construction of reasons guiding moral decision and action.

Kant, Immanuel. 1785/1959. *Foundations of the Metaphysics of Morals*. Translated by Lewis White Beck. New York: The Library of Liberal Arts, Bobbs-Merrill Company, Inc. German original, *Grundlegung zur Metaphysik der Sitten*, 1785.

Korsgaard, Christine. 1996. *The Sources of Normativity*. Cambridge: Cambridge University Press. A broadly Kantian theory of the foundations of moral values, specifically the "sources" of their "normativity," understood as including their moral claim on us.

——. 2003. "Realism and Constructivism in Twentieth Century Moral Philosophy." *Journal of Philosophical Research*. APA Centennial Supplement. A study of constructivism in contemporary ethical theory, including Kantian background.

Mandelbaum, Maurice. 1955. *The Phenomenology of Moral Experience*. Glencoe, Illinois: The Free Press. A study of phenomenological elements of ethics.

Mensch, James Richard. 2003. *Ethics and Selfhood: Alterity and the Phenomenology of Obligation*. Albany, New York: State University of New York Press. A phenomenological study of obligation, drawing on the concepts of self and other as studied by Husserl and others.

Mulligan, Kevin. 2004. "Husserl on the 'logics' of valuing, values and norms". In B. Centi and G. Gigliotti, editors. *Fenomenologia della Ragion Pratica. L'Etica di Edmund Husserl*, 177–225. Naples: Bibliopolis.

Rawls, John. 1980. "Kantian Constructivism in Moral Theory." *Journal of Philosophy* 88. An appraisal of the Kantian constructivist conception of moral values.

——. 1993. "Political Constructivism." *Political Liberalism*. New York: Colombia University Press. Rawls' account of a liberal, contractualist conception of the construction of a just political system.

——. 2000. *Lectures on the History of Moral Philosophy*. Edited by Barbara Herman. Cambridge, Massachusetts: Harvard University Press. Studies of the main ideas and figures in the history of ethics, by one of the premier political philosophers of the 20th century.

Sartre, Jean-Paul. 1943/1956. *Being and Nothingness*. Translated by Hazel E. Barnes. New York: Washington Square Press (a division of Simon and Schuster). French original, 1943. Paperback edition, 1992.

——. 1945/1956. "Existentialism Is a Humanism." In Walter Kaufmann, ed. *Existentialism from Dostoevsky to Sartre*. New York: New American Library (Times Mirror), 1975 edition.

Scanlon, T. M. 1998. *What We Owe to Each Other*. Cambridge, Massachusetts: Harvard University Press. A contemporary contractualist theory of the construction of those moral values that define obligation in the sense of what we morally owe to each other – reflecting a specific conception of "construction."

——. 2005. "Constructivism: What? And Why?" Text of a lecture. Manuscript draft.

Searle, John R. 1995. *The Construction of Social Reality*. New York: The Free Press. An analysis of how through collective intentionality we construct social institutions, which involve values (at least political values, and perhaps moral values too).

——. 1998. *Mind, Language and Society: Philosophy in the Real World*. New York: Basic Books. A study of mind, featuring consciousness and intentionality; social institutions, constructed through collective intentionality; and, finally, language as a social institution – offering a more concise account of social reality than in Searle 1995.

Zahavi, Dan. 2001. "Phenomenology and the Problem(s) of Intersubjectivity." In Steven Crowell, Lester Embree, and Samuel J. Julian, eds. *The Reach of Reflection: Issues for Phenomenology's Second Century*. Center for Advanced Research in Phenomenology, Inc. Electronically published at www.electronpress.com. An overview of intersubjectivity, including issues of empathy, with relevance for ethical theory. Drawing partly on Husserl's three volumes of writings on intersubjectivity (*Intersubjectivität* I, *Intersubjectivität* II, *Intersubjectivität* III), published posthumously in 1973 (not yet in English translation).

Nine

Husserl's legacy

In preceding chapters we studied Husserl's views in the core philosophical fields of logic, ontology, phenomenology, epistemology, and ethics, tracing their interconnections within Husserl's system of philosophy. In this chapter we look back on Husserl's work, on his overall philosophy. We consider the significance of Husserl's system writ large, taking its place in the long course of philosophy since Plato. We then survey Husserl's role in 20th-century philosophy, in the two traditions called "continental" philosophy and "analytic" philosophy. Then we consider implications of Husserl's results for more recent "analytic" phenomenology and philosophy of mind. In these respects, we assess what, from our perspective today, we should see as Husserl's paramount contributions to philosophy.

A SYSTEMATIC PHILOSOPHY OF OBJECTIVITY, SUBJECTIVITY, INTERSUBJECTIVITY

Husserl's legacy is a tightly knit system of philosophy, a system weaving together theories in logic, ontology, phenomenology, epistemology, and value theory, with a central role for the new science of phenomenology. What should we say is most significant, and most novel, in Husserl's system?

In a gloss, Husserl's system forms an integrated philosophy of objectivity, subjectivity, and intersubjectivity.

As we have seen in chapters preceding, Husserl developed a systematic philosophical theory of the essences of objects in the world at large (objectivity), acts of consciousness (subjectivity), and forms of culture (intersubjectivity). Major philosophers have long addressed these themes. The search for objectivity within the structure of the mind characterizes early modern philosophy from Descartes to Kant and beyond, while the social or intersubjective contributions to our knowledge and our humanity emerge from Hobbes and Rousseau in the social contract tradition of social-political theory, and from Hegel, Heidegger, Sartre, and more recent thinkers in the continental tradition. In the tradition of analytic philosophy, too, these themes have played their roles in philosophy of mind and language, notably in the writings of Carnap and Wittgenstein. Indeed, Donald Davidson, for whom language is the entry to mind and meaning, explicitly titled a book of his essays *Subjective, Intersubjective, Objective* (2001). In Husserl's work, however, each of the three idioms is prominent. Most important, Husserl's philosophical *system* digs deeply into each of these phenomena and into their interdependence.

If we track the flow of Husserl's ideas through the *Logical Investigations* and on into later studies from *Ideas* I and II to the *Crisis*, we see a detailed and evolving theory of precisely these three phenomena. Logic is itself the art and theory of objective forms of representation and inference, as Husserl emphasized. Moreover, logic is the heart of pure mathematics, where Husserl began his intellectual journey in perhaps the most purely objective type of investigation we know. Ontology is the theory of objective forms of objects in the world. Phenomenology is the objective science of subjective experience. Epistemology is the theory of the formation of knowledge, formed through reason and evidence or intuition, setting the standards for objectivity in our belief systems or theories, yet founded in our experience of seeing and reasoning and judging. The theory of the life-world specifies how everyday experience presents objects in our surrounding world, which is intersubjective, there for everyone, for "me" amid "others," the background for all our experience and all our objective knowledge formation. The scientific ideal of repeatability of observation already presupposes this form of intersubjectivity. Even the ideal of ethical principles presupposes that values are subject to intersubjective agreement, if only we understand how certain moral principles are formed and why they have a hold on us.

Thus, Husserl's grand narrative is a march from objectivity to subjectivity to intersubjectivity and back to objectivity. Specifically, Husserl moves from (1) the ideal of objectivity in "pure logic" and mathematics into (2) the study of objective structures of the world (which can be represented by logical constructions of meaning or language). Then he moves into (3) phenomenology, with its own objective methods for understanding subjective experience from the first-person perspective (as consciousness "intends" objects of appropriate types in the world). From there he moves into (4) the ideals of "reason" and "intuition" as grounding objective knowledge (achieved in perception and judgment about the world). He then moves into (5) the role of intersubjective experience in the *Lebenswelt*'s background of all the preceding ranges of theory or knowledge. And from the life-world he moves on into (6) social and ethical theory. On Husserl's detailed analyses, then, the necessary conditions of objectivity – in science, in everyday knowledge, in ethics, and in culture generally – lie in basic structures of subjectivity and correlatively of intersubjectivity.

In Chapters 3–8 we explored the interconnections among these ranges of philosophical theory in Husserl's system, following an overview of the system in Chapter 2. Husserl's remarkable achievement lies in the synthesis he wrought among these ranges of philosophy while crafting a central role for the new science of phenomenology. With these results Husserl takes his place on the short list of great systematic philosophers in history: Aristotle, Kant, Husserl . . .

Accordingly, over the course of our narrative in prior chapters, we have regularly noted the significance of Husserl's work in relation to the history of philosophy writ large. When looking to the legacy of a major thinker, we usually think in such historical terms, looking to past eras. However, reports of the death of Husserl's ideas are greatly exaggerated (to echo Mark Twain's remark about his alleged demise). Husserl's legacy reaches through the 20th century and into current philosophy of mind. Specifically, Husserl's impact on the last century of philosophy divides between the continental tradition and the analytic tradition, while his ideas are finding resurgent significance in contemporary philosophy of mind, where those traditions intermingle.

HUSSERL'S ROLE IN 20TH-CENTURY CONTINENTAL PHILOSOPHY

Husserl played a prominent and seminal role in the "continental" tradition of European philosophy throughout the 20th century. Husserl was the founder of phenomenology, which in turn was the progenitor of later movements in the continental tradition. The abiding concern of this tradition has been the meaning of things human, and Husserl laid out this theme in great detail within his own system of philosophy.

The *Logical Investigations* appeared in three volumes in 1900–1, and soon launched a vigorous philosophical movement centered on phenomenology. In 1901 Husserl moved from Halle to Göttingen and his first regular professorship. By 1903 philosophers in Munich formed an informal group to discuss and develop issues raised in the *Investigations*, emphasizing ontology along with a "realist" approach to the new discipline of phenomenology. In this group Adolf Reinach developed an ontology of states of affairs, including their role in law. This notion took shape in Husserl and other Viennese philosophers, and would be central in Ludwig Wittgenstein's *Tractatus Logico-Philosophicus* (1921) as the analytic tradition diverged from the continental. In 1907 a group in Göttingen formed a society for the development of phenomenology. In this group were Roman Ingarden and Edith Stein. Joining in an active Polish school of philosophy, Ingarden developed a phenomenology and ontology of works of art, defining an influential approach to aesthetic theory. Stein would later work with Husserl directly. Husserl's lectures and seminars continued to stir interest in ensuing years, and Husserl emerged as the leading philosopher in Germany. By 1913, with the publication of *Ideas* I, Husserl had absorbed the language of Kantian "transcendental" philosophy, prominent in different neo-Kantian "schools" of the academy in Germany. In 1916 Husserl took the primary Chair in philosophy in Freiburg, where he taught until his retirement in 1928. During these years a number of significant philosophers attended Husserl's lectures, studied with him, or worked as his assistant (a position in the German universities where a young scholar works with and for the "master" scholar). And so Husserl migrated from his origins in mathematics and the Brentano school of Viennese philosophy into the center of German philosophy and indeed of continental European philosophy. As the century progressed, phenomenology, Husserl's brainchild, formed the intellectual center of continental philosophy in one form or another. (Spiegelberg 1965 constructs a two-volume history of the phenomenological movement and its several "schools.")

Notable philosophers found their way to Husserl's door. Among his assistants at Freiburg were Edith Stein and later Martin Heidegger. Stein wrote a dissertation under Husserl on empathy (Stein 1916/1989), an astute analysis of the phenomenon and a paradigmatic study in the new phenomenology. Stein assisted Husserl in transforming the initial penciled version of Ideas II (prepared in 1912) into a manuscript in 1916, though Husserl still did not publish it. Also, Stein assisted Husserl in preparing his manuscripts on time-consciousness, later published under Heidegger's editorship. Stein's journey led from her early work in phenomenology to writing about cultural and theological themes and women's issues, before she died at Auschwitz in 1942; Pope John Paul II, formerly a Polish student of phenomenology (born Karol Wojtyla), declared her a saint in 1998. When Husserl arrived at Freiburg in 1916, Heidegger had completed his doctorate and was lecturing as a Privatdozent (private instructor). Heidegger collaborated closely with Husserl and served as Husserl's assistant before Heidegger left Freiburg in 1923 to teach at Marburg. When Husserl retired in 1928, Heidegger returned to Freiburg to assume the Chair vacated by Husserl. Though closely associated with Husserl, Heidegger sought to take phenomenology in a new direction in his Being and Time (1927/1962). On one level, Heidegger continued the practice of phenomenology inaugurated by Husserl. On another level, Heidegger sought to replace

Husserl in the German academy and, philosophically, to move phenomenology away from a purportedly "Cartesian" emphasis on consciousness, practiced by "bracketing" the world beyond consciousness, and toward a new form of phenomenology, stressing our "being-in-the-world," our "being-with-others," and what Heidegger called "fundamental ontology." Scholars have some-times called Heidegger's approach to phenomenology "existential" as opposed to "transcendental." Interpreters are still arguing about the extent to which Heidegger either continued Husserlian phenomenology with different emphases or undercut the funda-mentals dear to Husserl's heart. (Dreyfus 1991 stresses the discontinuities, emphasizing the practical and social dimension of Heidegger's approach, while Crowell 2001 emphasizes the conti-nuities, emphasizing the "space of meaning" and Heidegger's debts to Husserl.)

What is beyond dispute is the historical progression from Husserl's work to Heidegger's and on to subsequent "continental" thinkers whose work would not have been possible without Husserl's. Indeed, beneath the disputes over method and emphasis, all "continental" philosophers from Husserl forward work in a broadly phenomenological tradition as they interpret structures of meaning (differently conceived) in various ranges of human activity, from perception to political engagement. (The Introduction to Embree et al. 1997, by Embree and Mohanty, assesses the commonalities of the many figures and views that fall within the phenomenological tradition broadly conceived. Moran 2000 offers a current study of the main works of several classical phenomenologists and the progression of phenomenologically inspired thinkers, starting with Husserl.)

In 1929 the Parisian philosopher Emmanuel Levinas visited Freiburg, studying the phenomenologies of Husserl and Heidegger. When he returned to Paris, Levinas wrote on Husserl's theory of intuition and subsequently developed a novel phenomenology of "the face" of the other, leading into a religious sensibility informed by phenomenology. In 1933–4 two more Parisian philosophers, whose fame awaited, went to Germany to study phenomenology. Jean-Paul Sartre and Simone de Beauvoir studied

Husserlian phenomenology in Berlin, partly with Aron Gurwitsch, who subsequently taught phenomenology in Paris in the 1940s. Sartre became the archetypal writer-philosopher-activist of French existentialism. Sartre's *Being and Nothingness* (1943) is subtitled *An Essay in Phenomenological Ontology*; in that framework, a variant on Husserlian phenomenology, Sartre developed his famous themes of French existentialism, stressing our ultimate freedom of choice, our creation of values, and the ideal of acting in "good faith," a kind of existential honesty. Meanwhile, Beauvoir, lifelong friend (and sometime lover) of Sartre developed an existential ethics and wrote one of the major works of feminist theory, *The Second Sex* (1949), in which she characterized the male-dominant cultural perspective as presenting woman as "the other." Maurice Merleau-Ponty worked with Sartre and Beauvoir through the Second World War, producing yet another seminal work in *Phenomenology of Perception* (1945). Admiring the unpublished text of Husserl's *Ideas* II, Merleau-Ponty developed a rich analysis of the ways our experience is centered on consciousness of the body. His themes are actively pursued today in cognitive science and in cultural studies. In these works, French phenomenology expanded on the ideas developed in Austro-German phenomenology from Brentano to Husserl and beyond.

In Heidegger and then Sartre, phenomenology begat the movement of existentialism, which has had a broad popular appeal and contributed to a more public intellectual scene in France, as well as an existential style of psychoanalysis. In the second half of the 20th century, continental philosophy moved through subsequent movements, from classical phenomenology to existentialism to structuralism (the mind is structured like a language), poststructuralism (culture is structured in historical motifs), deconstruction (an indefinable practice of unearthing hidden, often contradictory cultural meanings), and cultural theory, including feminist interpretation.

In the continental tradition, the great thinker needs to "kill off the father" in order to proceed with his own creativity. Heidegger had to separate his conception of phenomenology as fundamental ontology from Husserl's transcendental conception of phenomenology (though Heidegger talks, even more than Husserl, of the "conditions of the possibility" of experience, the hallmark of Kantian transcendental philosophy). Sartre had to separate his "phenomenological ontology," the foundation of his "existentialism," from Husserl and Heidegger. Foucault and Derrida had to separate from Sartre and from the "structuralism" that came after Sartrean existentialism in Parisian intellectual life. And so on. There is something to this Oedipal impulse in the trajectory of continental philosophy. Perhaps this sensibility reflects Nietzsche's emphasis on the constancy of change and the singularity of historical moments and figures. On the other hand, there are important continuities in the continental tradition, as each successive thinker seeks meaning in what remains a broadly phenomenological approach, as distinct from the "scientistic" approach of the analytic tradition. In Husserl's own case, though he distinguishes his views from traditional theories (of Platonic forms, Cartesian dualism, the Kantian thing-in-itself, Mill's psychologism), nonetheless his training in mathematics looked to the development of philosophical ideas on the model of mathematical theories built on prior theories. In a cultural vein, continental philosophy remains both a dynamic shifting from one movement to its successor and an evolving phylogeny of phenomenology writ large.

In post-Second World War Europe Husserlian phenomenology has been studied, modified, and critiqued by a wide variety of "continental" philosophers writing in the wake of Heidegger, Sartre, and Merleau-Ponty. Husserlian phenomenology crossed the Atlantic in the 1940s, as Aron Gurwitsch left Paris for the United States, ultimately teaching for many years at the New School for Social Research in New York City, where Dorion Cairns also settled after returning to the States from extensive studies with Husserl in Freiburg. Gurwitsch presented phenomenology in his own terms, merging broadly Husserlian theory with Gestalt psychology (as did Merleau-Ponty, who had heard Gurwitsch lecture in Paris). Gradually, the study of Husserl and phenomenology spread throughout universities in the United States, particularly in the East, but also in the Midwest, notably at Northwestern. American philosophers, pursuing studies of Husserl and other classical phenomenologists, formed scholarly organizations, including the Society for Phenomenology and Existential Philosophy, the Husserl Circle, and the Center for Advanced Research in Phenomenology. "Continental" philosophy, rooted in Husserlian phenomenology, was cultivated thus in the new soil of North American university campuses. (Many pertinent studies of Husserl and Husserlian phenomenology – indicating Husserl's continuing legacy growing out of the "continental" tradition – are cited in the previous chapters, especially Chapters 5 and 6.)

HUSSERL'S ROLE IN 20TH-CENTURY ANALYTIC PHILOSOPHY

Running parallel to the phenomenological movement and its progeny in 20th-century "continental" philosophy was the tradition of "analytic" philosophy, which focused originally on logical theory. Husserl's role in 20th-century analytic philosophy is less well known than his role in the continental tradition. Much of the contemporary philosophical culture has "forgotten" Husserl's role in early analytic philosophy – in exactly the sense in which Heidegger said we moderns have "forgotten" things known to the early Greeks at the inception of Western philosophy. Alternatively, Husserl's role was "repressed," in a Freudian sense, by philosophers who came of age in the second half of the 20th century. By the 1950s, the traditions of continental and analytic philosophy had sharply separated, each viewing the other with suspicion. Continental philosophy lacked logical rigor, said the analytic philosophers; analytic philosophy lacked human relevance, charged the continental philosophers. And so Husserl's relations to the founders of the analytic tradition came to be largely forgotten or repressed.

In Husserl's day, however, there was no schism between "continental" and "analytic" philosophy. Nor were these terms used until several decades later. Indeed, Husserl moved naturally among those thinkers who are now seen as the founding figures of the analytic tradition. As we noted in Chapters 2 and 3, from the 1880s through the 1920s Husserl interacted with major players in logic, mathematics, and set theory. During his years in Halle, 1886–1900, Husserl worked with Georg Cantor, a founding father of set theory, even as Husserl developed his own philosophy of mathematics that appeared in *Philosophy of Arithmetic* (1891). Husserl communicated with Gottlob Frege, chief architect of the new logic of quantifiers and relational predicates, and the effects of the Husserl–Frege correspondence have been duly studied (recounted in Chapter 2). During his years in Göttingen, 1900–16, Husserl worked with David Hilbert, who was not only a leading mathematician (consulted by Albert Einstein), but also a seminal voice in the formalist view of mathematics as purely formal axiomatic systems. As we stressed, Husserl's *Logical Investigations* (1900–1) traversed much of the same philosophical terrain as the chief logical works of those formative years, before Alfred North Whitehead and Bertrand Russell produced *Principia Mathematica* (1910–13). Especially striking are conceptual connections between Husserl's *Investigations* and Ludwig Wittgenstein's *Tractatus Logico-Philosophicus* (1921) – even though Wittgenstein's historical links to Husserl are unclear beyond their common ancestry in Vienna. Suffice it to say that Wittgenstein's account of how propositions "picture" facts (existing states of affairs in the world) by virtue of "logical form" looks like a special formulation of key parts of Husserl's account of how ideal meanings represent objects in the world and how propositions represent states of affairs. In 1924–5 Rudolf Carnap attended Husserl's lectures, and Carnap's *Aufbau* (*Der logische Aufbau der Welt/The Logical Structure of the World*, 1928) draws significantly and explicitly on ideas in Husserl's transcendental phenomenology, even as Carnap builds a "logical empiricism" or "logical positivism" focused on ideal forms of language rather than ideal forms of experience. Pressing the modern empiricist program, Moritz Schlick, founder of the Vienna Circle, where logical positivism thrived in the 1930s, took Husserl seriously, as Schlick set his own epistemology in opposition to Husserl's doctrine of intuition of essences or *Wesenserschauung* (as Livingston 2004 stresses). Where the positivists looked to empirical science, Albert Einstein, in formulating relativity theory, consulted mathematicians including David Hilbert and Hermann Weyl, both of whom were conversant with Husserl. (Hilbert, as noted, was a colleague of Husserl's at Göttingen, and Weyl explicitly looked to Husserl's transcendental phenomenology as Weyl sought a mathematical formulation of relativity theory: see Ryckman 2005.) Alfred Tarski cites Husserl's *Logical Investigations* in his groundbreaking mathematical theory of truth for certain formal languages (Tarski 1933). To be sure, Husserl pressed his case for grounding logical theory in a phenomenological theory of intentionality, rather than an autonomous realm of linguistic signs, as seems assumed by many analytic philosophers. Nonetheless, Husserl's case takes its place in the vigorous debate of his day concerning philosophy of logic and language. (Husserl's role in what is now called analytic philosophy is studied in a number of works: Dreyfus 1982; Mohanty 1982; Smith and McIntyre 1982; Cobb-Stevens 1990; Coffa 1991; Dummett 1993; Richardson 1998; Friedman 1999; Hill and Rosado Haddock 2000; Fisette 2003; Livingston 2004; Ryckman 2005, 2006.)

In *Origins of Analytical Philosophy* (1993), Oxford philosopher of logic Michael Dummett held that what defined early analytic philosophy, beginning with Frege's work, was the thesis of the primacy of language. Bertrand Russell explicitly argued for grounding philosophy in logical analysis, and the new logic was built around a specific formal language. As the tools of this logical language were put to use, notably by Wittgenstein in the *Tractatus* and by Carnap in the *Aufbau* and later works, the focus on logic itself shifted to a focus on the nature of language. By mid-century, however, a new paradigm joined the older formal models: in philosophy we are to analyze the "logic" or "grammar" of ordinary language, so that classical epistemology, for instance, gives way to an analysis of how we ordinarily talk about sensations, beliefs, emotions, and other mental states. Wittgenstein's *Philosophical Investigations* (1953) set the agenda, following on years of discussions with philosophers in Cambridge and Oxford. Gilbert Ryle's *The Concept of Mind* (1949) appraised a variety of mental concepts as expressed in our everyday idioms of "believe," "see," and so on.

J. L. Austin furthered the new methodology of mid-century analytic philosophy. Now, it happens that Wittgenstein, Ryle, and Austin each called his own approach a kind of "phenomenology," albeit moving through analysis of language (rather than reflection on forms of consciousness per se). Here was Husserl's influence, perhaps at some distance, though Ryle explicitly wrote on Husserl. Meanwhile, in the United States, Wilfrid Sellars, familiar with both Husserl's *Logical Investigations* and the emerging Oxbridge sensibility, developed his own approach to mind through language, in *Empiricism and the Philosophy of Mind* (1956/2000), a work that has received renewed interest in recent years.

Analytic philosophy was influenced by Wittgenstein's early work in the *Tractatus* (1921) and again by his later work in the *Philosophical Investigations* (1953) and *On Certainty* (1949–51). It is not clear whether Husserl ever read Wittgenstein or whether Wittgenstein ever read Husserl. Yet there are important conceptual links between their views, and both philosophers shared a common background in Viennese philosophy and in the logical theory developing in their time. Indeed, models of representation, in language and/or thought, were very much in the air during their times. In the 1930s, moreover, in notebooks gathered as *The Big Typescript* (1933/2005), Wittgenstein explicitly wrote of "phenomenology" as "grammar," reflecting on visual space, color, pain, memory-time, "here" and "now," and the sense of self. Clearly, concepts from Husserlian phenomenology, and its antecedents in Viennese philosophy from Brentano to Mach, were in the air Wittgenstein was breathing. To be sure, Wittgenstein may have privileged language over thought or consciousness, while Husserl grounded language in the intentionality of consciousness. Nonetheless, there are structural similarities (amid differences) between Husserl's theory of intentionality and Wittgenstein's Tractarian theory of linguistic representation ("picturing"). Both focused on the fine structure of our experience and language concerning sensation, time, space, self, and so on. And there are conceptual ties between Husserl's account of the life-world's role in knowledge formation and the later Wittgenstein's account of the background

practices that ground our everyday knowledge. Both philosophers spoke of mathematical "manifolds," Mannigfaltigkeiten, in
mapping the representational power of a system of representation. (See D. W. Smith 2002 on intentionality vis-à-vis linguistic
"picturing"; D. W. Smith 2004: ch. 5 on background ideas and
practices; and D. W. Smith 2005 on the role of manifolds in a
model of representation that extends Husserlian and Wittgensteinian
models.)

In short, Husserl was in direct contact with early logical and
mathematical thinkers now perceived as the founders of modern
logical theory and so of the tradition of analytic philosophy.
Husserl and Frege critiqued their respective views on sense and
reference. Some of Husserl's views were explicitly taken up and
modified by Carnap, and are recognizable in early Wittgenstein.
Some of Husserl's ideas are cited by Tarski. Moreover, as we
observed in Chapters 2 and 3, Husserl's vision of "pure logic" as
the theory of theories, outlined in the Logical Investigations, is a philosophical vision of logic and metalogic as they would be developed
in technical detail in the works of Hilbert, Tarski, and Carnap. It is
as if these logicians were working out the mathematical details of
the philosophical vision framed by Husserl at the turn of the 20th
century. Meanwhile, Husserl was working out the philosophical
details of the vision, in his system of logic, ontology,
phenomenology, and epistemology, first mapped out in the Logical
Investigations in 1900–1. Husserl's philosophy of logic was distinctive, however, in seeking to ground logical theory in a
phenomenological theory of intentionality. Moreover, even
though Husserl developed his vision in a work whose title was
Logical . . . , his vision is much wider than what many philosophers
consider "logical." Contrary to a certain conception of "analytic"
philosophy, Husserl did not seek to reduce philosophy to logic in
anything like the usual sense. Rather, logic takes its place in
Husserl's system along with ontology, phenomenology, epistemology, in interdependence with these areas. (Many pertinent
studies of relations between Husserl and his contemporaries who
worked in logical theory are cited in previous chapters, especially
Chapter 3.)

"ANALYTIC" PHENOMENOLOGY IN HUSSERL'S WAKE

In the latter half of the 20th century, as philosophical logic developed new semantic models, Husserlian ideas on intentionality were reconnected with themes from logical theory, and Husserlian phenomenology took an "analytic" turn.

This "analytic" development of phenomenology took root in California during the 1960s, after a brief sojourn at Harvard. Dagfinn Føllesdal first studied mathematics at Oslo and Göttingen, and then wrote a master's thesis at Oslo in 1958 on Husserl and Frege, addressing Husserl's anti-psychologism. After completing a dissertation at Harvard in 1961, on reference and modal logic, under the direction of the logician-philosopher W. V. Quine, Føllesdal subsequently taught a course on Husserl at Harvard in 1962, 1963, and 1964, in which he drew parallels between Husserl's model of intentionality and Frege's model of reference (along the lines indicated in Chapter 6). Hubert Dreyfus, already working on phenomenology at Harvard since 1957, attended Føllesdal's Husserl lectures, completing his dissertation in 1964. In 1966 Føllesdal began teaching at Stanford as well as Oslo, and in 1968 Dreyfus began teaching at Berkeley, after teaching at MIT for several years. Meanwhile, Jaakko Hintikka, a pioneer in semantics for modal logics, spent the period 1956–9 at Harvard as a Junior Fellow in the Society of Fellows. During that time, when Føllesdal also arrived at Harvard, Hintikka developed a form of possible-worlds semantics for sentences of the form "a knows that p" or "a believes that p" (Hintikka 1962), followed in later years by further philosophical models of the logic of perception and intentionality as expressed in "a sees that p" (Hintikka 1969, 1975). In 1965 Hintikka began teaching at Stanford, while continuing also at Helsinki. In 1970 Ronald McIntyre and David Woodruff Smith (the present author) completed dissertations at Stanford, working with Føllesdal, Hintikka, and John Goheen, an astute reader of the history of philosophy. Those dissertations reconstructed Husserl's theory of intentionality, drawing on parallels with both the Fregean model of reference via sense and the Hintikkian "possible-worlds" model of intentional attitudes. (Smith and McIntyre 1982 extends results of those dissertations on the concepts of noematic sense and horizon, and Chapter 6 in this volume pursues those issues further, while addressing alternative interpretations of Husserl.) From 1968 until the present day, "California" phenomenology has evolved through recurrent discussion groups in Northern and Southern California. Early discussants included Føllesdal, Hintikka, McIntyre, (Woodruff) Smith, Dreyfus, Izchak Miller, John Haugeland, Richard Tieszen, and John Searle (whose views on intentionality were evolving along lines somewhat parallel to Husserl's). While Dreyfus and Haugeland have pursued ideas in Heideggerian phenomenology, Føllesdal and others have developed themes in Husserlian phenomenology. It is interesting to note that most of these philosophers studied mathematics or physics before they studied phenomenology, as Husserl himself did. Since 1991, this style of phenomenology has been addressed in regular symposia at the Pacific Division of the American Philosophical Association, under the auspices of the Society for Phenomenology and Analytic Philosophy (so named since 2004, formerly the Society for the Study of Husserl's Philosophy).

As "California" phenomenology evolved, "analytic" aspects of phenomenology also took root on the East Coast of North America in the 1950s and 1960s, with impetus from another direction, as J. N. (Jitendranath) Mohanty divided his time between Sanskrit studies and phenomenology. Mohanty studied Sanskrit philosophy in Calcutta. Then he studied mathematics and philosophy in Göttingen in 1952–4, where he met the quantum physicist Werner Heisenberg, and where he read widely in German-language philosophy and wrote a dissertation on Platonism, looking to Husserl. Returning to Calcutta, he continued work in both Sanskrit philosophy and European phenomenology. In 1964 Mohanty published a book on Husserl's theory of meaning (Mohanty 1964), which was reviewed by Føllesdal, and in 1972 he published a book on the Husserlian model of intentionality (Mohanty 1972). In 1970 Mohanty moved from Calcutta to Oklahoma and later to the New School in New York and on to Temple and Emory Universities, maintaining an active presence in phenomenology on the East Coast. But Mohanty looked beyond the continental European tradition to the analytic tradition, writing on Husserl and Frege (Mohanty 1982) and developing an explicitly "analytic account" of transcendental phenomenology in reflecting on classical Husserlian views (Mohanty 1989). Mohanty has also written extensively on relations between phenomenology and classical Indian philosophy. Thus, Mohanty's work forms a bridge between philosophy East and West – and between East Coast phenomenology and West Coast phenomenology.

In the 1970s another wave of "analytic" philosophy drew on Husserl's *Logical Investigations*. Three doctoral students in Manchester, England, worked on problems of ontology drawn from the early Husserl, which involved intentionality along with ontology and logical theory, reaching back to Bolzano and Brentano and philosophers influenced by those 19th-century Austrian thinkers. Kevin Mulligan, Peter Simons, and Barry Smith fanned out to teach and write in Salzburg, Geneva, and Germany. They organized numerous conferences and helped organize the European Society for Analytic Philosophy, where Husserlian ontology and phenomenology play a welcome role. Currently, Mulligan teaches at Geneva, Simons at Leeds, England, and Smith at Buffalo, New York. All three were visiting professors at the University of California, Irvine, between 1989 and 1992. (Smith and Smith 1995 includes essays that reflect interactions between the "California" school of phenomenology and this Anglo-European school of post-Brentanian philosophers.)

More recent developments of "analytic" themes in Husserlian phenomenology are informed by philosophy of mind shaped by cognitive science. Among recent philosophers working along these lines are Jean Petitot, Jean-Michel Roy, Bernard Pachoud, and the late Francisco Varela, working in Paris. Dan Zahavi, working in Copenhagen, joins classical Husserlian transcendental phenomenology with perspectives of cognitive science, as does Shaun Gallagher, working in Florida. And the list goes on, as Husserlian phenomenology is being developed, extended, and modified in relation to themes from analytic philosophy of mind and language. We turn next to philosophy of mind.

(Basic writings in the "analytic" style of phenomenology are found in Dreyfus 1982; Smith and McIntyre 1982; Smith and Smith 1995. Mohanty 1989 and Cobb-Stevens 1990 address analytic themes in Husserlian transcendental phenomenology. Petitot *et al.* 1999 gathers essays on Husserlian phenomenology in relation to recent cognitive science, from a 1996 conference in Bordeaux. Smith and Thomasson 2005 features essays that integrate Husserlian and Merleau-Pontian phenomenology with contemporary philosophy of mind. Reicher and Marek 2005 gathers essays on the interactions between phenomenology and analytic philosophy, from presentations at the 27th Ludwig Wittgenstein Symposium, held in Kirchberg am Wechsel, Austria, in August 2004.)

HUSSERLIAN CONTRIBUTIONS TO "ANALYTIC" PHILOSOPHY OF MIND

The philosophy of mind is that part of philosophy which studies the nature of mind. The mind–body problem – how the mind is related to the body – is central to philosophy of mind, and a traditional theme in modern European philosophy since Descartes. But this theme is also at home in the perennial philosophies that began in ancient India. Husserl came of age along with psychology, on the heels of modern philosophy. Following Brentano, Husserl defined phenomenology initially as "descriptive" psychology, that part of psychology – or theory of mind – that classifies and analyzes the basic types of mental activity, including perception, imagination, thought, emotion, and so on. Subsequently, Husserl defined phenomenology as the science of the essence of consciousness as experienced from the first-person point of view. His chief results, we know, featured the intentionality of consciousness, and much more. Clearly, phenomenology, in Husserl's hands, is a central part of the philosophy of mind. Indeed, if we are to tackle the mind–body problem, we must develop, on the side of mind, a characterization of the main types and properties of mental activity, notably conscious experience, and this characterization is the task of descriptive psychology or phenomenology. Furthermore, the relation between mind and body finds a distinctive analysis in Husserl's categorial ontology: the same event that I experience as an act of consciousness has a further aspect that science studies as an activity of neural processes in the brain, and these categorially distinct aspects of the event (moments or dependent parts of the event) are bound together in the event (a whole) by relations of ontological dependence. On Husserl's account, when I think or see or imagine something, this process is a whole that includes distinct "moments" (dependent parts) that fall, respectively, under the regions Consciousness and Nature, where the moment of experience (falling under Consciousness) depends ontologically on the moment of neural activity (falling under Nature). (Recall the survey of Husserl's ontology in Chapter 4 and the basic account of phenomenology in Chapter 5.)

The term "philosophy of mind" took root within the analytic tradition *circa* 1950, initially with little cognizance of Husserl's contributions. The mind–body problem was sharply defined in the 17th century, as Descartes argued that minds and bodies must be distinct kinds of "substances" since mind is characterized by conscious thought while body is characterized by spatiotemporal extension. But Cartesian dualism does not fit well with the naturalistic worldview, based in modern physics and biology. Accordingly, a new wave of philosophical theory about the mind developed in the second half of the 20th century. As the modern computer was developed in the 1940s and 1950s, philosophers and computer scientists came to think of the mind itself as a computing machine, where mind consists in the brain's running programs, just as a computer runs software. (Leibniz had already raised this model in the 17th century, and built a primitive "reckoning machine.") Since the 1970s empirical psychology has shifted from behavioristic analysis of stimulus and response to "cognitive science" models of how the mind processes information. The term "cognitive science" was coined in the mid-1970s as an umbrella term for theories of mind developing in empirical psychology, philosophy, linguistics, and computer science (especially artificial intelligence). Philosophy of mind today looks regularly to the experimental results of research in empirical cognitive science (for example testing what a person sees in a complex scene, in effect measuring the force of awareness and attention in what we see). Meanwhile, neuroscience developed increasingly detailed accounts of how different parts of the brain and nervous system perform particular functions, from perception to thought and emotions. In the background, moreover, was the success of modern physics, which encouraged a broadly materialist view of the universe, a "naturalism" that treats human beings and our minds as simply another part of the physical world of nature. In this context, philosophers of mind set to work, seeking a deeper understanding of how mind is realized in neural activity, including information-processing in a biological environment. (See Chalmers 2002 for many basic writings in philosophy of mind; and Armstrong 1999 and Kim 2000 for succinct recent appraisals of the field.)

Though Carnap (*Aufbau*, 1928) had addressed issues of mind in a sort of logical regimentation of phenomenological theory, it was Ryle's *The Concept of Mind* (1949) that brought "philosophy of mind" into its modern focus. Ryle analyzed types of mental activity as expressed in ordinary language, arguing that Cartesian *dualism* rests on a category mistake. When we know the behavioral manifestations or dispositions of a mental state, Ryle held, we know the state of mind; there is no categorially distinct entity, the mind, which is "the ghost in the machine." Ryle's view was sometimes understood as a "logical behaviorism," though Ryle rejected this characterization. By 1960, philosophers had proposed a more direct connection between mind and body. The *identity theory* held that each concrete mental state is identical with a concrete state of the central nervous system. Here was a strong form of *materialism*. But what if Martians landed, with a different physiology – could they not perceive and think? And what about machines that performed all the right computational operations – could not such computers, embedded in robots built like us, "think" and "see" and so on? By 1970, the strict materialism of the identity theory gave way to *functionalism*, the view that mind is not a physical process per se, but rather the function performed by a physical system: especially a proper form of information-processing, or computation, realized in any appropriate system, whether a biological organism or a computing machine.

By the mid-1980s, however, phenomenological properties of mind were gaining prominence (with or without the terminology of phenomenology). Philosophers of mind argued, on several grounds, that functionalism was inadequate. Important properties of mental states as we know them escape functional analysis. The subjective sensory properties, or *qualia*, that we experience in sensations of pain, of seeing red, and so on, are not addressed in a functional analysis: so long as the inputs and outputs of the system are properly correlated, it matters not how the state "feels" to the organism. *Consciousness* itself includes the property of "what it is like" to see, feel, and so on (as Nagel 1974 argued). But this feature of consciousness is not captured by functional analysis of the causal role or inputs-and-outputs of a mental state. *Intentionality*, on a Husserlian analysis, essentially involves the way a content or *meaning* represents something. But computation is strictly defined by the processing of purely syntactic symbols, so the computational model of mind as information-processing omits meaning, and does so by design. Further, part of what makes a mental state conscious, it seems, is the subject's *awareness* of experiencing the mental state. What is the form of that awareness? Does it consist in a form of *higher-order monitoring* of the state? This model has problems, so we need a further analysis of the form of awareness of experience. Following Brentano, Husserl argued against any higher-order consciousness of a conscious experience. Husserl's analysis of time-consciousness involved a form of awareness of an experience as it unfolds in time (see Chapter 5 in this volume).

These phenomenological aspects of consciousness, which Husserl treated in detail, have gradually come center-stage in analytic philosophy of mind. In this way, phenomenology is re-emerging, with or without the name, in contemporary theory of mind. Appropriately, Husserl's specific contributions are gradually being rediscovered and developed in the analytic tradition – or rather part – of philosophy of mind. These contributions include Husserl's rich analyses of intentionality, intentional content or meaning, consciousness, self-consciousness, subjective first-person perspectives on consciousness, temporal awareness, spatial awareness, sensory and intentional aspects of perception, bodily awareness, embodied volitional action, empathy and consciousness of others, intersubjectivity, the social or cultural sphere in the life-world, the role of values in experience, and so on.

A crucial part of the study of mind remains the classical problem of the exact relation between conscious experience and neural processes in the subject's brain. "Neurophenomenology," as Francisco Varela put it, will address this relation as neuroscience progresses in relation to phenomenology. Every day we read of new studies about, say, where a particular emotional state is coded in the brain, as evidenced in functional magnetic resonance imaging. But what is the nature of that correlation between subjective experience and electrochemical interactions in the brain – between the "transcendental" forms of consciousness and the "naturalistic" forms of brain process? The ontology of that relation, I find, is an application of Husserl's categorial ontology (per Chapter 4 in this volume). The same process that I *experience* from the *subjective* first-person perspective as a conscious experience (say, seeing a eucalyptus tree) is realized in a complex pattern of *neural* activity in my brain. Again, the same process which I experience as consciously volitionally hitting an inside-out crosscourt forehand shot to my tennis opponent's weaker backhand – my conscious intentional *action* – is realized in a complex pattern of neuromuscular dynamic activity in my body. Moreover, that same process is enacted in the *cultural* form of *intersubjective* life we call tennis. In short, numerically the same process has various aspects or "moments" (dependent parts) that instantiate, respectively, a form of conscious experience, a form of physiological activity, and a form of cultural activity. In Husserl's idiom, these three moments are instances of three distinct "essences" that fall, respectively, under the regions Consciousness, Nature, and Culture. What's more, there are ontological *dependencies* among these moments. To be sure, it is not easy to spell out the details of these categorially distinct aspects and their interdependencies. Yet there are well-honed tools of analysis to be drawn from Husserl's systematic approach to these phenomena. Here lies a distinctive contribution to our developing theory of mind, a theory that must integrate the phenomenological, the neurobiological, and the cultural. (My own sketch of the broad outlines of such a line of analysis is found in D. W. Smith 1995 and several essays in D. W. Smith 2004.)

(The relations between phenomenology and philosophy of mind are studied in a series of collections. Dreyfus 1982 addresses early convergences between cognitive science and Husserlian phenomenology. Smith and McIntyre 1982 explicitly presents Husserl's theory of intentionality as part of "philosophy of mind." Petitot *et al.* 1999 addresses in detail the relations between Husserlian phenomenology and contemporary issues in cognitive science and analytic philosophy of mind. Embree 2004 addresses contributions of Gurwitsch's phenomenology to contemporary cognitive science. Searle 1998 and 2004 stress the "first-person ontology" of conscious intentional experience realized in the brain. Livingston 2004 appraises pivotal points in the history of 20th-century philosophy of mind, with an eye to Husserl at some points. Zahavi 2005 studies subjectivity and self by drawing on key studies in classical phenomenology while looking also to recent analytic philosophy of mind. Smith and Thomasson 2005 addresses the contributions of phenomenology to contemporary issues in philosophy of mind. For more than a decade there have been large, interdisciplinary, biannual conferences in "consciousness studies" organized by the Center for Consciousness Studies at the University of Arizona, similar results appearing in the *Journal of Consciousness Studies*. Relevant issues are explored in a rather new journal, edited by Shaun Gallagher, titled *Phenomenology and Cognitive Science*.)

SUMMARY

Husserl once remarked that phenomenology is "an infinite task," forever unfinished. So too with Husserl's philosophical system as a whole. We have drawn a picture of the structure of Husserl's system: a complex theory with interdependent subtheories that fall under the traditional areas of logic, ontology, phenomenology, epistemology, and ethics. Through our reconstruction of Husserl's system, we have indicated ways in which one part of the system depends on others, drawing on that part which is Husserl's theory of dependence itself. Phenomenology, of course, is of central importance in Husserl's system, and we devoted two chapters to Husserl's phenomenology. Husserl's legacy, as just outlined, is far-reaching. Beyond the various lines of historical influence, however, three themes can be seen as guiding the development of Husserl's system: objectivity, subjectivity, and intersubjectivity. These interlocking phenomena recur in all of Husserl's salient concerns, in each of the areas of his philosophy. Accordingly, our study of Husserl's philosophy closes with an emphasis on this triad.

FURTHER READING

Armstrong, David M. 1999. *The Mind–Body Problem: An Opinionated Introduction.* Boulder, Colorado: Westview Press. A succinct overview of contemporary approaches to the mind–body problem, including Armstrong's version of materialism.

Bernet, Rudolf, Iso Kern, and Eduard Marbach, eds. 1989/1993. *An Introduction to Husserlian Phenomenology.* Evanston, Illinois: Northwestern University Press. Third paperback printing, 1999. Translation of the German original, *Edmund Husserl: Darstellung seines Denkens,* Hamburg: Felix Meiner Verlag, 1989. An overview of Husserl's philosophy, including (noteworthy for the present chapter) the structure of experience of "I," of the other, of the life-world, and of intersubjectivity.

Chalmers, David J. 2002. *Philosophy of Mind: Classical and Contemporary Readings.* Oxford and New York: Oxford University Press. A collection of writings in contemporary analytic philosophy of mind, along with some relevant historical selections.

Coffa, J. Alberto. 1991. *The Semantic Tradition from Kant to Carnap: To the Vienna Station.* Edited by Linda Wessels. Cambridge and New York: Cambridge University Press. A history of the development of semantics in logical theory, reshaping the received view of Carnap's role and indicating the roles of Bolzano and Husserl along the way.

Cobb-Stevens, Richard. 1990. *Husserl and Analytic Philosophy.* Dordrecht and Boston, Massachusetts: Kluwer Academic Publishers (now New York: Springer). A study of Husserl in relation to analytic philosophy.

Dreyfus, Hubert L., ed. 1982. *Husserl, Intentionality and Cognitive Science*. In collaboration with Harrison Hall. Cambridge, Massachusetts: MIT Press. Essays addressing Husserl's phenomenology in relation to Frege's logic and to contemporary philosophy of cognitive science.

Dummett, Michael. 1993. *Origins of Analytical Philosophy*. Cambridge, Massachusetts: Harvard University Press. A study of Frege and Husserl at the origins of the analytic tradition, emphasizing the role of language in the methodology of analytic philosophy.

Fisette, Denis. 2003. *Husserl's Logical Investigations Reconsidered*. Dordrecht and Boston, Massachusetts: Kluwer Academic Publishers (now New York: Springer).

Føllesdal, Dagfinn. 1969. "Husserl's Notion of Noema," *Journal of Philosophy*. Reprinted Hubert L. Dreyfus, ed. 1982. *Husserl, Intentionality and Cognitive Science*. Cambridge, Massachusetts: MIT Press. A succinct and seminal study of Husserl's theory of noema and intentionality in relation to Frege's theory of sense and reference.

Friedman, Michael. 1999. *Reconsidering Logical Positivism*. Cambridge and New York: Cambridge University Press. A study of the Vienna movement of logical positivism, featuring Carnap's key work and observing Carnap's relation to Husserl.

———. 2001. *Dynamics of Reason*. Stanford, California: CSLI Publications. A study of historical relations between Carnap, Cassirer, and Heidegger as they met at Davos and subsequently went in different philosophical directions.

Kim, Jaegwon. 2000. *Mind in a Physical World*. Cambridge, Massachusetts: MIT Press. A succinct account of recent physicalism, including Kim's contributions to the theory of supervenience (how mental states "supervene" on brain states without reduction).

Mohanty, J. N. 1982. *Husserl and Frege*. Bloomington: Indiana University Press. A study of the relations between Husserl and Frege.

Moran, Dermot. 2000. *Introduction to Phenomenology*. London and New York: Routledge. A study of the classical phenomenologists (Husserl, Heidegger, *et al.*) and their successors (including Arendt, Derrida, and others), indicating Husserl's influence on major thinkers in the 20th-century continental tradition, all presented as broadly phenomenological philosophers.

Petitot, Jean, Francisco J. Varela, Bernard Pachoud, and Jean-Michel Roy, eds. 1999. *Naturalizing Phenomenology: Issues in Contemporary Phenomenology and Cognitive Science*. Stanford, California: Stanford University Press. In collaboration with Cambridge University Press, Cambridge and New York. Contemporary essays on the implications of Husserlian phenomenology for cognitive science and philosophy of mind.

Richardson, Alan W. 1998. *Carnap's Construction of the World: The Aufbau and the Emergence of Logical Empiricism*. Cambridge and New York: Cambridge University Press. A historical study of Carnap's famous work, indicating relations to Husserl and others.

Ryckman, Thomas. 2005. *The Reign of Relativity: Philosophy in Physics 1915–1925*. Oxford and New York: Oxford University Press. A study of Einstein and others in the formation of relativity theory, including the role of Husserl's transcendental phenomenology in influencing Weyl's mathematical formulation of relativity theory.

Searle, John R. 1998. *Mind, Language and Society: Philosophy in the Real World*. New York: Basic Books. A study of mind, including intentionality, in the context of a form of naturalism, differing from Husserl on naturalism but sharing common ground on consciousness, intentionality, and collective intentionality in social formations (compare intersubjectivity in culture or *Geist* per Husserl).

——. 2004. *Mind: A Brief Introduction*. Oxford and New York: Oxford University Press. Searle's overall philosophy of mind, emphasizing the first-person ontology of consciousness and intentionality.

Spiegelberg, Herbert. 1965. *The Phenomenological Movement: A Historical Introduction*. Second edition. Vols. 1 and 2. The Hague: Martinus Nijhoff. A detailed history, in two volumes, of the early phenomenologists and their several traditions within the phenomenological movement.

Zahavi, Dan. 2001. "Phenomenology and the Problem(s) of Intersubjectivity." In Steven Crowell, Lester Embree, and Samuel J. Julian, eds. *The Reach of Reflection: Issues for Phenomenology's Second Century*. Center for Advanced Research in Phenomenology, Inc. Electronically published at www.electronpress.com. An overview of intersubjectivity, including issues of empathy, with relevance for ethical theory. Drawing partly on Husserl's three volumes of writings on intersubjectivity (*Intersubjectivität* I, *Intersubjectivität* II, *Intersubjectivität* III), published posthumously in 1973 (not yet in English translation).

——. 2003. *Husserl's Phenomenology*. Stanford, California: Stanford University Press. An overview of Husserl's thought covering the early logical period, the middle transcendental period, and the later life-world period. The perspective is broadly continental, indicating Husserl's influence on subsequent figures in the continental tradition of Germany, France, and other locales.

——. 2003a. "Husserl's Intersubjective Transformation of Transcendental Phenomenology." In Donn Welton, ed. *The New Husserl: A Critical Reader*. Bloomington: Indiana University Press. An argument that Husserl took the constitution of objectively existing things to rest on intersubjective structures of experience.

Zahavi, Dan, and Frederik Stjernfelt, eds. 2002. *One Hundred Years of Phenomenology: Husserl's* Logical Investigations *Revisited.* Dordrecht and Boston, Massachusetts: Kluwer Academic Publishers (now New York: Springer). Essays on the *Logical Investigations*, indicating their significance for contemporary philosophy, continental and analytic.

Glossary

The terms glossed below are technical terms or idioms, most of which are more fully explained in the chapters of the book. Most are drawn, in translation, from Husserl's texts; Husserl's original German terms are included in parentheses, where appropriate. Some terms below are drawn not from Husserl, but from philosophical or historical discussions relevant to the chapters.

abstraction (*Abstraktion*) an intellectual operation whereby one abstracts from an object some essence of the object.

abstract part a moment, or dependent part, of an object.

act (*Akt*) an act of consciousness, a conscious experience; specifically, a consciousness of some object.

adequacy (*Adäquatheit*) a measure of evidence; evidence is adequate when complete, so that there are no sides or aspects of an object that are not presented with intuitive fullness; for Husserl, perception is always inadequate.

adumbration (*Abschattung*) a variation in the appearance of an object of perception; for example, the same color of an object appears with different adumbrations under different lighting conditions.

analytic (*analytisch*) a proposition is analytic if its truth is determined by its meaning or conceptual content alone; for example, "a bachelor is unmarried" is an analytic proposition; Husserl, with Bolzano, is concerned with analytic propositions whose truth is determined by their logical form.

analytic philosophy the tradition in 20th-century philosophy (and beyond) that focuses, narrowly, on analysis of concepts and language that play in philosophy, or, broadly, on analysis of theories and arguments – with historical roots in Frege, Russell, Carnap, and other philosophers who began with logic and worked into metaphysics, epistemology, etc.

apodicticity (*Apodiktizität*) a measure of evidence; a judgment or experience is apodictic if while having the experience one cannot doubt the existence of its object.

apophantic (*apophantisch*) pertaining to judgment.

a posteriori a proposition is a posteriori if its truth can be known, or judged with evidence, only posterior to empirical observation or sensory perception; opposed to a priori.

a priori (*a priorisch*) a proposition is a priori if its truth can be known, or judged with evidence, prior to empirical observation or sensory perception; for Husserl, propositions in logic, in mathematics, and also in phenomenology are a priori.

axiology (*Axiologie*) the theory of good – a formal theory, for Husserl, applicable to values in different spheres.

background (*Hintergrund*) **of an object of consciousness** the range of properties and related objects lying in the background, or in the horizon, of an object of consciousness; for example, a perception presents an object against a background of further properties and objects; this structure of perceptual experience was emphasized by Gestalt psychologists influenced by Husserl, and by phenomenologists like Aron Gurwitsch and Maurice Merleau-Ponty.

background (*Hintergrund*) **of consciousness** the ground of consciousness and its intentionality; the surrounding world (*Umwelt*) or life-world (*Lebenswelt*) on which the intentionality of consciousness depends.

background sense the sense of objects that is implicit or presupposed in everyday experience, which helps to define the horizon of an object of consciousness.

body the physical or corporeal body (*körper*) is the human body *as* a merely physical object; the lived or living body (*leib*) is the body, my body, *as* a living body in which I act.

bracketing (*Einklammerung*) the method or technique of turning our attention from the objects of our consciousness to our consciousness of those objects, thereby engaging in phenomenological reflection; Husserl's proposed method for the practice of phenomenology; also called epoché.

categorical imperative Kant's basic ethical principle, "Act only on that maxim by which you can at the same time will that it should become a universal law"; Husserl uses the term "categorical imperative" more generally, for any basic ethical principle that serves as a ground norm for an ethical system, whence Husserl proposes to replace Kant's principle with the formal principle "Do the better."

category (*Kategorie*) a high-level form or formal essence of objects in general, such as the form Individual, Property, State of Affairs, Number, etc.; categories apply to objects in any material region such as Consciousness, Nature, or Culture.

certainty (*Gewissheit*) a measure of evidence; a judgment or experience is certain if one does not doubt the existence of its object.

cogito (*Cogito*) an act of consciousness; from Descartes' use of the Latin "*cogito*," meaning "I think."

completeness, logical in logic, a property of certain theories; a deductive theory is complete if and only if all true propositions in the theory are deducible from the axioms in the theory – where truth is a semantic property and deducibility is defined by syntactic rules of inference.

concept (*Begriff*) a type of sense, specifically a sense that can be a grammatical or logical part of a proposition, expressible in language by a predicate.

consciousness (*Bewusstsein*) conscious experience, that is, an act of consciousness, such as an act of perception, imagination, thought, emotion, volition, etc.; alternatively, a subject's stream of consciousness.

Consciousness (*Bewusstsein*) the material essence or region that encompasses acts of consciousness; here the term is capitalized when referring to the region.

constitution (*Konstitution*) the way an object is intended, hence "constituted," in consciousness, where an object is intended through a manifold of meanings (sense) that present the same object as having various properties (species, qualities, relations) – for example, presenting possible properties of the back side of an object presented in visual perception.

constructivism in ethics, the view that ethical or moral values are constructed, either through a process of practical reasoning about what to do or through choosing or willing what one will do, especially where one wills or reasons in an appropriate way (for example by following the Kantian categorical imperative).

content (*Inhalt, Gehalt*) the content of an act of consciousness, that is, "what" I experience as it is experienced or intended; an act's real content, or noesis, is a temporal part (moment) of the act, whereas an act's ideal content, or noema, is an ideal, nontemporal sense carried in the act by the noesis.

continental philosophy the tradition in 20th-century continental European philosophy (and its extensions elsewhere) informed originally by phenomenology in varying forms, featuring Husserl, Heidegger, Sartre, Merleau-Ponty, and others who wrote in their wake; more broadly, the tradition shaped by Kant and extending through the 20th century as Husserl and successors developed versions of phenomenology or critiqued and sometimes rejected variants of phenomenology.

culture (*Geist*) the range of cultural or social objects, activities, and institutions, including moral values: cultural objects have a historical aspect; the German term "*Geist*" literally means "spirit" and is sometimes so translated, but Husserl's usage emphasizes the social or cultural formation of "spirit."

Culture (*Geist*) the material essence or region that encompasses cultural or social objects, activities, and institutions, including moral values; here the term is capitalized when referring to the region.

dependence (*Unselbständigkeit*) the ontological relation or condition where one object depends on another object, that is, where the one object could not exist unless the other object existed, according to the essences of the given objects; literally "non-self-standing-ness"; also called foundation or founding (*Fundierung*).

eidetic variation the technique of varying the properties of an object in imagination or phantasy, with the aim of judging which properties are essential to an object of that type, an object with its eidos or essence.

eidos (Eidos) the shareable essence of an object, including its ideal species, qualities, or relations; the Platonic form of an object, "*eidos*" in Greek.

empathy (Einfühlung) understanding the experience of another subject or I; literally, "feeling" my way "into" the experience of another I; for Husserl, empathy is basic to our activities in the surrounding cultural or social world; now commonly distinguished from sympathy, where I feel with the other, coming to have similar feelings.

empiricism the theory that knowledge is founded ultimately in sensory perception, which confers all basic evidence on our knowledge claims.

epistemology the theory of knowledge.

epoché (Epoché) Husserl's basic method or technique for the practice of phenomenology; I bracket, or make no use of, the thesis of the existence of the world around me, and thereby I turn my regard or attention from objects in the world to my consciousness of objects in the world around me; adapting the Greek word "*epoché*," meaning "to abstain"; also called bracketing.

essence (Wesen) what an object is, including its ideal species or type, qualities, and relations, also called its eidos; for Husserl, essences belong to a unique category; here the name of a particular essence is capitalized when its categorial status is relevant, for example, "Man" or "Tree" or "Eucalyptus."

essential insight or intuition (Wesenserschauung, Wesenschau) intuitive comprehension of the essence of an object; also called eidetic intuition.

ethics the theory of moral values, of when an action is right or wrong, permissible or obligatory, praiseworthy or blameworthy, etc.

evidence (Evidenz) intuitive or evidential support for judgments or knowledge claims, providing intuitive fulfillment; also, an act of intuition or (self-)evident experience.

experience (Erlebnis) an act of consciousness, a lived experience.

experience (Erfahrung) a cognitive experience, that is, an evident or intuitive experience, which can serve as the basis of further judgments that form knowledge.

expression (*Ausdruck*) a sign or syntactic construction in a language, including words, phrases, or sentences.

fact (*Tatsache*) in Husserl's usage, any concrete, contingently existing object; specifically, an object in the region or category of Individual, the type of object that can have an essence – much as Aristotle defined particulars as what predicates are predicated of but what cannot be predicated of anything; distinguished from an existing state of affairs (*Sachverhalt*), for which some philosophers (following Bertrand Russell) have used the English term "fact."

feeling ethics (*Gefühlethik*) the ethical theory holding that an action is morally right just in case it carries appropriate feeling for others, or sympathy; promoted by David Hume, now called sentimentalist ethics, in English-language writers.

form (*Form*) a type of essence or eidos, namely a formal essence.

formal essence that type of essence which can be instantiated by objects in different material regions such as Nature, Consciousness, and Culture (*Geist*); formal essences include, for example, the forms Object, Individual, Property, Relation, State of Affairs, Number.

formal logic that part of logic, or logical theory, which depends only on the logical form of expressions or their meanings, thus the formal theory of signs or symbols in a language, including the theory of relations of inference or logical consequence among sentences or propositions, insofar as these relations are definable in purely formal terms; Husserl distinguished formal logic from transcendental logic.

formal ontology that part of ontology which deals with forms or formal essences, as distinct from material essences; formal ontology studies ontological forms such as Object, Individual, Property, Relation, State of Affairs, Number.

formal versus material a distinction Husserl applies at different levels, namely to expressions, to meanings, and to objects.

formalization the intellectual activity of moving from objects to their forms or formal essences; Husserl distinguishes formalization from generalization.

foundation (*Fundierung*) dependence, where one object depends on another object just in case the one object could not exist unless the other object existed, according to the essences of the given objects.

Geist the German term that can mean mind or spirit, including *Zeitgeist*, or spirit of the times; Husserl uses the term to mean the material region of cultural objectivities, including social institutions and moralities; the term can be translated directly as "spirit," but is translated here as "culture," since "spirit" carries different connotations in English (as the spirit is said to leave the body at death).

generalization the intellectual activity of moving from objects to their species or higher material essences; Husserl distinguishes generalization from formalization.

geometry, Euclidean the mathematical theory of space, originated by Euclid with his five axioms, where, in particular, parallel lines never meet.

geometry, non-Euclidean a mathematical theory of space with different properties than Euclidean space (for example like the surface of a sphere or of a saddle, in two such theories).

ground (*Grund*) that on which an object depends or is founded, specifically for its existence.

ground norm (*Grundnorm*) the norm or principle that defines what counts as a value in a given domain of values (for example moral values or aesthetic values).

horizon (*Horizont*) the range of possibilities left open for an object of consciousness, for example possible properties of the back side of an object as I see it and possible relations of the object to other objects; the horizon of an act of consciousness configures the object of consciousness as having possible properties and relations beyond those explicitly presented in the act, properties compatible with the content or noematic sense of the act.

horizon, inner that part of the horizon of an object of consciousness which includes possible further properties of the object, such as the size or color of the back side of an object of vision.

horizon, outer that part of the horizon of an object of consciousness which includes possible further relations of the object to other objects, such as the relation of an object of vision to objects behind it, say, objects that are not currently visible.

human being (*Mensch*) a member of the human species, a psychophysical natural object, with a living body (*Leib*), falling under the region Nature.

hyle (*Hyle*) the sensory part of a perceptual experience; also called hyletic data, or sense data, or sensory data; for Husserl, the real, temporal part (moment) of a perceptual experience that involves sensation and is given meaning or sense by noesis; from the Greek "*hyle*," meaning "matter," thus the "matter" of perception, which gains "form" through noesis.

hyletic data (*hyleticsche Daten*) the data of sensation, such as seeing colors or shapes, also called "sensory data" or "sense data"; the manifold of hyletic or sensory data in a perception form the hyle in the perceptual experience, where the hyle are given sense by noesis.

I (*Ich*) a subject of consciousness; the pure I, abstracted from its embedment in nature and culture; sometimes translated as "ego," but Husserl usually uses just the first-person pronoun "*Ich*."

implicit sense a sense that concerns an object of consciousness but is only implicit, not explicit, in the intentional content of the relevant act of consciousness intending the object.

independence (*Selbständigkeit*) the condition where an object does not depend for its existence on the existence of some other object; literally "self-standing."

individual (*Individuum*) a particular object, which can have essences, that is, species, qualities, or relations.

Individual (*Individuum*) the formal category encompassing individuals; here capitalized when referring to the category, as opposed to objects falling under the category.

intention (*Intention, Meinen, Vermeinen*) an intentional act of consciousness, intending some object in some way.

intentional object an object as intended in an act of consciousness; Husserl occasionally uses this traditional term as equivalent with the noematic sense of an act, or the object as intended, distinguished from the object which is intended.

intentionality (*Intentionalität*) the directedness of consciousness toward an object; an act of consciousness is a consciousness of something, and in that sense it is intentional.

intentionality, secondary in time-consciousness, one's secondary
  consciousness of one's primary consciousness of some object;
  the act is thus primarily directed toward its object while secon-
  darily directed toward itself – this form of consciousness toward
  itself Husserl analyzes in the structure of time-consciousness.

intersubjectivity (*Intersubjektivität*) the interaction of different
  subjects in the surrounding world, especially in our collective
  "constitution" of objects in nature or in culture; alternatively,
  the availability of objects to different subjects, especially the
  property of being perceivable or knowable by different subjects
  in different forms of consciousness, for example where different
  subjects can see the same object from different perspectives.

introspection inner inspection of one's conscious experiences, a
  technique used in empirical psychology in the late 19th
  century; Husserl distinguished phenomenological reflection
  from classical introspection.

intuition (*Anschauung*) direct, self-evident experience; empirical
  intuition is sensory perception of things and events in space
  and time, eidetic intuition is comprehension of essences (especially as achieved by eidetic variation), phenomenological
  intuition is reflection on the structure or content of consciousness as lived or experienced from the first-person perspective
  (especially as practiced by bracketing or epoché).

intuitive fullness (*Fülle, Erfüllung*) the character of evidence, or
  self-evidence, with which an object is "itself" given in intuition, or "bodily present."

judgment (*Urteil*) an act of judging that such-and-such, positing
  the existence of the state of affairs judged; knowledge is formed
  when judgments are supported by intuitive evidence.

  Kantian ethics the ethical theory, propounded by Immanuel Kant,
  holding that an action is morally right or obligatory just in case
  it accords with the principle Kant called the categorical imperative, "Act only on that maxim by which you can at the same
  time will that it should become a universal law."

kinesthetic experience consciousness of one's own body (*Leib*) and
  one's volitional bodily movement; related to what psychologists
  call proprioception, or body-awareness.

language a system of signs or expressions, with a grammar and semantics and practice, such as English or German; also, a mathematically defined language such as that of geometry, calculus, etc.

Lebenswelt the life-world, the world of everyday life, the surrounding world as experienced in everyday life; the German term is itself now sometimes used in popular writing.

life-world (*Lebenswelt*) the surrounding world as experienced in everyday life, including "spiritual" or cultural, that is, social, activities.

logic the study of valid inference; for Husserl, logic also includes what has since been called semantics, studying correlations between expressions, their meanings, and the types of object expressions represent by virtue of their meanings.

logical positivism or **logical empiricism** a movement in 20th-century philosophy, centered in the Vienna Circle in the 1920s and 1930s, holding that all knowledge is based in sensory experience (positivism, empiricism) and is structured or expressed precisely in the language of modern logic (logical) – featuring Moritz Schlick, Rudolf Carnap, and others.

manifold (*Mannigfaltigkeit*) a structured many-ness, a complex structure consisting (we may say today) of a set of objects together with a set of relations that may hold among those objects; Husserl borrowed the term from non-Euclidean geometries, and logicians later called such a structure a model (following Tarski).

mathematization when Husserl worried about the "mathematization" of nature, he meant the ontological assumption that the essence of natural occurrences is identical with (and exhausted by) the mathematical structures used, for example, in mathematical physics to calculate forces, motions, etc.

mathesis universalis the ideal of a universal mathematical language or calculus, a formal language representing, according to Husserl, the formal categorial structures of the world; Husserl borrows the term from Leibniz, and the notion traces to early geometers.

meaning (*Bedeutung*) the meaning of an expression, a meaning expressible by an expression in a language; Husserl holds that an expression expresses as its meaning a sense that is the intentional content of an appropriate underlying act of consciousness, though sense may be modified through its expression as meaning.

metaethics that part of ethical theory which concerns the nature of ethics, the status of moral values, etc.

metalogic in mathematical logic, the theory of symbolic languages and their logical properties, including what can be proved, represented, etc., in a given symbolic language; the details of metalogic were developing in Husserl's day, for example, in the work of his colleague David Hilbert, but many of the most famous results were developed after Husserl's time.

metatheory the theory of theories (Husserl's idiom), which would include metalogic (in mathematical logic) but also, in Husserl's conception of pure logic, simply the philosophical theory of how theories (systems of propositions) represent things in the world, drawing on Husserl's theory of intentionality.

mind all types of mental or psychic states or activities, including conscious experiences and (if so theorized) unconscious mental states; the German term "*Geist*" has different meanings, as in *Zeitgeist*, and Husserl generally talks of "psychic" states or of consciousness.

modality (*Modalität*) **of being** a mode or way of being for an object, specifically possibility or necessity or impossibility or (in some ontologies) actuality, especially as these apply to states of affairs; in modal logic these modalities are represented by the modal operators or sentence-modifiers "possibly_" and "necessarily_"; Jaakko Hintikka developed a variety of modal logic that treats the sentence-modifiers "*a* believes that_," "*a* perceives that_," etc. as modal operators.

modality (*Modalität*) **of judgment** a mode or way of positing an object in an act of judgment, for example with belief, with doubt, with certainty, etc.

modalizing (*Modalizierung*) varying the modality of a judgment, say, as one acquires further evidence concerning what is judged or judged about.

moment (*Moment*) a dependent part of an object, that is, a part that cannot exist unless the object exists; thus, an object that depends on another object for its existence; specifically, what Aristotle called an "accident" of a substance, for example this whiteness in this white vase; what some recent philosophers have called a "trope."

motivation (*Motivation*) a relation of evidential support offering some degree of probability; one experience or belief motivates another just in case the former provides intuitive evidence for the probability of the existence of the object posited in the latter; for example where a perception motivates a judgment about the existence of a presented object or state of affairs.

motivated possibility (*motivierte Möglichkeit*) a possibility for an object of experience or judgment where that possibility is motivated or rendered appropriately probable by prior experience or by relevant background beliefs; for example, when I see a table, the possibility that it has ten legs is not a motivated possibility, whereas the possibility that it has four or three legs is a motivated possibility.

nature (*Natur*) the range of objects and events and properties that occur in space–time and have causal properties.

Nature (*Natur*) the material essence or region that encompasses objects and events and properties that occur in space–time and have causal properties, that is, the region of objects in nature; here the term is capitalized when referring to the region.

noema the ideal content of an act of consciousness, including (1) the noematic sense embodying the way the object is intended, for example as a particular object "X" having such-and-such properties or "predicates," and (2) the thetic character of the act, that is, whether perceiving, imagining, or judging, etc.

noematic quotation a technique of phenomenological bracketing; by "quoting" the noema of an act of consciousness, we turn our regard or attention from the object of consciousness (prescribed by the act's noema) to the noema "quoted" (which prescribes the object).

noematic sense the component or part of an act's noema which embodies the way ("how," or "*Wie*") the object is intended, that is, as thus-and-so, as a particular object ("X") bearing certain properties ("predicates").

noesis the real content of an act of consciousness, "in" which the ideal content or noema occurs or is realized; the noetic part or moment of an act of consciousness, the part that consists in the act's intending or presenting an object in some way, a part that occurs in time, as does the act itself.

norm (*Norm*) any value, in a sphere or domain of values.

object (*Gegenstand, Objekt*) any entity of any kind or category; Husserl sometimes speaks of "objectivity" (*Gegenständlichkeit*), covering any complex type of object; also, any object of consciousness.

objectivity (*Gegeständlichkeit* or *Objektivität*) the property of being an object, especially a potential object of consciousness; alternatively, the property of knowledge or judgment that is properly formed or grounded in evidence or intuition.

ontology (*Ontologie*) the theory of what there is, and perhaps the ways objects exist (for example in space–time or not).

other I (*anderes Ich*) another subject.

part (*Teil*) a part of some object; a dependent part or moment (*Moment*) of an object cannot exist apart from the object, as, for example, this white in that white object; an independent part or piece (*Stück*) of an object can exist apart from the object, as, for example, the wheel of a bicycle.

person (*Person*) an individual in a social or cultural community, subject to moral values, in the life-world.

phenomena (*Phänomene*) in common usage, whatever occurs; in the original Greek, appearances, or what appears to us; in Kant's philosophy, things as they appear, that is, as they appear to us, especially in our forms of cognition defining space and time; in Husserl's phenomenology, objects as we experience them, what we experience, "the things themselves" – thus, in a technical sense, the domain of study in phenomenology.

phenomenological psychology the study of acts of consciousness (per phenomenology) as realized in nature (per psychology).

phenomenology (*Phänomenologie*) the theory or study of consciousness as lived or experienced from the first-person perspective;

especially, focusing on pure consciousness and its characteristic intentionality, its structure in the stream of consciousness, etc.

philosophy of language the philosophical theory of language, addressing reference, sense, truth, speech acts, etc.

philosophy of mathematics the philosophical theory of the nature of mathematics and mathematical objects.

philosophy of mind the philosophical theory of the nature of mind; especially the tradition in analytic philosophy that addresses, in particular, approaches to the mind–body problem.

philosophy of science the philosophical theory of the structure, aims, and methods of the various sciences, especially the natural sciences of physics, chemistry, biology, and empirical psychology; for Husserl, in effect, the theory of sciences in the widest sense, including mathematics, logic, phenomenology, as well as the natural sciences.

piece (Stück) a part of an object that can exist independently of the object.

Platonism in ontology, the doctrine that ideal objects such as forms or essences or numbers are not spatiotemporal and can exist independently of concrete, spatiotemporal objects that instantiate them; in logical theory, Platonism holds that logic concerns ideal meanings, including propositions and concepts, and the relations between such meanings, notably relations where one proposition logically entails another proposition.

positivism (Positivismus) the doctrine, popular in 19th-century philosophy, holding that all knowledge is modeled on the empirical or "positive" sciences, especially physics, chemistry, etc.; logical positivism specified further that knowledge claims should be not only founded in sensory perception, according to empiricism and positivism, but also expressed in a logically precise language, such as the new logic of the late 19th and early 20th centuries, following Frege, Peano, Whitehead and Russell, et al.

practique (Praktik) the theory of practice; a formal theory, for Husserl, applicable to different ranges of practice, especially in the theory of values.

pre-predicative experience a form of experience prior to predication; especially, seeing an individual, on the basis of which

one may form a predicative judgment that the perceived object
has certain properties.

predicative experience an experience such as judgment in which
a property is predicated of an object, or a relation is predicated
of two or more objects.

primary impression in time-consciousness, the current phase of
perceptual experience, which consists in a sensory impression
(for example of the present tone in a melody) that is joined
with retentions (of just-past tones just heard) and protentions
(of anticipated just-about-to-be-heard tones).

(pro)position (*Satz*) Husserl uses the term "*Satz*" sometimes to
mean proposition (a form of sense or *Sinn*) and other times, in
one specialized use, to mean the position taken toward an
object in an act of consciousness; a proposition is the noematic
sense of an act of, say, judging that such-and-such, whereas a
position in this sense is the noematic thetic character of the act
plus the noematic sense.

proposition (*Satz*) the type of sense that serves as the content of
an act of thinking or judging that such-and-such; the same
term is also used for sentences in a language.

protention (*Protention*) in time-consciousness, the immediate
anticipation in current experience of the just-about-to-occur
phases of experience and of their objects; for example, in
hearing a melody, the protention of anticipated imminent tones
while hearing the current tone; counterpart of retention.

psyche the mind, especially taken as an aspect of an animate
organism in nature; for Husserl, the psyche is studied in
psychology, whereas pure consciousness is studied in
phenomenology.

psychologism the view that logic (and thus mathematics) is a
matter of empirical psychology, specifying how we happen to
reason.

pure consciousness consciousness in abstraction from its realization in nature and culture; the region of pure consciousness is
the proper domain of phenomenology.

pure ethics formed ethics, which governs substantive or material
ethics; a form of metaethics.

pure I (ego) (*reines Ich*) I, the subject of an act of consciousness, the enduring subject of the experiences in the unified stream of consciousness; the subject in abstraction from his or her body in nature and role in culture, thus restricted to the aspect (part or moment) of oneself as playing the role of subject of consciousness.

pure logic logic, or logical theory, restricted to the study of ideal meanings or senses and their logical powers; for Husserl, pure logic is the theory of theories, where a theory is an ideal system of propositions; specifically, for Husserl, pure logic studies the forms or categories of expressions, the forms or categories of meanings, the forms or categories of objects, and the logical (= semantic) correlations among expressions, meanings, and objects, for example the correlations among sentences, the propositions they express, and the states of affairs these propositions represent.

pure phenomenology transcendental phenomenology; opposed to phenomenological psychology; pure phenomenology studies pure consciousness, that is, acts of consciousness in abstraction from their realization in nature and culture; pure phenomenology is practiced by the method of bracketing.

rationalism the theory that knowledge is founded ultimately in reason, which confers all basic evidence on our knowledge claims, even justifying reliance on sensory perception.

reduction, ontological the ontological doctrine that one kind of object reduces to another, for example that mental events or conscious experiences reduce to, or are fundamentally identical with, physical events in a brain.

reduction, phenomenological (*Reduktion*) Husserl's technique for practicing phenomenological reflection on conscious experience: also called bracketing or epoché; sometimes called transcendental reduction.

region (*Region*) a material essence or domain of objects with a certain range of essences; Husserl recognizes three such regions, namely Nature, Consciousness, and Culture (*Geist*).

relativity theory the theory in physics, launched by Albert Einstein, which holds (roughly) that matter and energy are defined in a system of space–time so that the mass, velocity, etc. of material objects are relative to that framework.

retention (*Retention*) in time-consciousness, the retaining in current experience of the just-past phases of experience and of their objects; for example, in hearing a melody, the retention of just-heard past tones while hearing the current tone; counterpart of protention.

semantics that part of logic (or linguistics) that concerns meaning, including the roles of meanings in reference and truth; after Husserl's day, logical theory was divided into syntax, concerning the form of expressions, semantics, concerning the sense or meaning of expressions, and pragmatics, concerning the use of expressions.

sensation (*Empfindung*) the temporal (partial) experience of sensing colors, shapes, sounds, etc.; for Husserl, sensation is a dependent part (moment) of a perceptual experience, which is given sense in the noesis, also a dependent part of the perceptual experience.

sense (*Sinn*) the ideal intentional content of an act of consciousness, prescribing what is experienced as it is experienced; Husserl also refers to the sense in an act as "the object as intended," distinguished from the object which is intended.

sense data (*Sinnesdaten*) or **sensory data** (*Empfindungsdaten*) the data of sensation, such as seeing colors or shapes, also called "hyletic data"; for Husserl, the real, temporal part of a perceptual experience that involves sensation and is given meaning or sense by noesis.

skepticism the epistemological doctrine that we cannot know such-and-such for certain; at the extreme, holding that we can never know anything, that is, with certainty.

solipsism the ontological doctrine that there exists only one thing, the self or mind, so that all objects are merely ideas in my mind.

space (*Raum*) the realm of spatial relations among things in nature, described mathematically by an appropriate system of geometry.

species (*Spezies*) an ideal kind or type to which an object may belong.

state of affairs (*Sachverhalt*) a structured object consisting of an individual having a property or essence, or two or more individuals standing in a relation; literally, "things related"; for Husserl, a state of affairs is the type of object that serves as the object of a judgment, and is represented by a proposition (Satz), the type of sense that serves as the noematic sense of an act of judgment.

State of Affairs (Sachverhalt) the formal category encompassing states of affairs; here capitalized when referring to the category, as opposed to objects falling under the category.

stream of consciousness (Bewusstseinsstrom) or **stream of experience** (Erlebnisstrom) the temporally structured flow (stream) of experiences or acts of consciousness; the term originated with William James, whom Husserl had read.

subject (Subjekt) an I (ego), the subject of an act of consciousness, that is, the being or object who plays this role in consciousness, thus in the relation of intentionality; for Husserl, to be a subject is to play this role in intentionality, not to be a purely mental substance (per Descartes) or a thinking organism (per biology) or a political subject (per political theory).

subjectivity (Subjektivität) the property of consciousness where it is experienced or lived through or performed by a subject, an I.

substrate (Substrat) an object that bears properties or essences, and so plays the role of individual in states of affairs, but is not itself an essence or higher-order object; for Husserl, a formal category akin to Aristotle's category Primary Substance, whence species, qualities, and relations are predicated of substrates but substrates are not predicated of anything.

surrounding world (Umwelt) the world around me or us as experienced in everyday life; equivalent with the life-world (Lebenswelt).

syntax that part of logic which concerns the form of expressions in a given language.

syntactical objectivity a complex object, such as a state of affairs "syntactically" formed from simpler objects such as individuals and properties; Husserl thus uses the term "syntactic" to apply not only to the forms of expressions, but also to the forms of complex objects represented by complex expressions.

synthesis (Synthese) the form of "constitution" wherein objects of different types are intentionally put together or synthesized as objects of consciousness; for Husserl, both active and passive synthesis is at work in the "constitution" of a given type of object of consciousness – by contrast, for Kant, the understanding synthesizes the products of sensibility by applying concepts to form cognitions of objects, especially objects in space and/or time.

synthetic a proposition is synthetic if its truth is not determined by its meaning or conceptual content alone; for example, "the moon revolves around the Earth" is a synthetic proposition.

systematicity the way a theory or philosophy hangs together systematically, as its parts are interdependent; Husserl's philosophy hangs together in such a way, though he does not use this term explicitly.

theory (*Theorie*) for Hussserl, a theory is an ideal system of propositions that are connected by relations of logical consequence (in an ideally complete axiom system) and concern objects in a specified domain, that is, the domain of objects represented by concepts or propositions in the theory.

theory of science (*Wissenschaftslehre*) or **theory of theories** the theory of what counts as a theory (*Theorie*) or a proper science (*Wissenschaft*); for Husserl, pure logic is the theory of theories or of sciences.

thetic character (*thetischer Charakter*) or **positing character** (*Setzung-Charakter*) the ideal character of an act of consciousness including its species (perception, imagination, judgment, etc.) and modifications of certainty or probability, intuitive fullness, clarity, attentiveness, etc., thus including its character of "positionality" (*Positionalität*) or "position" (*Satz*, as distinct from propositional sense, also *Satz*), that is, the character of positing an object in the way appropriate to an act of perception or judgment or imagination, etc., and with appropriate modifications thereof; for Husserl, an act's noema divides fundamentally into a thetic character and a sense (*Sinn*).

thing (*Ding*) an object in space (and time), thus in nature.

time-consciousness (*Zeitbewusstsein*) consciousness of the flow of time.

time-consciousness, inner consciousness of the temporal flow of experiences in the stream of consciousness.

time-consciousness, outer or **objective** consciousness of the temporal flow of things or events in space–time, that is, in nature.

transcendence (*Transzendenz*) lying beyond complete knowledge or intention; for example, a physical thing can be perceived from only one side at a time, and so its full essence is transcendent – there is always more to come, further properties that could be known or intended in further experiences of the same object.

transcendental a philosophical term whose exact meaning varies; Husserl uses the term to apply to aspects of consciousness, pure consciousness in abstraction from its connection with natural or cultural objects or activities; Kant used the term in reference to the necessary conditions of the possibility of cognition; Medieval European philosophers used it for the most universal of properties, including being and unity.

transcendental idealism Husserl's doctrine that all objects are in principle objects of possible consciousness, capable in principle of being intended through some appropriate meanings or noemata, and in that way relative to consciousness; Kant introduced the term for his doctrine that space and time are forms of our cognition, whence objects in space and time are phenomenal rather than noumenal, and so are relative to our forms of cognition.

transcendental logic logic, or logical theory, that is grounded in transcendental phenomenology, specifically in the theory of intentionality; for Husserl, formal logic addresses only the formal structure of expressions in a language and relations of inference or consequence that depend on form alone, whereas transcendental logic addresses the sense or meaning of expressions in the language, specifically where these meanings are drawn from the contents of intentional acts of consciousness, and so (in today's terms) transcendental logic includes semantics based in the theory of intentionality.

transcendental phenomenology that type of phenomenology which stresses the pure or transcendental structure of consciousness, in abstraction from its realization in nature and culture; in his middle and later works, Husserl stressed the transcendental conception of phenomenology, especially where practiced by the method of bracketing or epoché.

transcendental philosophy for Husserl, philosophy grounded in transcendental phenomenology; Kant introduced the term to mean philosophy that seeks the necessary conditions of the possibility of knowledge.

transcendental reflection phenomenological reflection, especially as practiced through bracketing or epoché.

truth (*Wahrheit*) the correlation of a sentence or proposition or judgment to the world; specifically, for Husserl, a proposition is true just in case it represents an existing state of affairs.

truth definition in logic, a formal specification of the conditions of truth for syntactical forms of sentence in a given language; this mathematical semantic conception of truth was introduced by Alfred Tarski in the 1930s and has become a standard form for the basic semantics of a language.

Umwelt the surrounding world, as experienced in everyday life; Husserl used this term in early works for what he came to call the life-world (*Lebenswelt*).

utilitarianism the ethical theory holding that an action is morally right just in case it promotes the greatest utility, either the greatest balance of pleasure over pain or the greatest happiness or well-being.

value (*Wert*) any value in a given sphere or domain (for example aesthetic or moral values).

Value (*Wert*) here capitalized when referring to the ontological category that encompasses values of all kind: Husserl assumes a distinct formal essence or category for values.

ways of givenness (*Gegebenheitsweise*) the variety of thetic characters in an act of consciousness, for example perceptual or imaginative givenness, intuitive fullness, clarity, attentiveness, etc.

world (*Welt*) everything that is; for Husserl, the structure of the world would be elaborated in terms of formal essences or categories, applied to objects in material regions.

X or **the determinable X** a component of the noematic sense of an act of consciousness; the determinable X prescribes the object itself, in abstraction from all predicates or properties of the object as intended.

Bibliography

HUSSERL'S WORKS

Philosophy of Arithmetic: Psychological and Logical Investigations with Supplementary Texts from 1887–1901. Translated by Dallas Willard. Dordrecht and Boston, Massachusetts: Kluwer Academic Publishers (now New York: Springer). 2003.

Early Writings in the Philosophy of Logic and Mathematics. Translated by Dallas Willard. Dordrecht and Boston, Massachusetts: Kluwer Academic Publishers (now New York: Springer). 1994.

Logical Investigations, vols. 1 and 2. Translated by J. N. Findlay. Edited and revised by Dermot Moran. London and New York: Routledge. 2001. German original, first edition, 1900–1; second edition, 1913, 1920. English translation, first edition, 1970. 1900/2001.

On the Phenomenology of the Consciousness of Internal Time (1893–1917). Translated by John Barnett Brough. Dordrecht and Boston, Massachusetts: Kluwer Academic Publishers (now New York: Springer). 1991.

The Phenomenology of Internal Time-Consciousness. Edited by Martin Heidegger. Translated by James S. Churchill. Bloomington: Indiana University Press. 1966. A translation of a shorter selection of the texts translated in the preceding volume.

Thing and Space: Lectures of 1907. Translated and edited by Richard Rojcewicz. Dordrecht and Boston, Massachusetts: Kluwer Academic Publishers (now New York: Springer). 1997.

The Idea of Phenomenology. Translated by William P. Alston and George Nakhnikian. The Hague: Martinus Nijhoff. 1970. German original, from 1907 lectures, published 1950.

"Philosophy as Strict [or Rigorous] Science." In Edmund Husserl, *Phenomenology and the Crisis of Philosophy*. Translated with an introduction by Quentin Lauer. New York: Harper Torchbooks, Harper & Row. 1965. German original, "Philosophie als strenge Wissenschaft," *Logos* I (1910–11).

Vorlesungen über Ethik und Wertlehre: 1908–1914. (Lectures on Ethics and Value Theory: 1908–1914.) Edited by Ullrich Melle. 1909–14/1988. Dordrecht and Boston, Massachusetts: Kluwer Academic Publishers (now New York: Springer). 1988. No English translation.

Ideas Pertaining to a Pure Phenomenology and a Phenomenological Philosophy, First Book: General Introduction to Pure Phenomenology. Translated by Fred Kersten. Dordrecht and Boston, Massachusetts: Kluwer Academic Publishers (now New York: Springer). 1991. German original, 1913. Called *Ideas I*. 1913/1983.

Ideas [toward a Pure Phenomenology and Phenomenological Philosophy, First Book]: *General Introduction to Pure Phenomenology.* Translated by W. R. Boyce Gibson. London: George Allen & Unwin Ltd.; and New York: Humanities Press, Inc. 1969. First English edition, 1931. A prior translation of *Ideas I*. 1913/1969.

Ideas Pertaining to a Pure Phenomenology and to a Phenomenological Philosophy, Second Book: Studies in the Phenomenology of Constitution. Translated by Richard Rojcewicz and André Schuwer. Dordrecht and Boston, Massachusetts: Kluwer Academic Publishers (now New York: Springer). 1989. Original manuscript dating from 1912, posthumously published in German in 1952. Called *Ideas II*. 1912/1989.

Ideas Pertaining to a Pure Phenomenology and a Phenomenological Philosophy, Third Book: Phenomenology and the Foundations of the Sciences. Translated by Ted E. Dlein and William E..Pohl. The Hague and Boston, Massachusetts: Martinus Nijhoff Publishers. 1980. Original manuscript dating from 1912, posthumously published in German in 1971. Called *Ideas III*. 1912/1980.

(*Lectures on Ethics and Value Theory 1908–1914.*) *Vorlesungen über Ethik und Wertlehre 1908–1914.* 1988. Edited by Ulrich Melle. Dordrecht and Boston, Massachusetts: Kluwer Academic Publishers (now New York: Springer). 1988. No English translation.

Analyses Concerning Passive and Active Synthesis: Lectures on Transcendental Logic. Lectures from 1920–6. Translated by Anthony J. Steinbock. Dordrecht and Boston, Massachusetts: Kluwer Academic Publishers (now New York: Springer). 2001.

Phenomenological Psychology: Lectures, Summer Semester, 1925. Translated by John Scanlon. The Hague: Martinus Nijhoff (now New York: Springer). 1969. German original, 1929.

Formal and Transcendental Logic. Translated by Dorion Cairns. The Hague: Martinus Nijhoff (now New York: Springer). 1969. German original, 1929.

Cartesian Meditations: An Introduction to Phenomenology. Translated by Dorion Cairns. The Hague: Martinus Nijhoff (now New York: Springer). 1960. First published in French, 1931; first German edition, 1950. Original manuscript, in German, 1929.

Experience and Judgment: Investigations in a Genealogy of Logic. Revised and edited by Ludwig Landgrebe. 1948. Translated by James S. Churchill and Karl Ameriks.

Evanston, Illinois: Northwestern University Press, 1973. Originally published in 1939, the manuscript prepared by Landgrebe in collaboration with Husserl, from a variety of Husserl's manuscripts. 1939/1948/1973.

The Crisis of European Sciences and Transcendental Phenomenology: An Introduction to Phenomenological Philosophy. Translated by David Carr. Evanston, Illinois: Northwestern University Press. 1970. Original German manuscripts written 1935–8. German edition first published 1954. 1935–8/1970.

Intersubjektivität I. (On the Phenomenology of Intersubjectivity.) Zur Phänomenologie der Intersubjektivität, Erster Teil: 1905–20. Edited by Iso Kern. Husserliana, vol. 13. The Hague: Martinus Nijhoff. 1973. No English translation.

Intersubjektivität II. (On the Phenomenology of Intersubjectivity.) Zur Phänomenologie der Intersubjektivität, Zweiter Teil: 1921–8. Edited by Iso Kern. Husserliana, vol. 14. The Hague: Martinus Nijhoff. 1973. No English translation.

Intersubjektivität III. (On the Phenomenology of Intersubjectivity.) Zur Phänomenologie der Intersubjektivität, Dritter Teil: 1929–35. Edited by Iso Kern. Husserliana, vol. 15. The Hague: Martinus Nijhoff. 1973. No English translation.

STUDIES OF HUSSERL AND RELATED ISSUES

Armstrong, D. M. 1989. Universals: An Opinionated Introduction. Boulder, Colorado: Westview Press.

——. 1997. A World of States of Affairs. Cambridge and New York: Cambridge University Press.

——. 1999. The Mind–Body Problem: An Opinionated Introduction. Boulder, Colorado: Westview Press.

Beaney, Michael, ed. 1997. The Frege Reader. Oxford and Malden, Massachusetts: Blackwell.

Beauvoir, Simone de. 1949/1952. The Second Sex. Translated and edited by H. M. Parshley. New York: Vintage Books, Random House. French original, 1949.

Bell, David A. 1990. Husserl. London and New York: Routledge.

Bernet, Rudolf, Iso Kern, and Eduard Marbach, eds. 1989/1993. An Introduction to Husserlian Phenomenology. Evanston, Illinois: Northwestern University Press. Third paperback printing, 1999. Translation of the German original, Edmund Husserl: Darstellung seines Denkens, Hamburg: Felix Meiner Verlag, 1989.

Beyer, Christian. 2004. "Edmund Husserl." In The Stanford Encyclopedia of Philosophy (2004 edition), Edward N. Zalta, ed. URL = http://plato.stanford.edu/entries/husserl/.

Block, Ned, Owen Flanagan, and Güven Güzeldere, eds. 1997. The Nature of Cosnciousness: Philosophical Debates. Cambridge, Massachusetts: MIT Press.

Bolzano, Bernard. 1837/1972. *Theory of Science: Attempt at a Detailed and in the Main Novel Exposition of Logic with Constant Attention to Earlier Authors.* Edited and translated by Rolf George. Berkeley and Los Angeles: University of California Press, 1972. A partial translation of Bolzano's *Wissenschaftslehre*; original German, 1837.

Brentano, Franz. 1874/1995. *Psychology from an Empirical Standpoint.* Translated by A. C. Rancurello, D. B. Terrell, and L. L. McAlister. London and New York: Routledge. English translation first published 1974. German original, 1874.

Bruzina, Ronald. 2004. *Edmund Husserl and Eugen Fink: Beginnings and Ends in Phenomenology, 1928–1938.* New Haven, Connecticut, and London: Yale University Press.

Burge, Tyler. 2005. *Truth, Thought, Reason: Essays on Frege.* Oxford: Clarendon Press.

Carnap, Rudolf. 1928/2003. *The Logical Structure of the World and Pseudoproblems in Philosophy.* Translated by Rolf A. George. Chicago and La Salle, Illinois: Open Court. From the German original, *Der Logische Aufbau der Welt*, 1928, known as the *Aufbau*.

Casebier, Allan. 1991. *Film and Phenomenology: Toward a Realist Theory of Cinematic Representation.* Cambridge and New York: Cambridge University Press.

Chalmers, David J. 2002. *Philosophy of Mind: Classical and Contemporary Readings.* Oxford and New York: Oxford University Press.

Churchland, Paul M. 1988. *Matter and Consciousness.* Revised edition. Cambridge, Massachusetts: MIT Press.

Cobb-Stevens, Richard. 1990. *Husserl and Analytic Philosophy.* Dordrecht and Boston, Massachusetts: Kluwer Academic Publishers (now New York: Springer).

Coffa, J. Alberto. 1991. *The Semantic Tradition from Kant to Carnap: To the Vienna Station.* Edited by Linda Wessels. Cambridge and New York: Cambridge University Press.

Crowell, Steven Galt. 2001. *Husserl, Heidegger, and the Space of Meaning: Paths Toward Transcendental Phenomenology.* Evanston, Illinois: Northwestern University Press.

Davidson, Donald. 2001. *Subjective, Intersubjective, Objective.* Oxford and New York: Oxford University Press.

Dreyfus, Hubert L., ed. 1982. *Husserl, Intentionality and Cognitive Science.* In collaboration with Harrison Hall. Cambridge, Massachusetts: MIT Press.

——. 1991. *Being-in-the-World: A commentary on Heidegger's Being and Time, Division I.* Cambridge, Massachusetts: MIT Press.

Drummond, John J. 1990. *Husserlian Intentionality and Non-Foundational Realism: Noema and Object.* Dordrecht and Boston, Massachusetts: Kluwer Academic Publishers (now New York: Springer).

——. 1992. "An Abstract Consideration: De-Ontologizing the Noema." In John J. Drummond and Lester Embree, eds. *The Phenomenology of the Noema.* Dordrecht and Boston, Massachusetts: Kluwer Academic Publishers (now New York: Springer).

——. 1997. "Noema." In Lester Embree, Elizabeth A. Behnke, David Carr, J. Claude Evans, José Huertas-Jourda, Joseph J. Kokelmans, William R. McKenna, Algis Mickunas, Jitendra Nath Mohanty, Thomas M. Seebohm, and Richard M. Zaner, eds. *Encyclopedia of Phenomenology*. Dordrecht and Boston, Massachusetts: Kluwer Academic Publishers (now New York: Springer).

——. 2001. "Ethics." In Steven Crowell, Lester Embree, and Samuel J. Julian, eds. *The Reach of Reflection: Issues for Phenomenology's Second Century*. Center for Advanced Research in Phenomenology, Inc. Electronically published at www.electronpress.com.

Drummond, John J., and Lester Embree, eds. 1992. *The Phenomenology of the Noema*. Dordrecht and Boston, Massachusetts: Kluwer Academic Publishers (now New York: Springer).

——, eds. 2002. *Phenomenological Approaches to Moral Philosophy: A Handbook*. Dordrecht and Boston, Massachusetts: Kluwer Academic Publishers (now New York: Springer).

Dummett, Michael. 1993. *Origins of Analytical Philosophy*. Cambridge, Massachusetts: Harvard University Press.

Embree, Lester, ed. 2004. *Gurwitsch's Relevancy for Cognitive Science*. Dordrecht and New York: Springer.

Embree, Lester, Elizabeth A. Behnke, David Carr, J. Claude Evans, José Huertas-Jourda, Joseph J. Kokelmans, William R. McKenna, Algis Mickunas, Jitendra Nath Mohanty, Thomas M. Seebohm, and Richard M. Zaner, eds. 1997. *Encyclopedia of Phenomenology*. Dordrecht and Boston, Massachusetts: Kluwer Academic Publishers (now New York: Springer).

Findlay, J. N. 1963. *Meinong's Theory of Objects and Values*. Oxford: Oxford University Press.

Fine, Kit. 1995. "Part–whole." In B. Smith and D. W. Smith, eds. *The Cambridge Companion to Husserl*. Cambridge and New York: Cambridge University Press.

Fink, Eugen. 1988/1995. *Sixth Cartesian Meditation: the Idea of a Transcendental Theory of Method*. With Textual Notations by Edmund Husserl. Translated with an introduction by Ronald Bruzina. German original, 1988, from a manuscript written by Fink sometime in the early 1930s.

Fisette, Denis. 2003. *Husserl's Logical Investigations Reconsidered*. Dordrecht and Boston, Massachusetts: Kluwer Academic Publishers (now New York: Springer).

Føllesdal, Dagfinn. 1969/1982. "Husserl's Notion of Noema." In Hubert L. Dreyfus, ed. *Husserl, Intentionality and Cognitive Science*. In collaboration with Harrison Hall. Cambridge, Massachusetts: MIT Press. Reprinted from *The Journal of Philosophy*, 1969.

——. 1998. "Husserl's Idealism." In Mercelo Stamm, ed. *Philosophie in synthetischer Absicht. Synthesis in Mind. (Festschrift for Dieter Henrich)*. Stuttgart: Klett-Cotta.

Frege, Gottlob. 1892/1997. "On Sinn and Bedeutung." In Michael Beaney, ed. *The Frege Reader*. Oxford and Malden, Massachusetts: Blackwell. 1997. German original, 1892. Key terms sometimes translated as: sense (*Sinn*) and reference (*Bedeutung*).

Friedman, Michael. 1999. *Reconsidering Logical Positivism*. Cambridge and New York: Cambridge University Press.

——. 2001. *Dynamics of Reason*. Stanford, California: CSLI Publications.

Grattan-Guinness, I., ed. 1994. *Companion Encyclopedia of the History and Philosophy of the Mathematical Sciences*, vols. 1 and 2. Baltimore, Maryland, and London: The Johns Hopkins University Press.

Gurwitsch, Aron. 1964. *The Field of Consciousness*. Pittsburgh: Duquesne University Press.

——. 1985. *Marginal Consciousness*. Edited by Lester Embree. Athens, Ohio: Ohio University Press.

Hegel, G. W. F. 1807/1977. *Phenomenology of Spirit*. Translated by A. V. Miller. Oxford and New York: Oxford University Press.

Heidegger, Martin. 1927/1962. *Being and Time*. Translated by John Macquarrie and Edward Robinson. New York: Harper & Row. German original, 1927.

——. 1927/1982. *The Basic Problems of Phenomenology*. Translated by Albert Hofstadter. Bloomington: Indiana University Press. 1982. Written in 1927; first published in German, 1975.

Hill, Claire Ortiz. 2002. "Tackling Three of Frege's Problems: Edmund Husserl on Sets and Manifolds". *Axiomathes* 13: 79–104, 2002.

Hill, Clair Ortiz, and Guillermo E. Rosado Haddock. 2000. *Husserl or Frege? Meaning, Objectivity, and Mathematics*. Chicago and LaSalle, Illinois: Open Court.

Hintikka, Jaakko. 1962. *Knowledge and Belief*. Ithaca, New York: Cornell University Press.

——. 1969. *Models for Modalities*. Dodrecht and Boston, Massachusetts: D. Reidel Publishing Company (now New York: Springer).

——. 1975. *The Intentions of Intentionality*. Dordrecht and Boston, Massachusetts: D. Reidel Publishing Company (now New York: Springer).

Hyder, David. 2002. *The Mechanics of Meaning*. Berlin: Walter de Gruyter GmbH & Co.

Ingarden, Roman. 1961/1989. *The Ontology of the Work of Art*. Translated by Raymond Meyer with John T. Goldthwait. Athens, Ohio: Ohio University Press. German original, 1961.

——. 1965/1973. *The Literary Work of Art: An Investigation on the Borderlines of Ontology, Logic, and Theory of Literature*. Translated by George G. Grabowics.

Evanston, Illinois: Northwestern University Press. German original, third edition, 1965.

———. 1975. *On the Motives which Led Husserl to Transcendental Idealism.* Translated from the Polish by A. Hannibalsson. The Hague: Martinus Nijhoff.

James, Aaron. Forthcoming. "Constructivism about Practical Reasons." *Philosophy and Phenomenological Research.*

James, William. 1891/1981. *The Principles of Psychology.* Introduction by George A. Miller. Cambridge, Massachusetts: Harvard University Press. Revised edition, 1981. First published 1891.

Kant, Immanuel. 1781/1787. *Critique of Pure Reason.* Translated and edited by Paul Guyer and Allen W. Wood. Cambridge and New York: Cambridge University Press. 1997. German original, first edition, 1781, second edition, 1787.

———. 1785/1959. *Foundations of the Metaphysics of Morals.* Translated by Lewis White Beck. New York: The Library of Liberal Arts, Bobbs-Merrill Company, Inc. German original, *Grundlegung zur Metaphysik der Sitten,* 1785.

Kaplan, David. 1989. *Themes from Kaplan.* Edited by Joseph Almog, John Perry, and Howard Wettstein, with the Assistance of Ingrid Deiwiks and Edward N. Zalta. Oxford and New York: Oxford University Press.

Kim, Jaegwon. 2000. *Mind in a Physical World.* Cambridge, Massachusetts: MIT Press.

Korsgaard, Christine M. 1996. *The Sources of Normativity.* Edited by Onora O'Neill. Cambridge and New York: Cambridge University Press.

Livingston, Paul. 2004. *Philosophical History and the Problem of Consciousness.* Cambridge and New York: Cambridge University Press.

Lynch, Michael P., ed. 2001. *The Nature of Truth: Classic and Contemporary Perspectives.* Cambridge, Massachusetts: MIT Press.

Mandelbaum, Maurice. 1955. *The Phenomenology of Moral Experience.* Glencoe, Illinois: The Free Press.

Martin, Wayne M. 1997. *Idealism and Objectivity: Understanding Fichte's Jena Project.* Stanford, California: Stanford University Press.

Meinong, Alexius. 1904/1960. "The Theory of Objects." Translated by Isaac Levi, D. B. Terrell, and Roderick M. Chisholm. In Roderick M. Chisholm, ed. *Realism and the Background of Phenomenology.* New York: The Free Press. 1960. German original, 1904.

Melle, Ulrich. 2002. "Edmund Husserl: From Reason to Love." In John J. Drummond and Lester Embree, eds. *Phenomenological Approaches to Moral Philosophy: A Handbook.* Dordrecht and Boston, Massachusetts: Kluwer Academic Publishers (now New York: Springer).

Mensch, James Richard. 2003. *Ethics and Selfhood: Alterity and the Phenomenology of Obligation.* Albany, New York: State University of New York Press.

Merleau-Ponty, Maurice. 1945/2003. *Phenomenology of Perception.* Translated by Colin Smith. London and New York: Routledge. 2003. First English edition, 1962; French original, 1945.

Mohanty, J. N. 1964. *Husserl's Theory of Meaning.* The Hague: Martinus Nijhoff.

———. 1972. *The Concept of Intentionality.* St. Louis, Missouri: Warren H. Green, Inc.

———. 1982. *Husserl and Frege.* Bloomington: Indiana University Press.

———. 1989. *Transcendental Phenomenology: An Analytic Account.* Oxford and Cambridge, Massachusetts: Basil Blackwell.

———. 1995. "The Development of Husserl's Thought." In B. Smith and D. W. Smith, eds. *The Cambridge Companion to Husserl.* Cambridge and New York: Cambridge University Press.

Moran, Dermot. 2000. *Introduction to Phenomenology.* London and New York: Routledge.

———. 2005. *Edmund Husserl: Founder of Phenomenology.* Cambridge and Malden, Massachusetts: Polity Press.

Mulligan, Kevin. 1990. "Husserl on States of Affairs in the Logical Investigations". Epistemologia, special number on Logica e Ontologia, XII, 207 234, (Proceedings of 1987 Genoa conference on Logic and Ontology).

———. 1995. "Perception". In B. Smith and D. W. Smith, editors, *The Cambridge Companion to Husserl* Cambridge and New York: Cambridge University Press, pp. 168-238.

———. 2004. "Essence and Modality. The Quintessence of Husserl's Theory". In M. Siebel and M. Textor, editors, Semantik und Ontologie. Beiträge zur philosophischen Forschung. Frankfurt: Ontos Verlag, 387-418. http://www.unige.ch/lettres/philo/enseignants/km/doc/EssenceModalityQuintessence.pdf

———. 2004. "Husserl on the 'logics' of valuing, values and norms". In B. Centi and G. Gigliotti, editors. Fenomenologia della Ragion Pratica. L'Etica di Edmund Husserl, 177-225. Naples: Bibliopolis.

Mulligan, K.; Simons, P. M.; and Smith, B. 1984. "Truth-Makers". In *Philosophy and Phenomenological Research* 44, 278–321.

Nagel, Thomas. 1974. "What Is It Like to Be a Bat?" In David J. Chalmers, ed. *Philosophy of Mind: Classical and Contemporary Readings.* Oxford and New York: Oxford University Press. First published 1974.

Nelson, Alan, ed. 2005. *A Companion to Rationalism.* Oxford: Blackwell Publishing.

Nietzsche, Friedrich. 1887/1998. *On the Genealogy of Morality.* Translated by Maudemarie Clark and Alan J. Swensen. Indianapolis and Cambridge: Hackett Publishing Company, Inc. Original German edition, 1887.

Olafson, Frederick A. 1967. *Principles and Persons: An Ethical Interpretation of Existentialism.* Baltimore, Maryland: Johns Hopkins Press.

Parsons, Terence. 1980. *Nonexistent Objects.* New Haven, Connecticut, and London: Yale University Press.

Petitot, Jean, Francisco J. Varela, Bernard Pachoud, and Jean-Michel Roy, eds. 1999. *Naturalizing Phenomenology: Issues in Contemporary Phenomenology and Cognitive Science*. Stanford, California: Stanford University Press. In collaboration with Cambridge University Press, Cambridge and New York.

Philipse, Herman. 1995. "Transcendental Idealism." In B. Smith and D. W. Smith, eds. *The Cambridge Companion to Husserl*. Cambridge and New York: Cambridge University Press.

Proust, Marcel. 1927/1999. *In Search of Lost Time*, vol. VI. *Time Regained*. Translated by Andreas Mayor and Terence Kilmartin. Revised by D. J. Enright. New York: The Modern Library. 1999. French original, *A La Recherche du temps perdu. Temps retrouvé*, 1927.

Putnam, Hilary. 1981. *Reason, Truth and History*. Cambridge and New York: Cambridge University Press.

——. 1987. *The Many Faces of Realism*. LaSalle, Illinois: Open Court.

Rawls, John. 1971/1999. *A Theory of Justice: Revised Edition*. Cambridge, Massachusetts: Harvard University Press. Revised edition of the 1971 edition.

——. 2000. *Lectures on the History of Moral Philosophy*. Edited by Barbara Herman. Cambridge, Massachusetts: Harvard University Press.

——. 2001. *Justice as Fairness: A Restatement*. Edited by Erin Kelly. Cambridge, Massachusetts: Harvard University Press.

Reicher, M. E., and J. C. Marek, eds. 2005. *Experience and Analysis. Erfahrung und Analyse. The Proceedings of the 27th International Wittgenstein Symposium*. Vienna: öbv a hpt.

Richardson, Alan W. 1998. *Carnap's Construction of the World: The Aufbau and the Emergence of Logical Empiricism*. Cambridge and New York: Cambridge University Press.

Roy, Jean-Michel. 2004. "Carnap's Husserlian Reading of the *Aufbau*." In Steve Awodey and Carsten Klein, eds. *Carnap Brought Home: The View from Jena*. Chicago and LaSalle, Illinois: Open Court.

Ryckman, Thomas. 2005. *The Reign of Relativity: Philosophy in Physics 1915–1925*. Oxford and New York: Oxford University Press.

——. 2006. "Husserl and Carnap." In Richard Creath and Michael Friedman, eds. *The Cambridge Companion to Carnap*. Cambridge and New York: Cambridge University Press.

Ryle, Gilbert. 1949. *The Concept of Mind*. New York: Barnes and Noble.

Sartre, Jean-Paul. 1938/1964. *Nausea*. New York: New Directions Publishing Corporation. 1964. French original, *La Nausée*, 1938.

——. 1943/1956. *Being and Nothingness*. Translated by Hazel E. Barnes. New York: Washington Square Press (a division of Simon and Schuster). French original, 1943. Paperback edition, 1992.

———. 1945/1956. "Existentialism Is a Humanism." In Walter Kaufmann, ed. *Existentialism from Dostoevsky to Sartre.* New York: New American Library (Times Mirror), 1975 edition.

Scanlon, T. M.. 1998. *What We Owe to Each Other.* Cambridge, Massachusetts: Harvard University Press.

———. 2005. "Constructivism: What? And Why?" Text of a lecture. Manuscript draft.

Schneewind, J. B. 1998. *The Invention of Autonomy: A History of Modern Moral Philosophy.* Cambridge and New York: Cambridge University Press.

Searle, John R. 1983. *Intentionality.* Cambridge and New York: Cambridge University Press.

———. 1995. *The Construction of Social Reality.* New York: The Free Press.

———. 1998. *Mind, Language and Society: Philosophy in the Real World.* New York: Basic Books.

———. 2004. *Mind: A Brief Introduction.* Oxford and New York: Oxford University Press.

Sellars, Wilfrid. 1956/2000. *Empiricism and the Philosophy of Mind.* Cambridge, Massachusetts: Harvard University Press. 2000. With a Study Guide by Robert Brandom. The title essay was first published in 1956 in Minnesota Studies in Philosophy of Science, vol. 1.

Siewert, Charles. 1998. *The Significance of Consciousness.* Princeton: Princeton University Press.

Simons, Peter. 1987. *Parts: A Study in Ontology.* Oxford: Oxford University Press.

———. 1992a. *Philosophy and Logic in Central Europe from Bolzano to Tarski.* Dordrecht and Boston: Kluwer Academic Publishers.

———. 1992b. "Logical Atomism and its Ontological Refinement: A Defense". In Mulligan, Kevin. editor. *Language, Truth and Ontology.* Dordrecht and Boston: Kluwer Academic Publishers, 1992, pp. 157–179.

———. 1995. "Meaning and Language." In Barry Smith and David Woodruff Smith, eds. *The Cambridge Companion to Husserl.* Cambridge and New York: Cambridge University Press.

Smith, A. D. 2003. *Husserl and the Cartesian Meditations.* (Series: Routledge Guidebook to Philosophy). London and New York: Routledge.

Smith, Barry, ed. 1982. *Parts and Moments: Studies in Logic and Formal Ontology.* Munich and Vienna: Philosophia Verlag.

———. 1994. *Austrian Philosophy: The Legacy of Franz Brentano.* Chicago and LaSalle, Illinois: Open Court.

———. 1996. "Logic and the Sachverhalt". In Liliana Albertazzi, Massimo Libardi, and Roberto Poli, editors. *The School of Franz Brentano.* Dordrecht: Kluwer Academic Publishers.

Smith, Barry, and David Woodruff Smith, eds. 1995. *The Cambridge Companion to Husserl*. Cambridge and New York: Cambridge University Press.

Smith, David Woodruff. 1970. *Intentionality, Noemata, and Individuation: The Role of Individuation in Husserl's Theory of Intentionality*. Doctoral dissertation: Stanford University, Stanford, California.

———. 1975. "Meinongian Objects." *Grazer Philosophische Studien*, vol. 1 (1975).

———. 1986. "Mind and Guise: Castañeda's Philosophy of Mind in the World Order." In James E. Tomberlin, ed. *Hector-Neri Castañeda*. Dordrecht and Boston, Massachusetts: D. Reidel Publishing Company (now New York: Springer).

———. 1989. *The Circle of Acquaintance: Perception, Consciousness, and Empathy*. Dordrecht and Boston, Massachusetts: Kluwer Academic Publishers (now New York: Springer).

———. 1995. "Mind and Body." In B. Smith and D. W. Smith, eds. *The Cambridge Companion to Husserl*. Cambridge and New York: Cambridge University Press.

———. 2002. "Intentionality and Picturing: Early Husserl *vis-à-vis* Early Wittgenstein." In Terry Horgan, John Tienson, and Matjaz Potrc, eds. *Origins: The Common Sources of the Analytic and Phenomenological Traditions* (proceedings of the Spindel Conference 2001). *Southern Journal of Philosophy*, vol. XL, supplement 2002; published by the Department of Philosophy, the University of Memphis.

———. 2003. "Phenomenology." In *The Stanford Encyclopedia of Philosophy* (Winter 2003 edition), Edward N. Zalta, ed. URL = http://plato.stanford.edu/archives/win2003/entries/phenomenology/.

———. 2003a. "Phenomenology." *Encyclopedia of Cognitive Science*. London: Nature Publishing Group, Reference, Macmillan Reference Ltd. URL = www.natur-ereference.com, www.nature.com, 2003. On CD. vol. 3.

———. 2004. *Mind World: Essays in Phenomenology and Ontology*. Cambridge and New York: Cambridge University Press.

———. 2004a. "The Structure of Context and Context-Awareness." In Lester Embree, ed. *Gurwitsch's Relevancy for Cognitive Science*. Dordrecht and New York: Springer.

———. 2005. "Truth and Experience: Tarski vis-à-vis Husserl." In M. E. Reicher and J. C. Marek, eds. *Experience and Analysis. Erfahrung und Analyse. The Proceedings of the 27th International Wittgenstein Symposium*. Vienna: öbv a hpt.

———. 2005a. "Rationalism in the Phenomenological Tradition." In Alan Nelson, ed. *A Companion to Rationalism*. Oxford: Blackwell.

Smith, David Woodruff, and Ronald McIntyre. 1971. "Intentionality via Intensions." *Journal of Philosophy*, vol. LXVIII, no. 18 (September 16), pp. 541–61.

——. 1982. *Husserl and Intentionality: A Study of Mind, Meaning, and Language.* Dordrecht and Boston, Massachusetts: D. Reidel Publishing Company (now New York: Springer).

Smith, David Woodruff, and Amie L. Thomasson, eds. 2005. *Phenomenology and Philosophy of Mind.* Oxford and New York: Oxford University Press.

Sokolowski, Robert. 2000. *Introduction to Phenomenology.* Cambridge and New York: Cambridge University Press.

Spiegelberg, Herbert. 1965. *The Phenomenological Movement: A Historical Introduction.* Second edition. Vols. 1 and 2. The Hague: Martinus Nijhoff.

Stein, Edith. 1916/1989. *On the Problem of Empathy.* Translated by Waltraut Stein. Washington, D.C.: ICS Publications. 1989. Prior edition of English translation, the Hague and Boston, Massachusetts: Martinus Nijhoff, 1970. German original, *Zum Problem der Einfühlung.* Doctoral dissertation, directed by Husserl, Freiburg-im-Brausgau, 1916.

Tarski, Alfred. 1933/1983. "The Concept of Truth in Formalized Languages." In *Logic, Semantics, Metamathematics.* Second edition. Translated by J. H. Woodger. Indianapolis: Hackett. From the German of 1936, from the original Polish of 1933.

——. 1944/2001. "The Semantic Conception of Truth and the Foundations of Semantics." In Michael P. Lynch, ed. *The Nature of Truth.* Cambridge, Massachusetts: MIT Press. 2001. Reprinted from *Philosophy and Phenomenological Research* 4 (1944).

Thomasson, Amie L. 1998. *Fiction and Metaphysics.* Cambridge and New York: Cambridge University Press.

——. 2005. "First-Person Knowledge in Phenomenology." In David Woodruff Smith and Amie L. Thomasson, eds. *Phenomenology and Philosophy of Mind.* Oxford and New York: Oxford University Press.

Tieszen, Richard. 2004. "Husserl's Logic." In Dov M. Gabbay and John Woods, eds. *Handbook of the History of Logic,* vol. 3. Amsterdam and Boston, Massachusetts: Elsevier BV.

——. 2005. *Phenomenology, Logic, and the Philosophy of Mathematics.* Cambridge and New York: Cambridge University Press.

Tomberlin, James E., ed. 1986. *Hector-Neri Castañeda.* Dordrecht and Boston, Massachusetts: D. Reidel Publishing Company (now New York: Springer).

Tragesser, Robert S. 1977. *Phenomenology and Logic.* Ithaca, New York: Cornell University Press.

Twardowski, Kasimir. 1894/1977. *On the Content and Object of Presentations.* Translated by Reinhardt Grosmann. The Hague: Martinus Nijhoff. 1977. German original, 1894.

Welton, Donn. 2000. *The Other Husserl: The Horizons of Transcendental Phenomenology.* Bloomington: Indiana University Press.

———, ed. 2003. *The New Husserl: A Critical Reader.* Bloomington: Indiana University Press.

Willard, Dallas. 1984. *Logic and the Objectivity of Knowledge.* Athens, Ohio: Ohio University Press.

———. 1995. "Knowledge." In B. Smith and D. W. Smith, eds. *The Cambridge Companion to Husserl.* Cambridge and New York: Cambridge University Press.

Willard, Dallas, and Barry Smith. 1997. "British Moral Theory." In Lester Embree, Elizabeth A. Behnke, David Carr, J. Claude Evans, José Huertas-Jourda, Joseph J. Kokelmans, William R. McKenna, Algis Mickunas, Jitendra Nath Mohanty, Thomas M. Seebohm, and Richard M. Zaner, eds. *Encyclopedia of Phenomenology.* Dordrecht and Boston, Massachusetts: Kluwer Academic Publishers (now New York: Springer).

Wittgenstein, Ludwig. 1921/1961. *Tractatus Logico-Philosophicus.* Translated by D. F. Pears and B. F. McGuinness. Atlantic Highlands, New Jersey: Humanities Press. 1992. London: Routledge & Kegan Paul, 1961, 1974. German original, *Logisch-Philosophische Abhandlung,* 1921. First English translation, by C. K. Ogden, 1922.

———. 1933/2005. *The Big Typescript TS 213.* Edited and translated by C. Grant Luckhardt and Maximilian A. E. Aue. Oxford and Malden, Massachusetts: Blackwell Publishing. German typescript, 1933; revised through 1937.

———. 1949–51/1972. *On Certainty.* Edited by G. E. M. Anscombe and G. H. von Wright. Translated by Denis Paul and G. E. M. Anscombe. New York: Harper Torchbooks, Harper & Row. First published by Basil Blackwell, 1969, from notebooks written in German during 1949–51.

———. 1953/2001. *Philosophical Investigations/Philosophische Untersuchungen.* Translated by G. E. M. Anscombe. Third edition. Oxford and Malden, Massachusetts: Blackwell Publishing. Original edition, with original German facing the English translation, first published in 1953.

Yoshimi, Jeffrey. 2004. "Field Theories of Mind and Brain." In Lester Embree, ed. *Gurwitsch's Relevancy for Cognitive Science.* Dordrecht and New York: Springer.

Zahavi, Dan. 1999. *Self-Awareness and Alterity: A Phenomenological Investigation.* Evanston, Illinois: Northwestern University Press.

———. 2001. "Phenomenology and the Problem(s) of Intersubjectivity." In Steven Crowell, Lester Embree, and Samuel J. Julian, eds. *The Reach of Reflection: Issues for Phenomenology's Second Century.* Center for Advanced Research in Phenomenology, Inc. Electronically published at www.electronpress.com.

———. 2003. *Husserl's Phenomenology.* Stanford, California: Stanford University Press.

———. 2003a. "Husserl's Intersubjective Transformation of Transcendental Phenomenology." In Donn Welton, ed. *The New Husserl: A Critical Reader.* Bloomington: Indiana University Press.

———. 2005. *Subjectivity and Selfhood*. Cambridge, Massachusetts: MIT Press.

Zahavi, Dan, and Frederik Stjernfelt, eds. 2002. *One Hundred Years of Phenomenology: Husserl's* Logical Investigations *Revisited*. Dordrecht and Boston, Massachusetts: Kluwer Academic Publishers (now New York: Springer).

RELATED TITLES FROM ROUTLEDGE

The Movement of Phenomenology
Simon Glendinning

Phenomenology is one of the twentieth century's most important philosophical movements. It is also attracting renewed interest from philosophers working within the 'analytic' tradition, often thought to be at odds with phenomenology.

In this bold and controversial book, Simon Glendinning explores some fundamental questions about phenomenology that are frequently overlooked. To what extent is phenomenology a coherent school? If it shares some methods and problems with analytic philosophy and continental philosophy, what makes it philosophically distinctive? Should phenomenology be considered in the larger context of 'post-Kantian' philosophy?

Beginning with an exploration of what it might mean to 'do phenomenology', Glendinning explores the phenomenologies of Husserl, Heidegger, Sartre, Merleau-Ponty, Levinas and Derrida, considering important topics such as ontology, existentialism, perception and the other.

He argues that we should consider phenomenologically informed philosophy apart from the history of the phenomenological movement itself, and argues that the main dividing line within philosophy now lies not between analytic and continental but scientific and conceptual.

Clearly and engagingly written, *The Movement of Phenomenology* is essential reading for students of phenomenology and contemporary philosophy.

ISBN 10: 0-415-22337-7 (hbk)
ISBN 10: 0-415-22338-5 (pbk)
ISBN 13: 978-0-415-22337-9 (hbk)
ISBN 13: 978-0-415-22338-6 (pbk)

Available at all good bookshops
For ordering and further information please visit:
www.routledge.com

Logical Investigations Volume 1 & 2
Edmund Husserl

Edmund Husserl is the founder of phenomenology and the *Logical Investigations* is his most famous work. It had a decisive impact on twentieth century philosophy and is one of few works to have influenced both continental and analytic philosophy.

This is the first time both volumes have been available in paperback. They include a new introduction by Dermot Moran, placing the *Investigations* in historical context and bringing out their contemporary philosophical importance.

These editions include a new preface by Sir Michael Dummett.

Volume 1 Pb: 0-415-24189-8 ISBN-13: 978-0-415-24189-2
Volume 2 Pb: 0-415-24190-1 ISBN-13: 978-0-415-24190-8

Available at all good bookshops
For ordering and further information please visit:
www.routledge.com

Routledge Philosophy GuideBook to Husserl and the Cartesian Meditations

A.D. Smith

'In this amirably clear and well-written commentary Smith takes us through the work Meditation by Meditation.' *Paul Gorner, Philosophical Books*

'Smith has done a sterling job. Husserl's terms are defined, his ideas clarified and discussed, and since the Guidebook closely follows the structure of the Cartesian Meditations, it really does guide the reader through the text . . . essential reading for anyone studying Husserl's text.' *Komarine Romdenh-Romluc, Mind*

Husserl is one of the most important philosophers of the twentieth century and his contribution to the phenomenology movement is widely recognised. The *Cartesian Meditations* is his most famous, and most widely studied work. The book introduces and assesses: Husserl's life and background to the *Cartesian Meditations*, the ideas and text of the *Cartesian Meditations* and the continuing importance of Husserl's work to Philosophy.

ISBN 10: 0-415-28757-X (hbk)
ISBN 10: 0-415-28758-8 (pbk)
ISBN 13: 978-0-415-28757-9 (hbk)
ISBN 13: 978-0-415-28758-6 (pbk)